PENGUIN BOOKS

ALL YOU NEED IS LOVE

Educated at Cambridge, Tony Palmer was music critic for the London *Observer* from 1967 to 1975. Articles by him have also appeared in the *New Statesman, The New York Times, Punch,* the *Spectator,* and many other publications, and he is the author of four books, including *Born under a Bad Sign,* a survey of popular music in the late 1960s. Mr. Palmer has directed more than forty television films and has made four feature documentaries for the cinema. Currently he is at work on a feature film about Richard Wagner. Describing himself as a "confirmed bachelor," he says he likes "Mozart, strawberries, and Earls' daughters."

Here is a sample of what the British press said about *All You Need Is Love:*

"Brilliant exposition . . . magisterial style . . . magnificent" — *Sunday Times*

"The descriptive passages are of the highest quality . . . outstandingly good." — *Economist*

"One of the most comprehensive volumes to appear on pop" — *London Evening Standard*

"This beautifully presented book is something of a triumph . . . the first well-planned . . . history of the people's music in the people's century, infuriating, stimulating, long overdue: and hugely welcome." — *Listener*

All You Need Is Love

The Story of Popular Music

Tony Palmer

EDITED BY PAUL MEDLICOTT

PENGUIN BOOKS

Penguin Books Ltd, Harmondsworth, Middlesex, England
Penguin Books, 625 Madison Avenue, New York, New York 10022, U.S.A.
Penguin Books Australia Ltd, Ringwood, Victoria, Australia
Penguin Books Canada Limited, 2801 John Street, Markham, Ontario, Canada L3R 1B4
Penguin Books (N.Z.) Ltd, 182–190 Wairau Road, Auckland 10, New Zealand

First published in the United States of America by Grossman Publishers 1976
Published in Penguin Books 1977

LIBRARY OF CONGRESS CATALOGING IN PUBLICATION DATA
Palmer, Tony, 1941–
All you need is love.
Includes index.
1. Music, popular (Songs, etc.)—History and criticism.   I. Title.
[ML3545.P32 1977]   780'.42'0973   77-7989
ISBN 0 14 00.4521 X

Printed and bound in the United States of America by
Halliday Lithograph, West Hanover, Massachusetts
Set in Linofilm Melior
Color illustrations printed by
A. Hoen & Co., Baltimore, Maryland

This book has been published in association with Theatre Projects Film Productions,
EMI Television Productions and Polygram (T.V. Division)

ACKNOWLEDGMENTS
"Blowin' in the Wind," Bob Dylan, © 1962 Warner Bros. Inc.; all rights reserved; used by
permission. "I Feel Like I'm Fixing to Die Rag," by Country Joe McDonald, © 1969
Tradition Music Co.; rights assigned to April Music Ltd. for the U.K. and Eire; used by
permission. "Keep on Smilin'," by Jack V. Hall, James R. Hall, Maurice R. Hirsch, John D.
Armstrong, and Lewis M. Rose, Copyright © 1974 No Exit Music Co. Inc.; reproduced by
permission. "Sympathy for the Devil," by Mick Jagger and Keith Richard, Copyright ©
1968 Essex Music International Limited; reproduced by kind permission. "You Never
Miss the Water Till the Well Runs Dry," by Paul Secon and Arthur Kent, Copyright 1947
by United Music Corp., Copyright renewal assigned to Arthur Kent Music Company,
Copyright © 1975; reproduced by kind permission.

The author gratefully acknowledges the permission to use the material from Storyville,
New Orleans, by Al Rose, copyright © The University of Alabama Press, 1974, and also
all of that material on jazz contained in the pamphlet New Orleans Jazz—What It Is and
What It Isn't (City of New Orleans, 1973), by Al Rose, and Al Rose's commentary on the
television series All You Need Is Love.

For

Contents

Prelude   xi

God's Children   /   *The Beginnings*   3

I Can Hypnotize Dis Nation   /   *Ragtime*   17

Jungle Music   /   *Jazz*   33

Who's That Comin'?   /   *Blues*   55

Rude Songs   /   *Vaudeville and Music Hall*   75

Always Chasing Rainbows   /   *Tin Pan Alley*   97

Diamonds as Big as the Ritz   /   *The Musical*   117

Swing That Music!   /   *Swing*   139

Good Times   /   *Rhythm and Blues*   157

Making Moonshine   /   *Country Music*   173

Go Down, Moses!   /   *Songs of War and Protest*   195

Hail! Hail! Rock 'n' Roll!   /   *Rock and Roll*   211

Mighty Good   /   *The Beatles*   231

All Along the Watchtower   /   *Sour Rock*   253

Whatever Gets You Through the Night   /   *Glitter Rock*   273

Imagine . . .   /   *New Directions*   287

Coda   309

Index   311

The idea for this book first came almost eight years ago, after I had completed a television film entitled *All My Loving*. The British Broadcasting Corporation wanted me to construct a documentary "explaining" popular music, which then, as now, seemed much talked of but little understood. The film, my second, achieved a notoriety that obscured its manifold weaknesses, not least of which was a lack of historical perspective. The criticism it unleashed, however, made clear to me the prejudice and ignorance amidst which we have gleaned our knowledge of the subject. My desire grew to reconsider popular music's progress at length and in detail. But the task of research appeared so monumental and so costly that I put it aside for fear of embarking upon an investigation I could never finish.

The opportunity to make a constructive beginning arose three years ago when I was asked to make a series of sixteen television specials "explaining" contemporary American popular music. The idea that a phenomenon as complex and diverse as popular music could be "explained" in sixteen, let alone sixty, television films is, of course, absurd. First, the weight of the material would demand a lifetime of study. Second, the subject is usually thought unworthy of prolonged consideration. Nonetheless, popular music remains — for me — perpetually fascinating; a knowledge of its bizarre, often tragic, saga is crucial to an understanding of contemporary social history. Could one imagine a world without Rodgers and Hammerstein, without Duke Ellington, or without the Beatles? But are these composers freaks, or do they belong to a continuing and developing tradition? If so, what? And how? And why?

In spite of the dangers, I accepted the television commission and began to explore the argument contained in this book. I interviewed over three hundred key protagonists, from performers to record producers, from critics to managers, from publicists to promoters, throughout the United States, Europe, and Africa. I shot almost a million feet of film and acquired as much again in archival material. Since films are thought to have scripts, I commissioned essays relating to each episode, hoping these would focus my attention on what was considered important. I had long since abandoned the notion of a chronological survey, which would have become, I suspected, merely a list of names and dates. Instead, I drew up a list of topics about which I wanted to know more — ragtime, jazz, swing, the musical, and so forth — to understand how each movement had developed and from where, what pressures it had undergone in that development, how each had influenced and contributed to the others, and what if anything that particular style entailed today. These essays, or scripts, written by an impressive array of authorities, were intended to provide the beginnings of this information.

The book, like popular music itself, therefore, is a synthesis of many influences; it is also the conclusion of several years of noisy and frequently unrewarding field work. Without the stimulus of the films and their scripts, the book might have remained unwritten. It is not the text of the films, although it expresses the same point of view. Nor is it a comprehensive survey of every name that has ever sung or strummed his or her way across a stage. It is not an apologia or a manifesto. Nor is it, I hope, mere hagiography.

To those who contributed essays I owe much gratitude, if only because they gave me opinions with which to disagree. They were: Paul Oliver on the blues; Rudi Blesh on ragtime; Leonard Feather on jazz; David Cheshire on music hall and vaudeville; Ian Whitcomb on Tin Pan Alley; George Melly on the twenties; John Hammond on the thirties; Stephen Sondheim on the musical; Humphrey Lyttelton on swing; Nik Cohn on rhythm and blues and country music; Charles Chilton on war songs; Jack Good on early rock and roll; Derek Taylor on the sixties; and Charlie Gillett on rock today. To those who patiently allowed me to interview them, at airports, backstage, in their homes, and on the beach, I am also grateful — in particular to the following, whose insight led me down alley-ways where otherwise I might not have ventured: Roy Acuff, Stanley Adams, Lester Bangs, Amiri Baraka, Dave Brubeck, Edward Cramer, Bing Crosby, Clive Davis, Jimmy Driftwood, Hal Durham, Benny Goodman, Brian Guinle, Seymour Heller, William Ivey, Lieutenant George W. Lee, Rouben Mamoulian, Paul McCartney, Jim and Amy O'Neal, Joseph Papp, Sam Phillips, Hal Prince, Dorothy Ritter, Al Rose, Ken Russell, Russell Sanjek, Pete Seeger, Artie Shaw, Phil Spector, and Jerry Wexler. There were many others, of course, in whose debt I shall always remain.

The films would not have been made without the continuing support of my two sponsors, Lord Delfont on behalf of EMI, and Tony van de Haar for Polygram: a unique and, I hope, not unfruitful partnership. Nor would the films have been undertaken without the devotion and hard work of my two producers, Neville Thompson and Richard Pilbrow, both of whom have had to endure more than their reasonable share of my temper. And probably the films would not have been conceived without Aubrey Singer, now head of BBC2 but at the time of *All My Loving* head of BBC Features. It was Singer who devised a world-wide television program called *Our World* on which the Beatles' song "All You Need Is Love" was first broadcast. Again, there have been many others who have seen the films through, including especially Jennifer Ryan, David Gideon-Thomson, Cyril Bennett, Paul Fox, Ann Ivil, Prof. Dr. Reiner Moritz, and Gail Geibel; again, to all of them my thanks.

Nor would the book have been finished so painlessly without the tireless labors of our picture researcher Anne Weldon who, together with her assistant Georgina Lee and Paul Medlicott, attacked the mountain of transcripts and related matter with the energy normally reserved for the Himalayas. Nor without the brilliance of my editor, Dan Okrent of Grossman/Viking, the expert guidance of managing editor Sophie McConnell, and the book's designer, the beautiful Jacqueline Schuman. Nor without the refreshing idealism of literary agent John Cushman. (I hope he takes the blame.) My thanks also to Juliet Clarke and Helen Howard for deciphering my handwriting; also to my assistant Annunziata Asquith for just being there.

Tony Palmer

Popular music is a paradigm of American culture: no one knows a song is good until the public says so—whereupon it can be stolen, reproduced, manufactured, and marketed for profit. Partly this attitude mirrors an acute inferiority; Americans have often looked to Europe, for example, because it seemed inconceivable that a culture as valuable could exist within their own shores. Partly it entails a naïve belief that the majority should and will decide the standard of excellence, although this ignores the difficult fact that popularization tends to diminish anything that has pretensions to Art. In its strivings for cultural respectability or commercial success, popular music thus finds itself crippled by a fundamental paradox. The more it is musical, the less it is popular; the more it is popular, the less it is musical. It may be possible to make a Ford look like a Cadillac, but you cannot make a musician sound like Louis Armstrong or Paul McCartney. The popular music industry has tried, repeatedly, to do with music what Ford attempts with cars. It works better with cars.

Popular music has in common with television and football great accessibility. Everyone, it seems, is an expert because the sound is so commonplace. Its history and development, however, remain obscure, even unknown. And in attempting to understand why the music is like it is, a knowledge of its past is essential.

That much of popular music is derivative, for instance, is irrelevant; the borrowing of ideas is not in itself a weakness in any art form. Bach used French and German dance tunes; Picasso incorporated every modish idea he came across; Shakespeare took something from everybody. The question is whether anything new is created by this absorption; whether, indeed, the whole became more than the sum of its parts.

Time and again popular music has been lost in some commercial helter-skelter because its practitioners have failed to accept and understand this process. Time and again the music industry, being a conglomerate, has been unable to prevent the ruination of individual talent, although it is upon the contribution of a remarkable collection of individuals that the industry finally depends. I have relied in the course of this book upon particular incidents and particular musicians or entrepreneurs to illustrate more general themes because I believe the story of popular music to be the story of individuals—struggling to survive in a milieu that reckons the individual, especially if black, an embarrassment.

All You Need Is Love

God's Children

On June 25, 1967, the technology of communications made possible a wonderful and historic event. Satellites stationed around the stratosphere were hooked—for the first (and only) time—into a single world-wide television network. Each country that boasted a television service was permitted to share in this unique enterprise; each was invited to contribute an item or items that represented their best to a program called, with dazzling simplicity, *Our World*.

As with many Historic Events, there were a few hitches. At the last minute most of the communist governments withdrew; in the Australian bush, there were some blackouts. But the venture was a triumph, or so we were told. It had been a "sedate dance around an electronic totem at the center of our global

---

Waiting by the Mississippi, c.1900.

Isaac Hayes, 1971. Born in Memphis, 1943.

village." America contributed an amusing diversion on the lesser known problems of pea farming in Prairie Hills, Wisconsin. Britain was more original. To an audience of over seven hundred million, simultaneously, all over the world, it gave its Beatles. "All You Need Is Love," they sang. And we believed them. It was the apotheosis of popular music. After that, where else could the popular song go — except down? Was it conceivable that any song would ever again achieve such massive and instantaneous promotion?

With unnerving accuracy, *Our World* had accidentally stumbled across a significant concept. Yes, it was plausible that what our world needed was love, and a lot of it. Yes, it was arguable that if such a program had to include some contemporary "popular" music, it

The Beatles bear the message.

might as well be by the Beatles. But by a peculiar twist — and here the element of chance enters in — the song happened to be a compelling example of the worst in "popular" music. The lyric, if that is the appropriate term, was mindlessly repetitive. The music began and ended with direct theft — although, in fairness, using excerpts from the "Marseillaise" and "Greensleeves" might have been an intended genuflection toward internationalism. The song was unmemorable, yet undeniably popular. Within three months, it had sold two million records. Not quite seven hundred million, of course, but a promising enough beginning.

"**P**op" is among the more maligned, misused, and misinterpreted words in the language. It is meant to signify popular; often, it has not. Much of what masquerades as popular music reaches only a tiny audience and is not intended to do any more. Popular music is not even what most people like. Janis Joplin sang popular music and most people — if by "most" one means the majority — did not like Janis Joplin. Van Cliburn's version of Tchaikovsky's First Piano Concerto, recorded in 1958, has outsold most pop music LPs. But Tchaikovsky is classical music. Yes, but it is also popular music. So why is Janis Joplin's music not classical music? Because it is popular music. And so on.

There have been as many definitions of popular music as there have been musicians performing it; the impression is that most people know, even if only intuitively, what is meant by the phrase. Usually, they do not. Can it be said, for example, that the Rolling Stones are of the same musical accomplishment as Duke Ellington? Probably not. Or that a guitarist like Eric Clapton is from the same school as Bing Crosby? Unlikely. But surely all are popular musicians? Stop anyone in the street and ask what pop music is, and the reply will almost certainly encompass long-haired kids, or loudness, or drugs. Some might venture the names of David Cassidy or the Osmonds. But the wealth of contemporary music remains unknown; the realization that Bob Dylan or Elvis Presley or Simon and Garfunkel are the inheritors of an immense tradition is outside the general knowledge. Aaron Copland once said that future generations, when listening to the Beatles, would hear the sound of the sixties. Other generations and ages have identified an era by its music, and this is a clue to understanding popular music.

The BBC, with characteristic thoroughness, reckoned it had cracked the problem in 1945–1946 when it devised (in the interests of culture) a uniquely simple division of its radio programming. There would be one channel devoted primarily to news and talk shows, called the Home Service; one—called the Third Programme—indulging in classical music (Tchaikovsky and friends); and one—calling itself the Light Programme—whose musical content would consist of "popular" music. Rock and roll would later be banned from this channel because it was thought disruptive, distasteful, and dissolute. "Popular" music was for easy listening, music without substance.

Later, when American radio stations began pumping out an unremitting sewage of pop/rock—because there was a vast audience for it and, for Americans, vast audiences equaled greater advertising revenue—the BBC decided to regroup. Having had various off-shore "pirate" radio stations declared illegal (their original sin had been to steal listeners who wanted to hear this thing called pop) the BBC decreed that henceforth there would be a new radio channel, called with dour inevitability Radio One, whose purpose was the dissemination of pop/rock. The Pink Floyd, however, were restricted to the Third Programme, along with Bach, Beethoven, and Tchaikovsky.

Such confusion demonstrates how difficult it is to define popular music. It might be said that any definition, especially one that depends on a causal chain of development, is irrelevant to enjoyment. That is true, but disappointing and fatalistic. And the need for a proper understanding is emphasized by the growing awareness that much of the accepted history of popular music is profoundly misleading, if not downright untrue.

It is commonly believed, for example, that rock and roll, rhythm and blues, jazz, and almost everything else categorized as popular music came from the coastal regions of West Africa. It did not. It is commonly believed that Storyville in New Orleans was the forcing house of jazz. It was not. It is commonly believed that when Storyville was shut down in 1917, jazz was booted out and its musicians took to the river and steamed north to Chicago. They did not. It is commonly believed that the blues are the cornerstone of all modern popular

music. They are not. It is commonly believed that the Delta, home of American Negro music, is located in and around the Mississippi River at New Orleans. It is not. The Delta, a smallish area bounded by the Mississippi River on the west and the Yazoo River on the east, is a hundred and fifty miles north of New Orleans. The paths of these two rivers roughly form a triangle much as do the main branches of the Nile; the area and its chief town take their names from the Greek letter Δ—Delta.

Such examples are trivial, but sufficient perhaps to make it worth reconsidering a few of the more fundamental assumptions about the origins of popular music. For two centuries, millions of Africans were torn from their villages and shipped to the Americas to work as slaves—not just in North America, but in Central and South America as well. Along the coast of West Africa, from Cape Verde to the Guinea, Ivory, Gold, and Slave coasts, around the Bight of Benin, and south to Angola, the slavers fought and bought to obtain their living cargoes. There is evidence in the survival of the Black Caribs of Surinam and in the dances and customs of Bahia that much African music and tradition were imported by slaves to the Americas. So it has always seemed reasonable to assume that since this music survived in South and Central America, then it must have done so in North America. After all, slaves for the North American markets are thought to have come from areas similar to those that dispatched slaves to South America; they must, therefore, have brought with them elements of a common musical past.

Drums, certainly, are a part of contemporary Afro-American music, as they are of Bahian and Trinidadian music. But, by African or even South American standards, drum-playing in the United States is elementary. It is no wonder. Drums were rigorously suppressed throughout the North American slave states because they could be used for sending messages of insurrection. The opportunities for sustaining a strong drum tradition, consequently, were negligible. Early blues made little use of drums, and drums were almost never heard in black American

music until well into the twentieth century—several decades after the supposed invention of the blues. The drum theory presupposes, moreover, that the Negro slaves brought to North America in the seventeenth and eighteenth centuries came from the coastal regions of Africa, where the drum was an important instrument. Mostly, they did not.

Africa is a vast continent, more than three times the area of the United States, which embraces a great range of topographic, climatic, and social conditions; it contains some five thousand peoples of widely differing cultures.

And it now seems probable that the blacks who became American slaves came not from the rain forests of the coasts, but from regions far north in the savannah, from an area known until comparatively recently as West Sudan. The coastal tribes were themselves slave traders, plundering the north and selling to the white European merchants who called at their ports. The Yoruba thugs who inhabited southern Nigeria opposed the abolition of slavery in the nineteenth century because, it is said (even in Nigeria), their entire economy depended on the slave trade.

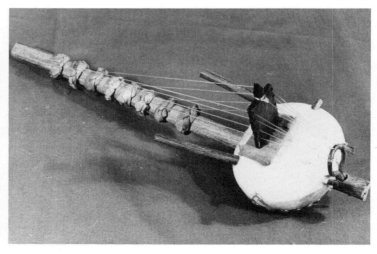

The principal musical instruments of the savannah were stringed — from simple monochords to the intricate *kora* and *seron* with over twenty strings. Particularly common was the *banya*. Thomas Jefferson, in his *Notes on the State of Virginia*, described the manufacture of a *banya* (precursor of the banjo) by a slave. Primitive banjos and fiddles can still be found in abundance in northern Nigeria, in Niger, and in the southern Sudan. Stringed instruments were also central to the Egyptian musical cultures, so it is possible that Egyptian merchants brought these instruments south and west on their trading expeditions several centuries before Christ. Thus, by way of the slave traders on the coast and the European entrepreneurs who sailed to the Americas, the Egyptian tradition was carried to New Orleans.

Whether it was the bongo or the banjo that the slave somehow managed to replicate in his new world, neither could have flourished in a white society that most blacks, at least in the beginning, viewed as only a temporary home. Gradually the Africans came to realize that they were never going home. They learned a new culture and a new language, and witnessed the inevitable disintegration of the threads that tied them to Africa. They became, against their will, black Americans. In order for them to live, black African culture had to die.

This is not to say that African culture made no contribution to the development of popular music. A musical characteristic of the savannah, for example, was the five-tone scale, part of a vocal tradition wherein a leader "preached" and was answered by a female and then a male voice. When Africans later heard the common Euro-American eight-tone scale, they selected from the unfamiliar instruments available to them those that approximated the voices of their own tradition. The leader picked the loudest: the cornet or the trumpet. The female voice

The original instruments, many still in use, and some of their descendants. *Top left:* a primitive xylophone; *bottom far left:* a gudu-gudu drum from Nigeria (note the leather drumstick); *bottom near left:* a Senegalese kora. Mail order goods quickly took over from the home-made musical instruments during the latter part of the nineteenth century.

became the clarinet; the male voice the trombone. And in an attempt to reconcile the five- with the eight-tone scale, the musicians produced "bent" or "blue" notes, familiar characteristics of jazz.

Many African languages, moreover, depend for their precise meaning upon pitch and tone quality. By merely altering the inflection of the voice, many Africans produce a multiplicity of definitions. African instruments, including the drum, reflected this ability. The talking drum (which survives today) appears to do just that, although it is less flexible than its stringed counterparts, upon which the most subtle of nuances can be discerned. Blues, bebop, and all manner of talking jazz clearly have a precedent —and it is not the bongos of the coast.

What of the idea that blues is the origin of jazz or ragtime or swing or even rock and roll? The notion is, if nothing else, misleading. To understand the blues, it is necessary to accept that it is not just music. A fit of the blues *is* the blues; the music gives this predicament voice and expression. To pretend that the blues is a single thread that binds together all popular music is nonsense. The earliest examples of ragtime, gospel music, and even jazz predate the earliest known instance of the form known as blues—the twelve-bar, three-line verse. English music hall entertainers and the composers of Broadway musicals owed little, if anything, to blues. The simplistic lineage argument has obscured rather than revealed the true influence of the blues. Blues only becomes comprehensible when it is recognized as a form with its own origin and evolution, rich enough to have colored popular music, but not the first link in a chain. It is a vigorous, profound tradition, with a life and development of its own, quite apart from whichever of its elements appears in other forms of popular music.

What of the idea that the blues were born in

Negroes were characterized invariably as happy dancing fellows; but apart from church services, dancing was often the only release. Both engravings date from about 1800, and are by unknown artists.

To understand the blues, it is necessary to accept that it is not just music.

slavery? The facts do not tally with this romantic view. Undoubtedly, the blues *feeling* or spirit can be associated with the oppression of slavery. But the recognizable blues harmonies that have been so consistently used by white musicians were unknown before 1895. When a bluesman says he is paying his dues from way back, he is fantasizing. That he is or has been poor is a consequence not only of his slavery, but of the failure of its abolition.

The predominant music of slavery was not the blues but the work song. These long, mournful, antiphonal songs accompanied the work on cotton plantations. Under the driver's lash, they set the time for hoeing or digging. The work leader sang a line and the gang responded in chorus in a song pattern similar to those of the African savannah. Otherwise, the slaves had few opportunities for social or emotional—or musical—release, except through their adopted church. Here they adapted what must have been incomprehensible Protestant hymns to their own vision of the promised land, just as their brothers were doing in Africa; the song "Swing Low, Sweet Chariot," whose origin is an eighteenth-century Methodist chant, surfaced in East Africa as well as in the Southern states of America. Eventually, as news filtered from the North that there was a land without slavery, a new note crept into these "spirituals": "Steal Away," for example, became a coded song of escape.

And what of the idea that jazz was born in a red-light district known as Storyville? The story goes—supported by encyclopedic evidence and the very best jazz authorities—that part of the French Quarter in New Orleans, designated in 1898 by a puritanical alderman named Story as an official area of prostitution, provided an environment within which jazz could flourish. Encouraged by wild times and dubious morals, the litany continues, the first bands put together a little ragtime, a dash of African rhythm, an improvisation on a classical march tune, a touch of libido—and then there was jazz.

Jazz critics have never hesitated to falsify

facts to accommodate journalistic needs. Storyville was not in the French Quarter, but several blocks north. Jazz was being widely played ten years before Storyville was conceived—and not just in New Orleans. Recent evidence suggests that a number of Texas cities including Houston and San Antonio sported instrumental street bands not dissimilar to those of New Orleans before 1898. Very few bands ever played in Storyville—there was little room for them in the saloons. The brothels employed solo pianists. That one or two musicians who subsequently became famous as jazzmen—such as Jelly Roll Morton and Tony Jackson—did play in Story-

ville has concealed the fact that, for religious reasons alone, the great majority would not have set foot in the area.

Jazz was an outdoor music, played by street bands for parades and picnics. As such, it was primarily functional. It was a product, moreover, not of a race, nor of a place. It is neither a black music nor a white music. It began as a collective improvisation, by an exceptional mixture of people, in an area whose musical culture was cosmopolitan and sophisticated. Had Daniel Boone turned south instead of west as he hacked his way across the continent, for example, he would have discovered not jazz but the French operetta. The first recognizable jazz came from Jack Laine's Reliance Band, formed in 1892, which toured all over the South and consisted of five musicians—two black and three white.

When Storyville was closed in 1917, its musicians—that is, its pianists—found themselves out of work. But the idea that they clambered aboard a passing steamboat and pushed off up the Mississippi toward Chicago, where they invented Chicago jazz, pausing briefly in Memphis to invent Memphis blues, is inaccurate. While it is true that U.S. Navy authorities banned music in Storyville—several years before the area was closed down and entirely as the result of a shoot-out in an insignificant lounge—it is not true that the majority of its musicians moved out of New Orleans as a result. They simply went on with their full-time jobs as laborers or farmhands; music, after all, was mostly a part-time employment. And a cursory examination of the most elementary school-room map will reveal that there was no navigable waterway between New Orleans and Chicago.

Those who traveled north went by train—the Illinois Central Railroad. They went not to make music but to find other work, in Chicago and

A sort of preservation. *Top left:* drummer at ease in New Orleans; *bottom left:* that city's Preservation Hall, where requests cost $1 for traditional tunes, $2.50 for others, and a fee of $5.00 is demanded from those who want the Saints to come marching in. *Facing page:* the way it used to be—to the cemetery, New Orleans style.

Detroit, in Cleveland and Pittsburgh. The significant change was not the "move upriver," moreover, but the change from country to city; from back-breaking labor in the fields to mind-breaking monotony on the new production lines spawned by Henry Ford.

So if the music did not come from Africa, except possibly in spirit; if ragtime and gospel were not founded on the blues; if slavery was not the mainspring of a developing black musical sensibility; if jazz was not a pimp's pastime in Storyville—what *did* create this revolution in music? The music that was heard around the turn of the century—first in the South, but soon all over America—would have as great an effect on twentieth-century culture as any other single influence. Like most revolutions, its causes were infinite. But its location was not. Popular music—in the sense of jazz, rock and roll, blues,

swing, soul, and their related progeny—began soon after and probably as a result of the Day of Jubilee, the freeing of the slaves, September 22, 1862.

After the Civil War, the victorious northern states decided to consolidate their victory by "reconstructing" the South on radical principles—which meant, of course, economic exploitation. With zeal and confidence, Northern politicians spoke of forty acres and a mule for every freed slave, as well as the chance and right to vote. For a moment, it looked as if their ideas might work. The slaves (and, incidentally, thousands of small white farmers) would benefit from the necessary break-up of the massive estates.

But the dream vanished in the reality. Opportunist Northern politicians went South to exploit the new voters. The scalawags and carpetbaggers found the blacks easily led. A man

whose whole life and livelihood had revolved around implicit obedience to one white man was unlikely to disobey another whose only request was the casting of a vote — what, after all, was a vote? Land for all was a fiasco. First, the plantations had been designed as giant operations: converting them into a myriad of small holdings reduced their crop potential and destroyed their economic balance. Second, the newly freed blacks were incapable of shifting instantaneously from laborers to landowners. They had no real grasp of farm organization and there was little chance that their dispossessed former masters would teach them.

As Reconstruction came to a close, repressive legislation, designed to cripple the political power of the blacks, was introduced by white Southern politicians. Poll taxes immediately disenfranchised thousands of blacks. The Ku Klux Klan, originally formed to intimidate Catholic immigrants, began a campaign of terror against those blacks who attempted to assert their rights. Laws were enacted to remove blacks even further from whites than most had been under the paternalistic plantation system.

As white ranks closed, segregation hardened into law. Blacks were not permitted to travel on the railroads, except in "Jim Crow" cars. Blacks were not permitted to stay in white hotels, or to

Dancing the slightly fantastic: Marian and Martinez Ramez demonstrate "jazz-dancing" at Palm Beach in the 1920s to an appreciative audience.

travel in white sections of trains, or to share lavatories or restaurants. Blacks had to use separate drinking fountains; they had to find their own doctors and dentists. And if they wished to speak with God, they had to do so out of sight of the whites and in their own churches. Blacks were roped off; they had no access to white entertainment, worship, transport, or life. They became unpersons.

There was, however, one important consequence of this barbarity: it turned the black community into itself, forcing it to rely on its own resources. From the harshness of segregation came the discovery of black identity. From an incoherent mass of peasants enslaved for generations arose the beginnings of a coherent culture. Black people, whose language and identity had been wrenched from them and made dependent upon their white masters, were now abandoned by white society. They had to look to themselves; they did so with dramatic effect, finding expression in the eloquent voice that was their music.

Within a few years, the South witnessed the birth of musical forms that owed much to Anglo-Scottish origin but now had a distinctive black character: instead of singing about white heroes, black balladists sang of Negro heroes. The boll weevil, a persistent crop wrecker, became the resister to white oppression. John Hardy and Railroad Bill carved their way through the white man's mountain. Jigs and reels of the plantation owners were adapted for dances and play-parties. "Musicianers" discarded the fiddle and banjo and wrote away for mail-order guitars.

Simultaneous with this outburst of secular music came the growth of an exhilarating, uninhibited religious music — the gospel songs. With roots in the Baptist Church, the Church of God in Christ was a Protestant religion in whose clapboard chapels and store-front converted sheds the congregation praised with the "timbrels and the horns," chanting ecstatic responses to the strained voices of the preachers. In effect, this shouting to the Lord was a mixture of the field hollers from plantation days and the only music previously allowed the slaves, their versions of English hymns. The work songs had almost died out after the Civil War and the end of collective farm labor. But they persisted in the penitentiary farms of Mississippi, Texas, and Louisiana, where slave conditions and group farming continued long enough for them to stay in the memory and provide the inspiration for a new and adaptable religious music.

There was another element: the minority of black freedmen and slaves hitherto employed in domestic service had been exposed to a European culture and mode of expression. They had heard formal sounds, such as parlor chamber music. They had also enjoyed, with their masters, songs made popular by traveling vaudeville shows and entertainments.

This emerging black culture did not improve social conditions, however, nor did much of it seem directed toward change. It remained essentially a reflection of the black state; a consolation for black people's disappointments; and, most important, an outlet for their emotions. At best, it helped them toward an understanding, even a toleration, of the problems that beset them.

But as segregation and oppression increased, as prejudice blossomed into hatred, as the blacks were consigned to the ghettos of the industrial North, their music gained in strength and urgency. When they traded the misery of the fields for the misery of production lines, their music changed.

The great locomotives of the Santa Fe and the Southern, the Illinois Central and the Texas and Pacific, thundered through the cottonlands of Mississippi and the timberlands of east Texas, belching their whistles. They had always been a symbol of escape; hence, the "Underground Railroad." Preachers took the smoking, fiery engines as a symbol of the Black Diamond Express—to Hell. But now the black worker hopped a freight train or "rode the rods" beneath the cars to carry himself to another place.

Traveling light, with his "easy rider" guitar

The black musician was considered by white society a loafer, a vagrant, irresponsible and unreliable.

and little else, riding the freights to another lumber camp or town where he could find food, liquor, and a place to sleep in exchange for his music, the black musician was considered by white society a loafer, a vagrant, irresponsible and unreliable. But he was admired in the black world for his anarchic view of life, for his freedom of movement, for his independence of spirit, which others could only long for.

The Southern style of fast piano, with bass figures of eight beats to the bar and sharp, ostinato improvisations, took its rhythms directly from the rattle of the railroad cars and its name from the impromptu gatherings of Southern migrants. This particular style, boogie-woogie, was the invention (first recorded in 1928) of Pinetop Smith. Boogie was to enjoy a brief period of commercial exploitation and popularization during the swing era, although without Pinetop Smith; he had sold his rights to a pair of hustlers (one white, one black) whose estates still collect a royalty every time the name "boogie-woogie" is used in the title of a recording or a published song. Pinetop was paid off with a dollar; three months later he was shot to death.

He was not alone in his fate. Blind Lemon Jefferson, a Texan with a flair for starkly poetic images, died derelict in a Chicago snow storm in 1930. Sonny Boy Williamson, a harmonica player, formed bands and recorded in Chicago —till, on the way back from a club in 1948, he was murdered. Neither man is important simply because of the manner of his dying; cultures always create heroes of the dead. But the world in which most musicians lived involved pressures outside their familiar experience, and they suffered because of them.

Thus many endured the lives they wrote music about—tough, often brutal. It is perhaps surprising that they managed to create a vibrant art in so dispiriting a milieu. But in the degradation of Northern industrial life, the black musicians found and asserted their identities. In their shared alienation, they transformed hith-

The New Masses Presents

AN EVENING OF AMERICAN NEGRO MUSIC

"From Spirituals to Swing"

FRIDAY EVENING, DECEMBER 23, 1938

Carnegie Hall

Conceived and Produced by John Hammond; Directed by Charles Friedman

---

Note: The following program is not in chronological order

Introduction

AFRICAN TRIBAL MUSIC: From scientific recordings made by the H. E. Tracy Expedition to the West Coast of Africa. THEME: Count Basie and His Orchestra.

I. Spirituals and Holy Roller Hymns

MITCHELL'S CHRISTIAN SINGERS, *North Carolina.* William Brown, Julius Davis, Louis David, Sam Bryant. SISTER THARPE, *Florida.* (Courtesy Cotton Club) with guitar accompaniment.

II. Soft Swing

THE KANSAS CITY SIX, *New York City.* Eddie Durham (electric guitar), Freddie Green (guitar), Buck Clayton (trumpet), Lester Young (clarinet and tenor saxophone), Jo Jones (drums), Walter Page (bass).

III. Harmonica Playing

SANFORD TERRY, *Durham, North Carolina.* Washboard playing by artists to be announced at the concert.

IV. Blues

RUBY SMITH, *Norfolk, Virginia.* Accompanied on the piano by JAMES P. JOHNSON, *New York City.*
JOE TURNER, *Kansas City, Missouri.* Accompanied by PETE JOHNSON, *New York City.*
BIG BILL, *Chicago, Illinois.* Accompanied by himself on the guitar.
JAMES RUSHING, *Kansas City, Missouri.* Accompanied by the KANSAS CITY FIVE. Freddie Green (guitar), Buck Clayton (trumpet), Lester Young (clarinet and tenor saxophone), Jo Jones (drums), Walter Page (bass).
HELEN HUMES, *Louisville, Kentucky.* Accompanied by the KANSAS CITY FIVE.

V. Boogie-Woogie Piano Playing

ALBERT AMMONS, *Chicago.* MEADE "LUX" LEWIS, *Chicago.* PETE JOHNSON, *Kansas City.* "A Cutting Session."

INTERMISSION

VI. Early New Orleans Jazz

SIDNEY BECHET and his NEW ORLEANS FEET WARMERS. Sidney Bechet (clarinet and soprano saxophone), Tommy Ladnier (trumpet), James P. Johnson (piano), Dan Minor (trombone), Jo Jones (drums).

VII. Swing

COUNT BASIE AND HIS ORCHESTRA. Count Basie (piano), Walter Page (bass), Freddie Green (guitar), Jo Jones (drums), Ed Lewis (first trumpet), Buck Clayton (second trumpet), Shad Collins (third trumpet), Harry Edison (fourth trumpet), Benny Morton (first trombone), Dickie Wells (second trombone), Dan Minor (third trombone), Earl Warren (first alto saxophone), Jack Washington (second alto sax and baritone), Lester Young (third tenor sax and clarinet), James Rushing and Helen Humes (vocalists). Arrangers: Eddie Durham, Count Basie, Albert Gibson, Buck Clayton, etc.

BASIE'S BLUE FIVE. Count Basie, Shad Collins, Walter Page, Jo Jones, Herschel Evans.

THE KANSAS CITY SIX. Eddie Durham, Freddie Green, Buck Clayton, Lester Young, Jo Jones, Walter Page.

erto loose adaptations of a white Southern culture into a music undeniably of their creation.

For years, none but a tiny minority of whites knew anything of this black music. It was different and separate. Only connoisseurs bought records of black music, and these were hard to come by outside the particular artist's immediate neighborhood. Black music seeped through when it was copied and vulgarized by white musicians.

But once the white music industry—the only music *industry*—realized there was something special about black music, it began to filch enthusiastically. The "King of Ragtime" was pronounced; his name was Mike Bernard and he was white. The "King of Jazz" was declared; his name, it happens, was Paul Whiteman. The "King of Swing" was Benny Goodman. Finally, Elvis Presley became "King" of rock and roll and rhythm and everything else, and he, too, was white.

Black music and black life have always been imitated in America, from minstrel shows in which whites covered their faces in burnt cork and aped the more "humorous" actions of nigger slaves, through the adoption of black dress and black slang (usually just as the blacks have moved on to new fashion and new language), to the copying of the blues form by contemporary white rock musicians. To be sure, it has not always been a one-way process: the cakewalk dance of the 1890s, for example, was a black attempt to impersonate the strutting style of dance thought typical of plantation owners in the big house. There were also extraordinary instances of black entertainers blacking up to perform as "nigger minstrels," although this was usually symptomatic of the grim realization that for a black man to succeed, he had to imitate the white man.

Left: almost a "Who's Who" of black music in the 1930s. Note the "scientific recordings" by H. E. Tracy—the West African connection is not such a revolutionary idea. Also note that four centers of jazz—New Orleans, Chicago, Kansas City, and New York—are well represented by names which became household words, but then were still struggling for "respectability." *Right:* uptown and downtown. William Hammerstein's Harlem Opera House; Carnegie Hall, where respectability was conferred on performers from Duke Ellington to the Beatles.

But mostly the black man and his music were easy meat for the white musician. LeRoi Jones, the black writer, politician, and chronicler of black music now known as Amiri Baraka, sees the process by which whites stole from blacks as inevitable and self-destructive. "Some white musicians have sung songs committed to changing society," he told me. "But when they've made a success of it, the rewards have encouraged them to become part of the society they criticize. If you get rich singing badly about society, you can't really sing badly about it any more. For the great majority of black musicians, however, the option of getting rich simply hasn't existed. For black people, it was always easier to be a failure. And in this way, their music has been preserved."

I Can Hypnotize Dis Nation

Ragtime was not the invention of a Jewish bandleader called Alexander. Nor was it the dream child of a Russian immigrant named Israel Baline, or Irving Berlin, as he became known with dubious chauvinism. "Alexander's Ragtime Band," however, was an indication that whatever the black musician invented, the white music industry was sure to steal. In 1911, Irving Berlin put his name to a catchy little ditty that was lyrically mediocre and musically indifferent. It was, nonetheless, a hit. That is, America took the tune to its heart and sang the hell out of it.

Soon there were "Red Peppers Rag," "Sweet Pickles Rag," "Sour Grapes Rag," "Chocolate Creams Rag." There were "Ragtime Skedaddle," "Ragtime

---

The Queen City Concert Band of Sedalia, Missouri, c.1891. Sedalia was named by General George Smith (who founded the Negro college that Joplin attended) after his daughter Sarah.

White couples dancing the cakewalk on the cover of Scott Joplin's most famous rag.

Chimes," "Ragtime Joke," and "Ragtime Insanity." There were "Mop Rag" and "Doll Rags," "Shine or Polish Rag," and "Smash-up Rag." These songs were musically hilarious, especially to those black musicians who had toiled for the acceptance of ragtime and were mostly excluded from this white bonanza. The market in spurious rags increased so rapidly that white society came to assume Berlin had started the whole damn thing. And when New York's song factory decreed that a newer fashion had arrived, ragtime was tossed aside and forgotten for half a century.

America of the 1870s was in a ferment of transition. Thousands were being drawn from the land by the promise of employment in the cities. The cities were life. People were hungry for amusement. Some found it at home, but most went miles for it on foot or by horse and buggy. White people had their entertainment and black people had theirs, and black entertainment was certainly not thought suitable or interesting for whites.

Except, that is, for one curious diversion. The nigger minstrel shows had begun as far back as the 1840s when white entertainers covered their faces in dark make-up (usually burnt cork) and mimicked blacks. Audiences found this parodying of blacks as dishonest, feckless, idle, and musically quaint immensely enjoyable. It occurred to very few that the shows were offensive.

It was not long thereafter that blacks themselves formed their own companies and performed all over the United States in front of white as well as black audiences. Some were not black enough to fulfill the expected image of coal-black niggers, so they, too, applied burnt cork in a demeaning but spirited attempt to prove they could sing and dance better than the white man. For a laugh, the black nigger minstrels parodied white hill country music — by syncopating it. The jig, the reel, and the hoedown, all staple fodder for country get-to-

Irving Berlin, born in Siberia, 1888, popularizer of ragtime, displaying the multitudinous fruits of his labors at a 1940 re-creation of Nigger Mike's Bowery Bar, where he had begun his career as a singing waiter. The event took place at the Astor.

gethers, were made ragged, and the dance step that resulted acquired the single description of "rag."

The music was primitive — a mixture of white folk songs and black work songs. Parody was its touchstone and the jug band — consisting of five-string banjo, empty liquor jugs, fiddle, and harmonica, all vamped over a wash-tub bass — its vehicle. In the pioneer states of Kansas, Arkansas, Oklahoma, and Missouri, such music found a ready audience. Encouraged by the success of the minstrels, black country jug bands multiplied, and their music was brought to town by itinerant musicians eager for employment in newly prosperous setlements of the Midwest.

Sedalia, in the center of Missouri, was one such community. It was not the hub of the universe, but had become the junction of an important railroad network that, in a comparatively short time, transformed a remote village into a thriving town. Work had lured many blacks, who found jobs in the commercial houses, in hotels, restaurants, and saloons, and on the farms that ringed the town. One opened up a barbershop, another ran a local newspaper. Others worked in the many clubs, including a bar on Main Street called the Maple Leaf. Main Street was the town's "sporting belt"; at sundown, the gambling houses and honkytonks were wide open and ready for business.

The wooden sidewalks thronged with loiterers and hookers.

Musicologist Rudi Blesh has reconstructed the scene inside the Maple Leaf. The "club" consisted of a large room dominated by a Victorian bar of carved walnut and filled with pool and gambling tables. The lighting was scarcely adequate to compete with the swirling tobacco smoke; hanging gas chandeliers seemed like beacons in a fog. The noise was immense. As the visitor's eyes became accustomed to the gloom, however, he would make out that the music he heard came from an upright piano in the far corner. There, on a plush covered stool, sat a black pianist. A quartet would gather around the piano and belt out a syncopated, close-harmony version of a popular song of the day. Without looking up from their dice games or poker hands, or from a delicate shot for the corner pocket, the men around the room would join in the chorus:

> Oh, Mr. Johnson, turn me loose,
> Got no money, but a good excuse,
> Oh, Mr. Johnson, I'll be good.
>
> Oh, Mr. Johnson, turn me loose,
> Don't take me to the calaboose,
> Oh, Mr. Johnson, I'll be good.

Mr. Johnson was popular slang for the law. Nobody wanted to finish up behind bars; life was better leaning on them, especially when there was an abundance of entertaining black piano players. These "professors" or "ticklers" drifted from town to town, playing at fairs and races and excursions, occasionally holding down jobs, performing in minstrel shows, meeting each other, exchanging ideas and borrowing snatches of melody and harmony from the country jug bands. Their music became the music of the brothel—relegated there because a race-conscious white society would permit no black musician a better platform. "We used to play in sporting houses," composer and pianist Eubie Blake told me, "and in bars. For ladies of the evening and gentlemen of leisure. We had to take our hats off, but they weren't nothing better than ignorant pimps."

But the principal musical activity of Sedalia was its brass band. This was the era of John

Orchestrated ragtime, by the Musical Spillers.

Philip Sousa and every Sunday afternoon in towns across the country local bandsmen would hold forth. Sedalia's pride was the Queen City Concert Band, led by cornetist Ed Gravitt, which had repeatedly proved its worth by demolishing all comers in band contests from Sedalia to Kansas City. A particular feature of the band was its orchestral offshoot, a seven-piece outfit organized and led by its trombonist W. H. Carter—who happened to be editor and publisher of the *Sedalia Times.* Disturbed one evening in his editorial reflections by the row coming from the Maple Leaf Club, Carter wrote: "We are informed that orders have been issued to shut down the piano thumping on Main Street." When nothing happened, he protested further. "Why is it not stopped? Someone answer the question."

The Concert Band, of course, continued to pump out its marches. But the sound coming from the Maple Leaf proved irresistible. The boys in the Queen City Concert Band began to work on so-called coon tunes like "My Coal Black Lady," "Dora Dean," and "Sweet Kentucky Babe." Overtures gave way to medleys of old plantation and "down South" songs. The orchestral section soon followed; quadrilles and schottisches were out, the two-step was in. Even favorite old waltzes took on a syncopation never dreamed of by Waldteufel or Strauss, although very much in the mind of the orchestra's new leader—Scott Joplin.

Joplin was born on November 24, 1868, in the

town of Texarkana on the Texas–Arkansas border. He was brought up with two brothers and two sisters in a poor but musical family. His father, a former slave, played the violin; his mother was a singer. Joplin, it seems, had an instinct for music from early childhood. By the age of eleven, his piano playing (self-taught) was the pride of the neighborhood. A German music professor, whose name has been lost, was so impressed that he gave the boy free lessons in the works of great European composers. But Joplin Senior became hostile to the music young Scott was playing, so the boy left home to seek a living in the only sure way available to a black musician—as one of hundreds of "professors" who furnished the entertainment for bar-parlors and bawdyhouses throughout the Southern and Border states.

He went to Sedalia and found he could continue his music studies at the new George Smith College for Negroes. After enrolling in the college, he took a job at the Maple Leaf Club to support himself. "Rags were played in Sedalia long before Scott Joplin settled there," one of his later pupils, Arthur Marshall, remembered. "But he got to making them really go." Not, however, into print. Joplin's first contact (in 1898) with the Sedalia music house of A. W. Perry & Son at 306 Broadway was disappointing. They had already published a "Maple Leaf Waltz" by a woman named Florence Johnson, and told Joplin there was no future for a piece entitled "Maple Leaf Rag"—unless, that is, the composer cared to change its name.

Joplin refused, and in December set off for Kansas City with a bundle of compositions under his arm. Carl Hoffman, a notoriously ungenerous publisher, bought a tune called "Original Rags" but passed up "Maple Leaf." It had, he said, no commercial potential whatsoever. Joplin returned to Sedalia with his dreams of publication temporarily abandoned.

Thomas Million Turpin (*top left*, in 1926) ran a pleasure complex in St. Louis. *Top right:* the site of his original Rosebud Café on Market Street. In the upstairs rooms and across the street were places of more specific entertainment. *Left:* members of the "Hurrah Sporting Club" seen behind the Rosebud. Third from the right in the front row is Louis Chauvin.

Then, one afternoon the following summer, a much respected local gentleman came in for a cool beer and a little amusement. Joplin was playing in the corner of the saloon. The customer, a white man, was much intrigued by the music he heard and asked Joplin to drop by his store next day with some of his compositions. Early next morning, Joplin sat down at a Jesse French upright and played his music. A deal was concluded and the "Maple Leaf Rag" was bought. John Stark, former ice-cream salesman, had consolidated his ambition to become a music publisher. From the meeting of John Stark and Scott Joplin in 1899 on, the history of ragtime revolves around these two men. Stark was indispensable to Joplin's vision: a white man, operating in the white world, able to bring reality to a black man's dreams.

It is important to understand the distinction between the rag and ragtime. "Ragtime" is a description that can, broadly, be applied to any music that is syncopated. Eubie Blake was able to play familiar "classical" music both traditionally and with a syncopated beat—the latter, as he told me, is "your ragtime." The rag, as it developed into what became known as the classic rag, was a written form. It had four sixteen-bar themes arranged systematically with specific harmonic relationships between each. Classic rags are intricate and hard to play, the natural product of a group of musicians whose livelihood depended on their skill at the keyboard.

Stark bought Joplin's rag for fifty dollars, plus royalties to the composer—good terms for the time. It was printed in St. Louis and went on sale in late September 1899. The only promotion was by Joplin himself, playing it for customers. But in its first dozen or so years, "Maple Leaf Rag" was to sell four hundred thousand copies—a phenomenal sale for a black composer. The first six months' sales alone were enough to decide John Stark's next move: to metropolitan St. Louis.

"Maple Leaf" made Stark one of the leading publishers in the state. Among other things, it enabled him to buy a printing press at 3615 Laclede Avenue where he could print whatever he chose to publish. Joplin soon followed Stark to St. Louis, bringing with him a new bride—a Sedalia widow, Belle Hayden. Joplin's life took on a new pattern, more to his liking than the honky-tonk circuit, and more in accord with the seriousness of his nature. He withdrew from active participation in the "sporting" world, though he maintained his friendships and contacts. Partly supported by the "Maple Leaf" royalties—as he was to be henceforth by his numerous compositions—he set up as a teacher while Mrs. Joplin supplemented their income by opening a boardinghouse.

One of Stark's first publications on the new press was also one of Joplin's finest compositions. Written in collaboration with Belle's dying brother-in-law, young Scott Hayden, it was called "Sunflower Slow Drag." It had been completed in Sedalia "during the high temperature of Scott Joplin's courtship," wrote Stark. Joplin was "touching the ground only in the highest places; his geese were all swans, and Mississippi water tasted like honey dew. . . . If ever there was a song without words, this is that article; hold your ear to the ground while someone plays it, and you can hear Scott Joplin's heartbeat."

Morgan Street, where the Joplins lived, was only three blocks from St. Louis' red-light district and its principal whorehouse, the Rosebud Café. Joplin was inevitably drawn to it by old acquaintances; it was, after all, the established rendezvous for every St. Louis or visiting pianist. They were all of an age—Joe Jordan, born in Cincinnati, was eighteen in 1900; Sam Patterson, St. Louis born, was nineteen; Charlie Warfield, from Tennessee, had come to St. Louis in 1897 at fourteen. Most gifted of all, Louis Chauvin—sometimes called "Bird Face"—was only seventeen.

Joplin, by now past thirty, had long since realized that the underworld was a doomed Bohemia for those who remained in it. If the whorehouse and saloon provided a haven for unrecognized genius, they provided a lotus also. It was easy—too easy—just to drift. It of-

fered refuge more than incentive. And so it was for Louis Chauvin, whose talent was brightest of all and with whom Joplin wrote "Heliotrope Bouquet." Patterson described him as "about five feet five and never above 145 pounds. He looked delicate, with his long, tapering fingers, but he was wild and strong. He never gambled but stayed up, drank, and made lots of love. He adored women, but treated them like dirt—he always had two or three. He loved whisky too, but only seemed to be living when he was at the piano. It's authentic, I guess, that he smoked opium at the last."

Chauvin died in 1908, after twenty-three days in a Chicago hospital, most of them in a coma. Joplin noted: "Chauvin died of complications." The *New Orleans Item* wrote of the atmosphere that pervaded and emanated from the bawdyhouses and saloons: "It was a day when the victims of the shadow-plague walked the streets of New Orleans and other great cities, living corpses, eyelids dropping in early paralysis, hands and body shaking with a palsy not caused by old age. It was a day when young sports decayed and died of the 'rales.' The younger generation hardly knows the word today. But old-timers remember it well."

For Joplin, Chauvin's death was further warning to stay away from the twilight world of the brothel and the honky-tonk, and a reminder. The success of the "Maple Leaf Rag" and other songs had enabled Joplin to continue his studies in composition and counterpoint. He was driven on by an instinctive realization that it was his responsibility to better himself. Not for him the tawdriness of the minstrel show nor the squalor of the gambling club. Social respectability, brought perhaps by commercial success, was an essential ambition. To achieve this he would have to prove he was more than a tunesmith. In 1903, an Eastern composer and journalist named Monroe H. Rosenfeld—writing in the St. Louis *Globe-Democrat*—noted: "St. Louis boasts of a composer of music who, de-

Chauvin's death was further warning to stay away from the twilight world of the brothel and the honky-tonk.

Scott Joplin c.1900.

spite the ebony hue of his features and a retiring disposition, has written possibly more instrumental successes than any other local composer. . . . But his . . . ambition is to shine in other spheres. He affirms that it is only a pastime for him to compose syncopated music and he longs for more arduous work. To this end he is assiduously toiling upon . . . an opera."

Joplin was not alone in this ambition. Another black composer, Harry Lawrence Freeman, had written over twenty operas, the first having been produced in 1893. None had ever been published, although Joplin and Freeman had formed companies like those of the vaudevillians to tour and promote their more "serious" music. Almost without exception, these companies had failed. In 1903, however, St. Louis was well into its planning of a World's Fair; Joplin intended to produce a grandiose work to celebrate the event and consolidate his reputation as a composer of stature. The handwritten orchestral parts represented weeks of unremitting labor by Joplin and painstaking copy work by Arthur Marshall. Marshall noted later: "As for the ragtime opera, *A Guest of Honor* was performed once in St. Louis, in a large hall where they often gave dances. It was a test-out or dress rehearsal to get the idea of public sentiment. It was taken quite well. I can't say just how far it got, as I was very eager for greater money. I left St. Louis for Chicago."

In fact, the opera got nowhere. The World's Fair was postponed until 1904, and the opera was not performed again. In the files of the copyright office in Washington, D.C., a card (dated February 18, 1903) reads: "Published by John Stark & Son, copyright 1903 by Scott Joplin." Despite this official data, *A Guest of Honor* was never published. A handwritten notation adds: "copies never received." All trace of the original manuscripts has vanished. Joplin is

presumed to have destroyed them.

Joplin's home life was no more fruitful than his work. A baby girl was ill from birth and lived only a few months. Joplin separated from his wife; Marshall remembered Joplin telling him: "My wife has no interest in my musical career." Saddened by the collapse of his household, Joplin dismissed his pupils. He no longer seemed able to compose. St. Louis and Missouri were finished for him. It was necessary, apart from any practical considerations, to look elsewhere. Perhaps to Chicago.

Joplin, of course, was not the only ragtime composer. Without doubt, he became the most famous black composer of his day, but there were many others. One was Blind Boone, born in 1864 in Miami, Missouri. Boone was a suc-

Top far left: Percy Warwick, aged 20. *Top near left:* William Krell, composer of "Mississippi Rag." *Bottom far left:* Arthur Marshall in about 1889. Joplin lived in Marshall's house when he first arrived in Sedalia, and gave the boy lessons. *Bottom near left:* Scott Hayden, Scott Joplin's brother-in-law, with whom he collaborated on several rags. *Right:* Jelly Roll Morton, aged about 18, in his days as a Storyville pianist.

cessful concert pianist, a successor to another black virtuoso, Blind Tom. Although (by repute) mentally backward, Blind Tom could repeat the most complex piano compositions after one hearing—including mistakes often planted to trap him. Blind Boone was a distinguished man with a prodigious technique—he was a renowned, albeit idiosyncratic, interpreter of classical music. On the side, however, he played ragtime and on retirement issued some of his rags under the title *Strains from the Alley*.

Nor was the publication of the "Maple Leaf Rag" the beginning of ragtime. "Rag Knots" by W. C. Coleman, a New Orleans composer, preceded it by ten years. The deluge of published rags had started in January 1897, with William H. Krell's "Mississippi Rag." The following December, Tom Turpin—whose Rosebud Café Joplin had eschewed—published "Harlem Rag." Nor was the sudden prominence of rag-

time a consequence of Joplin's apparent success. A dance craze, a white dance craze, had seized the nation. First performed by blacks on the plantations, the cakewalk had figured in the minstrel shows (white and black) as a "walk-around" finale danced by couples, with improvisations by each pair as they turned the corners of a square. The prize, awarded by acclamation to the most ingenious couple, was—by tradition—a cake.

"It was generally on Sundays when there was little work," said Shephard N. Edmonds, himself the son of freed slaves. "The slaves, both young and old, would dress up in hand-me-down finery to do a high-kicking, prancing walk-around. They did a take-off on the high manners of the white folks in the big house. Their masters, who gathered around to watch the fun, missed the point." But not the excitement. Later, white cakewalkers crowded the

beaches, invaded the ballrooms, took over the streets. Some considered it de rigueur to apply a little burnt cork and mimic the blacks who were mimicking the whites. Ragtime music, with its syncopation and jaunty air, proved well suited as an accompaniment. And when the dance—now promoted by the minstrel and vaudeville shows—attained its curious popularity in white society, ragtime went with it. By 1897, the demand was for rags, and more rags. Turpin, with his "Harlem Rag," was black; Krell, of the "Mississippi Rag," who knew nothing of ragtime other than its name and approximate tempo, was white.

The acceptance of ragtime, moreover, was urged forward by a white vaudevillian renowned for his close impersonation of Negro "qualities"—Benjamin Robertson Harney. Bruner Greenup, a prosperous St. Louis merchant, remembered him well: "Ben managed to

sit at the piano with a cane in one hand or the other and did a sort of tap dance with one or both feet and the cane. He came to my store one day and asked me to publish a song that he had put together. The song, now historic, was 'You've Been a Good Old Wagon, But You Done Broke Down.' It was the first syncopated song to be published in America. That is absolutely true. . . ."

Harney moved on to New York. A dozen of his ragtime songs were published, many with instrumental dance or cakewalk endings. Some became classics of a kind, although many had a familiar ring. One was called "Mr. Johnson,

The progress from ragtime. *Left:* James Sylvester Scott (second from right) played his piano in a small band; *center:* Tony Jackson and the Panama Trio, which produced singer Florence Mills (extreme right in photograph); *right:* James P. Johnson, whose development and mastery of "stride piano" set a style in Harlem for the 1920s.

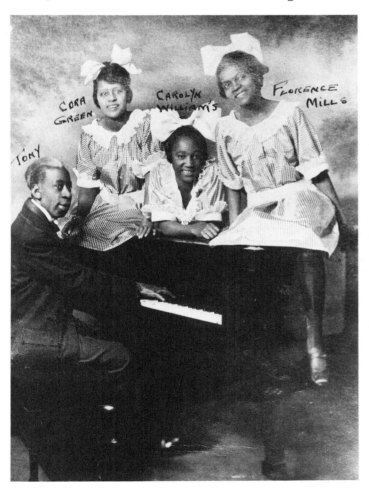

Turn Me Loose."

Harney was soon booked into vaudeville's top circuits and headlined as the "Inventor of Ragtime." His success encouraged a multitude of others and the New York *Police Gazette* decided it was time for a competition to decide

Sissle and Blake, the "Dixie Duo," known for their vaudeville appearances which lasted from 1917 to 1928. Eubie Blake (*left*, and at left in *right*), born in Baltimore on February 7, 1883, learned his trade as pianist in sporting houses and medicine shows. During his association with Noble Sissle (at right) he composed many standards, including "I'm Just Wild About Harry" and, in ragtime, "Chevy Chase" and "Troublesome Ivories." The two put together in 1921 a successful New York show called *Shuffle Along*, and in 1926 visited England. In 1928 Noble Sissle, born in Indianapolis on August 10, 1889, decided to take a band of his own back to Europe, where he made many recordings. He had already worked with Jim Europe's Society Orchestra as a guitarist and singer and with a U.S. Army band during World War I. During the 1930s Sissle's band included such musicians as Tommy Ladnier and Sidney Bechet; even Charlie Parker played briefly with Sissle. Sissle and Blake worked together again during World War II; Blake gave a solo performance at New York's Philharmonic Hall as recently as 1974, at age 91.

who was "Ragtime King of the World." The *Gazette* had a penchant for staging public contests, indulging its readers in everything from quail-eating to pigeon-flying, from oyster-opening to wrestling. Ragtime seemed a natural. "Many eyes are on the diamond studded trophy," the *Gazette* said in its issue of January 20, 1900. "The ragtime contest will settle a question much vexed . . . since the coon melodies became popular." After making assurances that "the best man will win, . . . an artist who belongs in an obscure country town has as much chance to win as anyone," the *Gazette* admitted that the acknowledged leader of the ragtime players was "Mr. Michael Bernard, leader of the orchestra at Pastor's, whose fame as a manipulator of the ivories has spread throughout the land. If ever there was a champ, he is one." The *Gazette* did not mention Scott Joplin. Being black, he was ineligible.

Mike Bernard won, not to anyone's great surprise, and soon the new "King" was traveling the circuits. Harney was eclipsed, but whenever he and Bernard met on the same bill, he would struggle wildly to win back his audience. With powerful emotion, he would render his more famous songs — including "The Cake Walk in the Sky" with its fanciful description of a "crap-shootin' coon — doomed for below [who] sneaked in the other way and bluffed Peter at the Gate." Audiences shouted and clapped and laughed until the tears ran down their faces.

As rags began pouring into the market, the demand for instruction grew. "Learn to play ragtime and be popular," read one advertisement. Another, published in the *Chicago Daily News* in 1903, carried the bold headline: "Ragtime Taught in Ten Lessons." The teacher was Axel Christensen, a twenty-two-year-old Dane.

"I secured quarters in the Athenaeum building," Christensen recalled later. "They were not so fussy there — as a matter of fact, the janitor asked me if I intended to sleep in the studio." Between 1903 and 1923, Christensen's schools spread across the continent with more than two hundred thousand enrollments. By 1935, the figure had grown to an amazing half a million and Axel W. Christensen was being

hailed as the "Czar of Rag-time."

Amid this bedlam, John Stark opened a New York office. It proved a tragic mistake; the provincial publisher could not compete with the experienced denizens of the big city. The commercial success of Irving Berlin's cheap imitation rag destroyed the hopes of men like Stark. Big publishers gobbled up little ones; they mobilized armies of white song pluggers to get their songs performed in vaudeville shows. Joplin fared little better than Stark. He, too, had followed the crowd—from St. Louis to Chicago and the Pekin Temple of Music, then from Chicago to New York—believing that his rags needed personal missionary work rather than exploitation by large publishing houses.

Stark and Joplin failed to grasp that in the cities of the North it was not the music that mattered; it was what sold the best. Black music was valued only insofar as it might fill the coffers of white publishers. When Stark's wife died, he decided to write off his New York venture. Sickened by the Manhattan Rialto, he closed his office and retreated to the printing press in St. Louis that the "Maple Leaf Rag" had bought for him. Joplin was dismayed and accused Stark of betrayal. For years after the collapse of his offering to the St. Louis World's Fair, he had been toiling on a second large-scale work. By 1911— the year Alexander "invented" ragtime—Joplin's piano version was ready. It covered two hundred pages and was called *Treemonisha*. John Stark turned it down.

The quarrel with his long-time supporter was symptomatic of something deeper. A slow and serious change in Joplin himself was beginning to worry his friends. Once a

It took fifty years of neglect and a hit movie called <u>The Sting</u> to restore ragtime not necessarily to its proper place, but at least to the attention of a fickle public.

man of even temperament, Joplin had become increasingly subject to alarming changes of mood. He would suddenly veer from apathy, verging on morose depression, to a hectic, almost feverish elation in which his energy seemed boundless and his concentration razor sharp. In his periods of depression, moreover, his skill seemed to desert him. He was like a child learning to play the piano. He would come to a halting stop, audibly correct himself, and start again. Those who had not known him before laughed at the spectacle of a man who said he had composed the "Maple Leaf Rag" but was unable to play it. Some began to doubt that he had actually written the compositions that bore his name: rumors grew that he had stolen the work of others. "I had heard so much about Scott Joplin," Eubie Blake told me, "but I had never heard him play. A club in Washington wired for him to appear and he told the guests 'I don't play.' But they wouldn't believe it and kept after him until he gave in. It was pitiful to hear."

Treemonisha contained twenty-seven complete musical numbers, including the overture and a prelude to Act III. Its subject was the Negro race, its moral that Negroes must rise above superstition and ignorance toward enlightenment in order to be fully human and exercise their own gifts.

With the herculean task of composition accomplished, Joplin undertook the even more formidable tasks of writing out the instrumental parts and securing money for the opera's production. During the long periods he worked on the score, he took in more and more pupils whose fees helped finance his composition, while he gave innumerable private run-throughs on the piano

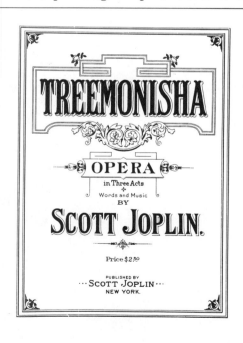

TREEMONISHA

OPERA
in Three Acts
+
Words and Music
BY
SCOTT JOPLIN.

Price $2.50

PUBLISHED BY
···SCOTT JOPLIN···
NEW YORK.

for potential backers. Eventually, the score finished, Joplin began auditioning; he was determined to put on one performance at his own expense to test public reaction and perhaps attract a financier. "Joplin got his whole cast set up," Sam Patterson remembered. "He worked like a dog training them."

A performance finally took place at a hall in Harlem in 1915. It was by a full cast, but without scenery or orchestra. Joplin played all the orchestral parts himself on the piano. *Treemonisha* made almost no impression. Without decor, lighting, or orchestral backing, the drama seemed thin and unconvincing, little better than a rehearsal. In any event, its special quality was lost on the Harlem audience that attended. They were sophisticated enough to reject their folk past, but not sufficiently aware for a return to it in art. *Treemonisha* was a terrible disaster, and was not heard again for over fifty years.

One revival of the opera by an enthusiastic cast began in Houston in 1975, moved to Washington, and finally to Broadway. The work itself seemed flawed, long and rambling, with only traces of the carefree elegance that marked Joplin's greatest work. He had allowed the memory of childhood mentors to overwhelm his own true invention, and equated respectability with an emulation of European masters. Sadly, he lacked time and health to develop beyond either.

Joplin never recovered from that night in Harlem. It crushed the hopes of a lifetime. The progress of his infirmity accelerated as though all inner resistance had gone. His physical coordination grew more uncertain, his periods of depression darker and more frequent. Finally, his second wife was compelled to have him confined to a madhouse. Before he went, Joplin destroyed hundreds of sheets of compositions. In the state hospital on Ward's Island in the East River off New York, he made notes feverishly on scraps of paper. Six months after he was committed, in the spring of 1917, he died. "Cause of death: syphilis, dementia paralytica."

The day of Joplin's funeral was long, the crowds impressive. The legend that the mourners' carriages each bore a banner with the name of one of his compositions is, like so many legends in popular music, untrue. The composer's widow rode in the leading carriage during the long ride to St. Michael's Cemetery in Queens, where Joplin was buried in an unmarked grave. Almost sixty years later, money was raised to inscribe an epitaph. It reads: "Scott Joplin, American Composer, November 24, 1868–April 1, 1917."

Ragtime did not die with Scott Joplin. But its beauty and strength had already been pillaged by New York's music publishers and promoters. It took fifty years of neglect and a hit movie called *The Sting* to restore ragtime not necessarily to its proper place, but at least to the attention of a fickle public. Joplin personified much that characterized the black man's struggle toward acceptance; his music laid the foundation for much that was to come, although it failed to achieve the respect for his people that Joplin had most especially desired.

John Stark, with profound insight, paid tribute to Joplin's predicament in his obituary. "Here is the genius," he wrote, "whose spirit—though diluted—was filtered through thousands of cheap songs and vain imitations."

Left: the original cover of Scott Joplin's ill-fated *Treemonisha*. *Above:* Carmen Balthrop in the title role of the Houston Grand Opera Company's 1975 revival of *Treemonisha*, surrounded by symbols of the fantasy world she is trying to banish forever from black consciousness. The production was cut for its Washington and New York performances.

Jungle Music

New Orleans was a ramshackle whirligig of a town, part French, part Negro, part Southern dude, part Northern carpetbagger, part Mexican, part Spanish, and part Indian. It was also a trading center and port, sprawled along the Mississippi on the Gulf of Mexico. No other town in the United States could boast such a cosmopolitan mix, or promise such an exciting welcome. It was noisy, dirty, hot, and smelly. And in this place, according to various Northern newspaper reports, was first heard a sound called variously "jass," "jasz," and "jazz."

Nowadays, the word "jazz" has little meaning. So many different styles of music—from Louis Armstrong to the Modern Jazz Quartet—have been labeled

Riverboat bandleader Fate Marable's Society Syncopaters, 1924.

Louis Armstrong, born in New Orleans, July 4, 1900, in England, 1932.

jazz that any sense of definition has been lost. Jazz now means anything that anybody chooses to call jazz—the music bellowed out today on Bourbon Street, for example, is no more jazz than the French Quarter was Storyville. It sounds vaguely similar to "authentic" New Orleans jazz, but is too loud and too fast. The loudness, at least, may not be the fault of the musicians. They are often required by the bar owners to play more lustily than the outfit next door because the loudest music attracts the most customers in off the street.

Many of these musicians learned their jazz from the first recorded group, the Original Dixieland Jazz Band. But the compositions played by the Original Dixieland Jazz Band were too long for the three-minute wax records of their day, so to accommodate the technical requirements of an infant recording industry, the band simply speeded up their music to make it fit. In live performances, as the band itself admitted, such speed would have been unthinkable.

Jazz was primarily a performing art; it has never lent itself easily either to arrangement or to sheet music. The determination to write down melodies and call them jazz came soon enough, but this was not in the spirit of the original music. "In a symphony orchestra," Bud Freeman says succinctly, "the listener is subservient to the orchestra, the orchestra is subservient to the conductor, and the conductor is subservient to the composer. But in jazz, the listener feels he is actively contributing to the music, actually making it himself."

All music is entitled to the dignity of definition and jazz is no exception. As it was heard in New Orleans after World War I, it possessed a definite and limited form. It consisted of any melody played by two or more musical voices,

A New Orleans "Crib House" on Basin Street, where musicians were a sideshow and the real business was prostitution. These brothels contained the likely origin for the term "jazz." The Cajun argot of Louisiana referred to prostitutes as "jazz-belles," a corruption of the Biblical "jezebels." Jelly Roll Morton once described the "jazz-belles" thus: "Some were real ladies, in spite of their downfall."

improvising collectively in two/four or four/four time, that was syncopated. Such a definition (or any definition for that matter) will not satisfy many people; aficionados of the extended, exploratory solo do not permit their heroes to be shackled by form. But before virtuosi boosted their images at the expense of cooperative musicianship, the style was not so loose. The word "jazz" may indeed have been Negro slang suggesting copulation, or merely an onomatopoeic reference to the sound of a New Orleans paddle steamer. But its meaning was clearly understood by all its early practitioners, as was its instrumentation and proper place in society. Without structure or purpose, it would have been anathema to anyone striving to attain respectability.

The growth of jazz was parallel to, but independent of, the development of other forms of music such as ragtime. From the French-derived military bands heard frequently throughout Louisiana in the second half of the nineteenth century, jazz bands took their bizarre combination of trombone, cornet, tuba, drums, and clarinet. To these they added the most commonplace Negro instrument, the banjo. Because of its instrumentation, jazz soon became the appropriate music for processions and parades; it was inconceivable that anyone could march to anything but a regular and steady beat. From the jug bands of homemade instruments that had proliferated after Emancipation, jazz musicians took over (in part) the function of providing music for dancing; a dance, too, required a consistent rhythm and pulse.

But the crucial influence jazz absorbed came from the European-oriented Creoles whom the racist policies of the South had forced out of white society and into black. Formerly hirelings and managers of the more prosperous plantations, these educated half-breeds carried with them a knowledge of and love for the classical music

In the brothels, music had the same function as wine, spirits, and striptease: it helped prepare clients for the main event upstairs.

of Europe. Probably more than any other single influence, this understanding of an academic musical tradition colored the development of what came to be known as jazz. Many of its earliest exponents—men such as Buddy Petit or Alphonse Picou—took care to emphasize their French Creole ancestry; even Jelly Roll Morton, whose claim to have "invented" jazz was as authentic as a three-dollar bill, frequently reminded everyone that his real name was Ferdinand Joseph La Menthe. The balance between know-how and instinct, between delicacy and ferocity, between technique and rule-breaking, became the hallmark of early jazz and resulted from this infusion of white culture into the black heritage. Any Creole music without form or definition would have been unthinkable. As George Shearing, the English-born American pianist, insists: "Everything, everything, whether jazz or classical music, literature or conversation, must have architecture and direction. And those who criticize us for confining jazz to such a requirement do not appreciate that in music, abandonment is fine, but indiscipline is death."

Jazz, therefore, was not the exclusive creation of a particular race; it was as much the white man's music as the black man's. Neither was it the exclusive creation of a place. Pianist Willie "The Lion" Smith swore he had heard jazz in the early years of the century played by brick-

workers as far north as Haverstraw, New York. W. C. Handy often said that the music of Memphis in 1905 was little different from that of New Orleans. Trombonist Wilbur de Paris made similar boasts for his home state of Indiana, as did Jimmy Rushing for Texas and Oklahoma.

While support for some of these claims is increasing, however, it remains true that all the elements that came to be recognized as prerequisites for jazz were present in New Orleans. As early as 1895, for example, Buddy Boldin—a barber as well as a musician—had enlivened the South by riding around in a horse-drawn wagon with a band not dissimilar in style or instrumentation to those that before long were known as "jass bands." And although there were other places farther north where blacks and whites lived close together, jazz appears not to have started in any of them. Perhaps the unexpected cultural mix of the South, particularly that of the better-documented New Orleans, was needed to encourage its beginnings.

What of Storyville, traditionally recognized as the cradle of this new music? On January 1, 1898, in an attempt to control prostitution, Alderman Sidney Story—whose own musical tastes ran closer to Johann Strauss than to emergent jazz—proposed a city ordinance to confine illegal trafficking to an area of New Orleans bordered on the north by Robertson and on the south by Basin Street. Sin, he said, was no longer discreet. The price for virgins had gone up to eight hundred dollars. Even a schoolteacher, Louisa Murphy, was making an easy living peddling her pupils. Henceforth, declared Alderman Story, evil would be contained. To his anger, the area of its containment became known as Storyville and flourished for almost twenty years until it was closed down in 1917.

The entrepreneurs of Storyville were in the sex business, of course, not the music business. Yet in the dance halls and cabarets (of which there were never more than five), music was es-

sential. In the brothels, though not a necessity, it had the same function as wine, spirits, and striptease: it helped prepare clients for the main event upstairs. From the madam's viewpoint, though, liquor was a more valuable stimulant — it sold at a profit. The musicians worked for tips. Happily for them, those out for a good time liked to prove their affluence by tipping generously.

The music varied from brothel to brothel. Often, a mechanical piano sufficed, and the patrons were expected to keep it primed with quarters. In most of the better houses, however, the music was supplied by a live pianist, one of whose functions was to accompany the ballads and song "parodies" (dirty lyrics sung to popular tunes of the day) beloved by the clientele. Sex, in all its permutations, was the dominant theme of many songs popular in or around the District. Jelly Roll Morton became famous for his repertoire of "variations" on standard songs. The sentimental ballad "Mamma's Baby Boy," published later by the Williams and Piron Music Publishing Company with lyrics fit for a church social, enjoyed great success in Storyville. The last lines in the published and authorized version are much concerned with such gentle concepts as the enormous degree of comfort, love, and joy that will be enjoyed by any girl lucky enough to share her life with Mamma's Baby Boy, if only she would realize it. The Storyville version was somewhat different; it ended:

> She handed him this line of sass —
> "If you don't like my Creole ways
> Kiss my fuckin' ass."

Kid Ory recorded the tune decades after under the title "Do What Ory Say," mumbling his way through the last line.

Storyville certainly gave employment to nu-

Top: King Oliver's Chicago-based Creole Jazz Band. Louis Armstrong joined the band in 1923, but his wife-to-be, Lil Hardin, was already its pianist; the "Jazz Wonder Child" is at Oliver's left in this picture. Among the other key figures in Oliver's band, trombonist Honoré Dutrey, clarinetist Johnny Dodds, and violinist Jimmy Palao are seen in this 1921 San Francisco picture. Bottom: Jelly Roll Morton and band, in a more "refined" period of the pianist's career.

merous musicians, who were visible and audible to anyone who passed through. Kid Ory and King Oliver furthered their careers in Storyville, although neither had begun there. But if all the musicians who are supposed to have played in Storyville — or who have claimed to have done so — had actually performed during the twenty years of its existence, then doubtless there would have been orchestras the size of the New York Philharmonic playing nonstop on every street corner. In fact, although a few bands existed in the cabarets and dance halls, the principal instrument was the piano. And at no time did the number of piano players exceed forty. The music they played was not jazz, moreover, but their own versions of concert classics (including, especially, "Tales from the Vienna Woods") or of the popular songs of the day (a favorite was "Bird in a Gilded Cage," another was "In the Gloaming," another "I'm Sorry I Made You Cry" — many were written in New Orleans). The musicians, except one, were all black. Only Kid Ross, who played for a time in the original Mahogany Hall (several blocks from its present imitation), was white.

Storyville was eventually closed by the Navy on the grounds that it was illegal to operate houses of prostitution within five miles of a military institution. Still, as a social experiment, it had not been without effect. There had been approximately 2200 registered prostitutes in 1898; in 1917, only 388 were left. During that time, New Orleans was the only American city able to reduce its police force, which it did by thirty percent. It was also the only city where the consumption of alcohol decreased. The piano playing and cabarets in Storyville had ceased some years before 1917, after the proprietor of the Tuxedo Dance Hall, Billy Phillips, had been shot to death following a bar quarrel; thereafter, music was considered a disorderly and unwelcome sideshow. But the syncopations and timbres used by the musicians in their attempts at parody — although regarded by upholders of the European traditions as "mistakes" — were among the true progenitors of the rhythmic and harmonic idiosyncrasies that soon characterized the music of the first jazz band to call itself such, the Original Dixieland Jazz Band.

This white quintet of part-time performers was musically illiterate. Only one member had any knowledge of notation, and none understood scoring. Yet they were, in 1917, the first to record "jass." One of their first hits, "Tiger Rag," was based on a French quadrille. "High Society" and "Muskrat Ramble," two other early jazz classics, were also old French tunes worked over by New Orleans musicians to give them a little extra flavor.

The Original Dixieland Jazz Band was led by a cornetist, Nick La Rocca, a carpenter by trade. Born in New Orleans in 1889, La Rocca has often been passed over in the story of jazz,

partly because his band had stopped playing altogether by 1926. Apart from a recording session in 1936, La Rocca himself forsook the music industry and returned to carpentry. Although the arrangements he and his fellow musicians performed were little more than mutilated versions of other music, La Rocca always complained that far too much credit was given to black musicians for having "invented" jazz. In the early days they never achieved anything like the commercial or public recognition he did.

La Rocca's band was the first to move north from New Orleans with any success, and before long began supplying America with its new dance music. It played New York in 1917 — at

Aldene

Reisenweber's Café—where, as purveyors of "novelty music," the musicians found themselves in ever-growing demand. Using titles such as "Barnyard Blues," "Ostrich Walk," and "Skeleton Jangle," La Rocca contrived to make jazz socially respectable, and harmless. New York publishers, recognizing the potential of La Rocca's "invention," began to remove the word "ragtime" from their sheet music and substitute the word "jazz."

Anything that had nonstop syncopation and encouraged the new craze for animal dances was now called jazz—the Turkey Trot, the Bunny Hug, and the Kangaroo Hop all became popular. None of these dances required formal training with a Dance Professor, and all symbol-

Fletcher Henderson graduated from Atlanta University in 1920, moved to New York to study for a master's degree in chemistry at Columbia University, and supported himself as a song demonstrator for a music publisher. Soon he became music director of Black Swan, and organized an outstanding collection of musicians, most important of whom was reedman-arranger Don Redman (extreme right). Henderson is here seated at the piano; saxophonist Coleman Hawkins is next to Redman. The Henderson band (including, at various times, Louis Armstrong, Benny Carter, and Rex Stewart) for five years was the headlined group at New York's Roseland Ballroom. Competition with the newly developing white bands (Paul Whiteman could pay Redman $100 an arrangement; Henderson paid $25) eventually undercut Henderson's primacy in New York. Later he thrived as an arranger himself—providing Benny Goodman, among others, with the greater part of his "book." His band was also to include such performers as John Kirby, Russell Procope, Sid Catlett, Roy Eldridge, and Jonah Jones.

ized an abandon thought appropriate by a post-war generation. The Pope denounced the Turkey Trot, but the antique dance he suggested as an alternative failed to set America ablaze.

La Rocca hit London. Then Paris. By the early twenties, every town and golf club across the United States had its jazz dance band. From small combos, these groups swelled to orchestras of thirty to forty players. With vaudeville dying, these dance bands filled the theaters with shows that included singers, acrobats, and dance troupes. The very best songwriters were encouraged to pen jazz; in 1924, George Gershwin contributed his "Rhapsody in Blue." Jazz had become America's music, though its origins, real or imagined, were ignored—except in two films that unwittingly spelled out the paradox of jazz's acceptance as a music worthy of the white majority.

The first (and well known) example was the "talking picture," Warner Brothers' *The Jazz Singer*, whose star—Al Jolson—was white, from the North, and renowned in vaudeville for his nigger minstrel routine. The second (now almost forgotten) was a film called *The King of Jazz*. Scene after scene of European music—from "D'you ken John Peel" to the massed balalaika bands of Smolensk, from *The Barber of Seville* to assorted Spanish fandangoes—descended gracefully into a smoking cauldron, there to be mixed by Svengali and the Sugar Plum Fairy, and to emerge as a tap-dancing, high-kicking troupe of Florenz Ziegfeld's best: yes, *Jazz!* The conductor of this musical gar-

Left: Leon Bix Beiderbecke, 1924. The Paul Whiteman recordings from 1927 to 1929 are valued today primarily because they bear witness to the extraordinary quality of Bix's cornet solos. The Whiteman orchestra's payroll *(above right)* indicates that Bix's weekly $200 salary was about average in the group; composer-arranger Ferde Grofé drew $375 a week, but Bing Crosby sang for only $150. *Right:* the "Austin High Gang"—Frank Teschemacher, Jimmy McPartland, Dick McPartland, Bud Freeman, and Freeman's brother, Arnie. Recordings made by the New Orleans Rhythm Kings inspired them to purchase appropriate instruments from the McPartlands' music-teacher father. The first four—clarinetist, cornetist, guitarist, tenor sax—joined with drummer Dave Tough, from nearby Oak Park High School, and collectively and individually played major roles in the white jazz boom of Chicago.

bage? Why, none other than the so-called King of Jazz himself, the white Paul Whiteman.

Meanwhile, a second exodus from New Orleans and the South had occurred, less spectacular than the first, although motivated for the same prosaic reason, the search for work. The poverty of the blacks, despite or often because of Emancipation, had continued unabated past the turn of the century. War manufacturing was concentrated in the North, further emphasizing the deprivation of the South. The first to suffer, as always, were the blacks. Traveling by rail, they journeyed to the most likely areas of employment. And the principal railroad from the South and West, the Illinois Central, led straight to Chicago.

Chicago was not, of course, the only northern city that held the promise of work, but Chicago seemed more glamorous, exciting. To a city already mob-ridden and promiscuous came the black musicians from New Orleans — by comparison, a sedate, relaxed, and, above all, cultured city. Those who came North were not, perhaps, the majority of musicians who had flourished in New Orleans, but a sufficient number to form a plenitude of bands on Chicago's South Side. The changes they helped initiate throughout the next ten years in a city that lacked peace, stability, and culture were central to the development and survival of jazz.

Chicago was no less segregated than the South. But its very flux and rapidly developing industrialization allowed a greater freedom of movement. Still, once again, blacks made their own entertainment and music — the white dance halls and beer parlors were mostly forbidden them. "All the great music was in their

Top left: Fats Waller; *top right:* Art Tatum. Oscar Levant called the highly trained Waller "the black Horowitz"; of Tatum, Waller said when the blind pianist entered a club where he (Waller) was playing, "I play piano, but God is in the house." *Bottom:* Paul Whiteman and Orchestra in the rooftop "Moonlit Terrace" of the Biltmore Hotel, 1934. The presence of an accordion and 5 violins gives an impression of the appeal Whiteman was seeking at this date; even in the Beiderbecke–Redman–Jack Teagarden–Bunny Berigan days, though, the Whiteman band was celebrated more for solo playing than for its ensemble work.

bars," saxophonist Bud Freeman told me. "We'd go to the South Side to their clubs, and we'd be half a dozen conspicuous whites. But they seemed to know we were there to hear the music and nobody bothered us. I remember one black doorman, huge—they said he weighed four hundred pounds—said to us: 'I see you little white boys is all out here to get your music lesson tonight.'" And among the musicians who played regularly in such clubs was a New Orleans trumpeter, Louis Armstrong.

The grandson of freed slaves, Armstrong had been summoned North in 1922 by his friend and mentor, Joe "King" Oliver, to the Lincoln Gardens on the South Side. Here, the excellence of his trumpet playing, although within the structural limits of jazz, transcended form. Indeed, so distinctive was his playing that before long he eclipsed King Oliver and became a soloist—an "eagle," Bud Freeman called him. The notion of jazz as collective improvisation was given a severe jolt, but not before Armstrong had made numerous records as an unnamed sideman accompanying such singers as Ma Rainey and Bessie Smith.

The importance of these sidemen (Armstrong was just one of hundreds) was unnoticed until the London *Melody Maker* (a jazz periodical founded several years before any American equivalent) recognized on these records a unique blend of composition and improvisation that was quite unlike the jazz that had been paraded by the Original Dixieland Jazz Band. The distinguishing factor, claimed *Melody Maker*, was the adroit contribution of the sidemen. Diligently, the magazine began digging up their names and ascribing to their talents the dubious epithet "genius." The first concert, as opposed to club appearance, ever given by Armstrong was at the London Palladium. And when Duke Ellington later traveled to England, he was astonished to discover that his jazz public knew the names and musical curricula of all his musicians better than he did himself.

It was the very nature of Chicago that provided Armstrong and his fellow musicians with the chance to develop the style and substance of their music. Since the advent of Prohibition (in

1919) and the subsequent growth of speakeasies and bootleg booze, jazz in Chicago had moved slightly underground. Trumpet players got the sack: they were too noisy and might attract inquisitive patrolmen. The new lead instruments were the clarinet and the cornet; solos, which tended to be quieter than ensemble playing, were preferred.

The speakeasies also offered an easy opportunity for whites to hear the music. "Al Capone would come in sometimes and give us twenty-dollar bills," another of these soloists, Earl "Fatha" Hines, recalls. "Other times he'd come in and close the joint down, give the boss man two thousand dollars, and make us play just for Capone. The different gangs used to try and outspend each other. East Side gang one night, West Side gang the next. Four to five thousand dollars thrown around just like that. There was an awful lot of money in Chicago then. Awful lot. Some of my band are still living in the homes they managed to buy at that time."

The emergence of these soloists also heralded a return to the older "call and return" pattern of work song and spiritual. The soloist and band would answer one another according to a prearranged pattern. This shift did not preclude improvisation or the sense of collective musicianship. But it encouraged a reliance on melody instead of the traditional three-part harmony of Dixieland. The soloist was required to play extended melodic lines and not just vamp as part of the band. Armstrong's temperament, that of the natural show-off, was ideally suited to exploit this tendency — as was that of a white cornetist, Bix Beiderbecke, who demonstrated by his effortless technique that a melody could be every note as fascinating as any harmony and that white musicians could initiate, not just imitate, jazz.

Leon Bix Beiderbecke learned most of his jazz at the feet — literally — of various black soloists in Chicago. Although little known in his brief lifetime, he has acquired legendary status since, not least because he was the first white jazz musician to be admired and copied by blacks.

Like the Creoles, he was influenced by classical composers, particularly Debussy. Maurice Ravel was a close friend, and from him Beiderbecke learned a sense of order and purpose that was instilled into the burgeoning canon of jazz. Beiderbecke's first recordings were made in 1923 for the Wolverines, with whom he journeyed to New York's Roseland Ballroom a year later. A season in St. Louis in 1926 with Frankie Trumbauer's orchestra at the Arcadia Ballroom, and a spell working with Jean Goldkette in Detroit, concluded in his joining Paul Whiteman's band, where he remained until 1930. Thereafter, odd jobs kept him busy until his death a year later — officially of pneumonia.

Soloists like Beiderbecke sought to group themselves in bands that, while retaining the semblance of the old Dixieland ensembles, allowed a new freedom of melodic improvisation. Their intuitive sense of togetherness enabled them to cook up what were called "head arrangements," music giving the illusion of spontaneity by the use of "riffs," repeated rhythmic and melodic patterns. Most important of these new groupings, if only because it attracted the most prominent musicians, including Armstrong, Coleman Hawkins, and Don Redman, was the big band of Fletcher Henderson.

Henderson had gone to New York City from Atlanta in 1920 for postgraduate work in chemistry, but instead took a part-time job playing piano with W. C. Handy. By 1923, he was leading his own band at the Club Alabam in New York, and a year later at Roseland on Broadway.

Ellington showed that it was possible to score jazz for a large ensemble of soloists without restricting their improvisational capabilities.

His was among the first of the large bands to acquire a reputation by playing jazz, and he began to record with many of the major black artists of the twenties — among them Bessie Smith, Armstrong,

Redman, and Benny Carter. Henderson's band was considered musically undisciplined; his greatest success was to come later as an arranger for others, such as Benny Goodman and the Dorsey Brothers. But his distinctive sound—the brass answering the reeds in harmonic counterpoint—became the model for many subsequent big bands. Count Basie, and later Artie Shaw and Goodman, prospered by Henderson's example. As did the greatest of these band leaders, Edward Kennedy Ellington.

Born April 29, 1899, into a middle-class home in Washington, D.C., Ellington had been a poster printer and designer while making money on the side providing a small band for local concerts and parties. Persuaded by Fats Waller—his strongest influence—to try his luck in New York, Ellington worked first for Ada "Bricktop" Smith and then at Barron's in Har-

lem. Before long, he was leader of his own group at the Hollywood Club on Broadway (later known as the Kentucky Club), and in 1927 secured an engagement at the Cotton Club in Harlem. It was from there, during a five-year stay, that he began to broadcast on national radio, which secured for him and his band notable popularity. In 1943, he performed the first of a series of concerts at Carnegie Hall (repeated annually until 1950), which saw his most determined efforts to introduce length, weight, and purpose into jazz music.

Ellington's performance on piano was not what established his reputation, although his skill was considerable. It was as a composer, arranger, and leader that he was incomparable. He showed that it was possible to score

The Ellington band, 1935.

jazz for a large ensemble of soloists without restricting their improvisational capabilities. But his importance for jazz was that he further demonstrated its development was not primarily the result of musical or historical accident (although both elements played an occasional role), but the result of contributions by a small but startling collection of individuals — Armstrong, Beiderbecke, and Henderson among them. Environment and chance affected these individuals, and Ellington, profoundly; but environment and chance were not sufficient to propel jazz along the particular course it took.

In fact, it was their triumph over circumstances that characterized the breakthroughs by these innovators. Ellington's music — despite its classical ambitions — was created for dancing. His band, like Count Basie's Kansas City-originated group, found early employment in the growing number of cabarets and dance halls. The compromises necessary to reach the larger white audiences, however, were considerable. Ellington sold forty percent of all his composition and performance fees to a white

promoter-manager. Armstrong sold fifty-one percent of his. Until the late forties, all black performers at New York's smartest night club — the Rainbow Room — were apparently still using the service elevator. Ellington's first recognition by Hollywood was in an Amos 'n' Andy movie. Earl Hines gave up classical piano when a friend pointed out there were no opportunities for a black on the white concert platform. Eddie South, the "Angel of the Violin," spent years in Paris and Budapest perfecting his technical mastery only to be told that the best employment open to him in America was in night clubs. And Dizzy Gillespie, who is not a bitter man, speaks of a time when he performed on the *Rudy Vallee Show:* "I came on and he said: 'Well, what do we have in the Ubanga department tonight?' He had no respect for our culture. He just thought of it as jungle music." "The whites," claims record producer John Hammond, "loused up a whole art form for twenty-five years."

Segregation and a sense of being cheated, however, did little to stop jazz. The music was neither morbid nor introspective. It bore witness to a triumph of the individual spirit over the most depressing of circumstances. After all, by the early thirties, most of the commercially successful bands were white. That is not to say the white bands were less musical than their black counterparts — Benny Goodman's big band was better rehearsed and more disciplined than any band Fletcher Henderson ever led. Nor is it to suggest that white musicians themselves supported segregation. Goodman had Henderson as one of his principal arrangers, and refused to accept bookings for segregated audiences. When he formed his first quartet, Goodman used two whites — himself and drummer Gene Krupa — and two blacks, Teddy Wilson and Lionel Hampton. "Being with Benny," Hampton says today, "we were able to play for the first time in the finest hotels and ballrooms in the country. It served a great purpose. It was wonderful."

Not all musicians were as lucky as Hampton, of course, and there was a growing resentment among blacks that something of theirs had been stolen. In tiny clubs along New York's Fifty-

Top: this unusual photograph, from the early 1940s, indicates John Hammond's remarkable position as entrepreneur-among-performers. Hammond, in the foreground, is lighting his cigarette; Earl Hines holds the bottle; Charlie Christian is at the rear of the table, on the left; Helen Humes wears a turban; Count Basie and Benny Goodman sit directly opposite Hammond. *Center left:* Ellington and alter ego Billy Strayhorn, who worked with Ellington from 1939 until his death in 1967. *Center right:* the guitarist Eddie Condon was responsible for a series of small-group concerts at New York's Town Hall in the mid-1940s; the club that bore his name became a vital source of mainstream jazz. Here, Condon leads a group including trumpeter Max Kaminsky, clarinetist Pee Wee Russell, trombonists Benny Morton and J.C. Higginbotham, and pianist Dave Bowman. *Bottom left:* one of the last photographs of guitar prodigy Charlie Christian (at left, with Don Redman and Count Basie), who died of drug-complicated tuberculosis in his early twenties. He played downtown evenings with Benny Goodman, and was present after-hours at Minton's in Harlem, where Thelonius Monk, Dizzy Gillespie, Charlie Parker, and Kenny Clarke were experimenting with a style that became known as bebop. Clarke told Nat Hentoff and Nat Shapiro that "he and Monk were hand in glove. If Charlie had lived he would have been real modern." *Bottom right:* Dizzy Gillespie, born in South Carolina, 1917. Asked how he felt about being so widely imitated, he replied: "It means that my life was worthwhile. I did something that somebody liked. So. There you go."

second Street, various musicians tried more intimate groupings whose very musicianship would defeat imitation. Fats Waller and Red Norvo, for example, led small units that played the same tunes as the bigger bands, but with greater emphasis on counterpoint and rhythmic complexity. John Kirby led a brilliant sextet that played lightly textured, carefully planned arrangements (mostly by his trumpeter Charlie Shavers) of classical pieces. Mixed with original works, these demonstrated not only the musical sophistication of black musicians, but also their daring.

Two men in particular developed a music whose technical complications were beyond the grasp of most white performers. After listening to a recording by Charlie "Bird" Parker and Dizzy Gillespie of a piece called "Shaw Nuff," one distinguished white musician declared: "Man, I can't *listen* that fast." "You could say that my relationship with Charlie Parker was pure joy," Gillespie told me, "because neither of us was the same musician before we met as after we had played together." The style was called bebop; critic Leonard Feather has devised academic origins for the word. "They [Parker and Gillespie] would take a conventional old tune like 'Whispering' and design a new swinging melody around its harmonic outlines, and retitle it 'Groovin' High.' The first two notes of that new melody had the same rhythmic feel as the synthetic word 'bebop.' " Gillespie insists that he never coined the word. "It was invented by the media. In fact, we used to talk our way through the melodies, very fast, just chattering away with anything that came into our heads. Often, this stream of words was brought to a full stop by a phrase like be-*bop*. It just seemed natural." The reaction to bebop was hostile—one Hollywood radio station actually banned it. "All they wanted was Dixieland," Gillespie told me. "They just hated our music." Soon after Gillespie's first Carnegie Hall concert, lovers of Dixieland resurrected an ancient New Orleans trumpeter, Bunk Johnson, bought him a new set of teeth and installed him with a bunch of fellow patriarchs in a Greenwich Village meeting hall.

Gillespie's co-religionist, Parker, was born in

Left: Billie Holiday as a young girl; *above, top*: Sarah Vaughan; *above*: Anita O'Day. Three apparently dissimilar singers, yet each claiming to be a "jazz singer." Holiday's voice is better known today than it was during her lifetime; Vaughan's distinctive contralto annually sells out New York's Avery Fisher Hall during the Newport–New York Jazz Festival. O'Day, who began in front of Gene Krupa's band, set a style of band singing that dominated the forties.

Kansas City on August 29, 1920, and had played baritone horn in the school band from age eleven. During the next twenty-four years, he became recognized as a major force in composition, arrangement, and improvisation. Some of his most influential records were those involving strings—pianist-composer Lennie Tristano once said of him: "If Charlie wanted to invoke plagiarism laws, he could sue almost everybody who's made a record in the past ten years." An awesomely serious, well-tutored musician, knowledgeable about Stravinsky and Schönberg, Parker was tormented by seeing his work imitated. His increased drug intake and his committal to Camarillo State Hospital for six months may well have been a result of this frustration.

By the time Parker died, in March 1955—a week after his last appearance at New York's Birdland, the jazz club named after him—bebop was already inspiring a host of followers. There were those who incorporated the subtleties of bop, but lowered its blood pressure to make it more acceptable. At a club known as the Royal Roost, trumpeter Miles Davis began playing his "cooler" music. Others abandoned form altogether. Lennie Tristano assembled a group that included saxophonist Lee Konitz and guitarist Billy Bauer and began an experiment called Intuition. His band ignored eight-bar patterns, tonality, melody, harmony—all of it in favor of unrehearsed exchanges between the musicians. The results were so odd that no record company would release them. Tristano had anticipated a style of free jazz that was not to be heard publicly for another decade.

Others sought refuge in classical forms to escape the confusion of musical anarchy. The leader of this movement, Dave Brubeck, was white. Again, the color of his skin did not indicate a lesser musicianship; but black men, in trying to remove jazz from the clutches of white show business, had taken the music beyond what many white musicians thought acceptable perimeters. According to the newest black jazzmen, form was dead. Even improvisation *within* form was dead—Brubeck recalls that Art Tatum's re-recording of "Lullaby of the

Leaves," completed shortly before Tatum's death, was identical note for note—including the "improvised" passages—with a recording Tatum had made years earlier. From this predicament, Brubeck and other individuals fought to revitalize jazz.

Brubeck struggled for years to get his ideas accepted. "Jazz had become overarranged," he told me, "with no *room* for improvisation. Still, I wanted to create within a known framework." His first major group—an octet—had only two jobs in two years, and one of those was nonpaying. Nobody would record him. Finally, Columbia Records signed him for some sessions, which produced the album *Time Out*. Columbia's president, Goddard Lieberson, liked two tracks in particular and wanted to release them as a single. It took a further two years for the single to reach the public, but Brubeck's patience was rewarded—"Take Five" and "Blue Rondo à la Turk" were enormously successful. The music was highly complex and impossible for dancing—indeed, that was not its intent. It was music for listening, although not always easy for that. Buddy Rich says he went to hear trumpeter Don Ellis once, when "time signatures were flying out of the window. I sat in the audience for about an hour, trying to find out what was going on. They played in eleven, thirteen, and twelve and a half. I became convinced I had gone to a mathematics class."

John Lewis worked toward the same ends as Brubeck. A highly sophisticated and cultured middle-class black, Lewis with his Modern Jazz Quartet evolved a style of music more akin to European chamber music than to any previous notion of jazz. His "Blues in A Minor," for ex-

Dizzy Gillespie told me: "You could say that my relationship with Charlie Parker was instant joy. Because everything he did was joyful, funny. Playing with him was the most stimulating experience I ever had. Neither of us was as good a musician before as we were when we played together. It was a perfect relationship." *Top left:* Dizzy, 1940. His bent trumpet started life through an accident at a party, he claims. It has no musical significance. *Center left:* Parker, joyful. *Top right:* Parker, with Miles Davis, who began playing with him at the age of 19. *Right:* Max Kaminsky, Lester Young, "Hot Lips" Page, Parker. Young's tenor playing was a trademark of Count Basie's band. His style still dominates saxophone playing.

ample, contains a bass figure similar to a Passacaglia by Purcell. Lewis defends his approach by maintaining that "there is a cross relationship between jazz and the rest of Western music. It is one of my obligations to try and express the capabilities of our music. Expanding the instrumentation and taking down the barriers between jazz and classical was one way of doing this."

The Modern Jazz Quartet, says Leonard Feather, had a "delicate artistry which brought a rare eclecticism to its repertoire under the guidance of its pianist and musical director John Lewis, who would as soon play a Bach Prelude as a work by Gillespie or Monk." Jazz, in other words, had become the intellectual province of critics and scholars. It had lost touch with those elements that previously had given it sustenance: collective improvisation mixed with composition, and a style that allowed individual inspiration yet retained outlines understood and accepted by all.

It might be argued, of course, that John Lewis and his quartet allowed just such a freedom. But splendid as a composition like "The Golden Striker" may be, its irregular beat and harmonic deviousness remove it from the realms of popular music. Chico Hamilton, whose quintet included a classical cellist and flutist, achieved much the same effect. Ornette Coleman, an alto saxophonist from Texas, slowed down or speeded up the tempo of his quartet at will, thus destroying all sense of regular meter or symmetry. In satisfying themselves, the musicians secured for jazz a minority role. Once a mainspring of popular music, jazz has become an esoteric side show: fascinating, often stimulating, but ultimately redundant. Saxophonist John

Coltrane, for example, occasionally seemed happiest when working in one chord for forty-five minutes.

None of this is to deny jazz the right of development away from its limited origins. After all, a musical form that depends exclusively on its original definition must wither and die through lack of flexibility. "I never did try to play anything the same," Earl Hines told me. "I always challenged the piano. I was *always* exploring — in fact, if you see me up there on the stand smiling, I'm lost! You can never master a music. You've always got to be reaching out for something new." But newness is not inimical to form, any more than freedom is a consequence of anarchy. When interviewed for this book, Dizzy Gillespie was playing at a Playboy Club before a mostly white audience — of twelve people. Gone are the days when Earl Hines could

boast that jazz was a language understood by everybody, "from the ghettoes to the palaces of Kings and Queens." Perhaps the Playboy Club is the inevitable, and sadly appropriate, dead end for jazz.

Facing page: the Cotton Club in 1938. Cab Calloway says of the Cotton Club: "It was a huge, famous, beautiful place where they had the greatest shows, the most beautiful gals, and the most greatest music you could ever hear." *Top left:* the original Dave Brubeck Quartet (drummer Joe Morello, saxophonist Paul Desmond, Brubeck, bassist Eugene Wright). Brubeck had to twist clubowners' arms to persuade them to let Desmond play a date; the standard bar instrumentation in the early 1950s was bass, piano, drums. *Below left:* the Modern Jazz Quartet. Pianist John Lewis (second from left), who also played with Dizzy Gillespie, completed work on his master's degree and organized a group that relied equally on Bach and Bird. Vibraphonist Milt Jackson is at right; Connie Kay is at left; Percy Heath is seated. *Clockwise from center top:* Cannonball Adderley, Charles Mingus, Thelonius Monk, John Coltrane — influential in the fifties, overlooked in the seventies.

4

Who's That Comin'?

"Blues" is a word that needs thinking about before it can be understood. It is sixteenth century in origin, an abbreviation of "blue devils," or melancholia. Musically, it is wholly black and wholly folk music. The blues is also a basic emotional response to an oppressive environment, a song of the alienated. It was, and is, quite unlike ragtime or jazz. The latter were communal sounds, sung or played to entertain the community. The blues, on the other hand, was born in loneliness. It was never a music of protest; it was always a music of accommodation, of coping with the realities of living in a socially and economically segregated society. The blues did not challenge white supremacy; the singer reconciles himself with himself, recognizes his own personality—and rejoices in it. The blues is a recognition of the human condition, a statement of identity.

It has been acknowledged that popular music in the twentieth century would have been very different without the blues. Still, musicians and critics

Bessie Smith.

have been slow to appreciate the real importance of its creation and development: its special meaning for a particular race, lately in exile and in chains, then in a more subtle bondage.

You never miss the water till the well's run dry,
You never miss the water, Lord, till the well's run dry,
You never miss your baby till she says "Goodbye."

It expresses the desolate sense of having no right to be where you are. The battering the human spirit takes when it strains to ascend toward its true purpose: this is the subject matter of the blues.

Blues is also a way of playing music that uses a particular structure—verses of twelve bars and three lines, sometimes repeated, to convey a particular attitude of mind. It was the last of the new musical forms to develop at the end of the nineteenth century, and flourished particularly in the Delta area of northern Mississippi. After the end of the Civil War and the breakup of the larger plantations, many freed slaves in the Cotton Belt, which stretched from Texas to Georgia, stayed in the countryside they knew best; many worked the same crops. The nature of that crop and the way it was cultivated engendered some of the basic elements of blues. Cotton required group labor: the continual hoeing or topping of the cotton rows, as well as the ensuing harvesting, were best done by gangs of workmen. The heavy soil made it monotonous, wearying work. The only relief, it seemed, was the songs chanted in the fields, songs telling of the disappointing and hungry lives of these black workmen scraping the bare sides and bottom of the economic pot.

In content and texture, these songs provided the source material for the blues. The use of flattened thirds and sevenths, the apparent freedom of expression, the characteristic bends and turns of the voice, all derived from the work songs predominant throughout the South. The

W. C. Handy, born in Florence, Alabama, in 1873, was musical director of the Mahara Minstrels for many years before he discovered the blues. Blind from his early twenties, Handy concentrated on developing his considerable business interests while conducting a celebrated running battle with Jelly Roll Morton over which of them had "invented" both jazz and the blues.

blues singer spoke for himself; his way of singing and playing expressed what he felt. The tradition was oral—no one dreamed of writing down, let alone profiting from, a folk music heard and comprehended by all.

Impoverishment again pushed blacks north in search of work. Those who had worked on the cotton plantations were drawn inevitably to the center of the cotton trade, Memphis, just north of the Delta. Like every other migrant population before and since, the workers finished up at night in the clubs and drinking houses and brothels; in Memphis, these were found on Beale Street. Lieutenant George Lee, a veteran of the Street, remembers "a gorgeous and melodramatic avenue of vice, of commercial ambition, of low comedy and sweet melody. Innumerable gambling dens were strung out along the main stem where hundreds of people lost their fortunes on the roll of a dice." As in Chicago, Prohibition was a boon. "I remember when Beale Street was better than Paris, Chicago, or New York," Memphis Slim told me. "All the musicians would leave those cities and come to Beale Street, that's how much it was blooming. Whisky was about fifteen cents a bottle. Policy was wide open. So was gambling, although controlled by Italians. It was better than Las Vegas."

Lieutenant Lee recalled when Beale Street was forced by the city fathers to go "dry"—after a fashion. "The club called Hole in the Wall," he told me, "had two trash cans outside loaded with pints and half-pints of whisky. If a man wanted to buy some, he went into the bar and first paid the bartender. The bartender then gave the man standing by the trash can a signal, and the man outside fished out the right-size bottle from the can. That's how you got your liquor. But when the garbage trucks come along, it was a sight. You'd see them frantically rolling the trash cans *inside* so that the garbage men wouldn't cart them away. When the truck passed, out came the cans again and business resumed as before."

Drinkers and gamblers needed entertainment and music. And on Beale Street, there was no shortage of music, twenty-four hours a day. In any one hour, dozens of musicians played there, or looked for a chance to perform: Memphis Slim recalls that the crush was so great that he could only get a daytime job playing piano. Beale Street became the natural headquarters for all those musicians who had come in from the countryside to seek work. Before long, as its fame and notoriety spread, these same musicians, when not performing Beale Street, traveled all over the mid-South, playing at dances and similar functions. And one entrepreneur—named, appropriately, Cash Mosby—ran three excursions a week from the countryside to Beale Street, each one loaded with Delta blacks eager to try their gambling luck and visit the whorehouses. Wednesday night was white people's night, but Thursday and Saturday were the most crowded—"those were the nights when the domestic servants and the workers in the Memphis silk stocking business got paid and had their evenings off," Lee remembers. "They brought their wages to Beale Street—and Beale Street obligingly took them away."

The music became the Street. It was devil's music and not fit for decent ears. Blacks and whites who professed respectability would never descend to Beale Street except "to observe." They ignored the sound, until a band led by a Memphis black, W. C. Handy, played in the summer of 1908 at a subscription dance for some whites at Croxdale, Mississippi, about twenty-seven miles from Memphis. Having struggled through every traditional tune they could think of, Handy's band was finally removed from the stage when a group of whites announced that they could not endure Handy's polite music anymore; they preferred their own. Whereupon, a country band (complete with jugs) began playing rowdy versions of plantation work songs and dances. Peering over the heads of an enthusiastic audience, the deposed band leader saw more money being thrown down during one number than his band was earning for the entire evening. "Suddenly," Handy wrote later, "I saw the beauty of the native sound." The Memphis Sound (as it became known) was, from the very first, the sound of coins hitting the floor.

Handy had gained most of his musical experience working with and for an assortment of nigger minstrel troupes, among them the Mahara Minstrels. Like other "composers" on the minstrel circuit, he recognized that if the black

Looking north on Main Street, Memphis, a few blocks from Beale Street.

man's rough poetry were polished, if his personal anguish were diluted to an acceptable level, if his musical limitations (which some considered his strengths) were broadened to include the more popular syncopated jazz style, there was a reasonable chance that more of his music would reach a wider audience. Above all, the minstrels were crucial in the development not of a style of music, but of an understanding of how the black man might penetrate white sensibilities. The minstrels were not especially a manifestation of white racism or Uncle Tomism or cultural snobbery or social ridicule; rather, they were the medium through which the last, but most essential, element of black music reached its compromise with white society.

Chastened by his experience in Croxdale, Handy returned to Memphis pondering how best to combine these different musical threads. Events, in the shape of a mayoral election, provided his opportunity. The three candidates each hired a street band to liven up their campaigns; Handy was employed by Ed Crump, one of the first modern politicians to earn the name "Boss." But when Crump was elected, he made a pass at becoming a reformer and threatened to close down gambling on Beale Street. So Handy changed a few words of Crump's election song:

"Crump, he don't allow no easy riders now;
I don't care what Mr. Crump don't allow;
I'm going to the 'Bow' House anyhow."

Handy also changed the title of the song and called it "Memphis Blues." He had found a winning formula: take the spirit of the blues; play it like country music; hot up the tempo; sweeten the words and. . . . Diligently, Handy steeped himself in country ballads, traditional blues, gospel works—anything and everything that could be heard in and around Memphis. Later apologists have claimed that Handy "attempted to put a folk idiom into notation" and achieved the "first popularization of a music hitherto outside the music business." But the tunes which Handy pieced together from existing music he called his own.

Whites loved it. Handy's music seemed to them a departure from convention-bound society; they thought of it as something new and fresh and American. Middle-class blacks, such as Handy, also saw the music as a step forward —out of Beale and onto Main Street. By comparison, jazz was for the brothel, or at least the speakeasy. "Jazz isn't music," Lieutenant George Lee says today. "Jazz is just a kind of

tempo—a rapid tempo. Not like the blues and its lazy rhythm. Jazz is not music but a style. Blues is music."

Handy went North to New York where he discovered that he was not the messiah of modern music he had come to believe. He was told that his music did not have the right tempo. New York publishers were still coping with ragtime and learning about jazz. Handy got a hundred dollars for "Memphis Blues" and was told to be grateful. He would, subsequently, spend a quarter of a century buying back the copyright. First, though, he formed his own company and published "St. Louis Blues," the cornerstone of his fortunes.

The blues Handy incorporated came from a variety of sources, which were not always in mutual sympathy. There was country blues, mostly a spontaneous individual expression played by itinerant (often blind) street-corner musicians, guitarists who offered entertainment in the "juke joints" and on rural front porches, and pianists who performed in barrel houses and "recreation parlors." Some stayed in the South, like Whistling Alex Moore or Bukka White; some migrated to the cities of the North and East, like Big Bill Broonzy and Blind Lemon Jefferson.

Then there was urban blues, sometimes called jazz blues, developed partly on Beale Street, where the gamblers demanded something more for their money than the self-pitying ramblings of an ex-cotton picker, but more importantly in New Orleans. Jazz blues, no doubt influenced by the noisy bands that now littered the streets, was mostly instrumental. But with several instruments involved, the music was less flexible than the solo, self-accompanied vocal tradition of the country singer. When a blues vocal chorus does appear in jazz, it lacks —even when drawn from the common stock of blues imagery—the intensity and anguish of the country singer. In brothel songs, for example, the emphasis (not unnaturally) is on provocation and sexual titillation. Whereas country blues was sexually explicit, jazz blues offered a more genteel invitation to "go upstairs." Urban

musicians ignored or rejected the back-home vocal blues because it was crude. As Sweet Emma Barrett, the New Orleans pianist and singer, put it: "*Strictly* blues players? Never did have much to do with them at all. I can't tell you nothing about them. I never did pay them no mind. Fact is, I didn't like their blues."

Then there was vaudeville blues, a direct product of the minstrel shows. The singers— mostly women—succeeded through "acting the blues," much in the style to be made popular by Ma Rainey and Bessie Smith, in reconciling the rural vocal blues tradition with the predominantly instrumental tradition of New Orleans. It

Left: Ma Rainey with her Georgia Jazz Band in 1925. Rainey mostly worked on the southern black circuit in theaters, and in tent shows, occasionally venturing to New York for dates; "Hot Lips" Page played briefly in her band. *Above, top:* members of W. C. Handy's band; *above:* Handy with George Avakian and Louis Armstrong in 1954. Handy died in 1958.

was not so much a musical compromise as a desire on the part of traveling entertainers to present their audience with a sound they would recognize in a style that would dazzle them. Before long, numerous white artists, such as Sophie Tucker, recognized the potential of such material and gave blues the possibility of even wider dissemination. Still, it was not a person, or a group of people, or even a place that proved the unifying force and cataclysmic influence in this multiplicity of styles. It was a machine.

The phonograph had been invented by Thomas Edison in 1877. For some years, it had been thought of as a novelty. But by the turn of the century—and with the growing use of more convenient flat discs instead of cumbersome cylinders—it had become a profitable source of home entertainment. The more prosperous citizens of the black community bought machines and records, although before 1920 only a handful of black artists were recorded. Of these, all were either straight singers or gospel choirs whose appeal was directed primarily at a white public; even W. C. Handy, by now famous for "St. Louis Blues" (it was soon to be selected as the imperial battle song by the Emperor of Abyssinia), did his best to conceal the color of his skin. Nobody seems to have been aware that a growing black audience was waiting for the chance to buy recordings of its "own" music.

Although Handy was associated with the first black-owned record company, Black Swan, the man who brought together the new machine and its new audience was a young Negro entertainer, composer, and entrepreneur named Perry Bradford. He became convinced there was an audience for black artists and, through his persistence, eventually persuaded Fred Hager, a white executive at OKeh studios, to allow a young black night club singer to record two of Bradford's own compositions, "That Thing Called Love" and "You Can't Keep a Good Man Down." Hager had wanted to use Sophie Tucker for the recording, but she was under contract to another company, so Bradford and his night club singer won the day. The record was released and sold well enough for Hager to realize he had discovered a new and unexploited mar-

Ex-vaudevillian Bessie Smith; *above, top:* 1923, and *right,* 1925. On her earliest records, as an acceptable signal that she was black, Smith was billed as a "comedienne." *Above:* John Hammond, born 1911; arguably the white man who has done most for black music (besides discovering such as Bob Dylan, encouraging such as Benny Goodman, and recording an unrivaled cross section of twentieth-century popular musicians). Born into a wealthy family (Hammond Organs and the Vanderbilts), Hammond made skillful use of his privileges to indulge his musical tastes: as a boy he used to cut short his classical music lessons to head for Harlem; he was the only white person in the audience at the Alhambra, where he heard Bessie Smith for the first time in 1927. Hammond became a personal friend of many

black musicians in the late 1920s and started writing jazz reports for the British-based magazine *Gramophone* in 1930, switching to *Melody Maker* in 1931. He organized a variety of jazz performances including one celebrated jam session at the Mt. Kisco Golf and Tennis Club (WASP outrage only restrained by the fact that Hammond's father was president of the club). In 1933 he began to assemble jazz musicians for England's Columbia Gramophone Company; throughout the 1930s he encouraged mixed bands, with mixed success; in 1938, on the eve of the opening of Barney Josephson's Café Society in New York City, Hammond staged Carnegie Hall's second major jazz concert (Goodman's swing concert was first): "From Spirituals to Swing."

ket; all three returned to the OKeh studios to cut another of Bradford's songs. In the first month of its issue, the new disc sold seventy-five thousand copies. The flood gates were open. The song was called "Crazy Blues" and the singer, Mamie Smith.

In retrospect, it is difficult to understand the impact of "Crazy Blues." Mamie Smith, on record at least, sounds dreary, even bored. Notwithstanding the presence of Willie "The Lion" Smith on piano, the song is as musically undistinguished as it is historically important. Almost all the newly formed recording companies understood the message and began to sign up every black cabaret artist in New York they could find. Singers like Lucille Hegamin, Edith Wilson, and Rosa Henderson were among the first. Each, however, wished to appear "sophisticated" in her performance; so for all their period charm and witty accompaniments, the records communicate little sense of involvement. The singers reshaped and, consequently, diluted the music. The high sexual content was delivered with coy innuendo. They remained detached, acceptable, "vaudeville blues" singers.

In the early stages of blues recording, scouts from the North combed the South searching for talent. These scouts had little knowledge or understanding of the quality of what they heard; they would record a singer and, if the music sold, go and record him some more. The scouts discovered, however, that most blues singers were preoccupied with local styles and subjects and did not sell nationally—at least, that was the excuse offered by the recording companies for the comparatively poor compensation paid the singers. Many were given only a few dollars, or a bottle of whisky, for their trouble, and then sent home. Memphis Slim says that "most of the blues singers didn't know what 'royalty' meant. I didn't know until Roosevelt Sykes told me I wasn't getting any. I was playing with Big Bill Broonzy at the time, and he hadn't told me. Perhaps he wasn't allowed to. So when I started asking for royalties, I got boycotted."

Despite the apparent commercial success of Mamie Smith, she made little money out of

recording. But making a phonograph record remained the ultimate ambition of almost every blues singer and player, regardless of origin. Even those who had stayed behind in the mid-South—partly through a determination not to get involved with white show business, and partly because white show business would not tolerate them as they seemed altogether too rough—yearned for recording contracts. It was, after all, their passport to the wider world. The belief, incidentally, that these uncompromising artists somehow embodied a more "authentic" music earned them the description "classic blues" singers.

Such musicological posturing has obscured an important consideration. Critics of popular music are obsessed by the need to load the music and its development with a philosophical importance that is alien to it. Thus, some have wished to elevate all blues artists of the twenties into the "classic" denomination. Others, who insist true blues is so primitive that no commercial phonograph company would touch it with a barge pole, dismiss those who recorded as mere vaudevillians. Often, artists from both schools played the same material. Often, after the success of certain "classic" singers, the so-called vaudeville singers would roughen up their style to achieve the semblance of authenticity. Musically, the crucial distinction worth noting is that vaudeville singers—even the most eminent—*acted* the blues. Classic blues singers simply performed them.

Ma Rainey, the most vociferous of those singers who had remained in the mid-South, was thought by her fellow black performers the ugliest woman in the business. Known as the "Mother of the Blues," she had introduced rural blues songs into her minstrel show as early as 1902. She remained, throughout her life, close to the country blues of her origins and frequently chose to record with a jug band as support, perhaps unwilling (or unable) to develop her art beyond its earthy, self-contained boundaries. Nervous about traveling north, she rarely ventured as far as Chicago (where she recorded occasionally for Paramount) and never beyond it. Unfortunately, the Chicago studios were technically inadequate; her records are an ordeal to appreciate. She herself was squat and flamboyant, although her songs possessed a certain charm and naïveté. Their warmth merited her motherly title, as did her encouragement of numerous protégés—among them a tall, fat, scared-to-death seventeen-year-old named Bessie Smith.

Born very poor, Bessie had sung in her local chapel from childhood (no self-respecting black singer ever passed up on the claim to have had a gospel background). At the age of nine, she had won a singing competition and spent the prize money on a pair of roller skates, only to get thumped by her mother for the waste. Ma Rainey spotted her in another competition and put her in the Rabbit Foot Minstrels, some said to teach her, while others claimed it was to ensure that a talent greater than her own did not challenge her own supremacy.

Bessie was performing with the minstrels in Philadelphia, before an enthusiastic audience

---

Left: Columbia advertisement for New Orleans' Willie Jackson. *Right:* the legendary Blind Lemon Jefferson, whose wanderings took him all over the southern states. Born in Texas in 1897, Jefferson spent much time in New Orleans and Dallas, where he made some of his early recordings.

Cordially Yours
Blind Lemon Jefferson

of Southern immigrants, when Columbia got wind of her increasing popularity. Carried along by the new-found phonographic obsession with almost anything black, they dispatched a white recording executive (Frank Walker) and his black associate (Clarence Williams) to find Bessie Smith. She had had several auditions with other companies, but usually failed them on the grounds that she was too earthy for white sensibilities. Her first session with Williams and Walker produced only two cuts. "Gulf Coast Blues," which Williams had written himself, was coupled with a version of "Downhearted Blues," written by another vaudevillian, Alberta Hunter, who had already scored a success with her own recording of the song.

Bessie's version of "Downhearted Blues" surprised everyone, including herself. Within a few months, it had sold over eighty thousand copies; within two years, she commanded two thousand dollars for a personal appearance; and throughout the remainder of the twenties, Bessie Smith was *the* blues singer. The vaudeville artists who had preceded her now lived in her shadow, and she would brook no rival. Yet, and artistically it may have proved her strength, she remained unknown to most white blues fanciers. Her visits to the white world of High Bohemia were social disasters. She lacked, or deliberately rejected, the ability to flatter those who wished to establish their liberal credentials. She remained of her people, almost a caricature of their virtues and failings. At a time when it was fashionable to be light-skinned, Bessie deliberately chose very black lovers. To Bessie Smith, black was unashamedly beautiful.

At first, she loaded herself with jewels and feathers. Later, she learned to simplify her appearance and to work, quite consciously, at achieving that moment of perfection when feeling and technique are fused. On either side of that synthesis lay folk art, with its unwitting charm, and the mannerism which results when technical virtuosity takes precedence over feeling. Her material ranged from intensely poetic blues to mediocre pop songs, including the occasional silly risqué number. But, a few mediocre tracks aside, she infused everything with an unparalleled grandeur and humanity. She seemed able to impart the sadness of mortality, the instability of happiness, the craving for certainty, the self-destructive pursuit of temporary oblivion. Offstage, however, she remained in many ways a simple person. She would offer to help Frank Walker's wife with the housework, for instance, if one of his children was sick. Bessie was a big woman who drank a lot—not usually the spirits she sang about, but home-brewed liquor. And she was quite handy with her fists.

After her years of triumph in the twenties

came the Depression. At first, it seemed, her records and appearances would be even more successful — after all, gloom was the hallmark of both her music and the era. But in her success was planted the seed of her decline. Encouraged by her example, or at least by the amounts of money being made off her, the recording companies began sending more and more expeditions to the South. New artists were cheaper; new recording companies undercut their competitors; sales of the professionals began yielding to those of amateurs. Even the blues themselves were changing. In Kansas City, against heavy riffing, male singers like Big Joe Turner and Jimmy Rushing were using a powerhouse beat far removed from the irregular, apparently spontaneous moaning favored by the "classic" singers. The young hipsters began to look on Bessie and her lesser sisters as passé. "High yeller" chorines were in fashion; a black chorus girl became known as a "Ma Rainey." Almost incidentally, the Depression also wiped out parts of the recording industry. Bessie's company (Columbia) was sold to another company, which then went bankrupt. Suddenly she was making no new records and earning no royalties from her old ones. When she made her last appearance at the Apollo Theatre in Harlem, she earned just two hundred and fifty dollars.

In September 1937, Bessie left Memphis, and took Route 61 south toward a show she was booked to join in Huntsville, Alabama. She was being driven by Richard Morgan, her lover and manager who had been one of Philadelphia's top bootleggers during Prohibition. The road was dark and, like so many in that part of the country, seemed endless. After sixty-five miles, it narrowed. There was a huge truck. The car slithered off the road and turned over. "It was a horrible mess," said a witness — a doctor — who arrived shortly after, with Bessie "lying out there in the open with maybe a pint of blood on the highway. Her arm was partially severed — but if that had been her only injury, surely she would have survived."

John Hammond, Bessie's record producer who was waiting for her at Huntsville, believes she could have been saved. The story, including the famous incident that she was refused admission to a white hospital, is very confused, Hammond says now. "Clearly she died through loss of blood — and that occurred because of terrible delays." Certainly, it took long enough to get the injured Bessie Smith to a hospital. On the way to Memphis, where there was a black hospital, the car in which she was being taken was involved in another mishap, which further delayed medical attention. By the time she arrived, it was too late. Whatever the true facts, it is a shoddy story.

Despite the myths that arose soon after her death, she was not given a pauper's funeral. On

From left to right: 1. One String Sam, itinerant Chicago blues singer. 2. Furry Lewis, born in Tennessee, 1893, protégé of W. C. Handy. (He recalls Handy as "a real fine fellow who always treated everybody right.") Beale Street bluesman, Memphis resident for over 75 years, Lewis performed with the Rolling Stones during their 1975 tour of the U.S., and travels now with the Memphis Blues Caravan in their bus whose destination is always marked as "Heaven." 3. Victoria Spivey, born in Houston, Texas, 1910, longest survivor of the classic blues tradition, a performer with many bands from the 1920s to the 1940s. In 1975, recalling Bessie Smith, she told me: "I was proud to work for her, she was good to everybody; she once said to me in Cleveland, Ohio: 'You're gonna sing "Blacksnake Blues" for me real good tonight or I'm gonna break your neck.' She was a wonderful woman." Spivey starred in King Vidor's early black talkie, *Hallelujah*. 4. Helen Humes, born in Louisville, Kentucky, 1913, blues shouter and big-band singer. Her 1975 return to New York re-established her as one of the more formidable jazz singers.

the contrary, she was buried in a coffin lined with pink velvet. Over seven thousand mourners were present. Benefits were held to raise money for a suitable headstone and a check was handed over to Jack Gee, her separated husband, who supposedly made off with the proceeds. Her funeral was reported in a Philadelphia paper:

Two heavily veiled women wept steadily. In the strained silence, the breathing of the men was plainly audible. The clergyman cleared his throat softly, "I am the resurrection and the life. . . ." The casket slid down into the grave. A woman screamed, and the broad shoulders of Jack Gee heaved and writhed as he buried his face in his hands. Hoarse sobs broke from his lips. "Bessie! Oh, Bessie. . . ."
"Earth to earth, ashes to ashes. . . ." The minister closed his book. The mourners faltered forward to cast their flowers into the grave. Bessie Smith Gee, late Queen of the Blues, was but a memory.

The airtight vault was guaranteed against corrosion or leakage for one hundred years. The grave remained unmarked for thirty-three.

On Friday, August 7, 1970, another ceremony took place at the Mount Lawn Cemetery, Sharon Hill, Philadelphia. In front of a small crowd, the Reverend Wycliffe Jangdharrie (wearing a dark suit and sunglasses) lifted a borrowed raincoat

to unveil a modest tombstone. In execrable taste, it had engraved upon it the following words:

THE GREATEST BLUES SINGER IN THE WORLD
WILL NEVER STOP SINGING
BESSIE SMITH
1895–1937

The stone, which cost five hundred dollars, was paid for by two people. One was a Mrs. Juanita Green, a registered nurse and owner of two Philadelphia nursing homes who, as a small girl, had sometimes helped Bessie around the house. The other was the rock singer Janis Joplin. Because of "professional commitments," but more likely because of a genuine desire not to be accused of using the occasion as a publicity stunt, Joplin had stayed away. Yet, as her own work and life demonstrated, she had begun to feel an almost frightening empathy with Bessie. Singer Dory Previn later said of Janis: "She bought a stone for Bessie Smith — but she forgot she had not paid for her own."

Bessie Smith is probably more important to an understanding of the blues than any other single artist. She revitalized an essentially folk idiom and gave it the dignity of form. She gathered together the various elements of that idiom with coherence and purpose. By her example, she prevented that form from being stolen away. She was too magnificent a performer, too idiosyncratic, altogether too vulgar, for easy

Far left: Jimmy Rushing, jazz-blues singer whose relationship with Count Basie dates back to when they were both with Bennie Moten's band in Kansas City. *Near left:* Roosevelt Sykes, born in Helena, Arkansas, 1906, has lived for many years in or near New Orleans. Sykes once said: "I came to Chicago for no special reason . . . after 37 years I left Chicago for no certain reason; since then, just call me 'international.' " *Near right:* Houston Stackhouse, southern blues man, known to have got as far north as Chicago in a good year. *Center right:* Memphis-based Bukka White, whose father was born in New York, says: "The blues originated behind the mule, but there's no race in it; no reason why a white boy shouldn't play blues just as good as a black boy." *Far right:* Sleepy John Estes, born in Ripley, Tennessee, 1903, once told an interviewer: "I'm now married to my second wife. I had three, but her husband come and got the last one."

imitation. She demonstrated by these very qualities that much of the work of W. C. Handy was little more than an attempt to beat the white man at his own game, to out-publish him, to absorb—even steal—before others had the chance.

Bessie Smith's artistry gave shape to a music that might otherwise have lapsed into crass self-indulgence. To feel the blues and merely "do your thing" was not sufficient. Without betraying her roots, Bessie reached out toward the universality necessary for any art. In this, of course, she was not alone. She held her place in a developing tradition, but was, at the same time, the inspiration of countless unnamed singers and guitarists isolated in the Delta. Her singing took the style it did because she was born of a certain class and color, in a particular place and a particular time. Many apologists, white and black, have wanted or needed to believe the numerous myths that surround her life; blues people are notorious liars. But without her, the blues might have become the property of white song merchants and whitened Negroes. She managed to delay that process long enough to allow her successor to emerge.

In 1933, John Hammond had been invited to the opening of a new club in Harlem called Monette's where his attention had been seized by a girl he describes as "a luscious, slightly overweight seventeen-year-old—who sang like an instrumentalist. She added her own special touches and, if she caught sight of somebody she liked, she would put a totally different inflection in her song. Pop singers just didn't do that sort of thing in the 1930s." Hammond asked to speak to the girl and discovered she came from Baltimore; her name was Billie Holiday.

Billie was always vague about her past. Hammond asked if she was related to Clarence Holiday, who played banjo and guitar in Fletcher Henderson's band. "She looked at me with the most awful contempt and said: 'Yes, he's my old man.'" When Hammond later asked Holiday why he had never said anything about his extraordinary daughter, his response was: "For God's sake, John, don't talk about Billie in front of the other guys, they'll think I'm old. Hell, she was something I stole when I was thirteen."

Her early years were spent as a "maid" in a brothel. She was sent to jail for prostitution at fourteen, and soon discovered an affection for cocaine and heroin. She was brought to New York by her mother and began working in such Harlem clubs as Jerry Preston's Log Cabin. For Hammond, she became a crusade. He took dozens of musicians and recording executives to hear her—including Benny Goodman, who was persuaded to make two records with her in December 1933. They were not successful, and Hammond tried for over a year to arrange another

recording date. This time she sang her own versions of current popular songs with Teddy Wilson.

Hammond takes up the story. "If Bessie Smith had lived, she would only be eighty today—she would have made a marvelous comeback from the Depression. Bessie drank, of course, but there was no suggestion of drugs in her life and her voice was in tremendous shape when she died. But Billie abused her voice—and herself. There was only a shred of her voice left before she died." Hammond recalls that he and his fellow record men were worried about the amount of dope Billie smoked in the studio. "And," Hammond says, "she was a patsy for good-looking pimps. She never had any luck with men, although she had some extraordinary men working flat out to help her." She also had some less than extraordinary men in her private life who went flat out to exploit her.

Inevitably, the life she seemed determined to lead squandered her opportunities. Her father died in 1934, her mother in 1940. There had been little warmth in Billie's relationship with her mother, but her mother's death hit her hard. From then on, in Hammond's words, "she went from one terrible guy to another. And all of them wanted to make money off her." During World War II, she went to prison again, for drug offenses. She sang with Count Basie and Artie Shaw and throughout the late forties and the fifties toured extensively as a solo performer. She gave a benefit concert at the Phoenix Theatre in Manhattan in June 1959, but collapsed soon after and was taken to a hospital where she was arrested again for narcotic addiction—on her deathbed.

If Bessie Smith was the singer whose example ennobled a folk tradition, Billie Holiday was the singer whose life spelled out the implications of

If Bessie Smith was the singer whose example ennobled a folk tradition, Billie Holiday was the singer whose life spelled out the implications of that tradition.

that tradition—a constant reminder of what the blues was and had been. Her art was exquisite and unique, her voice spilling over with rough melancholy, expressing a sorrow too deep for words. She spoke for countless generations who had suffered; but equally she spoke for others, with heroic pessimism, about love abandoned, love forgotten, love denied, and love rejected. She touched a chord beyond race or creed or time. And yet, she was utterly of her race and her creed and her time. The drugs, which gave her consolation, eventually crushed her. But they were the means by which her life, as she saw and understood it, was made tolerable.

In 1939, at a New York restaurant named Café Society, Billie sang a bitter song called "Strange Fruit," which talked of bodies hanging from Southern trees. The audience loved it. Café Society was the first New York club in which black and white were able to enjoy themselves together, the first that deliberately ignored segregation. But it should not be forgotten, and Billie Holiday never did forget it, that New York in the thirties was as racist as Memphis. John Hammond remembers that if there were blacks in the audience of any show he was producing, even if they were his own guests, the theater owners would threaten him. "If you wanted to go out for dinner with black friends—and not many did," Hammond says, "you would have to telephone the restaurant in advance to check if it was okay. If a black worked in downtown Manhattan and wanted a haircut, he would have to go all the way back to Harlem to get one. No restaurants or bars would admit blacks, outside their own neighborhoods. And it didn't do to get sick. Hospitals were rigidly segregated, even in Harlem. One time, I think in 1937, Jo Jones—playing with Count Basie's band—badly needed attention. He had a neurological disturbance and the sensible place to go was the Neurological Institute right up on 168th Street in Harlem. It was only because the resident psychiatrist happened to be a music fan and knew

Big Bill Broonzy, despite appearances here, was an acknowledged master of tough, searing blues. Born in Scott, Mississippi, in 1893, he went north to Chicago but received his widest recognition on a European tour in 1951. He died in 1958.

who Jones was that he let him in. Jones was thus the hospital's first black patient."

Many places of entertainment would not allow blacks through their doors. The Rainbow Room, properly renowned for its band music (Ellington, Basie, and Armstrong all played there), informed its musicians that they must not be seen by the white clientele, except on the stage. Harlem's biggest theater, the Alhambra, was closed to blacks; and the Cotton Club, a theater in the center of Harlem whose fame rested on its exclusively black entertainment, would allow no blacks in its audience through most of the thirties. When the management did finally relent, it set up special reserved areas for blacks —at the rear, and behind pillars.

A consequence of this segregation was that most whites rarely heard authentic black music. What was served up for white audiences was usually an emasculated version of the real thing. Even when the Apollo Theater began to put on black shows, few of the white music critics went to listen. The Apollo, incidentally, was the biggest house in Harlem, with more than eighteen hundred seats. Originally a white burlesque house, it had attempted (with Bessie Smith) to stage black entertainment as early as 1932. But its audiences were unaccustomed to hearing black music so publicly—most of the more famous musicians had already gone where the money was—and Bessie Smith's two-week engagement was not a success. The theater reverted to white comedy. But when its chief rival, the Lafayette, closed down, the Apollo secured a weekly radio spot, called *Amateur Night*, at 11 p.m. every Wednesday on WMCA and began to broadcast black music. Radio was the first way in which a large white audience had access to noncommercial black music.

Black musicians had to depend upon a handful of individuals, such as John Hammond, to make their music available in undiluted form. Barney Josephson, a shoe salesman from New Jersey, was so shocked by the continuing segregation of black and white that in 1938 he decided to open his own night club where both races would be allowed, on stage and in the audience. He was lucky in that he met Hammond, probably the white man who knew black music best at this time. Hammond was able to secure

Top: left to right: Billie Holiday, Ruth Etting, Mary Lou Williams, each more glamorous, and perhaps more adept, than their rougher compatriots. Etting, born in David City, Nebraska, in 1905, was an accomplished white blues singer, but was more often described as a "torch singer"—another not-so-subtle signal. Williams is better known as a jazz pianist, although her preoccupation with gospel indicates the overlap between blues and jazz—as does the improvisatory quality of Holiday's singing. *Right:* Memphis Slim lives in Paris now because, he says, "it's a wide-open city, just like Chicago and New York in the old days."

the best acts for Josephson, and as a result, Josephson filled his Café Society—all 210 seats—three times a night from the very opening. He even got some favorable press.

He had his problems, of course. Some patrons were disgusted at seeing blacks in their midst. It was all right to be served or entertained by them, he was told, but sitting next to them was going too far. "We come to a night club to be entertained, to be amused, and to have fun. And we don't want to sit around with these nigs. What are you doing with all these damned nigs?" One businessman told Josephson: "Barney, I don't care anything about your filling this joint up with niggers—after all, to me a buck is a buck. The only thing that bothers me is that there are more white dollars around than black. So you mustn't offend the white dollars. If you can get both, of course, that's good enough."

Occasionally, Josephson would expect, almost provoke, trouble. Like that song by Billie Holiday about lynching and bodies on trees. Joseph-

Dylan showed, perhaps unintentionally, that there was little room for real progress in the blues.

son used to insist she sing it as her last number, to leave the audience with something to think about. One night, as the applause died away, a woman rushed backstage and punched Billie, tore her costume, and told her never to sing that song again. She was a Southerner, and as a child of twelve had watched a black man being hanged from a tree. She had never forgotten and did not wish to be reminded. According to Josephson, Billie first swore at the woman, then the two women burst out sobbing.

Some trouble Josephson did not provoke. When Senator Joseph McCarthy began investigating America's morals, those who had declared for truth rather than prejudice were suspect. Anxious to avoid censure, segments of the New York press began a campaign to protect itself. Among those who felt the whip, if only because it had been previously encouraged, was Café Society. Critics on some of the papers wrote about its new acts only to attack them. "At Café Society, the proletarian hangout in the Village," one review began. Artists who accepted an engagement at Café Society were subject to blacklisting. Rumors spread that FBI agents took seats at the club to see who was there. Health and fire inspectors were sent in for "routine checks," always at the busiest time of the evening; state liquor inspectors would shoulder their way to the bar with their phials and measuring devices and so disrupt normal business. Café Society was forced to close.

In the thirties and forties, there was no business like show business—as long as you were white. For a while, ragtime had been a cornerstone of the white music industry. Jazz had taken its place. Spirituals had been bastardized for performance on white concert platforms. Blacks had either "adjusted," like Armstrong, or died in obscurity, like King Oliver. Basie went into swing; Ellington went classical; Parker and Gillespie, lost in their own brilliance, hurtled toward a limbo, dragging their followers with them. It was young white musicians who, in the fifties and sixties, enthusi-

astically espoused the blues. And it was they who finally killed it off.

They were determined to be progressive, whatever that meant, to burst through what they conceived as music's frontiers. White music lacked roots, they said; it lacked a tradition, and a steely sense of injustice. So the blues became the musical jingoism of white youth from Tokyo to Liverpool to New York. As the blues became popular currency, most of the original blues singers simply gave up. Revolution had never been their intention. Their music had adapted to circumstances—like moving to the city, or picking cotton in Mississippi—but it never "progressed." After all, where was it to go? Experience showed that blacks were lucky to make more than a bottle of whisky for their efforts. That was what their music was about: it was not the music of progression, but of oppression. Young blacks rejected the blues. What was the point of complaining? It was time for action.

But the blues trickled on, even if disguised. Elvis Presley had a riotous success with "Hound Dog," written by Jerry Lieber and Mike Stoller, and originally recorded as a blues number by Willie Mae Thornton. Big Bill Broonzy got a hero's welcome when he toured Europe in 1951. And by the sixties, major tours were being organized under such seductive titles as American Negro Blues Festival. Hordes of indifferent white guitarists said they played the blues— while they were being busted for dope, photographed with groupies (occasionally they married them), and getting richer and richer. Memphis Slim moved to Paris and bought a Rolls-Royce.

The biggest blow, however, came from a lean and scrawny kid from Minnesota. Bob Dylan (né Zimmerman) had a wheezy voice and was described as a "natural poet." In fact, like W. C.

Handy before him, he took directly from the blues and the Okie songs of the Depression. He worshiped Woody Guthrie and won a massive international following as the spokesman of a generation that liked to think of itself as fearless. Certainly, he had a genuine affection for the blues and wrote and performed some powerful songs. If that was the blues (and he said it was), then his young fans liked it and copied it. Here was a new idol telling how it was.

But how was it? Young white listeners believed Dylan spoke for them. What he sang related directly to their own experience, so they claimed. But to young blacks or the poor of any color, he said not a word. In spite of his declared dislike of the bourgeoisie, his was a middle-class music. Dylan showed, perhaps unintentionally, that there was little room for real progress in the blues. The music of Chicago and Memphis and the Delta had been tough and spirited, but only enough to hold out hope for the good times that might lie ahead. The blues did nothing to change—and were not intended to change—the conditions from which they had grown. In the end, an increasing number of blacks abandoned the blues; the white popular music industry kept the name, but lost the music.

Top left: the Rev. Robert Wilkins, a manifestation of the seemingly paradoxical relationship between the blues and gospel. *Bottom far left*: Big Joe Williams, a major force in the development of mid-South blues. *Bottom left*: Jesse Fuller for years maintained a link between folksong, protest song, and the blues. *Right*: Johnny Woods, still in the Delta, still poverty-stricken, still playing the blues.

Rude Songs

Frances Gumm was born in a trunk at the Princess Theater, Pocatello, Idaho — so she sang. She was not black; she did not play a guitar, she was not born in New Orleans. But Frances Gumm was, and still is for many people, the essence of popular music.

Actually, she was born in a hospital, the Itasca, in Grand Rapids, Minnesota. By the time she was sixteen, Miss Gumm had signed with MGM, changed her name to Judy Garland, and starred in twelve movies. She grew fat, was christened "Little Leather Lungs," and was told by an executive: "You look like a hunchback." She was under psychiatric treatment from the age of eighteen; psychologists were her parents, the camera her lover. By twenty-three, she

English music hall artists, 1864.   Josephine Baker.

was already once divorced. "Call me unreliable," she sang, "but it's undeniably true, I'm irrevocably signed with you." With whom, it was none too clear.

She grew thin, almost haggard, and flicked her hair back like a boy's. The orange sequined suit she liked to wear made her jaunty: a pantomime principal boy, lost in a back street. Her performance remained stunningly alive, although she herself seemed dead. With hand on hip, she tottered and stomped and prowled, tigerish and restless, her great brown eyes darting among the audience for a friendly face. "I haven't been taught anything new since silent movies," she croaked. She kissed her musical director. He smiled. He indicated the band. They smiled. She smiled. We all smiled. She pretended to listen for requests from the audience, her ear cocked as if she were a cheeky schoolboy expecting a wallop. "What do you want? Okay, darling, we'll come to that."

She wrestled with the microphone wire, wandered around the stage as if in search of somewhere to put it. She offered the microphone to the audience and invited them to join in. At one performance, a woman actually seized it and sang "Over the Rainbow" herself, whereupon the audience jeered and hooted for the woman to continue. "I love you all," Garland cried. She drank and toasted herself. Her words became more and more slurred. Her hands appealed, shouted, implored: "I'd like to hate myself, but I can't." She was greedy for applause. Her new husband was dragged on and kissed while she sang: "For once in my life, I have someone who needs *me*." She smoked, borrowed a handkerchief, looked amazed by the applause. Her little finger went to her mouth in a well-rehearsed sob of joy.

It was all perfect—and meaningless. The shoddy, tarnished world that had created her had also destroyed her. In her, a whole gaudy age of show biz that believed glamor was a good

enough substitute for talent became apparent. Her raucous masculinity, for all its fashionable and legendary attraction, gave her and her tradition away at last. Judy Garland was the apotheosis of those countless generations of wandering players who had provided white entertainment for the working classes. From street corner to beer house, from Palace of Variety to brothel, these vaudevillians had sung and danced all manner of ballad and bawdry for the edification of those too poor to afford higher-class divertissements.

"**M**usic hall" as a term means what it says — a hall, originally a drinking room or pub or tavern, in which music is heard. The music competes against the drinking. From this atmosphere came numerous offspring called, variously, burlesque, vaudeville, and variety.

Above: the Gumm sisters, c.1930; Frances (Judy Garland) is the smallest. *Right:* the cross-cultural appeal of black caricature, represented in an English poster from the 1890s.

Tony Pastor, a great American vaudevillian, used—but hated—the term "vaudeville." He considered it a sissy term for what was, after all, variety. He maintained that his rivals used the term "vaudeville" to boost the alleged superiority and respectableness of their own "variety" theaters. In fact, music hall and variety, vaudeville and burlesque, were hardly different and often interchangeable venues for the presentation of popular song and popular singers for financial gain.

The tradition was British. In the eighteenth century, many a tavern had been enlivened by such entertainment. Sadler's Wells, now an esteemed auditorium for opera and ballet, was one. At one end was a stage for the performers (comics were the most popular); at the other, a collection of booths where the drinkers lurked. The liquor sales paid for the music. To discourage these "entertainments," the British Parliament passed an act in 1751 requiring each pleasure haunt to obtain a magistrate's license. The measure had the contrary effect: larger and more prosperous taverns lived up to their new dignity by employing musicians and scenery, while smaller taverns avoided the license by forming "harmonic clubs." Profits from the licensed premises, moreover, led to the building of variety theaters of increasing size and glitter capable of producing elaborate scenic effects.

The spread of urbanization following the British industrial revolution brought a growing demand for "entertainments"; it always seemed worth risking prosecution for the profits that could be had from booze. In fact, the profits were so substantial that publicans looked to expand their operations: wherever possible, buildings adjoining taverns were acquired and adapted into "music houses." And in 1852, Charles Morton—a publican known later as the "father of the halls"—opened the first music hall behind the Canterbury Arms in Lambeth, just south of the Thames. Collins's Music Hall, founded at about the same time by a chimney sweep, opened in the north of London in Islington.

By the mid-nineteenth century, the terminology was confused and confusing: unlicensed premises evaded the licensing laws altogether by changing into "burletta," or burlesque houses—that is, theaters where a certain number of songs were contained within a play. "Saloon" then became the name for a place of popular entertainment, while "music hall" signified a concert hall. "Variety" was an evening of mixed plays; a "vaudevillian" was a performer in burlesque, music hall, variety—or vaudeville—whatever that might be.

But no matter its description, the entertainment devolved around a select number of themes. Popular song and drink, for instance, have always gone together. Today, the relaxation of state and federal laws have again made it easier for theaters to allow their patrons entertainment and drinks at the same time. In the music halls of Victorian England, performers usually fought a losing battle with customers more interested in boozing (and gambling) than listening. An obvious solution was to sing about drinking—preferably with a catchy chorus that everybody could bellow.

Preeminent among the drinking-song brigade of the 1870s was one George Leybourne. Tall and dashing, Leybourne was in great demand by hall managers—not least because the bar profits rose sharply after he had sung his biggest hit of all, "Champagne Charlie." The words were a satire on the raffish man-about-town or "heavy swell" represented by Leybourne, who always managed to imbue his songs with the appearance of good fellowship. But he had a rival, known as the Great Vance, who scored a notable success with a ditty entitled "Clicquot, Clicquot, That's the Wine for Me"—set to the tune of "Funiculi, Funicula." Leybourne was prevailed upon to work his way through an entire wine list, with commercials for Moët et Chandon, Cool Burgundy Ben, and (reflecting surely

no more than a passing fad) lemonade and sherry. "Champagne Charlie," however, remained the firm favorite—doubtless because Leybourne received a weekly subsidy to buy champagne for everybody at the end.

Leybourne himself was not above the occasional drink. Oswald Stoll, then manager of the Parthenon in Liverpool, recalled that one day he despaired of his wayward star ever arriving at the theater. "I went round to his lodgings, and in a sordid room found him huddled up in an arm chair, half comatose. I shook him and cried: 'Come, Mr. Leybourne! All your friends are waiting for you.' I shall never forget the bitterness of his outburst. 'My friends?' he cried. 'I have no friends. Curse the men who call themselves my friends!' I got him to the hall, however, and there again he just collapsed. . . . But when the band played his opening music, he sprang to his feet, a new man, full of life and

Left: the Canterbury Arms Music Hall in Lambeth, London, generally recognized as the first "true" music hall. It opened its doors in 1852, and closed them before this packed house in 1912. *Right:* Marie Lloyd—"Our Marie," born in 1870, a London Cockney.

charm. He sang five songs and was applauded to the echo."

Despite the occasional lapse, George Leybourne was the first popular singing star outside of the opera houses to be concerned with his "image." Suitable clothes and a carriage and four were to be provided at all times; he felt it essential to maintain his man-about-town air wherever he was seen. One British vaudevillian remembers: "When I was young, I thought they were all millionaires with Rolls-Royces waiting at the stage door. It was a bit disillusioning when you got to the other side of the footlights and saw the realities." The reality for George Leybourne was that he died from "dissipation and disillusion" when he was but forty-two.

The tradition of the drinking swell did not die with Leybourne. Dean Martin's "Little Old Wine Drinker Me," with only minor emendations, could have been sung at any time in music hall history. Just as, in the 1960s, Ray Davies' "Alcohol," written for The Kinks, could have been a clarion call for the Salvation Army. Drink, says Davies, is entirely responsible for the breakup of the happy home. He would have found many sympathizers among the reformers of early-nineteenth-century England.

Another well-used theme was Empire and expansionism. Since it went without question that the British Empire was a good thing, songs with an Imperial theme guaranteed success. In the 1880s, a singer called Leo Dryden presented patriotic ballads, educationally. For the song "Great White Mother," he would dress as a Red Indian Chief; as a rajah for "India's Reply"; as an Australian for "The Miner's Dream of Home."

After drink and Empire, the most common subject matter in these music halls was nostalgia for a home left long ago to seek work in strange places. Many of the audience had left their birthplace to do just that and the most

Left: Lillian Russell *(top)* and the so-called Nigger Minstrel of Eastbourne *(bottom)* show the contrast between the elegant and the absurd. *Right:* Nellie Wallace, in pages from an early "fan booke." The music hall artists had devoted audiences who feasted on the face-to-face rapport crucial to the music hall atmosphere.

Truly Yours Nellie Wallace

Mrs Twankey - Aladdin

Warwick Brooks 350 OXFORD ROAD MANCHESTER.

I was born on a Friday

"Oh! I was afraid."

"Down by the Riverside,"

Debenham SOUTHSEA

UDIOS 22, BEDFORD STREET, STRAND, LONDON

HANA

Warwick Brooks 350 OXFORD RO

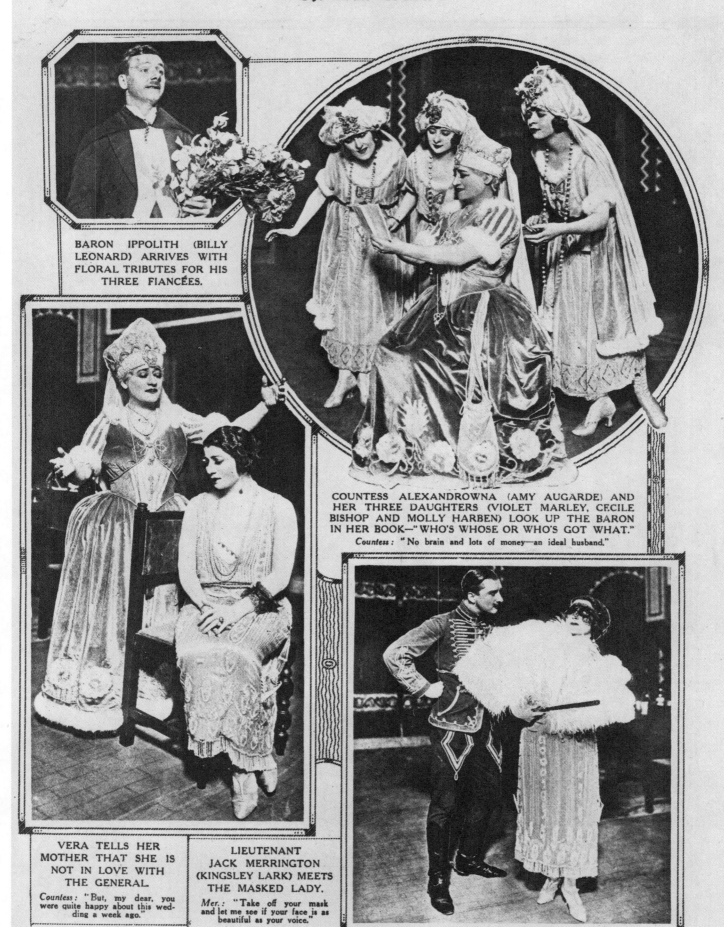

BARON IPPOLITH (BILLY LEONARD) ARRIVES WITH FLORAL TRIBUTES FOR HIS THREE FIANCÉES.

COUNTESS ALEXANDROWNA (AMY AUGARDE) AND HER THREE DAUGHTERS (VIOLET MARLEY, CECILE BISHOP AND MOLLY HARBEN) LOOK UP THE BARON IN HER BOOK—"WHO'S WHOSE OR WHO'S GOT WHAT."

Countess: "No brain and lots of money—an ideal husband."

VERA TELLS HER MOTHER THAT SHE IS NOT IN LOVE WITH THE GENERAL

Countess: "But, my dear, you were quite happy about this wedding a week ago."

LIEUTENANT JACK MERRINGTON (KINGSLEY LARK) MEETS THE MASKED LADY.

Mer.: "Take off your mask and let me see if your face is as beautiful as your voice."

popular ballad was called simply "Home Sweet Home." It was sung everywhere—Adelina Patti had no qualms about introducing it into the lesson scene of Rossini's *Barber of Seville* at New York's Metropolitan Opera House in 1891. Even the Scottish comedian Harry Lauder made it one of his theme songs—it seemed just the thing expatriate Scotsmen throughout the world loved and wanted to hear. As a result, Lauder became more popular in America, Canada, South Africa, Australasia, and London than in Scotland itself. "Home Sweet Home" combined evocative, straightforward lyrics with a simple, catchy melody. Add to these the personality of men like Dryden and Lauder, and the mixture seemed irresistible.

America did not have the same tradition of pubs and drinking houses as Britain. But it did have, of course, a similar market for spontaneous, back-street entertainment. Other than itinerant banjo players, the first such entertainers to organize themselves into troupes were the white nigger minstrels.

Again, the inspiration came out of Britain, where blacked-up minstrels had been popular since the beginning of the nineteenth century, although usually as part of a much larger show. A performance consisted of an all-male group of singers and instrumentalists sitting and/or soft-shoe dancing in a half-circle facing the audience, their faces daubed to give the illusion of absurd, albeit noble savages. Interspersed with the songs was a cross-talk between the two lead minstrels, the Interlocutor and Mr. Bones. Again, a dominant theme was Home Sweet Home and a longing for the good old days when the social order was assured, when a man knew his place—even if it was slavery—and all was well with the world. Such a theme might be developed throughout an entire first act, although relieved in the second by assorted variety turns.

British entertainers, among them the minstrels, often toured the East Coast of America. With its considerable slave population, America found the shows appealing. As early as 1822, one Charles Mathews had blacked-up to borrow (or steal) from a black performer a song called "Possum up a Gum Tree" for his routine, "A Trip to America." Another white vaudevillian named Thomas Rice, although he never appeared with a minstrel company (he preferred farce), provided the most commonly accepted origin of the term "Jim Crow." Rice was touring with Ludlow's Summer Company in Louisville, Kentucky, when (according to his friend Edward Connor) he noticed "back of the theatre was a livery stable, kept by a white man named Jim Crow. The actors would look into the stable yard from the theatre, and were particularly amused by an old decrepit Negro who used to

MISS VESTA TILLEY IN KHAKI

Left: from *Music for All* magazine. *Right:* Vesta Tilley often performed in male drag, but particularly when called upon to do her part for recruiting.

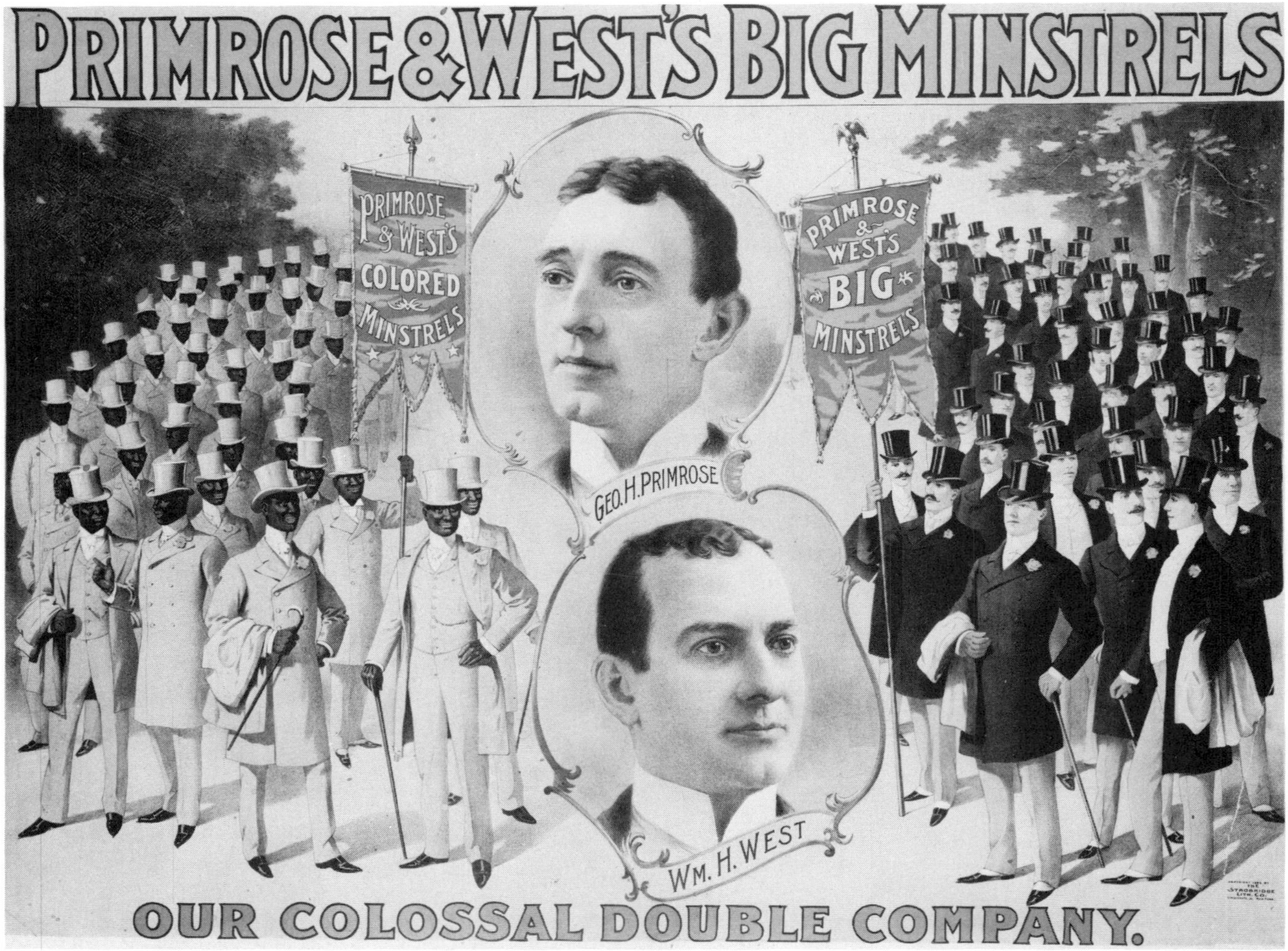

PRIMROSE & WEST'S BIG MINSTRELS
PRIMROSE & WEST'S COLORED MINSTRELS
PRIMROSE & WEST'S BIG MINSTRELS
GEO. H. PRIMROSE
WM. H. WEST
OUR COLOSSAL DOUBLE COMPANY.

do odd jobs for Crow. He was very much deformed, the right shoulder being drawn high up, the left leg stiff and crooked at the knee, giving him a painful, at the same time laughable, limp. He used to croon a queer old tune with words of his own, and at the end of each verse would give a little jump, and when he came down he set his heel a-rockin'. He called his song 'Jumping Jim Crow. . . . ' Rice watched closely, and saw that here was a character unknown to the stage. He wrote several verses, changed the air somewhat, quickened it a good deal, made up exactly like Daddy, and sang it to a Louisville audience. They were wild with delight, and on the first night he was recalled twenty times. . . .''

None of this entertainment, of course, was considered proper. The variety theaters, in particular, were regarded with suspicion. William Hammerstein (son of Oscar II) passes on tales of his grandfather's exploits as a New York promoter: ''In spite of the fact that he ran a vaudeville house—and ran it a bit unethically sometimes—he was a man of great moral viture. He would never allow his wife to go there. And, though he made money out of them, he would *never* allow theater people to come to the house.''

The British were equally condescending. A Mr. Anstey, writing in *Harper's New Monthly*

Above: the unusual sight of a mixed company. Whites would share the stage in blackface, but almost never with blacks. *Top right:* the vaudeville staple, a cross-talk act, at the Fifth Avenue Theatre, New York. *Bottom right:* Harry Lauder, who was knighted for his successful use of Scottish sentimentality.

Magazine in 1890, noted: "The audience is not a distinguished looking one. The fringe is made up of gay young clerks, the local 'bloods,' who have a jaunty fashion in some districts of wearing a cigar behind the ear. Large ham sandwiches are handed round by cooks in white blouses, and when a young woman desires to be very stylish indeed, she allows her swain to order a glass of port for her refreshment. Taken as a whole, the audience is not remarkable for its intelligence."

Nonetheless, there were many aspects of the music hall that made it socially intriguing and kept it vigorous. There was the growing cult of the male impersonator, the most renowned of whom was the British star Vesta Tilley. She fascinated both men and women. Male impersonation had been an integral part of minstrelsy and the English theatrical tradition since the seventeenth century, although few had spent as much time and money perfecting that art as Miss Tilley. Her suits and uniforms were fashioned by leading tailors so correctly that it was she, rather than any of her male theatrical contemporaries, who was considered the very model of the fashionable young man. Possessed of a tremendous showmanship—her overture was sometimes played two or three times before she entered—she made no attempt to sing like a man. Instead, songs such as "Burlington Bertie" gave a woman's view of the men she represented.

There were also female impersonators, whose asexual attraction had Greek and Egyptian antecedents. Impersonations of comic servants, harridans, and aged wives and widows were usually supplied by famous comedians otherwise noted for their nonfemale parts—in England, comedians such as Dan Leno and George Robey; in America, performers like Julian Eltinge, who reintroduced an almost pre-Restoration style of impersonation. Eltinge presented himself as a convincingly glamorous woman in vaudeville and film between 1900 and 1928, and through his example, the English tradition of sexual ambivalence in variety shows passed into American theater. Judy Garland was only a step away.

Sex was not the only quality that attracted people to the music halls. The excitement of visiting a place of entertainment thought to be a hideaway of the underworld proved irresistible. The London Theatrical Managers Association boomed its disapproval. "The Music Halls," it announced in a broadside published in 1904, "are permitted to have smoking and drinking in the auditorium, and standing in the corridors; their performances are not subjected to censorship; they are, moreover, permitted in many instances to have what are called 'promenades,' and in other ways they enjoy those free and easy attributes which have become associated with the music hall. It seems scarcely in accordance with the rights of man that any class of the community should claim that, by breaking a law sufficiently often, they can make a law unto themselves." The "promenades" referred to were lobbies in the music halls where "high-class" prostitutes were allowed to solicit, in exchange for a fee paid to the management.

There was in addition the question of accent, a matter of intense and inverted preoccupation among the class-ridden societies of late-nineteenth- and early-twentieth-century Britain and America. Although the Victorian music hall drew its performers from all parts of the British Isles, the East End of London was regarded as the richest storehouse of talent and the Cockney accent was the most imitated. Later, when modern drag artists attempted to re-create the old songs for contemporary audiences (whether British or American), they always used Cockney as a proof of their authenticity.

It is remarkable that an East London accent—occasionally barely comprehensible to a West Londoner—should have been the passport for many an English music hall star to America. Sam Cowell, for instance, was an actor who performed popular songs in a Cockney dialect dur-

Left: St. Louis–born Josephine Baker introduced *le jazz hot* to Paris in *La Revue Nègre* in 1925, and was known thereafter as the "Dark Star" of the Folies-Bergère. She became a French citizen in 1937, and remained (despite occasional "retirement") a figure of enormous popularity until her death in 1975. *Right:* the center, still, of the vaudeville-music hall world—the London Palladium.

ing the intermissions of Broadway plays. Albert Chevalier was another. Although in no way a Cockney—he was born in West London of a French father and a Welsh mother—Chevalier was typical. After working twenty years in burlesque, melodrama, and pantomime as a low character comedian, he made his music hall debut at the London Pavilion in 1891. Three years later, he transferred to New York, was a hit, and spent the next years touring the United States and Canada.

Music hall's ultimate fascination, however, came from an unexpected source—the chance approval of the British Royal Family. Queen Victoria once asked the bandmaster at Windsor Castle the title of a particularly intriguing piece. "That is from the music halls,

Facing page: a bespectacled Bob Hope, English-born (in 1904), Cleveland-bred, as part of an act called "Two Diamonds In The Rough," in the early 1920s. *Top left:* black vaudevillians thrived mostly as dancers; Buck and Bubbles were an above-the-title act. *Center left:* Bud Flanagan (with Chesney Allen, at right) was as popular in England as George Burns and Gracie Allen *(bottom left)* were in America. The latter appeared with Fred Astaire *(above right)* in *A Damsel in Distress*, a film in which a pained Joan Fontaine (it was her first starring role) tried to carry the romantic interest while her co-stars danced, somersaulted, and frolicked circles around her. Paul McCartney told me he wanted to put a Bud Flanagan statue on top of every fire hydrant in London.

Ma'am," said the bandmaster. "Yes, but what is it *called*, my man," spake the Queen. After a pause, and no doubt a cough, the embarrassed official replied: " 'Come Where the Booze Is Cheaper,' Ma'am." Victoria's son Edward, Prince of Wales, showed his appreciation of individual female performers often and famously. And a private visit to the Holborn Empire when Edward became King caused much adverse comment—although Dan Leno, Albert Chevalier, and Bransby Williams all received the command to entertain the King at Sandringham. George V even attended a matinee of a new opera house financed by the original Oscar Hammerstein, and called—without permission—the London Opera House. As George stepped from the royal carriage, Hammerstein was so overcome that he forgot all the protocol in which he had been carefully schooled and rushed forward shouting: "Hello, King. I'm glad you could come." Quite unruffled, King George shook Hammerstein firmly by the hand and said: "It's very nice of you to have us." The present William Hammerstein told me that his great-grandfather had to pay his bona fide opera singers by rifling the cash boxes of his son's vaudeville houses.

With the accession of George V and the attendant coronation festivities in 1911, there were the usual command galas at Covent Garden for opera and ballet and at His Majesty's Theatre for drama. It was a surprise when a similar honor was announced for the "variety profession," as it was now fashionably called. The date set was for midsummer, at the Edinburgh Empire. Alas, a few weeks before the time appointed, fire destroyed the building. It also nearly killed the idea of a command performance. Another date was suggested (in May 1912), but again postponed, this time because of court mourning. Fi-

Proudest products of New York's Lower East Side were Sophie Tucker *(top left)* and Fanny Brice *(bottom near left),* both stars of the Ziegfeld Follies. More characteristically Bricean is the picture *(bottom far left)* where, in her "Baby Snooks" guise, she cavorts with Judy Garland. Though his shows were noted for their "glorification of the American girl," Florenz Ziegfeld's greatest box office draws were less than beautiful. They relied, instead, on what is music hall's most tendentious quality: personality. *Below left:* Woody Herman was a child vaudevillian, whose act consisted of a creditable imitation of bandleader Ted Lewis; as it turned out, Lewis was much more the vaudevillian, Herman the accomplished bandleader. *Below center:* Max Miller worked English music hall stages for decades. *Below right:* Gypsy Rose Lee (born Rose Hovick) worked an American equivalent of music hall, the burlesque house, before moving into legitimate theaters and literary salons after the 1941 publication of her best-selling mystery novel, *The G-String Murders.* Her memoirs, *Gypsy,* were the basis for a Broadway show of that name.

nally, the Palace Theater was chosen and the performance took place on July 1, 1912. By now a prosperous London theater owner, Oswald Stoll said: "The Cinderella of the arts has gone to the ball."

All the stars of the day were included. If not in the main program, they "walked on" in the final tableau called "Variety's Garden Party." Only Marie Lloyd was missing. Those in charge thought their newly won respectability might be endangered by the vulgarity of "Our Marie." It was, however, entirely music hall's loss. "Every performance of Marie Lloyd is a performance by command of the British Public," she announced with justification. Her songs had strength because they appeared to come

"Every performance of Marie Lloyd is a performance by command of the British public," she announced with justification.

straight from the experience of the singer. At the peak of her popularity (in the 1890s), she impersonated roguishly demure young ladies singing "The Boy I Love Is up in the Gallery," emphasizing the words with hefty nudges, winks, and flashing grins. She drew the audience in and began an affair that had resounding consequences. Audiences began to identify with their favorite singer, just as singers became identified with their most popular song. When Edith Piaf later sang *"Non, Je ne Regrette Rien,"* one knew she spoke for herself. Abandoned as a baby, blinded as a child (her sight was restored miraculously at the shrine of St. Teresa), she worked as a street singer, lived through the

534-2/53

murder of her first lover and manager, was involved with the Resistance during World War II, made several marriages, was victimized by alcohol, drugs, and ill health. Her life was, in short, extraordinary. Many of her songs were written about her and for her. Her audience knew she had suffered, and loved her for it.

Danny La Rue, a present-day English female impersonator, feels the same contact. Compared with that of Piaf, his career has been garlanded with roses. "But life on the road is hard," he told me. "The Saturday nights packing up, the opening nights on Monday—traveling to absolutely everywhere. Hundreds of miles for very little money. You *have* to love it. The audiences make it possible. They were *always* there, regularly. Every time you went back to a hall, there was the butcher and his wife in the same seats as before. Music hall was a family of audience and artists." Even that apparently liberated, mature, and ultrasophisticated Frenchwoman, Juliette Greco, tells the same story. "To sing is not just work or pleasure, it is my vitamin. The thing that keeps me going," she says, "is that people come and listen to me. It is very physical, very emotional. After a performance, I am completely empty. I don't exist any more. It's a drug. I am so happy when I sing that I forget everything else. I come in the theatre, go on stage, and it is finished, all rubbed out. Again, I am myself. It's like a fire. Love, that's it."

Long before World War I, the vaudevillians had ceased to be lords of the popular song; other, more immediate, methods of promoting songs had developed. Vaudeville had countered the new devices with a greater emphasis on sensation. The result had been frivolity. The content of its songs became gibberish—songs like "Ta-ra-ra-boom-deay," on which Lottie Collins' entire contemporary reputation and posthumous fame rests. Adapted from an American song first heard in a New Orleans brothel and called "Ting-a-ling-boomderay," the English version had been introduced by Miss Collins into her pantomime at the Grand Theatre in Islington, where it was an instantaneous hit. Soon all the errand boys were whistling it, and she embarked upon extensive tours throughout the world to promote it. Part of the song's popularity was due to a surging chorus sung by the audience while Miss Collins whirled around the stage in a frenzy of can-can and high kicks. Holbrook Jackson, an enthusiastic young socialist, saw Miss Collins as a symbol of youth, kicking the stuffiness out of Victorian England. Another saw her act as a religious, dervish-like ritual. In fact, almost everyone was trying to see up her skirts.

After 1918, in a society increasingly caught up in economic, social, and political turmoil, the tradition of music hall in both Britain or the United States seemed to embody little except trivia. Its multiple strands—drink, nostalgia, accent, drag, minstrels, bawdry, and the iden-

Left: the Ziegfeld Follies. *Right:* Ziegfeld himself, in Florida.

tification of singer with song — were not broken, however, and came together for one last fling in the person of Mae West. At heart, she was a burlesque who mocked the whole absurdity of sex. She alarmed moralists by declaring that Love was a subject fit only for laughter. She parodied the Edwardian vamp and perfected the technique of fixing all the blame on the audience for seeing something rude in her material. Neither Miss West nor her male English contemporary Max Miller needed to use actual words to gain their effects. They raised their eyebrows when the audience laughed — at an apparently rude reference — and they raised them when the audience did not. Either way, they got a laugh.

The tradition staggered on, giving sustenance to a host of unknowns who became stars in other media. Eddie Cantor, Bob Hope, Rudy Vallee, all started in vaudeville. So, incidentally, did Irving Berlin. But when, in 1942, New

Plus ça change: an original Ziegfeld girl *(top left);* the modern equivalent, flourishing in Las Vegas today *(top center),* where Liberace *(top right)* represents the latest in a very long line. *Right:* Edith Piaf was certainly more of a singer than Sophie Tucker, but Tucker's Ziegfeld-packaged appeal was predicated on the same belief as that of Piaf: an unerring sense of, and commitment to, the audience.

York's Palace Theatre decided to stop its twice daily performances, vaudeville and music hall (it was said) finally succumbed to the power of the talkies and breathed its last. Music hall had *officially* died, however, on May 2, 1937, when the management of New York's Gotham Theatre was put on trial for breaking the obscenity laws by presenting striptease. The theater lost and Mayor La Guardia ordered the closure of all burlesque theaters in New York. Then again, music hall died once more in 1966 when London's Windmill Theatre—"We never close"—closed. For sixty years, it had provided nonstop entertainment of clowns, jugglers, nudes, and a few songs. Now, it was silent. Vaudeville, said the pundits, was no more.

Perhaps it truly died with Judy Garland. She never gave a concert; she conducted a séance. "We love you, Judy," shouted the audience. "I love you, too," came the response. The affair between audience and singer was consummated in her swaggering performance. She had endured much, and didn't mind telling you. Although she had dazzled the world through her movies, she finished up in drinking and gambling clubs on both sides of the Atlantic. "Audiences," she said, "have kept me alive." They also fed on her agonized and well-publicized past—her teen-age stardom, her tantrums, her wonderful alcoholic voice with its frequent crackups, her broken contracts, her four busted marriages (to men increasingly younger than she was), her suicide attempts, and her aches and pains. The audience *knew* that life had beaten her up but had not destroyed her. Her survival gave her power—and sex appeal.

And then, at the end of each performance, she would sing that song: "Somewhere, over the rainbow, blue birds fly. Birds fly over the rainbow, why, oh, why can't I?" She would sit cross-legged, lit by a single spotlight, alone in a great emptiness. No more gimmicks, no more show. Just a little girl who has been put down but who has refused to give in. Her voice croaked a little, sighed a little. No more noise, no more smiles. It was pathetic and lonely and dignified—but her audience carried on, leering

and gossiping. "You made me love you; I didn't wanna do it," she would sing.

Today, only one great palace of variety remains—Las Vegas, Nevada. In its early days, Liberace told me, "the hotels would supply free breakfast and even free rooms because they wanted your custom at the tables. All that has changed: now the hotels are all so alike that they can only try to outdo each other in the pretentiousness and vulgarity of their shows. Thousands of dollars can be spent on a single costume, millions on a presentation. But it's the same old story: drag them in and give them a show. The more vulgar it is, the better they like it. I was weaned on vaudeville," Liberace adds. "Alas, it's not what it was."

But the spirit engendered by music hall did survive and was to prove crucial in the development of rock and roll; and the theatrical traditions it embodied and preserved were to contribute substantially to the development of what some claim to be America's major art form, the musical. Before there was musical theater, however, a more raucous influence lurched across the stage, making a noise much like its name— Tin Pan Alley.

METRO - GOLDWYN - MAYER PICTURE
THE
BROADWAY
MELODY
ALL TALKING
ALL SINGING
ALL DANCING
ASTOR THEATRE

Always Chasing Rainbows

Tin Pan Alley wrote songs to make money, and to supply the needs of vaude-ville. "It may sound a little immodest," song writer Irving Caesar says, "but you'd be amazed—perhaps you shouldn't be—that most of my songs that sold were written in less than fifteen minutes. 'Tea for Two' was written in less than four minutes. 'I Wanna Be Happy' in about twelve minutes. 'Swanee'— George Gershwin and I wrote that in about fifteen minutes while there was a card game going on in the parlor. 'Just a Gigolo'—no, that took me overnight, that required a little work." Irving Berlin wrote a song a day. Harry von Tilzer wrote over three thousand in his lifetime. Fred Fischer wrote so many that his mind went to pieces. One day he asked a neophyte writer: "Wanna see a joke?"

The melody played on Broadway *(left)* was forged by immigrants who began their uptown move from Ellis Island *(above)*.

and hurled a heavy typewriter out of his fifth-floor window.

To survive in the Alley, it was not necessary to be musically literate. It was not even necessary to be musical. Some, like Gershwin, could write you a rhapsody. Others, like Irving Berlin or Lewis Muir, couldn't read a note and played in only one key. Berlin's key was the unusual F sharp. He had a special piano made that could transpose at the flick of a lever. Lewis Muir's key was C major. When demonstrating "Waiting for the *Robert E. Lee*," Muir had an assistant waiting for his shout of *"Now!"* to switch the piano from the C verse into the F major chorus.

Victor Herbert was another poor pianist — he played as though he had club fingers, according to Irving Caesar. "I wrote quite a few songs with George Meyer, for example. Great song writer, but he, too, couldn't play the piano. He was one-fingered — well, almost one-fingered. But he was a great melodist." Harry Woods had no left hand, merely a stump. Nevertheless, he insisted on banging out a rhythmic vamp that sounded (it is said) rather jazzy.

Many songs were written by committee. The early-twenties hit "Yes, We Have No Bananas" is the work of at least seven writers. Ian Whitcomb, an English singer and historian of Tin Pan Alley, has traced its group origins. "Frank Silver played for Irving Cohn's New York Dance Band. One night he was at a girl friend's house romancing her on a couch . . . or at least, he was trying to, except the girl's kid brother kept squealing a nonsense phrase: 'Yes, we have no bananas.' Eventually, Silver asked the child where he'd picked up the phrase. 'From the fruit seller down the street — the guy who can't speak no English.' 'Come over to the piano, kid, and let's work.'" Silver took the results to Irving Cohn, and soon it was a popular request. They then took it to Shapiro and Bernstein, publishers, where the staff boys doctored it a bit, adding a word here and a note

there. Among the contributors were Hanley and McDonald ("Trail of the Lonesome Pine"), Lew Brown ("The Best Things in Life Are Free"), and Shapiro and Bernstein themselves. Among musical phrases that went into the patchwork tune were quotes from "My Bonnie," "Aunt Dinah's Quilting Party," "The Bohemian Girl," "An Old-Fashioned Garden," and "The Hallelujah Chorus."

"Bananas" became the rage of 1923. *Time* magazine devoted an article to it. David Niven says he first experienced love in the embraces of a West End prostitute while the song was playing on her boudoir gramophone. In Weimar Germany, the song was known as *"Ja, Wir Haben Keinen Bananen Heute."* Hitler was reported furious when he realized that the song had been devised by Jews.

If the Alleymen were often musically backward, they had other qualities. They claimed to be servants of the people who put their ears to the street and listened. Then, of course, they sold back what they had heard, in song form and at a profit. Black, white, yellow, ragtime, jazz, blues, anything and everything was grist for their mill. Veteran Alleyman Mickey Addy

From left to right: Stephen Foster, born in Pittsburgh, 1826; Irving Berlin; Chas. K. Harris composed, published, and posed.

remembers a lyric writer who would sit all night drinking coffee in New York restaurants. "He'd just go and sit next to a group of fellows and every time one of them made a crack he'd write it down in his notebook as a title. He must have had seventy or eighty titles. And when anyone needed a song, he'd have a title ready."

This obsession to make money from the entertainment of others has always gripped the American imagination. It was focused at the turn of the century, however, by Chas. K. Harris, who published a little book of rules entitled *How to Write a Popular Song*. A dignified figure with wax moustache, wing collar, and tweed suit, Harris looked like an entrepreneurial Kaiser Wilhelm. He was proud of the business to which he belonged: song manufacturing. Indeed, so well had he studied his craft that he could, it is said, determine in advance how many sheet music copies his songs would sell. To his readers he advised: look at newspapers for your story line; acquaint yourself with the style in vogue; avoid slang; know the copyright laws.

Harris knew exactly what he was talking about. In the early 1880s, he had put up a sign outside his shop: "SONGS WRITTEN TO ORDER." His work tool was a banjo, and on it he had carpentered songs for births, deaths, marriages, junkets—anything. Maximum price: twenty dollars. He worked hard, and one day arranged for his three-verse story ballad, "After the Ball," to be inserted into a variety show called *A Trip to Chinatown*. The song had nothing to do with Chinatown, but insertion was getting to be standard practice. Good exposure for your song. If it clicked, then everyone was happy. Some shows were sure-fire for years on the strength of one hit. And "After the Ball" was an instant hit from the first night. Harris was publisher as well as author-composer, and within a year, the song was bringing in twenty-five thousand dollars a week; within twenty years, sheet sales topped over seven million. It was translated into every known language. Harris never had another hit, but he lived nicely off this single work for the rest of his life.

"After the Ball," written and published in 1892, was also the first million-seller to be con-

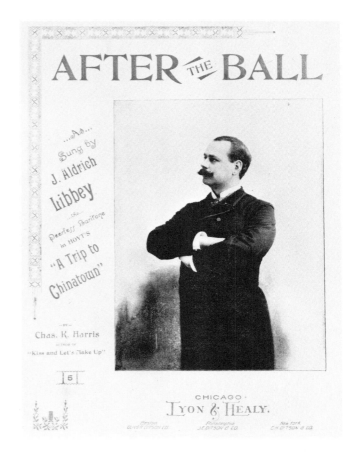

ceived and marketed as a million-seller. Its content was simple enough, yet dramatic: a little maiden climbs on an old man's knee and asks him why he has no babies and no home. He replies that he had a sweetheart once but caught her kissing another—at a ball. He couldn't forgive her and wouldn't listen to her explanation. Years later, after her death, the man he saw her kissing tells him he was her brother. That's why the old man is lonely, has no home at all, because he broke her heart—after the ball.

> *Many a heart is aching*
> *If you could read them all;*
> *Many the hopes that have vanished,*
> *After the ball.*

The idea of mass-producing ready-made songs to sell to the millions did not originate in America. European street hawkers had been doing a brisk trade in topical songs about murders, disasters, and illicit love for decades—in London, Paris, and Berlin—and established

music publishers had done well with their simplified versions of operas. And since Victorian America had already imported French chateaus brick by brick, why not import European musicians and their know-how? First attempts were inconclusive. One particular harp player declared the natives "supremely vulgar." Whereupon he found himself stranded in Montana, without a booking, and with two arrows in his instrument.

Admittedly, music publishers did have their occasional hits — Stephen Foster's plantation songs sold extremely well — but this seems to have happened almost by accident. The publishers were a sleepy lot whose catalogues were stuffed with too much music. Like any old country store, they kept everything somewhere — only they weren't sure exactly where. So

when they had hits like "Camptown Races" or "The Old Folks at Home," they were unable to exploit them. Foster even became embarrassed by his songs — he was deeply affected by an attack upon his music in *Dwight's Journal of Music* wherein his tunes were condemned as "only skin deep, hummed and whistled without musical emotion."

Most song writers were not as fortunate as Foster, however. They were a motley lot who sold their songs where they could for a few dollars. Failure drove them to the bottle. They

Above: Tin Pan Alley, in its 42nd Street incarnation. *Color pages:* when selling a song meant selling sheet music, when there was no radio and consequently no disc jockeys to do the selling, the packaging was all-important. The following early sheet music covers demonstrate the nature of the sell — sentiment, racism, star appeal, patriotism — as well as the importance of illustrative skills.

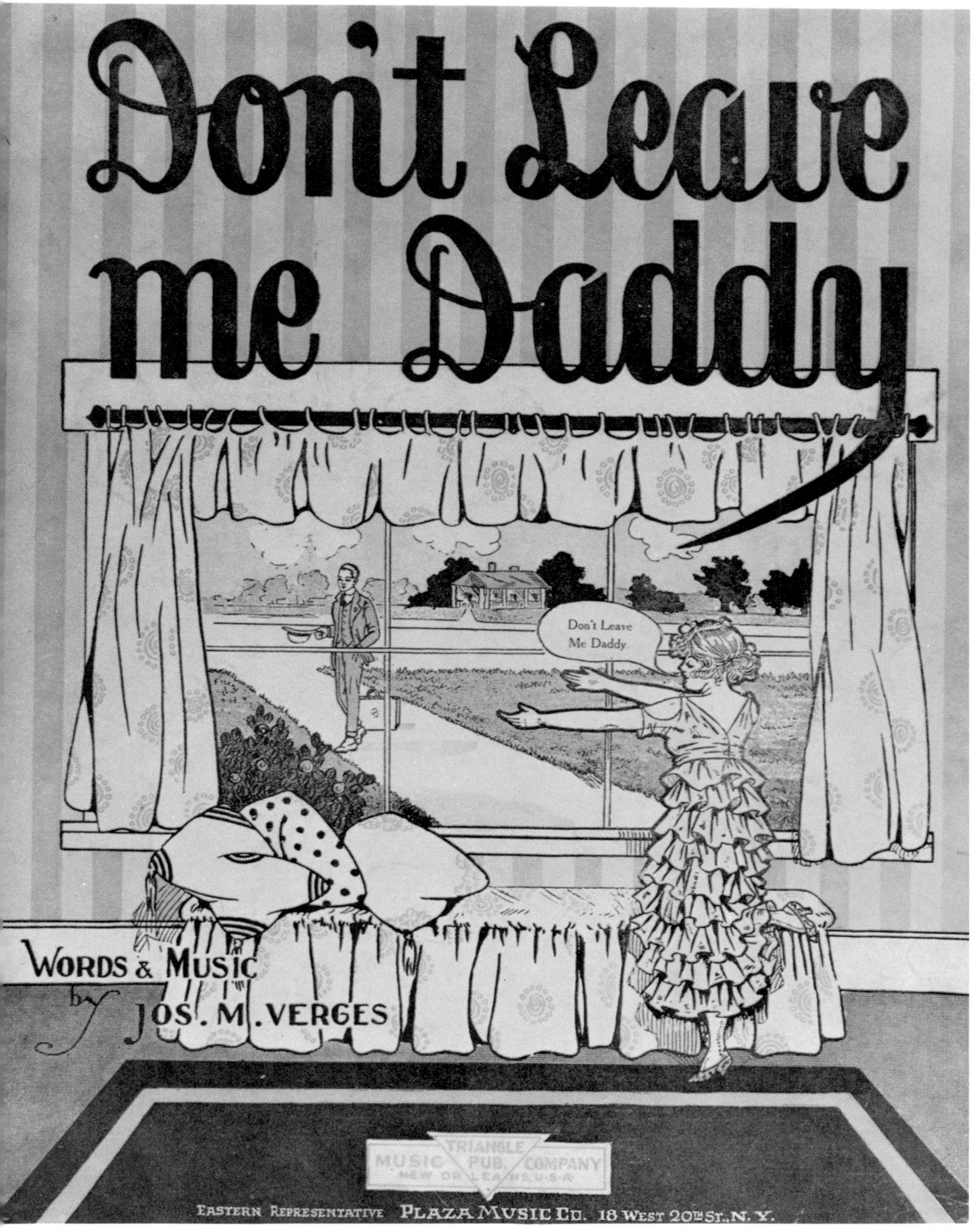
Don't Leave me Daddy
Don't Leave Me Daddy
Words & Music by Jos. M. Verges
Triangle Music Pub. Company New Orleans, U.S.A.
Eastern Representative Plaza Music Co. 18 West 20th St., N.Y.

CHILI SAUCE

THAT TANTALIZING
RAG·TIME·SONG

Words & Music By H. A. Fischler.

COMPOSER OF

"RASTUS" ———— RAG
"NIGGER TOE" ———— RAG
"PEPPER SAUCE" ———— RAG
"CHILI SAUCE" ———— RAG
"BLACK WASP" ———— RAG
"HOT SCOTCH" ——— RAG ETC

CHILI SAUCE

50 VANDERSLOOT MUSIC PUB. CO. WILLIAMSPORT PA. 50

DOWN WHERE THE SWANEE RIVER FLOWS
WORDS BY
CHAS. McCARRON AND
CHAS. S. ALBERTE
MUSIC BY
ALBERT VON TILZER
FEATURED WITH GREAT SUCCESS BY
AL JOLSON
IN THE WINTER GARDEN PRODUCTION
"ROBINSON CRUSOE, JR."
PRICE SIXTY CENTS
BROADWAY MUSIC CORPORATION
WILL VON TILZER PRESIDENT
145 WEST 45TH ST. NEW YORK
PUBLIC PERFORMANCE OF THIS WORK WITHOUT WRITTEN LICENSE FROM THE COPYRIGHT PROPRIETOR IS PROHIBITED

THAT MESMERIZING
MENDELSSOHN TUNE
MENDELSSOHN RAG
Successfully Sung by
GOFF PHILLIPS
Words and Music by
IRVING BERLIN
5
TED SNYDER Co.
MUSIC PUBLISHERS
112 WEST 38 St. NEW YORK.

PRETTY BABY

SONG

As Originally Introduced in the SHUBERT PRODUCTION "THE PASSING SHOW" OF 1916

LYRIC BY
GUS KAHN

MUSIC BY
TONY JACKSON
AND
EGBERT VAN ALSTYNE

6

JEROME H. REMICK & CO.   NEW YORK   DETROIT

RESPECTFULLY INSCRIBED TO
GEN'L JOHN J. PERSHING
AND THE MEN OF THE A.E.F.

PERSHING'S CRUSADERS

MARCH MILITAIRE

BY E.T.PAULL

SPECIAL U.S. OFFICIAL DESIGN USED BY COURTESY OF COMMITTEE ON PUBLIC INFORMATION

PUBLISHED BY E.T.PAULL MUSIC Cº 243 WEST 42nd ST.

NEW YORK

LONDON, ENG.
B. FELDMAN.

CHICAGO, ILL.
F. J. A. FORSTER CO.

NEW YORK
CROWN MUSIC CO.

NEW YORK
ENTERPRISE MUSIC CO.

NEW YORK.
PLAZA MUSIC CO.

TORONTO, CANADA.
W. R. DRAPER.

J. A. ALBERT & SON, SYDNEY, AUSTRALIA.

LITH BY A.HOEN & CO RICHMOND VA

PIANO SOLO
PRICE 50¢
FOUR HAND
PRICE $1.00

Copyright
MCMXVIII.
By E.T.PAULL
COPYRIGHT FOR ALL COUNTRIES

THE SENTIMENT OF EVERY AMERICAN MOTHER

AMERICA
HERE'S MY BOY

WORDS BY
ANDREW B. STERLING

JOE MORRIS MUSIC CO.
145 W. 45TH St.   NEW YORK

MUSIC BY
ARTHUR LANGE

WE'RE GOING OVER

by ANDREW B. STERLING, BERNIE GROSSMAN & ARTHUR LANGE

JOE MORRIS MUSIC CO., 145 W. 45th ST. NEW YORK

The Nine Founding Members of ASCAP

GEORGE MAXWELL

SILVIO HEIN

LOUIS A. HIRSCH

RAYMOND HUBBELL

VICTOR HERBERT

NATHAN BURKAN

GLEN MacDONOUGH

JAY WITMARK

GUSTAVE KERKER

were vagabond individuals, splendid isolationists. James Thornton, for example, often fell off the stage while performing, drunk. In his alcoholic haze, he saw men with crab's legs; yet the same man would write "My Sweetheart's the Man in the Moon." He died broke. Then there was Charles Graham. He died in 1899 in Bellevue Hospital's alcoholic section. Yet he wrote songs like "Two Little Girls in Blue." Hart Danks expired in a New York flophouse, leaving a note that read: "It's hard to die alone." Yet he wrote carefree, glorious songs like "Silver Threads Among the Gold." Foster himself ended up in the Bowery. One day, he fell over a wash basin, drunk. Someone took him to the hospital, where he died. Someone else found a manuscript in his pocket. It was "Beautiful Dreamer."

The ubiquitous Chas. K. Harris, on the other

hand, was determined that such a fate would not befall him. With the success of "After the Ball," he moved to New York and opened an office. He soon became involved with a bunch of ingenious businessmen who were establishing themselves in the pop sheet music publishing trade. They were a new breed, observed Harris, quite unlike the Victorian crowd. They did not mind the occasional "ain't." Harris was astonished. But, like them, he was astutely aware of one cardinal fact: the American industrial revolution had created "the masses"—those millions who had flocked, and were flocking, to the cities from farm, mountain, and plantation to find work. These new urban folk needed entertainment, ready-made, off the peg. A tune for every mood—washing the gritty bits of hard life away, as it were. Chains of music halls and vaudeville theaters, rows of restaurants decorated with dance orchestras, alleys of saloons and cafés featuring singing waiters and honkytonk pianists, were springing up overnight. And all needed cheap music cheaply. The new pop

Tin Pan Alley was built by money (*upper left*, one of Irving Berlin's early royalty statements) and a closed brotherhood (*lower left*, an ASCAP annual dinner at Lüchow's; *right*, the organization's founding members).

publishers were there to provide it. The central question remained: who was going to write the tunes?

Again it was Europe that supplied the answer. Not for the first time, Europe's poor made America rich. Between 1880 and 1910, twenty million arrived. It was a heavy time for accents. Native-born Americans were scared of these aliens, these "dangerous and corrupting hordes." They were the beaten races, those whom the gods had rejected. Americans were especially hard on the Jewish immigrants, treating them only a little better than they treated blacks. Finding established businesses such as banking closed to them, these immigrants invaded the emerging rogue industries of mass entertainment: movies, vaudeville, and pop

music. They brought guts, nerve, and a remarkable facility for assimilating American culture. They also gave America its songs; more accurately, they sold them.

Many of these new musicians couldn't read a note of music; most had begun their business lives as salesmen. Isadore Witmark had sold water filters; Joe Stern and Ed Marks had peddled neckties and buttons, respectively; Leo Feist had been in the corset trade. Like the men who founded the movie industry at about the same time, many were from Middle and Eastern Europe. From the Imperial German Navy came Fred Fischer, who wrote a song called "Chicago." A Russian, Wolfe Gilbert, wrote of "Waiting for the *Robert E. Lee.*"

Like Jews in Europe, they formed their own ghetto. Journalist Monroe Rosenfeld was commissioned in 1900 by the New York *Herald* to write a story about this new song writing business—a trade in which he dabbled himself—and called upon one of its more eminent practitioners, Harry von Tilzer. The windows of Harry's office were open, and it was hard to be heard above the babble of pounded pianos waft-

Success, not musical quality, was the prerequisite when song pluggers, song demonstrators, and sheet music designers were king. With the development of radio, success could be instant. Hoagy Carmichael, who wrote the overnight sensation "Stardust," poses as His Master's Voice (*right*); Irving Berlin, Jerome Kern, Victor Herbert, Gene Buck, John Philip Sousa, Chas. K. Harris, and Harry von Tilzer (*center, from left to right*) gave the dog—and the nation—even more to listen to.

ing in. "Those are my friends and rivals," shouted Harry, "assembling tomorrow's cashertos [his variation on 'concerto']. You know, hit tunes. It's always reminded me of kitchen clatter, just like tin pans. Hit tunes out of out-of-tune pianos. Get me?" The story sounds a little crazy, and is. But Rosenfeld's series of articles was a modest success and the title caught on. Where the hits were made, night and day, on out-of-tune pianos, that was Tin Pan Alley. "Not *too* out of tune," remembered Irving Caesar, a doyen among Alleymen. "But they didn't sound too far removed from a tin pan to a passerby with a sensitive ear for music."

Curiously enough, no two publishers have ever agreed on the exact location of Tin Pan Alley, except that it was usually in close proximity to the source of the next dollar. In 1900, it was centered around New York's Twenty-eighth Street, an area in which many music hall singers and vaudevillians lived. But as the city

No two publishers have ever agreed on the exact location of Tin Pan Alley, except that it was usually in close proximity to the source of the next dollar.

developed, the music publishers moved uptown, to be nearer their potential market. Mickey Addy claims it was not even christened "Tin Pan Alley" until it had arrived at Forty-sixth Street, between Broadway and Sixth Avenue. And when radio became an important factor, Tin Pan Alley regrouped around radio's production centers: RCA in Radio City and CBS at Fifty-second Street and Madison Avenue. For his part, Eddie Rogers, a British song plugger, scorns all American claims. "It really started in Denmark Street in London," he told me. "There were only twelve publishers in those early days, but literally hundreds of artists looking for songs. When they came down Denmark Street, they'd get dragged into one of the houses to hear the new song, and all the pluggers from the other houses would grab dustbin lids and kettles and bang them together to kill the plug. *That's* why it was called Tin Pan Alley. It had nothing whatsoever to do with America."

Wherever its origin, Tin Pan Alley publishers

always clustered together. They came to work in the same street, they married into one another's families, they lived with one another. They manufactured their own incestuous environment. "I remember a song I sang as a little kid in a minstrel show," Irving Caesar told me. " 'In the Land of the Buffalo, Where the Western Winds Do Blow'—all about the land of the buffalo. Probably the fellow who wrote it had never been west of New York. But he *did* have imagination."

The Alleymen turned the song business into big business. They hired "staff arrangers" who were kept busy scoring stock arrangements in any key for any size orchestra for any occasion;

the arrangers would amuse themselves by seeing how many times they could change key in one tune. Such arrangements were given away free to all artists—in this way, the publishers were certain that a pit orchestra would be able to play a new number instantly, which meant that a pit singer would be more likely to try it out on his or her audience. And the audience would buy the sheet music for the parlor piano at home.

Next they used pluggers. In early Alley days, the publisher would trudge around to the night spots himself, lugging a caseful of sheets, wining and dining performers and orchestra leaders before slipping them his latest songs. Ed Marks, proprietor of one of the largest publishing houses, has told of these rounds. "The Alhambra Music Hall was expensive because you had to buy drinks for the boys in the band and there were twenty-six of them. The Haymarket was

Yet another picture of the clan. The trade paper that published this picture identified each man with first initial, last name, and most famous composition, then added: "G. Verdi (*Aïda*) and R. Wagner (*Siegfried*) could not attend."

dangerous. Bullets flew frequently and you could only get in by joining a club called the Welsh Rabbits, and that cost another round of drinks for the boys." Marks used to take a fellow called Louis the Whistler with him. Louis was brilliant at insinuating Ed's tunes into nearby ears. Anyway, Marks couldn't play the piano.

But by the 1910s, with money beginning to flood in, the publishers no longer had to leg it for themselves. They could afford to hire pluggers—men such as Harry Cohn, who later became president of Columbia Pictures. He was known simply as the "Crude One." Jack Warner, one of the famous motion picture brothers, was another.

The pluggers' costume and demeanor were important—the flashier the better. Addy recalls that he often introduced himself to vaudeville managers as an Austrian count. They were impressed. "The guy's got *class*," they would say. Addy also grasped the importance of dress. He wore a fresh carnation every day and he says he introduced the turtleneck sweater in 1914. Others would sport trousers with different-colored legs, but this failed to have the desired effect.

A typical day would see the pluggers—armed with song sheets—swarming out of the Alley buildings in mid-morning. Some would take to the street in truckloads, literally, to warble at sidewalk crowds. Others would raid Lower East Side synagogues in search of singing boys with large lungs and rabbinical voices who could be planted in music hall audiences to get up at a prearranged moment and sing whatever was the hot text of the week.

In the evenings, the pluggers invaded music halls and vaudeville theaters, showering human and animal acts with songs, flowers, and chocolates. Others descended on political rallies, cycle races, and billiard saloons. Addy liked to campaign aboard a horse and cart with a band consisting of three Hawaiians and three Americans, all armed with megaphones and selling sheet music at five cents a copy. His prime was

Sunday night at Coney Island, where he lined up with other pluggers for what was called "publishers night," in which one plugger after another was given the freedom of the fair. A plugger named Charlie Fisher was known as Leatherlung; his voice, without the aid of amplification, could be heard in the next county.

Another outlet was the fast-growing movie business. Illustrated song slides began to be screened during the intermission, an idea originated in the 1890s by a theater electrician. Ed Marks had founded his publishing house on the success of the "Little Lost Child Song." This tragic story, told in three verses, was illustrated by gaudy magic lantern slides, and Marks sold a million sheet copies. By the 1920s, these song slides had become a permanent fixture between shows. And among those who pumped out new songs under the silver screen, while his plugging partner conducted the audience in appropriate lyrics, was George Gershwin.

Above all, and mostly because the song pluggers were always out and about, the Alley continually gathered first-hand knowledge of exactly what the public wanted. When they shouted a new song and got only a lukewarm response, they questioned their audience to find out what was wrong. Back at the office, they instructed the writers on what needed changing. It was eyeball to eyeball with the customer.

It was also eyeball to eyeball with the artist. When a music hall performer was persuaded to accept a particular song, he or she became its most effective plugger. After all, a vaudeville show might go on tour throughout the United States for up to fifty weeks, thus guaranteeing almost a year of nation-wide exposure. "Every Monday and Thursday we would go to the theaters, see what the performers were singing, and see if they needed a new song to put into their act," Mickey Addy told me. If a singer became interested in a ballad, he might say yes, but what he really needed was a comedy song for

Pluggers would raid Lower East Side synagogues in search of singing boys with large lungs and rabbinical voices who could get up and sing whatever was the hot text of the week.

his act. The pluggers would report back and a comedy song would be written for nothing, so long as the singer guaranteed he would sing the ballad as well.

"We used to demonstrate the song to the artist in such a manner that it made him the big man," Addy remembers, "although eight times out of ten the demonstrator was a better singer than the performer. Take Al Jolson: he wasn't a singer, he was a stylist, a great salesman. But he didn't have a voice. Georgie Jessel and Eddie Cantor were the same. Take Rudy Vallee, there's another one. He used to sing through his nose." For his part, Vallee says: "Strangely enough, most of the *demonstrators* didn't have good voices. Nor did most songwriters, although they loved to demonstrate. Irving Berlin had a horrible voice — yet he insisted on demonstrating his own songs."

Even after the introduction of radio, the technique remained the same. Bing Crosby says that the pluggers would turn up wherever he was appearing, whether at a theater or a radio station. "They'd come to your dressing room to demonstrate whatever song their company was concentrating on. They were all nice guys, interesting and colorful, some of them old vaudevillians whose acts had flopped. They could sing and dance, they knew all the jokes. It was an amusing interlude. And they always had the same line: 'Bing, I promise you, this is going to be the number one song, there's no question about it.'

"With certain writers, of course — the Cole Porters and the Rodgers and Harts and the Gershwins — nobody had to persuade you to sing that kind of material," Crosby remembers. "Songs being sung onstage in shows that were hits were a natural choice — if you could get a hold of them, it could be a big break for you. But occasionally, you took songs that you wouldn't otherwise have sung just because you had been well sold by an engaging plugger."

And the singer, of course, could be bought. Orchestras had their arrangements paid for. Publishers would pay traveling companies of vaudevillians to perform only their songs. Band leaders and artists received gifts. And a common way of rewarding an artist was to cut him in on the royalties, as though he had written the song. Rudy Vallee says that the publishers simply told him: "We've put your name on it and we want you to perform it." "We never discussed royalties. It was a technical matter. Never anything exorbitant — a penny a copy, and my percentage of the mechanical royalty. Simple as that. Might sign a contract, might not. They just said: 'You're going to get it.' And that was that." It is doubtful that any of the songs bearing Al Jolson's name as co-author was written by him. Sometimes, Jolson agreed to let his name be used provided there were other inducements. Once, he graciously accepted from a publisher the small gift of a race horse.

Another publisher, Leo Feist, furnished and decorated a house belonging to singer Gene Austin at a cost of between ten and fifteen thousand dollars, and then gave him a Cadillac. "Because anything Gene touched turned to gold," Vallee now explains. "Austin was worth at least three or four hundred thousand dollars to any publisher, and they thought nothing of giving him five or ten thousand dollars' worth of gifts." Later, when Vallee himself ran a popular radio show, Mickey Addy says, "He'd put a star on his show and the next thing you'd know, there'd be a new boat up on Vallee's estate called *Banjo Eyes* after the song by Eddie Cantor. Everything on Vallee's estate had been given him, from tennis courts to peanuts."

It was essential that the Alleyman — whether plugger, demonstrator, composer, lyricist, or publisher — remain versatile. Should dream songs become popular, then it was all hands to the dreams. "Meet Me Tonight in Dreamland," "When I Met You Last Night in Dreamland," "You Tell Me Your Dream and I'll Tell You Mine." The Alleymen knuckled down to the job so fast and so well that they began to number their works — "Dream Song No. 1," "Dream Song No. 2," "Dream Song No. 3," right up into the hundreds. The content was unimportant, so long as it sold.

The American Federation of Musicians, among others, had long advised against the playing of ragtime. In 1914, the *Musical Courier*

had damned it as obscene, lewd, and "artistically and morally depressing." But the denizens of Tin Pan Alley never questioned its morals for a second. Irving Berlin once said: "You know, I never did find out what ragtime was." Still, he wrote it. Whatever it was. And it was commercial. His colleagues began writing ragtime in reams. There was even a Ragtime Shakespeare. "*Everything* in America is ragtime," noted Berlin. When jazz hit New York around 1919, the Alleymen decided that this, too, was ragtime, only more ragged. They removed the word "ragtime" from their lyrics and substituted the word "jazz."

But it was the vast number of topical songs that demonstrated beyond question Tin Pan Alley's unsinkable versatility. When the *Titanic* sank, Alleymen sang of its demise: "Just As the Ship Went Down." New inventions—cars, planes, radios—found equal favor: "Come Away with Me Lucille in My Merry Oldsmobile" and "There's a Wireless Station Down in My Heart." Lack of acquaintance with the subject matter was no hindrance; sometimes it was a positive advantage. Irving Caesar told me

The Gershwins, and colleagues. *Left:* Ira (at piano) with E. Y. Harburg (left) and Arthur Schwartz, conveniently posed while "composing" in behalf of United China Relief in 1941; *right:* the brothers with playwright Guy Bolton.

that Stephen Foster had never seen the Swanee River. "Foster was from Pittsburgh. And when George Gershwin and I wrote 'Swanee, How I Love Ya,' *we'd* never seen the Swanee River either. We'd never been south of the Battery in New York. When we did finally see the river, however, on a trip down to Florida, it was a good thing we had written the song first because the Swanee turned out to be just a nice muddy stream." The moral was simple, Caesar explained. "Anyone could write a popular song, that's no great shakes. But to be able to write a song any time of day or night, that's what a pro had to be able to do. I wrote songs *any* time, on a bet." Personal expression was irrelevant. Al Bryan wrote a song in 1915 called "I Didn't Raise My Boy to Be a Soldier." It was a peace song; America was not yet in the war. But England was, so for the English edition, Bryan simply altered the words to "I'm Glad My Boy Grew Up to Be a Soldier."

When America did enter the war in 1917, Tin Pan Alley had its finest hour. The song makers were called upon by the President himself to fill the breech. Stirring, chauvinistic songs, which sent the soldiers merrily to the front lines, were the order of the day. "Goodbye Broadway, Hello France" was published within the week; the Alleymen immigrants were determined to be more patriotic than native Americans, as if to prove their worth as citizens of their adopted land. They would chase the Kaiser all over Europe: "We Are Coming, We Are Coming, in Yankee Doodle Style" and "We Don't Want the Bacon, What We Want Is a Piece of the Rhine."

The war was treated as one great vaudeville show. More songs were produced than at any time before or since. After the war, the sheet music publishers would have to fight a rearguard action against new money-making vehicles—records, radio, dance bands, and talkies. But for the moment, it was boom, boom, boom. In 1917 alone, more than two *billion* copies of pop sheet music were sold. It cost a publisher about twenty-five hundred dollars to print a first run of ten thousand, and each copy sold for fifty cents. A publisher could make a hundred thousand dollars clear from a million-copy sale. And by this time, a five-million sale was not uncommon.

The Alley was safe only as long as it preserved its monopoly. But in 1920, radio began commercial operations. At first, the Alley seemed well suited—yet again—to fulfill a need. Radio's listeners appeared to like a good dance tune best of all, and the Alley thought it could provide as many as were required. Radio was insatiable, however, and devoured material at an unbelievable rate; hits withered and died in only a few weeks. A new brand of song, ultrasimple and bland, was pushed. Radio engineers informed song writers that a range of five notes around the middle of the piano was the most suitable for high-quality broadcasting. "So we simply adjusted ourselves to the cleffing of ether material," says one old Alleyman. "Some moonlight here, a touch of roses there, and all painted the color of cheap hamburger. You know—beige!" Any song that appeared too spicy for family audiences was banned, the first one to suffer being "How Could Red Riding Hood Have Been So Very Good and Still Keep the Wolf from the Door?" It was very perplexing for old-time song men. Ed Marks was pessimistic: "Song is a tough intangible. It may even weather radio—the most disastrous of all mechanical developments which have so altered

our Tin Pan Alley!"

Radio companies refused to pay publishers for the right to play their music on the air. They claimed that all they were doing was broadcasting "ether," and anyway, they were *honoring*

As important as the fruits of success was the publicity engendered by them. *Clockwise from upper left:* a stately George Gershwin at the Warburg family estate; Bert Kalmar in his California peach orchard; Al Jolson and his wife, dancer Ruby Keeler, in well-posed leisure; the House That Radio Built for Rudy Vallee.

the Alleymen with free plugs. Almost in retaliation, the Alleymen got organized. They had already grouped themselves into a performance rights society called the American Society of Composers, Authors, and Publishers. According to the current ASCAP president, Stanley Adams, the society had come into being when composer Victor Herbert had decided in 1914 to sue Shanley's Restaurant in New York. Shanley's band had been playing Herbert's music to attract people into the restaurant, but not a penny of the subsequent profits found its way into Herbert's pocket. The Supreme Court found for Herbert. In its early days, ASCAP was concerned primarily with restaurants. It was not until about 1921 that the association actually collected any money—and then only after more litigation. The introduction of radio provoked another series of court cases—again settled in ASCAP's favor. The monopoly seemed secure.

Then came another threat, in the guise of the phonograph record. From 1924, fans could listen to their singing idols on electric recordings. Print was becoming redundant. Hits were learned off 78 rpm records; the record companies were now having the million-sellers. The composers still profited, of course, but new techniques and new production methods were needed to accommodate the new requirements. The self-perpetuating club that had dominated Twenty-eighth Street, or Thirty-second Street, or Forty-sixth Street, or wherever was not properly equipped: a million discs could not be handled through a brownstone. But Chicago, with its rapidly expanding industrialization and supply of cheap labor, could manage. Parts of the record business moved west, and although ASCAP continued to protect its composers and publishers, there was nothing it could do to keep all of the new industry in the family. From Chicago, men with microphones set off south and west to discover a music other than that manufactured by Tin Pan Alley. And it was music not owned by ASCAP.

The biggest threat of all, however, came from far away, from the mystic land of Hollywood. Movies and popular music had always been

Left: producer Jack Warner with Dr. Lee De Forest, inventor of the device that made talkies possible, and one of the men credited with the invention of radio. *Above:* Rudy Vallee crooned into his microphone; Helen Kane boop-boop-a-dooped into hers. *Below:* almost a family reunion for the progeny of the Hollywood–Tin Pan Alley romance: from left to right, Darryl Zanuck, Louis Silvers, Irving Berlin, Lloyd Bacon, Al Jolson, Jack Warner, Albert Warner.

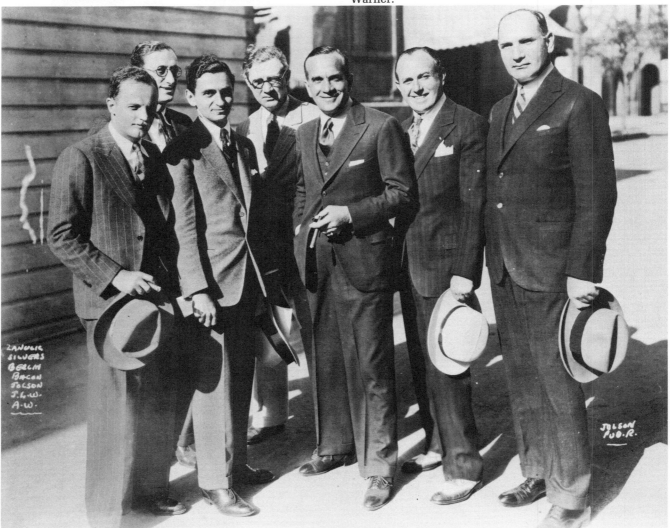

connected since pluggers had invaded movie palaces; they worked well together, of course, because they both reflected popular taste. Movie makers needed background music for their silent pictures, and the Alley cooperated by inaugurating campaigns to associate "theme" songs with particular pictures. "Charmaine," for example, was heard in minor and major keys throughout screenings of *What Price Glory?* In 1927, when Warner Brothers decided to risk its failing fortunes on talking pictures, it bought seventy percent of the new Vitaphone Corporation, formed to make popular music shorts, and rented the original Oscar Hammerstein's Manhattan Opera House. The ubiquitous Al Jolson sang, and *The Jazz Singer* revolutionized the movie industry. Hitherto silent actors burst into song, and mammoth Hollywood revues were tacked together by major studios anxious to take advantage of this latest trend.

Hollywood, therefore, needed cheap music and in bulk. The Alley, tottering under the impact of records and radio, responded enthusiastically. Warner Brothers bought up the cream of the Alley houses and Hollywood soon owned most of America's popular published music. The song writers trekked by train across the continent, seeing for the first time the Land of the Buffalo that they and their colleagues had written about from their vantage points in New York office buildings. "It was all very educational," composer Harry Warren, one of the trekkers, remembers. For here were real harvest moons, and June nights and Gal Sals. "Every studio had a staff of song writers," Warren told me. "There must have been twenty-five at Fox alone. I don't know where they all came from — out from under rocks probably." But, protected from the fierce wind of the Depression, they began writing even lusher music than they had in New York. Now they wrote of sitting on top of a rainbow, sweeping the clouds away, and tiptoeing through the tulips. As Ian Whitcomb notes, they had stepped through the looking glass with Alice, into the cock-eyed world of celluloid.

Harry Warren: "Every studio had a staff of song writers. There must have been twenty-five at Fox alone."

The Hollywood musical of the thirties was made possible because the movie companies had acquired a considerable backlog of Tin Pan Alley songs that they were eager to sell in films. A performance on network radio of a "theme song" became the most important medium for promoting the movie from which it came. The hits of the thirties were from motion pictures. During those years, it was thought, families spent their evenings in one of two ways: either they went out to the movies, or they stayed home and listened to network radio. The motion picture business made its money by attracting an audience through the box office; the radio networks made theirs by delivering an audience to the advertisers.

Both were struggling to secure a majority, and the Alleymen and their protectionist organization ASCAP benefited either way. Until, that is, the size of their audience suddenly stopped increasing. In the late thirties, the accumulated years of economic depression finally took their toll. Hollywood discovered that the gross audience was actually diminishing. Its financial stability was threatened; its rivals must be curbed. And its chief rival was radio.

The solution was simple. ASCAP, now controlled by Hollywood, owned most of the songs that radio played and would demand that the royalty paid by radio to ASCAP members be doubled. Since radio would be unable to pay this vast increase, radio would no longer benefit from ASCAP's songs. Radio *sans* music would become less attractive to audiences and advertisers. The movie's share of both would, inevitably, increase.

ASCAP was sure its strategy would work. ASCAP music, claimed its secretary, was America's music and that was that. "We own all the best writers," they said. Except, that is, all those who because of ASCAP had been excluded from the charmed circle — the hillbillies and the blacks. ASCAP had never involved itself in country music for the straightforward reason that anything not written by ASCAP peo-

ple produced no returns. But for every girl who was seduced in the rumble seat of a car to a performance by Bing Crosby on the radio, there was another who experienced the same delights listening to Roy Acuff singing live on the Grand Ole Opry radio network. Hitherto, ASCAP was New York and Los Angeles. These were the centers of production, the centers of exploitation. ASCAP had no wish to extend the franchise. After all, its income in 1939 was $4.3 million, divided between 125 publishers and about 1200 writers. Who needed change?

But in seeking to limit radio by doubling its fees, Hollywood-controlled ASCAP made a profound blunder. By the time its license with the broadcasters ran out at midnight, January 1, 1941, the radio stations had organized their own performing rights society: Broadcast Music, Incorporated. For its catalogue, BMI chose music previously ignored by Tin Pan Alley and joined the Chicago record manufacturers as they combed the South for material. Whereas ASCAP had only collected on live performances on the radio networks, BMI promised it would collect for live *and* recorded performances. For the first time, artists who had little chance of being heard on a major show could obtain some financial return from records they had made or from appearances on local radio stations. And those who benefited immediately were the hillbillies, who by now had their own well-established network of local country radio shows, and the black musicians, who for years had been recorded for little or no financial reward. The ASCAP monopoly was broken and the absolute domination of Tin Pan Alley came to an end.

The Alley suffered a further setback. For years, many of its writers had profited from the work of others. When jazz was popular, the Alleymen adapted its beat. When blacks produced the blues, Alleymen attached the word

Left, from top: Eddie Cantor, Bing Crosby, the Boswell Sisters. Cantor sang, danced, clowned, and rolled his eyes; Crosby groaned; the Boswells chirped. *Right:* it is sometimes forgotten that Judy Garland's first, greatest, and most especial talent was her ability to sing.

"blues" to their song titles. As rhythm and blues developed, Tin Pan Alley tried to use that also. Likewise hillbilly music. But now, because of BMI, the authentic music itself was being heard throughout the States. Suddenly, an authentic audience was dictating what became popular. It was no longer sufficient for a radio personality such as Rudy Vallee to bestow upon a song his imprimatur. The new audience wanted the real thing, and Rudy Vallee was not it.

ASCAP was forced to back down. By the end of 1941, a new agreement was signed and ASCAP's boycott was lifted. But it was too late. The barbarians were all over the airwaves.

At its best, Tin Pan Alley had seemed to reflect and affect everyday life. But electricity and Hollywood isolated its song writers from the sound of the street; it took rock and roll to restore the vital connection, but that was much later. The hype the Alley pioneered is still central to the industry known as pop music. Don

Kirshner, one of the most successful modern-day entrepreneurs, looks back on the old Alley techniques with admiration: "Their salesmanship was irresistible. An artist might find after he'd lived with a song that it wasn't too good after all. But when two pluggers sat down at the piano and sold it, the artist just had to buy it. In any business, the name of the game is promoting your product. Being commercial. And winning." Song writing, as practiced by Tin Pan Alley, was part of a money-making business. And money was made by producing songs that could be packaged and sold in the largest possible numbers. Tin Pan Alley ripped off the American sensibility and reduced it to a low common denominator.

Nonetheless, a song like E. Y. Harburg's "Brother Can You Spare a Dime" expressed the Depression mentality better than a hundred books. Songs could and did represent the growth of a country, and crystallize what was in people's hearts and heads. Many of Tin Pan Alley's products were fun, even delightful, and occasionally substantial. But Tin Pan Alley squandered its great opportunity. It took apparent blackmail to expose the apparent greed of a white, Jewish-dominated, New York–oriented clique that perpetuated the money-making machine. The songs it peddled were not the white equivalent of black music. The boast—"tell me what a nation is singing, and I'll tell you what they are thinking"—turned out to be a lie.

Facing page: Ruby Keeler trips across the insane, brilliant excess of a Busby Berkeley set. Berkeley's style of film-making was a cul-de-sac; with each succeeding film, he found it more and more difficult to surpass himself and remain within the confines of decency. It became apparent that what had once been the most startling aspect of the early "All Talking! All Singing! All Dancing!" pictures—namely, its music—had become irrelevant. More recent gasps from Tin Pan Alley emanated from Phil Spector *(top),* who sang as a member of a group called the Teddy Bears before he became a producer; Lieber and Stoller *(center),* who wrote "Hound Dog" for Willie Mae Thornton and made a fortune when Elvis Presley "covered" it; and the Monkees *(bottom),* force-fed the rudiments of guitar playing, manufactured for a weekly television series by Broadway producer Burt Shevelove and here—appropriately—suspended from a marionette master's strings.

WS-25?

Diamonds as Big as the Ritz

Before World War I, the recording industry was a novelty, movies were silent, and radio had not been invented. The most rewarding outlet for a new song writer was in the music halls, and that could be a wearying business. Vaudeville artists were constantly in need of good, fresh material, which they were expected to supply themselves. Yet a song plugger had to loll around outside a star's dressing room whistling or shouting a new song until someone acknowledged his existence. "That's not a bad song you've been hollering under my window for the last six days," the star would say. "What's it called?" "It's called 'Shine on Harvest Moon.'" "Well, maybe I'll try it out."

Just as vaudeville had become a market for song merchants, so had revue,

Left: Rogers and Astaire in *Shall We Dance.*

another of musical theater's antecedents. Unlike vaudeville, the material in a revue was the producer's responsibility. A revue producer said: "We're going to do a revue all in yellow. Now, who can we get? Let's get Ethel Waters and Fred Allen and Clifton Webb. And, darling, *you* start designing some yellow costumes and then let's get a couple of songs from Jerome Kern and a couple from this young Gershwin." Performers often worked in both vaudeville and revue, but most of the prominent composers — such as Gershwin and Porter — did not. A revue was predicated on comedy sketches and songs, while vaudeville concentrated on "turns" — magicians, animal acts, and comedians — with Tin Pan Alley songs sandwiched between the tightrope-walking dog and the performing seal. Revue had artistic pretensions; vaudeville did not. Jerome Kern placed his songs only in revue; Irving Berlin wanted both.

Burlesque, or farce with a few songs, presented a further chance to be heard. Although as old as Plautus, burlesque did not make an impact on America until 1868, when a redoubtable English rose named Lydia Thompson appeared in New York with an entertainment entitled *Evangeline*. Consisting mostly of an endless troupe of girls in flesh tights playing "male" roles, and comedians in baggy pants and red noses who sang and told unsavory jokes, *Evangeline* was a hit. Its language and style were accessible. Unlike the eighteenth-century dramas of Edmund Kean, unlike the caricatures offered by nigger minstrels, here were *real* people, talking *real* English (or at least American). They were in need of popular songs to amuse their audience.

As the power of Tin Pan Alley increased, it attracted song writers who were not content to rely upon the whims of a particular performer or management for acceptance of their songs. This new breed wanted the social respectability usually reserved for that other notable European import, the operetta. Operetta satisfied a yearning for Art, which in nineteenth-century America had to be foreign (indeed, being foreign was sufficient). Johann Strauss and Offenbach were clearly foreign. Gilbert and Sullivan were, best of all, English. And all, according to Leonard Bernstein, "led the American public straight into the arms of operetta. All three were

national versions of the same thing: Gilbert and Sullivan with their British comic opera, Offenbach with his French *opéra bouffe*, and Strauss with his Viennese operetta."

It seemed essential that operetta be fancy and removed from any taste of the familiar; that its characters be improbable; and that its language be archaic, although elegant. Nonetheless, operettas like Franz Lehár's *The Merry Widow* swept the American public away, inspiring a dozen pale imitations by Middle European songwriters recently arrived in the United States. Rudolf Friml, Sigmund Romberg, and Emmerich Kalman used lyrics that were unspeakable (sometimes literally), but their music raised the audience's expectations to a new level of accomplishment. Operetta scores were complex and elaborate partly because musicians such as Friml and Romberg (who later wrote with Oscar Hammerstein II) were operatic composers by inclination who had resigned

Top: Charles Winninger *(center left)* in the original production of *No, No, Nanette,* as dissimilar from the Kern-Hammerstein revolution as it was characteristic of the pre-*Show Boat* era. Later, Winninger became *Show Boat's* Captain Andy in 1927. *Bottom left:* the first Rodgers and Hart score written for Hollywood was *Love Me Tonight* (1932). In bed is Maurice Chevalier; director Rouben Mamoulian gives him pre-shooting instructions. *Bottom right:* the styles of the twenties survived into the seventies as a revival *(Irene, Nanette);* in the fifties, spoof was the vehicle. *The Boy Friend* (shown here) was the outstanding example.

themselves to what may have seemed the second-rate task of achieving something more than vaudeville although less than opera. For the ambitious song writer, the extended form operetta entailed was the perfect opportunity for fulfillment.

Vaudeville, revue, burlesque, and now the culturally aspiring operetta. It is often said that operetta, being European (and thus Art), gave shape and purpose to an otherwise disparate collection of entertainments, interchangeable in content, indifferent in style, and insupportable in musical achievement. But for the musical theater to attain true stature required more. It required — in fact, demanded — an integration of music, words, dancing, and book. Unity of form became an essential for musical theater, and the struggle toward that unity its massive accomplishment.

The first step toward that integration had taken place long before the invention of Tin Pan Alley. In 1866, an epic called *The Black Crook* arrived in New York. Originally a somber and Germanic melodrama, it had been bought for presentation at Niblo's Garden in New York City by a producer named Wheatley. At the same time, a French ballet company landed in New York to find that the theater in which it had been booked to dance had burned to the ground. Wheatley had a bright idea: why not merge the two productions? *The Black Crook* lacked music, and the French ballet company lacked a stage. So Niblo's Garden was transformed, bits of music and dance were thrown into *The Black Crook,* and the show was on. This revolutionary though bizarre oeuvre lasted five and a half hours each night; it ran for a year and a half in New York and twenty-five years more on the road.

The Black Crook showed it was possible to

bring together music and melodrama, plus a few specialty acts such as dance, without damaging any of them. What's more, the public adored it. The extravaganza had benefited, of course, from the infusion of Foreign Art (the French ballet company); but the possibility that music hall might engender something more than a vaudevillian romp was clear. *The Black Crook* was, in effect, the first variety show with a story.

Burlesque had already demonstrated the commercial appeal of entertainments in the vernacular, and when (in 1890) the show called *A Trip to Chinatown* was pieced together from songs and dances familiar to the audience, including Chas. K. Harris's "After the Ball," another hit was assured. *A Trip to Chinatown* was a revue with a plot, presented in the style of music hall, with the outrageous glee that was a hallmark of burlesque.

The gap between European Art and American vernacular music, however, was bridged most skillfully by Oscar Hammerstein II (grandson of the vaudeville manager) and Jerome Kern. Schooled in European classical music, Kern had always and deliberately used American "native sounds" in his songs — folk and ragtime, jazz and music hall. Hammerstein was the first writer to grasp the need to translate plot and dialogue into a language that everyone could and would understand. Stephen Sondheim, a protégé of Hammerstein's, says: "His work tended to make people think of him as an unsophisticated, platitudinous hick, whereas he was a highly intelligent, strongly principled, very firm-minded, and philosophic man. Which is just what his work seemed not to be." Hammerstein was consumed by the search for an area between operetta and revue, between music drama and music hall. Maybe there was something in between, something unmistakably American as opposed to European, something that had purpose and coherence and was not just a mere collection of songs.

Show Boat, which opened in 1927, was an operetta in form; but instead of princes and counts and disguised lovers in the best Ruritanian tradition, it presented recognizable peo-

---

Rouben Mamoulian's progress with *Love Me Tonight* and the work of fellow European emigrés such as Ernst Lubitsch enabled the cameras to do more than photograph a stage production. *Top: The Gold Diggers of Broadway* (1929) represents what they had to triumph over. *Bottom:* the first of Mamoulian's Broadway triumphs was the Gershwins' *Porgy and Bess;* it had a naturalism previously avoided by the Broadway audience.

ple in familiar situations. The technique remained that of Friml, Lehár, and Romberg, but the style was new. It took its insistence on a vernacular language from burlesque, and its reliance on "contemporary" music from revue. Quite ironically, it was produced by that embodiment of all that was Ruritanian, Florenz Ziegfeld. The story, taken from a book by Edna Ferber, was another striking aspect of *Show Boat.* It concerned the South and black oppression and considered the problem in an intelligent and humane manner. Yet it also managed to be witty, charming, full of beautiful songs, and commercially successful.

Still, after *Show Boat,* Broadway continued as a glittering song supermarket, an easy way for Tin Pan Alley to plug its material. Every composer wanted to make it in one of the growing number of theaters housed on side streets off the Great White Way. The turnover became fast and furious. An investment in a show could bring a handsome financial return in a couple of weeks; if a show ran for six months, it was a huge hit. A year's run was almost unbelievable. Rodgers and Hart composed two shows a year; Kern did the same. If a number failed in one show, the producers simply hauled it out and kept it aside for the next.

Even during the Depression, most song and show writers retained a notably gilded view of their world—usually explained away with the excuse that in times of gloom, what America needed was escapism. Some, like Cole Porter, found themselves trapped aboard a roller-coaster of triviality from which the only escape seemed commercial, if not artistic, suicide. Porter was rich, witty, and urbane. As Robert Kimball points out, his lyrics were "as refreshing a tonic as Broadway had imbibed since the days of the legalized cocktail." He invented his own fantasy world, and then laid it on the customer. Love is genuinely "the best, the crest, the works"; occasionally, it is also painful, evanescent, or tragic. But Porter never achieved the biting simplicity of Lorenz Hart. He was brilliant, but also foolish. His songs never hurt like those of Harburg—they were altogether too flashy, like the silk he always wore. Nor did he

understand the full potential of the musical and the need for a larger design. His shows were the same at the end of his life as they had been at the beginning: frothy collections of songs. That is not to detract from their magic. But, along with Berlin, he did not (or could not) contribute to a form whose survival would come to depend upon its development. He remained a song writer who provided songs for the stage. His English counterpart, Noel Coward, did make some attempt to bridge the gap between operetta and colloquial musical comedy. Essentially a playwright, Coward grasped the necessity of relating songs both to each other and to

Top left: Billy Rose (with Charles MacArthur and Ben Hecht) was the embodiment of a breed of producers who claimed to be "showmen." The production they are contemplating here is *Billy Rose's Jumbo. Bottom left:* at a rehearsal of *On the Town,* the director George Abbott (arms folded, center) shares a moment with his young collaborators. Writer-performer Betty Comden sits at left; her partner, Adolph Green, wraps his arms around Nancy Walker and Sono Osato; choreographer Jerome Robbins speaks to Abbott; composer Leonard Bernstein sits behind Robbins, hand on chin. Green, 28, was the oldest among them; Walker, the youngest, was 22. *Above:* Gertrude Lawrence and Noel Coward. These two, more than any other non-Americans, imitated most successfully the American musical stage. Coward, a playwright, composer, lyricist, and performer, was among the more versatile theatrical figures to emerge in Britain between the World Wars.

the plot. But he, too, was betrayed by his very sophistication, by the chic little world of his own creation. Eventually, time simply passed him by.

The 1931 show, *Of Thee I Sing,* by the brothers Gershwin, managed to impart social criticism but in a more colloquial manner. Lighthearted though it was (Sondheim says Ira Gershwin wouldn't know how to sting if his life depended on it), it became the first musical to win the Pulitzer Prize. The book, by George S. Kaufman and Morrie Ryskind, was almost more important than the music. But, through the merging of operetta and revue techniques as demonstrated in *Show Boat,* something new had happened to the music: it had become more serious. As long as a musical comedy was just songs, it had been enough to be just a song writer. But now, the song writer found himself called upon to be a serious composer, fully con-

versant with the musical demands of effective comment and able to write extended musical sequences.

George Gershwin was able to meet that demand. His brother, Ira, remembers that there was never a time when George was not trying to further his academic studies; no matter how occupied he was with theater or film work, George always found time to take lessons or analyze the work of "serious" composers such as Schönberg, whom he knew personally and much admired. Gershwin, of course, was not the only one to benefit from a classical training; Porter, Kern, and Rodgers had all endured formal musical educations. But Gershwin was definitely the most interested in trying to write so-called symphonic pieces. As early as 1924, Paul Whiteman had asked Gershwin to write some "symphonic jazz" for a concert Whiteman was arranging at New York's Aeolian Hall. Gershwin composed *Rhapsody in Blue* in ten days, and despite (or perhaps because of) its success, he was accused of being unable to write for the orchestra: Gershwin had asked Ferde Grofé to orchestrate the piece. So he dashed off a prodigious number of works to silence his critics — the piano *Concerto in F, An American in Paris,* his *Second Rhapsody* — and scored each for orchestra himself.

For his own part, Gershwin seemed bemused

Left, above: the three children of vaudevillian Lew Fields: Herbert, Dorothy, and Joseph. Dorothy, who worked alone as well as in collaboration with each of her brothers, was a lyricist-librettist-screenwriter who prospered in the otherwise male-dominated world of musical theater. Her lyrics to Jerome Kern's songs for the Astaire-Rogers film *Swing Time* included the Academy Award–winning "The Way You Look Tonight." *Left, below:* Agnes De Mille rehearses Bambi Lynn (actress Jan Clayton watches) for the ballet sequence of *Carousel. Top and center right:* these two curious pictures of Lorenz Hart and Richard Rodgers show that the press agents' idea of men-at-work had a certain predictability. Ideas seem to be coming more freely to the gesticulating Hart in the earlier photo. *Bottom near right:* Rodgers (hatless, at piano) demonstrates a point about the score of *Babes in Arms* to star Mitzi Green, the show's producers, and choreographer George Balanchine (seated, right). Balanchine's contribution to the musical stage was his ballet for Rodgers and Hart's *On Your Toes,* "Slaughter on Tenth Avenue." *Bottom far right:* among Oscar Hammerstein's pre-Rodgers collaborators, Jerome Kern was foremost. Although the collaboration proved most fruitful during *Show Boat,* it also found favor in *Sunny* (1925) and, here, in *Music in the Air* (1932).

by his talent and regarded his music (according to brother Ira) "with almost mystical wonder." Sondheim says: "I don't know how important Gershwin thought his music was when he was writing. I would love to know. I would love to know if he thought of *Porgy and Bess* in the same way that Leonard Bernstein thought of his *Mass*, or whether he thought of it as 'Jesus God, I bet this show doesn't go because it's got all those blacks in it.' " At the time, it didn't go; it lost seventy thousand dollars in its first production. Gershwin never realized a cent from it, although he had sweated blood over it.

For its creators — Gershwin, his lyricist brother Ira, librettist DuBose Heyward — the real tragedy of *Porgy* was that no one knew what it was. Its subject matter was similar to that of *Show Boat* — the plight of blacks. Rouben Mamoulian, the Armenian emigré film maker, brought back from Hollywood to direct, considered it semioperatic in form. "Originally, there was a lot of recitative patterned on the Italian style," Mamoulian told me. "I talked to George about it and said: 'This really doesn't belong because the rest is so authentic, so American, so black and so rhythmic.' " Gershwin thought of *Porgy* as a "folk opera," whatever that means.

The novelty of *Porgy and Bess* was that it was ninety-five percent song. *Show Boat* had been constructed along the familiar lines of

scene-then-song, scene-then-song. But *Porgy* was nearly all music—replete with themes identified with particular characters or situations, all interrelated in a musical pattern unique to this particular show. Its dramatic language, however, proved too complicated for the Broadway audience of its time. "We are not an aria country," Alan Jay Lerner says. "We are a song country." But Gershwin tried to expand and heighten that song idiom by involving that which sustained it. Whereas "Summertime" epitomized the traditional function of song in the theater—a pause in the action, a moment of musical reflection, a casual divertissement—other songs, such as "Bess You Is My Woman Now," contributed to the action, advanced one's understanding of character, were linked by recitative and *leitmotif*, and were causal in the development of plot.

Although it appears that Gershwin did not fully comprehend what he had stumbled across, the point was not lost on Mamoulian. But before either had the opportunity to capitalize on the lessons learned, Gershwin died and Mamoulian returned to Hollywood. While rehearsing for a performance of his Piano Concerto, Gershwin collapsed. A malignant brain tumor was diagnosed and Gershwin never regained consciousness after surgery. He was dead at thirty-nine. John O'Hara said: "George died on July 11th, but I don't have to believe it if I don't want to."

During the 1930s, Oscar Hammerstein remained obsessed by his chosen task of bringing seriousness to the musical stage but succeeded only in writing failures that satisfied him even less than they satisfied the public. With Jerome Kern, he had considered writing a musical based on a play of the early thirties by

Top: on the set of *Shall We Dance*, George Gershwin plays for Astaire and Rogers, while dance director Hermes Pan, director Mark Sandrich, Ira Gershwin (behind George), and musical director Nathan Shilkret look on. Although Astaire was, for the most part, his own choreographer, he depended on Pan in most of his movies to coordinate, rehearse, and criticize the numbers. *Center:* Cole Porter and director Sidney Lanfield flank Rita Hayworth, here on the set of *You'll Never Get Rich*, one of Astaire's post–Ginger Rogers films. *Bottom:* Irving Berlin, Astaire, and Rogers.

Lynn Riggs called *Green Grow the Lilacs*, about the settlement of the Oklahoma Territory. Hammerstein was attracted by its celebration of the simple virtues embodied in opening up a new state; Kern was not interested and the project had been abandoned.

Riggs' play had originally been staged by the Theatre Guild of New York. By 1940, the Guild was sliding toward bankruptcy and decided to revive and/or sell off the rights to many of its erstwhile productions. It approached Richard Rodgers and asked him to put a show together with his long-time partner Lorenz Hart. Hart was ill and unwilling to make the attempt. The Guild was disappointed but brought in Hammerstein — Rodgers had written just with Hart for twenty-five years — and signed Rouben Mamoulian to direct.

From the start, the opinionated Mamoulian caused trouble. In his contract, he stipulated that the production he had in mind would not be a conventional musical comedy. "I tried to express my ideas about dance, music, and words. And, of course, they said: 'Fine, fine, just do what you think best.' " After a week of rehearsals, choreographer Agnes De Mille had prepared the first dance number for Mamoulian's inspection. Everyone was enthusiastic — except Mamoulian. "I saw it. And I said: 'Agnes, this is all wrong. This is ballet. Number one: you won't have an empty stage. Number two: the principals have to be in it. Number three: cut out the ballet and make it more an American folk expression.' And, of course, she almost died." It has to be remembered that Mamoulian, to whom little credit for the success of *Oklahoma!* has been given, may well be attempting to restore the balance of critical praise in his favor; in fact, De Mille's dance sequences were considered among the more startling examples of the show's innovation. Mamoulian's version of the story has it that in rehearsal she screamed: "You're ruining my dance, and you're ruining me." Mamoulian continues: "She complained to Dick Rodgers, who came to me and said: 'Why don't you leave her alone? Give her an empty stage. After all, a ballet's a ballet.' I said, 'No, in this case, a ballet

is *not* going to be a ballet.' Before long, Agnes was saying what a sour bitch I was and that I was an even greater tyrant than her uncle, Cecil B."

The function of dance in the show was not the only problem. Rodgers grumbled that it was impossible for his characters to be singing while they moved about the stage. Why could they not come to the front of the stage in the usual way and "present" the songs to the audience? Hammerstein alone seems to have understood Mamoulian, and he hoped his lyrics would profit from Mamoulian's insistence. "Make the dialogue rhythmic and rhyming," Mamoulian had told him. "When the emotions are ready, then we'll go into a song."

But by the time rehearsals were complete, Mamoulian was a villain. "My friends and associates would hardly talk to me," he remembers. "Everyone always now says how happy *Oklahoma!* must have been. In fact, it was the most agonizing experience of my life. I lost sixteen pounds." Opening night in New Haven was almost the end. After the performance, Mamoulian saw a group standing around Rodgers, De Mille, and Hammerstein, all pointedly ignoring him. "Finally, they said: 'We've tried to reason with you, we've tried to tell you that nobody wants this highbrow so-called integrated musical play. It's got no specialties, no dancing girls, nothing. It will be a disastrous flop.' " Mamoulian went home.

Again according to Mamoulian, at two o'clock in the morning, the phone rang and he was invited to the post mortem. The Theatre Guild wanted the whole ragbag restaged. Mamoulian: "Was I being the big Hollywood director, coming back to prove I was better than them all, I asked myself? I decided to trust my intuition. I said: 'I know you all have a big stake in this, and in order to show you that I'm not being capricious and following an idle whimsy, I will promise that if I am wrong — and all of you are right — I will never, never direct on the stage again.' " Faced with such an uncompromising affirmation, the opposition wilted. Richard Rodgers was working with a new lyricist for the first time; Agnes De Mille was anticipating her first chance on Broadway; the Guild was close to bankruptcy. Hammerstein's son William remembers that Mamoulian's contract included the phrase "the way I want it." And that was that.

The show moved to Boston—its advance sales were insignificant. Next door, Mary Martin was packing in the audience with specialty numbers and dancing girls galore.

Oklahoma!'s first night in New York, March 31, 1943, could also have been its last. Scores of friends were given free tickets, but the theater was still only half full. The following morning, however, after a collection of ecstatic notices, a queue formed outside the box office that remained a permanent feature for the next five years. The show ran for 2212 performances, the longest run achieved on the Broadway stage up to that point. Above the theater, the poster advertising the show displayed the names of Rodgers, Hammerstein, and Mamoulian in large letters. There were no "stars" in the cast and the Theatre Guild only had a line at the bottom that read: "Supervised by the Theatre Guild— Theresa Helburn and Lawrence Langner." After the first night, Walter Winchell saw painters at work on the poster and assumed that they were adding the names of a happy young cast. In fact, they were blocking out the Guild's credit—and painting it back in, ten times the original size. Hammerstein considered the runaway success with characteristic drollery. He took a full-page ad in *Variety*, listing his recent flops, and adding: "I did it before and I can do it again!" Mamoulian, for his part, remained silent.

Compared with that of *Show Boat* or *Porgy and Bess*, the subject matter of *Oklahoma!* was trivial. Theatrically, however, it was a work of dazzling invention. Mamoulian recalls an article that Hammerstein wrote for a Boston newspaper while the show was previewing: "He wrote about me standing over him and Dick Rodgers with a club, saying: 'Integrate! Integrate! Bridge, I want a bridge here!' You must remember," he continues, "that music, dance, and the spoken word and dramatic action are each a vital yet separate element in theater. When you go to a play, however, you miss the

music. Go to a grand opera, and you miss the spoken word. You hear recitative and you're grateful it's in Italian or German, which most people do not understand. If they did, they would have gone home years ago because the words are so silly. So you start thinking, Why not combine? Why not aim for total theater? It's good to have diversity: kitchen comedy, high drama, tragedy, farce, great music. But why not put all those forms together? Normally, before, you had a dramatic scene, people talking, pretty much kitchen dialogue. Then suddenly one of them got up and started singing. A convention, but it was ridiculous. Or another scene, comedy perhaps, when suddenly, *boom!* a dancer is pounding around the stage. It's idiotic. But suppose you had a dramatic scene with a rising emotion where *nothing* could top the spoken words except a song? Or, in dramatic action, you bring it to as big a climax as you can, which inevitably leads to a dance that lifts the whole endeavor to an even higher level. This integration of form is essential to any activity wishing to describe itself as art."

In *Oklahoma!* Mamoulian's insistence on art, and Rodgers' and Hammerstein's extraordinary ability to provide it, had some results. None of the major songs could be taken out of the show without rendering the story unintelligible. Every song furthered the plot or one's understanding of a character. Previously, it had been customary—as in vaudeville—to start shows with a big "production number" while people shuffled late into their seats or noisily unwrapped their chocolates. *Oklahoma!* starts with a solo, offstage. Onstage, a girl churns butter. In the distance, we hear a young man singing—in waltz time—"Oh What a Beautiful Morning." The first-night audience was

---

No performers—or, for that matter, no composers, lyricists, or directors—made such an impact on musical films as did Fred Astaire and Ginger Rogers. They worked with the Gershwins, with Porter, with Kern and Fields, with Irving Berlin. They danced spunkily *(top left)*, in *Swing Time*; romantically *(top right)*, to Berlin's "Cheek to Cheek" in *Top Hat*; and grandly *(bottom)* "inventing" the carioca, in *Flying Down to Rio*, their first film. Someone, reputedly Katharine Hepburn, once described them as "the perfect partnership; she gave him sex appeal, and he gave her class."

staggered and listened in utter silence.

Hammerstein fully acknowledged the contribution of his predecessor, Richard Rodgers' former partner: "If it hadn't been for Larry Hart," he said, "none of us would have felt free to write colloquial lyrics. He took the way people talked and put them into lyrics. That doesn't mean much, but in the early twenties, nobody had ever done it." Stephen Sondheim says: "Most rock artists have no idea who Lorenz Hart was. They tend to think they have a patent on expressing themselves. Crap!"

After *Oklahoma!*, Mamoulian returned to Hollywood. A fellow European-born movie director, Ernst Lubitsch, told him: "This was the first musical I ever saw on the stage where the people were not complete idiots." But Hollywood, of course, managed to undo the accomplishment. When Mamoulian saw a rough cut of the film of *Oklahoma!*, "it nearly broke my heart: it was a pedestrian western, with a

few songs attached. Totally naturalistic and no style. The lessons of integration had been ignored." Indeed, they had never been assimilated. Ever since the movie companies had bought Tin Pan Alley, they had pumped out a veritable flood of musical pictures. Most of these had been a jumble of songs, plus production numbers thrown in for effect and with little concern for plot or characterization. Such considerations were altogether too complex for the movie factories, and quite beyond the musical capabilities of most ex-Alleymen who had journeyed from Manhattan to the West Coast in search of gold. Anyway, Hollywood always knew when it was on to a good thing. Of course, the movies were good; thousands of people went to see them, didn't they? And, of course, the music was wonderful; ninety percent of the top-selling songs of the thirties and early forties came from the movies, didn't they?

Some composers had gone to Hollywood because the movie industry represented another important outlet for new songs, especially with the demise of live theater during the early Depression. Porter, Kern, and the Gershwins had all gone west for the opportunities Hollywood promised. "I don't think they did it just for the money," Stephen Sondheim says, "although it was an advantage to be paid a fee in advance instead of having to wait until your stage show became a hit. I think they did it for the experience and because working in Hollywood meant

The ethereal Astaire had competition only from the gymnastic Gene Kelly, born in Pittsburgh, 1912—here in the "Broadway Melody" number from the least embarrassing of Hollywood musicals, *Singin' in the Rain* (top left). Eventually, the "small" Hollywood musical was replaced by cumbersome monsters; the conversion from stage to screen was all that mattered. The conversion was clumsy at best, at worst distortive. (When *Pal Joey* was filmed, its score was replaced by a grab bag of Rodgers and Hart's "greatest hits.") *Bottom left:* from the film version of *Oklahoma!*; the painted backdrop couldn't fool the most myopic city dweller. *Below: Damn Yankees,* on stage, where there would seem little point in attempting to create the illusion of an actual ball park.

that your songs had a chance of being widely played."

But for many, Hollywood was a frustrating experience. "In a stage production," E. Y. Harburg says, "the author has a right to discuss and advise the director. But in a film, the author has no rights. In fact, the director and producer can ban you from the set—which they did." As produced on Broadway in 1947, Harburg and Burton Lane's *Finian's Rainbow* was a tough, satirical show. But for Hollywood, it presented a problem. Harburg says of Hollywood: "They divide the United States up into red-necks and skull-heads, Middle West, and South and East, the hicks and the slickers. Then they come up with an 'average.' Eighty percent of the money came from Hicksville—so they had to please Hicksville in order to get their money back. For twenty-five years, Hollywood would not touch *Finian's Rainbow* unless they could change the subplot about a senator who makes himself black to understand better the lives of the poor people who have elected him. They were scared they would lose the whole of the South—a huge proportion of their audience." Harburg refused

Whereas Rodgers and Hart wrote smart "city" shows, Rodgers and Hammerstein were more bucolic. They preferred Indian territory (*Oklahoma!*) and county fairs (*Carousel*), indeed, anywhere that resonated with homey, small-town virtues. *The Sound of Music* (above) featured Mary Martin in the Alps; *South Pacific* (right) took her far away in miles, although not in emotional values.

to make the change, and for years the film was not made.

The movie moguls also noticed that *Finian* lacked a "formula." Nobody gets killed or drowned, there is no automobile accident, no chase at the end—in fact, no "real drama." So why not have a character working in a laboratory and inventing a new sort of cigarette that doesn't hurt your throat? Why not? "It was a namby-pamby ridiculous idea," Harburg explained. It helped to destroy his musical, as Hollywood adaptations would destroy so many others, altering them, dismembering them, diminishing them.

It was inevitable that the merchandising mania that had infected Tin Pan Alley would have traveled to Hollywood with its grubby practitioners. Equally, it was inevitable that the revue form of musical theater—beloved of vaudeville and music hall—should have found its latter-day fulfillment with the movie moguls. Hollywood has been blamed for almost everything in its time, including the demise of music hall. But it was Hollywood, with its predilection for the frivolous, that temporarily preserved that tradition. Hollywood musicals of the thirties, forties, and early fifties often featured romantic re-creations of vaudeville; Busby Berkeley made film after film plotted around vaudeville shows; Bing Crosby and Bob Hope were small-time vaudevillians in their "Road" pictures; in Gene Kelly's first film, *For Me and My Gal*, and in his greatest, *Singin' in the Rain*, he plays song-and-dance men. Hope had started his career in vaudeville; so had Jolson and W. C. Fields, the Marx Brothers, and Fred Astaire. They all brought with them a repertoire of vaudeville and revue techniques that they were able to present in a polished and technically accomplished manner on film. Mae West's presence alone was evidence that burlesque in Hollywood was still alive. The anachronisms of musical theater—including the passion for Balkan provinces exemplified by Jeanette MacDonald–Nelson Eddy movies—survived in cloud-cuckooland long after they had been abandoned by Broadway.

Composers and directors continued to be se-

duced by the medium, moreover, although usually to their chagrin. Ken Russell tells of the fate of his lightweight movie *The Boy Friend*. "It didn't fit into the required two-hour movie-house slot," he says. "But instead of asking me to trim it—which I would have done because I knew it was too long—the distributors simply took out reel nine. Which meant they took out a whole section of plot development, including two whole numbers. And then trimmed every other number. Next, they said: 'This isn't a very good musical, is it?' Of course it isn't. MGM had fucked it up, and that's why now it isn't a very good musical. The movie companies would rather spend two million dollars on promotion parties for people who have nothing better to do, than spend it on getting a decent sound system into their cinemas so films can be properly appreciated."

Since the success of his film *Tommy*, says Russell, "I can just see those raspberries in Hollywood who've never even heard of rock music. Beverly Hills is probably full of them right now. They've got six scripts apiece and they haven't the faintest idea what to do with them except eat them." When Leonard Bernstein's show *On the Town* was seized upon by Hollywood, only four of his own songs were retained and writers were brought in to compose a batch of replacements. The Hollywood version of Rodgers and Hart's *Pal Joey* dropped three songs and added three lifted straight from *Babes in Arms* and *On Your Toes*.

Although *Oklahoma!* had explored the use of dance as a means of developing plot, it was not the first musical to have done so—"Slaughter on Tenth Avenue" from *On Your Toes* was choreographed by George Balanchine. (The show was about a ballet dancer, so it required ballet sequences.) But it did help to establish the possibility of communication through dance on the musical stage, a possibility later enhanced by *Oklahoma!* and *On the Town*. Frank Loesser's *The Most Happy Fella* (1956) contained most of its plot within the musical numbers. Arthur Laurents, who wrote the book for *West Side Story* (1957), wanted to replace dialogue

altogether, which is exactly what composer Leonard Bernstein, his lyricist Stephen Sondheim, and choreographer Jerome Robbins occasionally achieved. Sondheim says: "Arthur had written a libretto for the prologue which Jerry Robbins didn't know what to do with. The entire prologue—which is seven minutes long, but took us three months to write—was devised with complex lyrics. Then Arthur said he had the feeling the whole thing might be more effective *without* the lyrics. Jerry said: 'Suppose a Jet comes onstage and two Sharks attack him and then four Jets attack two Sharks and then six

Left: Rex Harrison and Julie Andrews (aged 21 at the time) in *My Fair Lady*, 1956. *Above, top:* Zero Mostel celebrated his reprieve from the entertainment blacklist in *Fiddler on the Roof* (1964). These shows, successes commercially and artistically, had literary origins, as did many of Broadway's postwar triumphs. *Hello, Dolly! (above)* not only drew upon Thornton Wilder's *The Matchmaker*, but managed to extend its run by imitating itself: here, Pearl Bailey takes the Carol Channing part in the all-black production.

Sharks attack him and then four Jets attack two Sharks and then six Sharks attack four Jets and then build it until there is a free-for-all. This will set the scene for much of the subsequent action.' Bernstein and I agreed, Jerry expanded it and that is how the prologue of *West Side Story* came about. You are still told the story, as we had all agreed, but without a single word being either sung or spoken. But, at the end of the seventh minute, you have been given the entire exposition — and all through dance."

Into the sixties the musical — on Broadway, if not in Hollywood — appeared secure as a vital, growing art form as well as a viable commercial proposition. *Hair*, in 1967, seemed a natural progression; it allied the integrated form with a new musical language. In fact, it set the clock back forty years. In some ways a rewrite of one of the most popular shows in American musical history, *Hellzapoppin'* (staged originally in 1939), *Hair* was a revue. It was successful because of its glorious music, but also because revue was such an old art form that it seemed new; Rodgers and Hammerstein and the maturation of musical theater had made sure of that. *Hair*, which seemed startling because for twenty-five years audiences had become accustomed to musicals telling them a story, is about a young man who is going into the army. Or something. And there are nudes at the end of the first act. The only connection be-tween the songs was that the people who wrote them liked them. They tell little of plot, character, or action. As for dance, that was spontaneous — which, of course, was what the youth culture was about. Or should have been. Or something. Galt MacDermott, its composer, has few illusions about its philosophy. "It just amused me," he says. "The guys who wrote it had an attitude that was original. There was a lot of preaching in it, which I didn't take too seriously. The approach to sex, race, and dope seemed slightly outrageous at the time, but also slightly ridiculous."

Although *Hair* did nothing to advance the musical as a form, it did have other and perhaps more lasting consequences. Its producer, Joseph Papp, had been untouched by all that Broadway entails. "I was never close to the musical theater as a child," he says. "In fact, I hardly knew it existed. I came from a very poor neighborhood and the music I knew best was the music of the street, and then maybe some songs from the movies. Broadway was out of my class entirely — Broadway meant money, so we never even thought about it."

Nor was Papp interested in rock music until James Rado and Gerome Ragni brought him twelve sheets of a script and he suggested that MacDermott put some music to it. But whereas *Show Boat* was sophistication of subject matter, and *Oklahoma!* sophistication of technique,

Hair was simply what Broadway audiences hoped rock music might be about—a little dirty, a little freaky, but good and wholesome underneath. As such, it had nothing at all to do with the musical. But it did convey the impression that youth had brought to the musical the classless vigor that alone could revitalize what was thought to be a floundering tradition. Sadly, that proved to be an illusion.

Partly this was because the economics of presenting a musical had become a nightmare. Far more shows are closed within a week—or never even reach Broadway—than achieve any success at all. For once, the excessive demands of stagehands, actors, and musicians have crippled their creation. John Kander and Fred Ebb's *Chicago*, for example, required thirteen musicians to play onstage; the American Federation of Musicians demanded that twenty-six of its members be assigned to the show. So, every night, thirteen musicians were paid to remain totally silent. The Broadway revival of Bernstein's *Candide*, which was scored for twelve musicians, involved the restructuring of the theater, which considerably reduced the number of available seats. But since the number of musicians required by the union contract is determined by the theater's *original* number of seats, once again, thirteen idle musicians earned a full rate for their evening's "work."

Bob Fosse, who directed *Chicago*, says: "The show cost nine hundred thousand dollars to produce—you can make a movie for that. And when you look at *Chicago*, you wonder, Where did nine hundred thousand dollars go? Admittedly, a hundred thousand of that was due to a postponement. But when I started directing ten years ago, you could do the same show for three

hundred thousand." Harold Prince, another major Broadway producer-director, affirms that it is becoming increasingly difficult to find backers. "It gets easier when you have had some successful shows to your name, but you constantly have to go out and beat the bushes for new people to put up money." *Follies*, one of Prince's more lavish productions, became a cult show and ran for 522 performances. It lost $650,000. Everyone had assumed it was profitable—until it closed.

"The trouble with traditional Broadway producers," Joseph Papp told me, "is that they are hogbound by their own tradition and end up making mistakes. They will try to reproduce some other success, or try a gimmick that will draw the audience in. But they don't know, they really don't know." *Hair* succeeded not because it was a revolutionary musical—it was not—nor because it changed the nature of the Broadway audience—it did not. The Broadway audience is as middle-class and middle-aged as it always has been. Social and economic change go together, according to Papp, and the theater must always reflect the spirit of a particular class at a particular time if it is to have any validity. And any sale of tickets.

The paraphernalia of Broadway success, in process and after the fact. *Far left:* Peter Arno's rough sketch for the poster logo for *The Pajama Game. Center left:* a "wheel of fortune" in Harold Prince's current office. Each sector of the wheel contains the names of two Prince productions. As Ruritania had been replaced by snazzy New York, and as New York had been replaced by faraway exotica, so exotica itself has taken on a new vitality in recent years. Joseph Papp *(near left)* was responsible both for *Hair (above left),* and *A Chorus Line (above right).* In the former, the cast exposed their bodies; in the latter, it was claimed, their psyches.

Swing That Music!

CARNEGIE HALL PROGRAM
SEASON 1937-1938
FIRE NOTICE—Look around *now* and choose the nearest exit
to your seat. In case of fire walk (not run) to *that* Exit. Do
not try to beat your neighbor to the street.
JOHN J. McELLIGOTT, *Fire Commissioner*

CARNEGIE HALL
Sunday Evening, January 16th, at 8:30
S. HUROK
presents
(by arrangement with Music Corporation of America)
BENNY GOODMAN
and his
SWING ORCHESTRA
I.
"Don't Be That Way"...*Edgar Sampson*
"Sometimes I'm Happy" (from "Hit the Deck")........*Irving Caesar* &
Vincent Youmans
"One O'clock Jump"...............................*William (Count) Basie*
II.
TWENTY YEARS OF JAZZ
"Sensation Rag" (as played c. 1917 by the Dixieland Jazz Band)
E. B. Edwards

~~~~~~

PROGRAM CONTINUED ON SECOND PAGE FOLLOWING

"The thing about jazz," Artie Shaw says, "was that white musicians learned very early on it was an escape from boredom. We would be playing the most miserable Tin Pan Alley songs. Things like 'Marie Lou'—you can't believe that song, it was so asinine. Tunes like 'Ain't She Sweet,' 'There She Goes, on Her Toes'—whatever the hell it was called—'Five Foot Two, Eyes of Blue.' Those sort of songs. Terrible. 'If You Knew Susie'—awful music. The quality was not important. But that's what we had to do. So in order to survive, when nobody was looking or when the leader went off to the john, we would improvise to see what we could do with this rubbish. That was the beginning of *our* jazz."

By the early thirties, Tin Pan Alley had scraped the bottom of its ragtime

Jitterbuggers at the New York World's Fair, 1939.

and jazz. Record sales had slumped from one hundred million in 1927 to a mere six million in 1931. Even the word "jazz" was no longer in favor. "It is a word of sarcasm," the London *Melody Maker* told its readers. "It signifies everything that is old-fashioned." The "jazz" that had accompanied the noisy twenties seemed inappropriate after the Wall Street collapse; the Depression needed sweeter and more soothing sounds. Jazz was banished whence it was thought to have come—to the Prohibition-created network of dives and speakeasies in Chicago.

In fact, as we have seen, true jazzmen had never left their underground habitat. But the Depression ensured that a considerable number of white "jazz" musicians, for whom employment was suddenly limited, joined them. Conditions were often hazardous, especially since gangsterism offered a risky patronage. "We would see those rods come up—and duck," Eddie Condon said. "At the Triangle Club, the boss was shot in the stomach one night, but we kept on working. After that, he walked sort of bent over." Woody Herman says he was shot in the leg on his first night as a teen-age bandsman in Chicago. But to relieve the frustration of the Depression, and to escape the music Tin Pan Alley was producing, white musicians flocked to wherever black jazzmen were making their music. "Whenever I got a week off," Artie Shaw recalls, "I'd go up to Chicago and sit at the feet—literally, at the feet—of these guys, on the edge of the bandstand and watch these cats like Louis Armstrong doing what he was doing." Shaw himself got his first break when he landed a job with Red Nichols, a white band leader who worked in midtown New York. But he spent all his spare time up in Harlem listening to black musicians such as pianist Willie "The Lion" Smith.

The attraction of black jazz for the growing number of white musicians who wished to play in that style was obvious. "Black jazz was less constrained," Shaw says, "less influenced by the heritage of white men who, whether they knew it or not, had been brought up on Palestrina, Mozart, and Beethoven. Black musicians didn't have to read music. They played heads long before heads became popular. But what the white musicians brought to jazz was a kind of discipline and training—and, of course, an acceptance."

The white music industry was in need of a new fix, the white musicians were in need of a new style that satisfied both them and their public. The black bands of Chicago, in an attempt to gain recognition on their own terms, had begun performing popular tunes of the day in a jazz style. But there was little hope that such arrangements, by Fletcher Henderson or Benny Carter or whomever, would reach a large audience except

Benny Goodman may not have invented the music, but he brought to it great popularity; his sidemen (including Harry James, Lionel Hampton, and Gene Krupa) went on to lead successful bands of their own. *Above:* Goodman leans on Artie Shaw. *Top right:* Goodman at Atlantic City's Steel Pier, in 1936, with Helen Ward. Harry James is kneeling next to Goodman. *Bottom right:* a rapturous crowd at New York's Paramount Theater, 1939.

through a white band. John Hammond, then a young recording executive and fervent jazz fan, was told by a European company to find a band that might supply the white music industry with its next bonanza. Hammond and his employer, the Decca Record Company, were convinced a market existed—in both Europe and America—for white dance bands that played popular tunes, but with the lilt and syncopation and excitement of jazz. Hammond's need was answered by a diffident, indecisive, but especially gifted young clarinetist, Benjamin David Goodman.

Goodman had been a working musician from the age of thirteen. His first recorded solo, at age seventeen, in a piece appropriately called "He's the Last Word," revealed a master technician. He, too, had had some classical training with a German professor and was equally at home playing clarinet concertos and improvising jazz. Like Shaw, he joined Red Nichols and later had some success in Ben Pollack's band at the Venice Ballroom in Los Angeles. His first experi-

ence as a leader, however, came when he was asked to organize a group to back the popular singer Russ Colombo. The group included the pianist Joe Sullivan and a young drummer named Gene Krupa. "It was," says Goodman, "quite a good little jazz band." It was Hammond who urged Goodman to put together a regular performing combo along similar lines.

The band—consisting of five brass pieces, four saxophones, rhythm guitar, bass, and piano (with Goodman, of course, playing clarinet)— was duly formed for an engagement in 1933 at Billy Rose's Music Hall in New York. Goodman remembers it as a difficult time. "It was kind of tough to go in there and get this group to play and drill them and rehearse them," he recalled.

Left: Earl Hines played an eleven-year stand at Chicago's Grand Terrace from 1929 to 1940. Hines himself, born in 1903, in Duquesne, Pennsylvania, now plays with a small group that tours eleven months of the year. *Right:* Artie Shaw's Gramercy 5, the band within a band, took its name from a telephone exchange. Standing next to Shaw is Roy Eldridge, second only to Louis Armstrong among jazz trumpeters.

"Sometimes players just wouldn't turn up. It was so frustrating." In fact, the band got the sack after a couple of months—but not before it had won an audition for a network radio show sponsored by the National Biscuit Company. Called *Let's Dance*, the show lasted for twenty-six weeks and the music was much enlivened by Goodman's new arranger, the black band leader Fletcher Henderson. "The arrangements were unique," Goodman says. In fact, Henderson had used the same arrangements—of tunes such as "King Porter Stomp," "Sugarfoot Stomp," and "Down South Camp Meeting"—for his own band ten years earlier.

When the radio stint ended, there was little to suggest that success for Goodman was imminent. He secured an engagement at the Roosevelt Hotel in New York, filling a spot usually occupied by Guy Lombardo's Royal Canadians and their "sweetest music this side of heaven." On opening night, the Goodman Orchestra was given two weeks' notice.

The band took to the road and headed west,

where it was met with total indifference. "We got to Denver, Colorado," Goodman told me, "which was an absolute catastrophe. There was virtually nobody in the hall and the people only wanted waltzes. Well, we couldn't play waltzes, so we just had to continue playing what we could." The tour was a failure. By the time the band got to its last date—at the Palomar Ballroom in Los Angeles, in August 1935—their attitude, according to Goodman, was, What have we got to lose? Almost scared to play at all, they decided to let loose with the best they had. "From the moment I kicked them off," Goodman says, "the boys dug in with some of the best playing I'd heard since we left New York."

No one will ever know what, in one night, turned a dismal tour into a triumph that supposedly launched an era. The music was not new. Other white bands, in particular that of the Dorsey brothers, had tried blending jazz with a big-band line-up; other bands had even used Henderson's arrangements. "I don't know *what* it was," says Goodman, "but the crowd went

Above: Ella Fitzgerald and the extraordinary drummer Chick Webb. Fitzgerald, born in Newport News, Virginia, in 1918, joined Webb in her mid-teens, and they reigned as king and queen of Harlem's Savoy Ballroom until Webb, hunchbacked and tubercular, died in 1939. Fitzgerald "inherited" the band and kept it together for three years before going on her own. Although she was unrivaled among "girl singers," the requirements of a swing era band brought stiff competition. *Facing page: clockwise from top left* are Ivie Anderson, who sang with Duke Ellington—her first recording in 1932 was "It Don't Mean a Thing (If It Ain't Got That Swing)"; Maxine Sullivan, who sang with Benny Carter and turned "Loch Lomond" to swing; Dinah Washington, more a blues singer than a band singer; Billie Holiday, in 1954—"I don't think I'm singing," she told Nat Shapiro and Nat Hentoff. "I feel like I'm playing a horn."

wild and then—*boom!*" Goodman, that August evening at the Palomar, had—in Duke Ellington's words—"done the right thing at the right time in front of the right people."

The Palomar Ballroom was certainly the right place. It was one of the first West Coast ballrooms to be hooked into network radio. Night after night, the microphones stationed around the ballroom transmitted the dancers' enthusiasm as much as the band's performance. "Radio was just beginning to spread out," Goodman added, "and it seemed to me that I could work along and secure a pretty good living in that field."

Back in New York after a nation-wide tour and another radio series, this time the *Camel Caravan* from Chicago, the Goodman band checked into the Pennsylvania Hotel. The management, with some asperity, asked the musicians to turn down the volume. But "when the crowds started to come and kept on coming, we didn't hear much more comment about the band being loud." The band was booked for the regular "live" spot at the Paramount Theatre, doing stage shows from ten-thirty in the morning onward between screenings of the movie. When the musicians arrived for a seven o'clock rehearsal on the morning of their first day, they found two hundred youngsters already in line at the box office. All through the first showing of the movie there were restless noises and whistles coming from the auditorium. And when the band finally emerged—blasting away on the slowly rising stage—the noise, according to Goodman, was "like Times Square on New Year's Eve." As they launched into one of the "killer-diller" arrangements—with Gene Krupa whipping himself into a damp frenzy at the drums, and Harry James soaring away with his trumpet—the effect was explosive. Seeing the kids beginning to jump out of their seats and start dancing in the aisles, the theater manager rushed out of his office. As soon as the ushers saw him, they snapped to attention and saluted. "To hell with that!" he shouted, "Get down there and stop those kids from killing themselves!"

Goodman's success encouraged a frenzy of

dance bands: Bob Crosby, with his Dixieland flavor, Woody Herman and his "Band That Played the Blues," Shaw, James, and Krupa would all, in time, have their own bands. All had one thing in common: for the first time, they brought to the whole of America a music that was black in origin, black in design, and black in spirit. Goodman, although white, was too good a musician to interfere with a black heritage he knew well and respected; and before long, he took steps to ensure that blacks shared in his good fortune. His rapid popular success prevented (for a while) Tin Pan Alley from diluting and rendering gutless a music that had

punch, vitality, and optimism. Goodman fathered the first healthy cross-fertilization between black and white culture. The press decided. Goodman was King, the King of Swing.

To this day, Goodman is casual about the origin of the term "swing." During that disastrous trip to Denver, he says, he was approached by a reporter. "He wanted to know what we called the band. So I said: 'Benny Goodman and His Orchestra.' The reporter was horrified and said: 'You can't have that.' And he reeled off the names of other bands like Fred Waring and His Pennsylvanians and Guy Lombardo and His Royal Canadians, and Coon Saunders and His

Night Horse. It couldn't be just Benny Goodman. . . . . So Gene Krupa, who was standing by me, said: 'Why don't you call it the Swing Band?' So I said fine, we'll call it the Swing Band. Big deal."

But as Goodman himself admits, the terms "swing" and "swinging" were not confined to jazz. The Viennese waltz, played in the right place and in the right conditions, undeniably swings. So does the Hungarian tzigane or the Scottish reel. Even the black singers and musicians of revivalist churches and chapels—who disapprove of rag, jazz, and blues as the work of the devil—swing exceedingly when possessed of the spirit. Critic Henry Pleasants says swing was like flying—the feeling was much the same as when an airplane, in the prejet era, suddenly took off after roaring down the runway. Swing was always physical, and always closely allied to dancing: the musicians provided the familiar melodic strains above a steady, rhythmic foundation that the dancers used as a framework for their own improvisations. Swing was thus the inspiration for most modern dance crazes, from the jitterbug to jive. But, as Artie Shaw points out: "We don't just say: 'Listen to that, isn't it good?' We've got to give it a name. It's the human penchant for labeling. We don't say: 'That's a pretty bird.' We call it an oriole. The bird doesn't know it's an oriole. All it knows is it's got wings, if flies—and it swings." Swing was not a form, like jazz. It was a style, a mood.

News of Goodman's success crossed the Atlantic where, in England at least, dance bands had been in vogue for some years before Goodman played at the Palomar. The best of them—Bert Ambrose, Lew Stone, Jack Hylton—considered themselves rather superior to their "sweet band" counterparts in the United States. Despite a considerable enthusiasm for jazz among European musicians, however, there was no tradition of native jazzmen to spark these bands into life. Further, it was inconceivable that the smart London or Paris hotels that employed the big bands would welcome hordes of scruffy swing fans. Bert Ambrose once acknowledged a request for a tune written on a

pound note with a curt refusal—written on a five-pound note.

But even if Europe had no swing craze of its own, it did make a contribution to the swing era. By the end of the twenties, Europe already knew more about jazz than America. The immense popularity of jazz records from America—many of which, incidentally, featured a mixture of black and white musicians unthinkable on the American stage—had fostered a new discipline: jazz criticism. In 1932, some while before Krupa named Goodman's band, a Belgian lawyer and jazz enthusiast called Robert Goffin produced a book entitled *Aux Frontières du Jazz.* Two years later Frenchman Hugues Panassié published a critical work entitled, in curious franglais, *Le Jazz Hot.* Both attempted to define jazz and outlined as much of its history as was known.

Newspapers and periodicals followed suit and, before long, clusters of European jazz fans huddled together in cellars that became known as "hot clubs" or "rhythm clubs." There, armed with fistfuls of records, magazines, and passionate opinions, they worshiped. "Real jazz," they insisted, had nothing whatsoever to do with the commercial excesses of swing. They preferred "jam sessions" wherein groups of musicians would improvise for hours, perhaps on a familiar standard, playing the "way they felt" and for "the love of it."

Goodman and others took note. Goodman, at least, had always cherished those moments of rich improvisation by small groups. As early as 1929, he had recorded a trio set and always maintained a "band within a band," even with his largest ensembles. Most of the swing bands followed his example—Tommy Dorsey had his Clambake Seven, Bob Crosby his Bob Cats, Artie Shaw his Gramercy Five. Goodman's trio and quartet were the most significant, however, because of their personnel.

The trio had started from a chance meeting with the black pianist Teddy Wilson. Goodman sat down to jam with Wilson and it sounded good. It sounded even better when Gene Krupa joined in, and the trio cut a couple of records. The trio also played as an adjunct to the Goodman band during radio shows from the Congress Hotel in Chicago. Shortly after, the band was in California. Teddy Wilson took Goodman and Krupa to hear a friend of his, Lionel Hampton, who, encouraged by his band leader Louis Armstrong, had mastered a new instrument known as the vibraharp. As Hampton remembers it: "One minute I'm playing, then there's Teddy playing the piano. A minute later, Benny has sat down next to me with his clarinet and about another minute later, Gene's at the drums." The Goodman Quartet.

Goodman took his black and white quartet right onto the stage, thus flouting years of racial taboos.

It was a historic combination because Goodman took his black and white quartet right onto the stage, thus flouting years of racial taboos. Ironically, Goodman recalls: "When some hotel managers found out, they'd come straight up to see if there was any bad reaction. But when they found a lot of business and the place jumping, they were *perfectly* willing to go along with it." Again, the other bands followed Goodman's example. Before long, Woody Herman, Charlie Barnett, and Artie Shaw all had black musicians in their bands. "I was quite often threatened by theater operators and managers," Woody Herman says, "that if I didn't have an all-lily-white band, my contract would be torn up."

The pop stars of the thirties were not singers, like the idols of today, but instrumentalists. Most of the big bands were crammed full of jazz musicians who had previously been denied the creative opportunities being opened up to them. Not only could they now play the music they wanted, they could also get paid exceedingly well for their trouble. But this acceptance had a price. Most bands played fifty weeks a year. The more popular the band, the more it had to travel. Woody Herman recalls that a one- or two-week engagement was greeted with enthusiasm—"It was a chance to get your laundry done"—although longer engagements involved several shows a day, sometimes as the live attraction in a movie house. The movie moguls who had bought up Tin Pan Alley had found yet another way of squeezing money and promotion out of their products. Benny Goodman: "The films were terrible as a rule. But when we'd been playing in a movie house for a few days and cramming in the audience, the movie company would take out an ad in the

Far left: Benny Goodman backs "Liltin'" Martha Tilton in Atlantic City, 1938; *near left:* the Andrews Sisters. Both Tilton and the Andrews became famous for versions of "Bei Mir Bist Du Schoen." Certainly, both characterized swing, but the similarity ended there. Tilton was a prototype, with a voice that did, indeed, lilt; Patti, Maxene, and LaVerne were rambunctious, highly stylized performers who adapted the qualities of swing instrumentation to the capabilities of the human voice.

local paper saying what good business the *movie* was doing."

The movie house performances were never a holiday. Bands played five or six shows, from ten in the morning until one o'clock the following morning, seven days a week. Buck Clayton explained to me how even this arrangement was exploited: "We might start with an hour-long show in the morning. Then, if there was a big crowd, they'd only put on a short film, maybe

forty minutes. That's when you rushed out to get breakfast. After that, it was straight on through the day. If the crowds were good, they'd cut the movies short. You were lucky if you had half an hour for supper. You never had time to relax and enjoy yourself. You just didn't have time for anything."

Then there were the fans. Mostly screaming.

Above, left: Billy Eckstine came out of Earl Hines' band to front his own, for which he played trumpet and valve trombone as well as sang. Unnervingly popular, the Eckstine band was the first so-called modern swing unit: its players, at various times, included almost all creators of bop, including Charlie Parker, Dizzy Gillespie, Miles Davis, and Art Blakey. *Above, right:* Tommy Dorsey's Pied Pipers, featuring Jo Stafford and Frank Sinatra. The latter acknowledged that his singing style derived from vocal imitation of Dorsey's trombone playing. *Near right:* Miss Peggy Lee, 1941. *Center right:* Frank Sinatra and Nat King Cole, 1946. Sinatra was earning $75 weekly singing for Harry James in 1939 when Dorsey signed him up; by 1943 he had supplanted Bing Crosby as the world's most popular singer. By the time this picture was taken, he was a solo performer—the first popular singer to follow this route—a film star, and probably a millionaire. Cole was important on 52nd Street in the early 1940s, playing piano (particularly blues) and leading a trio before he attained national success as a singer. *Far right:* Jimmy Dorsey and Tommy Dorsey in 1934, before personal acrimony and different musical styles caused them to split up and lead separate bands. Although both were successful, Tommy had a much sharper sense of business. He even hired the advertising agency of Batten, Barton, Durstine and Osborne to promote him and the band.

Artie Shaw hated them. "One time, during an appearance in Philadelphia, I was informed on the first day of our engagement that there had been such a drop in attendance at the Philadelphia schools, the Board of Education had lodged a formal complaint with the police. After the first show, I tried to leave my dressing room to go out for a breath of fresh air. I was told by the doorman not to attempt going into the street. I asked him why not. He opened the stage door—just a crack—so that I could look outside. The whole street was jam-packed with kids. Traffic was completely halted and there were half a dozen mounted policemen trying to disperse this rioting mob of youngsters."

Benny Goodman began to have the same misgivings. "Anyone who really wanted the kind of adulation we got was out of his mind. We never encouraged any of that noise. In fact, we wouldn't play if people were noisy. We'd say: 'We'll start to play when you quiet down, so shut up. You *can't* listen to us and make all that noise.' "

The jazzmen themselves, moreover, were not the mature, seasoned performers that their later and continuing fame might suggest. Benny Goodman was only twenty-six when he hit the jackpot at the Palomar; Artie Shaw was just twenty-four when his success was earning him thirty thousand dollars a week. The record that confirmed his stardom, incidentally, had originally been a filler. "We had a real rouser on the other side—a version of the 'Indian Love Call' that I'd arranged as a proper flag-waver," Shaw says. "But it didn't happen at all." The "B" side, however, taken from a Cole Porter musical that had failed, became one of the most popular arrangements of swing. It was "Begin the Beguine."

The confusion was not helped by overzealous agents and managers. The event that came to be regarded as the absolute peak of the swing era, for instance, started out as a stunt. In 1938, Goodman's press agent saw the possibility of acquiring a little "class" for the band (and more publicity, of course) by staging a formal concert. Goodman said he thought it was a crazy idea; they were a dance band. But the agent kept on insisting until finally Goodman agreed. Sol Hurok, the impresario, was persuaded to put his

name to the venture; his actual contribution was a worried letter to Goodman asking him to make sure the boys were on their best behavior. His concern was understandable—after all, the band was about to play Carnegie Hall.

Swing had arrived. The band played well; Goodman led a jam session featuring stars from the Ellington and Basie bands, and the audience danced in the aisles. But, as Goodman says: "We had that sort of crowd already at the Paramount." The band played a couple more concerts, including a second at Carnegie Hall later in 1938, but Goodman was determined: "I just didn't think my music should be played in a

Bands sold the seats. Thus, the movie companies kept their houses filled, and profitable. Later, the movie companies put the bands *on* celluloid—there was *The Benny Goodman Story, The Glenn Miller Story, The Fabulous Dorseys*, besides numerous other swing-based "biopics." Occasionally, a movie would be rewritten to include an otherwise irrelevant band sequence. *Center left:* Woody Herman and his "Band That Played the Blues," in 1938, six years before the formation of Herman's first "Thundering Herd." *Bottom left:* Bob Crosby (third from left) and the Bob Cats, 1941. *Above:* in the 1941 production, *Las Vegas Nights*, Frank Sinatra (third from left), Buddy Rich (next to actress Constance Moore, center), and Tommy Dorsey (behind Moore, in front of slot machines).

concert hall. So I said no more. I'm going to play for dancing.''

The concert at Carnegie Hall highlighted the dilemma of swing. The audience's behavior, especially in those austere surroundings, proved that the music was for dancing. The Carnegie Hall gimmick convinced many that the music's ultimate *raison d'être* was to make money. Within months of Goodman's Carnegie Hall debut, Artie Shaw left the stand in the middle of an engagement and lit off for a holiday in Mexico — never to return, so he said. *The New York Times* reported it: ''Any commentary that might occur to us would be lost in the Shakespearean sweep of Mr. Shaw's exodus: the kind of spectacularly irreverent farewell to his work and former associates that even the timidest soul must occasionally dream of, a beautifully incautious burning of all his bridges behind him.'' For months, the musical press had crackled with Shaw's tirades against corruption in the music business, against the greedy demands of agents. But no one was quite prepared for the apparent finality of Shaw's gesture.

Today, Artie Shaw is no longer certain he did right. ''We were playing in dance halls, but we were playing concerts,'' he told me. ''I broke the

record at the old Palomar. We had nearly ten thousand people there — I'm sure it was past the legal limit. You could have walked across the ballroom on people's heads. Nobody danced. On the other hand, I wanted to play concerts — but my agent wouldn't consider it. And when the bands got into the movie theaters where the audience *could* sit and listen, they didn't. They shouted and screamed — and danced. In fact, we played the best we knew how when it was quiet. All we cared about was that everybody shut up and let us play. The only time I didn't like playing was when the audience got in my way, when they made so much noise you couldn't hear yourself.''

The endless one-night stands; the ecstasy of the fans; the impossibility of changing a tune from show to show because the audience insisted on hearing exactly what they'd heard before. '' 'Begin the Beguine' is a pretty nice tune,'' Shaw told me. ''But after you've played it five hundred times in a row, it gets a little dull. If you are reduced to packaging what you do as a commodity, and involved in selling it to a vast audience, you are in serious trouble. I decided that if I didn't quit, I would be incapable of living with myself. At first, I thought I couldn't quit. I was booked solid—about a million dollars' worth of contracts. My lawyer said I'd be sued to death if I left. I suggested insanity might be a defense. He said: 'What kind of insanity?' My reply was: 'If a nice American boy walks out on a million dollars, wouldn't you say he was insane?' "

Shaw was not the only band leader who quit. Goodman stopped and started his bands almost as often. Once he had back trouble and was out of action for several months; more than once, he says, "I just wanted to break up the routine." In pursuit of jackpot-winning combinations, star instrumentalists were traded around like latter-day football players: Dave Tough went from Dorsey to Goodman, Bud Freeman from Goodman to Dorsey, Buddy Rich from Shaw to Dorsey. Gene Krupa and then Harry James left Goodman to form their own bands.

Denied its unique ensemble quality, the music itself began to change. Goodman's success was such that what he played began to solidify: the fans wanted the arrangements they knew. The best bands, like Goodman's, had always been rigorously rehearsed, but allowed time and space for wild improvisations. Now, the improvisations were getting rehearsed. Artie Shaw: "I couldn't stand debasing my music so that it could be understood by a mass audience who didn't know what I was doing. And finally, you've got to come down to people's level for them to understand and stay with you. Your agent and your manager and your publicity man and your fan club will tell you that you've got to compromise. So the music gets to be pap, and when it gets to be pap, you've had it. Music is one thing and business is another," Shaw concludes. "When you start making music into a commodity and selling it to the masses, then you've lost something very precious. You've gained something, of course—which is money. But to do that, you have to start using labels. And 'swing' became just another of the labels given to the mass market of popular music."

Tin Pan Alley pounced. Big bands would

Bing Crosby: "If you got on a national network regularly, I don't care how good or bad you were: if you were audible, you had to be successful."

swing higher than ever. On radio, the major cigarette companies—Chesterfield, Lucky Strike, Old Gold—scrambled to sign up bands for their sponsored shows. Meanwhile, the networks of CBS, Mutual, and NBC fought for the right to broadcast hotel and ballroom dates. Bands dominated the airwaves. The recording industry had never seen a boom like it. Sales were the highest in over ten years. In 1941, one record topped a million sales, an immaculately arranged ditty that achieved an international popularity far in excess of anything even Goodman had achieved. The song was "Chattanooga Choo-Choo," and the band that of an indifferent "jazz" trombonist, Glenn Miller.

Miller had been well schooled. Like Goodman, he had played with Ben Pollack. But he had always been overshadowed by more gifted instrumentalists, like Jack Teagarden. When he finally put his own band together in 1939, he arranged that all press photographs would show him with trombone at the ready. But he rarely took solos in front of his band and never cut loose with the fierce improvisations that were characteristic of his rival Tommy Dorsey. Nor did his band ever manage the uninhibited, extroverted style that brought Benny Goodman's audiences to their feet. Long before he became a major in the United States Army, Miller had imposed a quasi-military discipline on his instrumentalists, even to insisting that they display a regulation length of handkerchief above their breast pockets whenever they came on stage.

But Miller's treacly blend of clarinet and saxophone, although the antithesis of jazz or swing, was exactly what the merchants felt comfortable selling: it packaged well, it was eminently respectable. When Miller joined the Army in 1942, his choice radio spot went to Harry James. Gone were the high-flying jazz solos that had rocked the Goodman band. "You Made Me Love You," James' band sang and played with a melancholy sigh that seemed a denial of everything he had pioneered six years earlier with Goodman.

James had one lucky break. Soon after he started his own band in 1939, he heard on the radio a young man singing with a local group. Impressed, he drove out the next day to find the singer. "No," said the manager of the roadhouse where the broadcast had come from, "we don't have a singer. But we have a waiter who acts as MC and sings—a bit." Harry James signed the young man on the spot, having made a vain attempt to persuade him to change his name—James didn't think the public would ever remember someone called Frank Sinatra.

Unfortunately for James, his band was not successful enough to keep the ambitious youngster. Despite a strong rapport with James, Sinatra left within months to join Dorsey—the "sentimental gentleman of swing"—whose suave trombone phrasing was to have such a formative influence on the Sinatra style. But James decided that no self-respecting band should be without a singer who "crooned." Most bands of the swing era had featured singers; the vocals of Helen Ward, for instance, had been a considerable element in the popular appeal of Goodman's first big band. But in the early days, the singers had had to rely on lung power to reach their audiences. Bessie Smith, Sophie Tucker, and even Al Jolson may have had their intimate moments, but they never "crooned." If they had, they would have been inaudible.

Mildred Bailey, who was married to the vibraphonist Red Norvo, singing at Barney Josephson's Café Society.

Rudy Vallee was the first popular singer to bring "intimacy" to his performances, and it says much for his appeal that he was able to sustain a glamorous image in front of his band while singing through a tin megaphone. Radio and recordings gave the illusion of being close to the singer, although it was Vallee himself who pioneered a primitive public address, which he later described in a letter to fellow band leader Paul Whiteman: "I borrowed an old carbon mike from NBC," he wrote, "and hooked up a homemade amplifier with some radios. I'd got a sort of electronic megaphone. By the by, I had the legs sawn off the radios so they don't look so strange."

While Vallee was fooling around with bits of wire, another singer—also with Whiteman—was perfecting the art of singing into an electric

microphone, confidentially. Curiously, he was known as the Young Belter; as time went by, however, he became the Old Groaner—Harry "Bing" Crosby. "In the early days," Crosby says, "everybody that sang with the band always sat in with the band. And generally they played an instrument. For example, in the Whiteman band of the late twenties, there were three who sang: Johnny Fulton, who was a very fine trombone player; Charlie Gaylord, who played a fair violin; and Skin Young, who could make a pass

---

The Count Basie Orchestra, 1954, on its way to Sweden. Second from left, front row, is Lester Young. Basie's organization, despite inevitable changes in personnel and in style, still plays. *The New Yorker* commented on a 1976 performance by noting the fine acoustics of the room Basie was playing. And then dismissed the acoustics as irrelevant: "Basie's orchestra *is* a sound system."

at a guitar and get away with it." Crosby admits he "couldn't play anything, but I had to hold an instrument so they gave me a thing they called a packhorn—it's a kind of raincatcher; looks something like a French horn, only it's used in marching bands. Well, I found where the mouthpiece was, so in some of the big arrangements I'd put in a few little licks—oompahs—generally out of tune. Whiteman took a pretty dim view of this, and finally gave me a violin with rubber strings. I became quite expert at faking that, had a very good bowing technique. They said my bowing was excellent, though I wasn't too strong on the pizzicato."

Crosby spent a year and a half at the Cocoanut Grove in Los Angeles with Whiteman and later sang with Beiderbecke, Ellington, and Armstrong. But, as he says: "Radio was the single most important factor in my career. If you got on a national network regularly, I don't care how good or bad you were: if you were audible, you had to be successful." The bands made the careers of singers possible and thus staked out their territory for the next decade. But then came the fight between ASCAP and BMI; with no license to broadcast live music, many radio stations used records. In retaliation, the American Federation of Musicians—under the bellicose leadership of James Caesar Petrillo—called a strike, claiming that the union had a right to collect a fee on every disc played. The band leaders argued against such a move with some desperation. But from August 1942 they were forbidden to enter recording studios.

The strike dragged on for over a year, during which time the recording companies could not afford to cease recording. So they turned to the only musicians who were not members of the union—the singers. Vocal backings replaced instrumental accompaniments; "crooners" emerged from their relative anonymity; trios and quartets like the Andrews Sisters and the Ink Spots made their mark. The Andrews Sisters were particularly skillful at impersonating all the instruments of the orchestra. As they became increasingly popular, old recordings those singers had made with bands before the strike were re-released, with the singer pro-

moted to top billing. One of Sinatra's first big hits, for instance, was a song he had recorded back in 1939 as a new boy with Harry James, "All or Nothing at All."

The strike ended in October 1943; the union claimed its settlement would generate three million extra dollars "for the advancement of musical culture." But the initiative had been lost: most recording companies preferred house bands. If nothing else, they were safer. Musical directors like Nelson Riddle took their solos with the rest of the band, if only to demonstrate that a "leader" was redundant.

Some of the bands survived. In the recording studio, Goodman's small groups continued to feature top jazz players; critics agree that some of Goodman's line-ups in the mid-forties were musically the best he ever had. But in 1946, as if in a concerted gesture of surrender, Harry James, Tommy Dorsey, Woody Herman, Les Brown, and Jack Teagarden all dissolved their bands. (Goodman had already disbanded in 1944, but with him nothing was permanent.) A year later, Louis Armstrong—who had been the inspiration for so many of them—also turned his back on the big bands he had fronted for years and reverted to the smaller line-ups of his earlier New Orleans days. "Most people," Woody Herman told me, "went underground. Many of the people in our business had made a lot of money. Now the money was harder to make. So they would work a while, and when it got difficult, they would rest." At the end of 1947 Petrillo struck again. "No one can expect a musician to play at his own funeral," he said. Never again would jazz and popular mass entertainment be on such intimate terms.

"We created a monster," Artie Shaw says. "Or rather, other people created it for us, although we were willing. But you could not have the kind of career we had in those days, and still have a semi-sane life. My choice was between having a life or having a career. The price of the career was proving too great. And I wanted a life." But then, so had the black man from whose music the white man had profited yet again.

To Don Redman a Swell Pal Wishing you Luck & Success In What Ever you do or go So Sincerly Deek 4 Ink Spo

Hoppy

Kenny

Chas

9

Good Times

people of one of the grandest
mineral regions on this continent
should not fail to establish a school
of mines.

The peaks of the Cumberland, the
Clinch, and the Smoky, furnish

Berry Gordy was once a production line worker in Detroit. Now he is boss of a multi-million-dollar black show business organization, which proves that to escape the ghetto it is necessary to beat the white man at his own game. As founder and inspiration of a record label and style known as Motown, Gordy has been responsible for a horde of black artists—among them the Supremes, Martha and the Vandellas, the Miracles, the Marvelettes, Stevie Wonder, and the Temptations—whose financial success is almost beyond measure.

This complete reversal of black musical fortunes, however, has been achieved at considerable risk to the black man and his music. Gordy first unveiled his formula in 1959. Take a simple repetitive tune, a simple-minded

The Ink Spots, 1936.

lyric, box them in with an impersonal, unswinging background, add the coyness of socially manicured, sexy black singers, and success is guaranteed. Well, not quite. His first major group, the Supremes, had numerous flops before "Where Did Our Love Go?" established them, him, and the sound they purveyed as the new voice of black music. It was called "soul" or, in its less political mode, "rhythm and blues." "It's not a music," said Mitch Miller of Columbia Records. "It's a disease."

Gordy insisted that successful packaging should include his employees' accommodations, hair styles, make-up, clothes, and private lives. He meticulously preened his artists for international love. "Our relationship was like a marriage," Gordy's high priestess, Diana Ross, once said, while out of her spindly, predatory body crackled hit after hit—seven gold discs in 1967 alone. In their neat little trouser suits, the Supremes ooohed and aaahed with immaculate togetherness. They pouted and hitched up their breasts. With lacquered wigs and blasted smiles, they ensured—along with Berry Gordy and his music factory located in a Detroit building called Hitsville, U.S.A.—that the emasculation of black music would be finally completed. Sluiced, desecrated, and then laid waste, the blues—thanks to Brother Gordy—lost what little authenticity remained. "Well," said Miss Ross, "you can only live one dream at a time."

Gordy's victory was not inevitable, although its cause may have been just; big-band music, with its colossal rewards in white swing, had seemed seductive. Yet, increasingly, black performers concentrated on making a music, a sound, that was truly their own. The origins of that music were in blues, jazz, and ragtime. But the sound had changed with its new urban surroundings. In its rural form, the blues had been a personal testament, an exorcism. But in the city, private meditation took too long and was drowned out by the roar and bustle. To match that noise, the blues had become loud and brash. The music might still involve self-expression, but its primary function was to entertain.

Chicago again provided the stimulus. By the late forties, the heyday of Prohibition and gangland warfare was long over. But in clubs like the Roosevelt on the West Side, the Checkerboard on the South, Pepper's, Queen Bee, and a hundred other dives and bars elsewhere, city blues made itself heard. The solo country singer was turned off the stage by groups loud with drums, pianos, and amplified guitars held together—and thrust forward—by a heavy relentless beat. From time to time, the singer might attempt a little social comment—a tale of hard luck and trouble—in the traditional blues manner. The sense of real anguish, however, was gone. The intensity was no more. Washboard Sam sang: "I've been treated wrong." But whether he had been or not, whether his entire race had been or not, was irrelevant. One young

man, come north from Dallas, epitomized the new spirit. Among the first bluesman to use an amplified guitar on record, T-Bone Walker leered like a blues Cab Calloway. "As he played," one old Chicago club owner says, "Walker would bop up and back across the wires, do the splits, and man, he could strut just like a burlesque queen." He would hold his guitar behind his neck, push it between his legs, and then, crouching low, begin to grind it against his groin. He made it clear that the electric guitar equaled sex.

"Black people never knew if they would get back to their beds at night in good enough order to survive another day," Jerry Wexler, one-time top recording executive with Atlantic Records, says. "After all, they lived in a very dangerous and hostile culture. They didn't have time for the nuances of behavior or morality that were the hallmarks of WASP society." Wexler, who was largely responsible for the commercial recognition of this new sound, was pessimistic about the consequences. "It had always been a question of making love or not making love, of being downcast or seeking revenge. Now, black people chose the latter."

Within the ghettoes, the music became the

Word, and the Word was spread. In every city, new record companies sprouted like vinyl-coated mushrooms. Most were known as Independents, quite separate from the major national recording companies that had previously insinuated their way into the ghetto. The Independents were mostly black owned and black controlled. Their markets were local. Many operated in garages or back rooms and basements. Their "executives" worked from the back seats of their own cars. With no overhead and no serious life-expectancy, such companies could afford to gamble. A failed record meant the loss of only a few hundred dollars; the major companies risked thousands. Consequently, the Independents could give a hearing to anyone who could hold a guitar or open his mouth. For the Independents, a sale of five thousand records was an extraordinary success.

These little companies lived close to their audience—they *were* their audience—and quickly developed a shrewd idea of what would be popular. If it sold, they repeated the dose. If it didn't, too bad. Many companies folded, but some took root, among them, Specialty in Los Angeles and, most influential, Chess in Chicago. Before long, news of this activity reached New York. Some of the major record companies already had a particular division for dealing with black music—the Bluebird label, for instance, was a subsidiary of the RCA Victor Record Company; its sole function in the thirties had been to record the blues. Concentrating mostly on rural styles (although it had also recorded the harder, more extroverted sound of Sonny Boy Williamson and Washboard Sam), it had enjoyed good sales to blacks in the South. Other national companies were started for the specific purpose of recording this newer, more aggressive music now emerging from the ghettoes. The most adventurous of these was Atlantic Records, founded by the Turkish Ambassador's sons, the brothers Ertegun, and aided by Jerry Wexler.

Columbia "New Process" Records
REG. U. S. PAT. OFF.

BLIND WILLIE JOHNSON

THIS Race artist's singing of Sacred Songs and Hymns is remarkable for its simplicity and melody. It's the sort of singing that grips you and holds you, having a strain of the spiritual in it. Blind Willie Johnson usually plays his own accompaniments on a guitar.

The demand for his recordings, places him in the front rank of Race artists. He is of course, an exclusive Columbia artist.

MOTHER'S CHILDREN HAVE A HARD TIME / IF I HAD MY WAY I'D TEAR THE BUILDING DOWN	14343-D	75c
IT'S NOBODY'S FAULT BUT MINE / DARK WAS THE NIGHT—COLD WAS THE GROUND	14303-D	75c
I KNOW HIS BLOOD CAN MAKE ME WHOLE / JESUS MAKE UP MY DYING BED	14276-D	75c

REV. T. E. WEEMS

| IF I HAD MY WAY I'D TEAR THE BUILDING DOWN—*Singing Sermons* / IF I HAVE A TICKET LORD CAN I RIDE? | 14254-D | 75c |
| THE DEVIL IS A FISHERMAN—*Sermons with Singing* / GOD IS MAD WITH MAN | 14221-D | 75c |

MADE THE NEW WAY—ELECTRICALLY
[22]

Advertisements for "Race artists." As late as 1955 some record companies never included black performers in their general lists of available music: it was unthinkable that a white audience would be interested.

"It was really very simple," Wexler explains. "We were recording black music, performed by black artists, to be sold to black people." Wexler became increasingly embarrassed by the dismissive name—"race music"—given to this music during the late forties. A variety of euphemisms replaced the term: record companies would produce a "Sepia Series," for instance, or an "Ebony Series." "Some of us in the music department of *Billboard*, where I worked at the time," Wexler says, "thought this was a bit odious. So we started a little campaign to come up with a new idea. 'Rhythm and blues' was our designation, and it caught on. As a description, however, it meant little. The music was not particularly rhythmic and it was almost never true blues—that had been left behind in the rural Southern states of America. Of course, 'rhythm and blues' was also a euphemism. It meant the music of black people."

Recording was often a casual business. An engineer and his producer would arrive in a Southern or Midwestern town and pass the word they were "entertaining," while they visited local clubs to hear what they hoped was music in the raw. Few had much knowledge of recording or electronics; many just set up a few microphones and hoped for the best. Most were enthusiasts—amateur musicologists first, entrepreneurs second. Much of their early success depended on chance encounters. "We were lucky," Wexler said. "We happened to find artists like Ray Charles and Joe Turner, LaVern Baker, Ruth Brown, and Clyde McPhatter, all of them among the very best black artists of that era. Their records turned out to have a guaranteed minimum sale, which, again, gave us the

Wexler and Chess unearthed musicians in the middle and late forties who were arrogant and brawling and came on like prize fighters. They were back-alley studs.

financial security to make more recordings."

Above all, Wexler and his colleagues discovered there was a bewildering range of material unknown and unheard outside the ghettoes of its origin. Full-lunged shouters like Joe Turner and Bullmoose Jackson; crooning Clarence Brown; virtuoso guitarists like B. B. King; big-band blues artists like Billy Eckstine. Each city, each ghetto, had its own musical heroes, although Chicago remained a mecca for them all. The success of Chess Records drew men from all over and especially from the South, whence came Little Walter, Elmore Jones, Muddy Waters, and, eventually, Howlin' Wolf.

As in earlier migrations, some musicians were also drawn to New Orleans, where the sound was softer and more relaxed. Jimmy Reed and Fats Domino moved south from upstate Louisiana; Bobby Bland arrived from Texas. Competition for artists in both Chicago and New Orleans became fierce. "We would go all through Chicago," Wexler told me, "even though that was the province of Chess Records. It was not uncommon for us to see if we could snatch someone from under Leonard Chess's nose. Anyway, he'd come to New York and do the same to us."

Whatever the location, and whatever the musical and regional variations in the sound, Wexler and Chess heard a common voice. With only a few exceptions, the musicians they unearthed in the middle and late forties were arrogant and brawling and came on like prize fighters. Like back-alley studs. The stumbling, incoherent soliloquies of the old rural singers belonged to another world. The music was now one long Rabelaisian boast, defiant in bad times, rampant in good. By their own admission, the star performers were just that, especially in bed. Muddy Waters was the "Hoochie Coochie Man." Howlin' Wolf would suddenly freeze, gesture to the prettiest girl in the room, and yell: "Shake it for me, baby." And she would.

Gospel? *Top*: the Fisk Jubilee Singers made their first concert tour in 1871. Fisk University, founded in Nashville in 1866, continues to support a choir today. *Bottom left*: Sister Rosetta Tharpe performed throughout the South. Occasionally, during the 1930s, she appeared in New York, including a series of appearances at the Cotton Club in Harlem, 1938–1940. *Bottom right*: Mahalia Jackson, born in New Orleans, 1911, the most celebrated of solo gospel singers.

The music was profoundly different from the gentle pleasantries of white pop—the difference between an endless diet of whipped cream and a bunch of people digging for a plate of ribs and coleslaw. But there was also an emotional difference. "Little white girls are a huge influence in the buying of records and the setting of

pace," Jerry Wexler explains. "A white girl from suburban Scarsdale who might chance upon a Big Bill Broonzy record, or a Leroy Carr record of 'In the Evening When the Sun Goes Down,' gets the image of this huge and threatening black man with a blue work shirt all sweated at the armpits. Such an image is just not part of her consciousness. She is terrified by it and, because of her polite white upbringing, finds it hard to make an empathetic connection with it. And so she rejects it."

For the first time, white audiences stayed away. Older band leaders like Lucky Millender or Tiny Bradshaw or Erskine Hawkins had been, by any standard, wild. But now, multicolored spotlights lit up grotesquely costumed bandsmen. The blues singers screamed and the ballad singers wept; the drums thundered as if from the jungle, while the frenetic, almost ritualistic, behavior of players like Illinois Jacquet roared to a climax. Clutching that most sexual of all instruments, the tenor saxophone, Jacquet would bend slowly backward, his head touching the floor, his instrument erect before him, shrieking riff upon riff just as loud and as high as he could go. Although many of the new performers were limited, their music had urgency, venom, and a compelling sense of involvement. Their energy was boundless. "Keep on churnin'," cried Wynonie Harris in one terrible outburst, "until the butter comes. . . ."

The Staple Singers (above, top), the Golden Gate Quartet, with their manager (above), and the James Cleveland Singers (near right) were among the gospel groups who moved from church to concert stage. Roebuck "Pop" Staple, who holds a guitar in the picture above, picked cotton in the South as a boy and found success in Chicago as performer, arranger, and entrepreneur. Facing page: if the Mills Brothers (left) were a whitened form of gospel style in the 1930s, the Shirelles (center) and the Drifters (right) were both of a highly cosmetized variety a quarter century later. As with many other early groups, the terminology is confusing: recently, there have been three different touring groups calling themselves the Drifters, each performing the group's well-known songs; only one of these can boast an "original" Drifter in its lineup, the others none at all.

Inevitably, this scarcely disguised assault and battery palled. The music was crude and the sexual machismo began to seem repetitive. Those white entrepreneurs who had strayed into this particular black territory discovered that the market was reaching saturation—or, perhaps, satiety. By the early fifties, a more subtle sound was required, if only to sustain the momentum. What was needed was a form that would impart style to the raunchy, cocksure noise that had stirred the loins of Chicago. Black music had such a form, although it came from a most unlikely source—the church.

Blues and gospel had always maintained an uneasy relationship. Both had similar roots. The majority of itinerant or professional blues singers usually claimed some experience of church singing and often included quasi-religious songs in their performances. Testifying to the Lord was a moment of abandon; emotional display in church was a sign of devotion. The greater the display, the greater the supposed devotion. Gospel singing was the zenith of this devotion, a formalized expression of communion with the Lord. The star singers were leaders in this communion, as eloquent as preachers, as rigorously trained, and as painstakingly rehearsed. No matter how abandoned they might sound, even to the faithful, their effects were calculated to the last shudder. They might seem possessed as they howled and wept,

but their harmonies were spotless and they never missed a beat. Passion had become a style, and a necessity.

Rhythm and blues—all roughness and guts—remained, despite the virtuosity of some performers, essentially an unschooled music. Gospel, on the other hand, had finesse as well as excitement. Any secular rhythm and blues singer wishing to impart a measure of class to his act began to imitate his more formal gospel brethren. Part of Ray Brown's style, for instance, clearly devolved from country blues, but he delivered that style in a high, emotional, and extravagantly pained voice that was pure gospel. As he wailed and sobbed his way through songs like "Good Rockin' Tonight," his posturing was a direct copy of the preacher-singers who wailed and sobbed every Sunday in church.

Gospel not only gave rhythm and blues confidence, but it also helped provide its sound. Gospel singing had long been dominated by groups that sang in close harmony. Apart from occasional soloists such as Mahalia Jackson or Sister Rosetta Tharpe, those who packed the black churches throughout America were groups like the Dixie Hummingbirds, the Golden Gate Quartet, the Five Blind Boys from Mississippi, and the Soul Stirrers. They were versatile performers; their music ranged from slow ballads to joyful cries of praise. Although their "message" (if that is what it was) remained

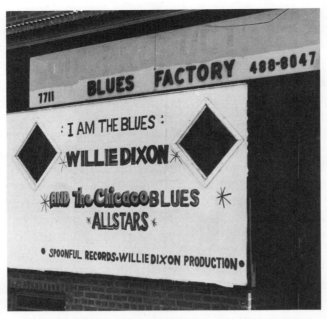

pointedly religious, their records began to sell almost as well as those of the noisier and less sophisticated rhythm and blues performers.

The Ink Spots had already peeped into the white market and made money by offering sweet harmony and joyful sounds. Being the first to achieve any notable success, they had acquired among their fellow blacks quasi-mythic status. But it was Billy Ward, a black New York gospel singing instructor, who achieved the first successful synthesis when he decided in 1950 to assemble a group of his best pupils and cash in. Ward, however, had not bargained for the singer whom he had chosen to lead the group, Clyde McPhatter. McPhatter refused to settle for mere imitation and threatened to go. Ward was forced to allow McPhatter his gospel-trained technique of high, free-flowing tenor over a solid, steady, close-harmony foundation, the two parts answering each other in call and response much as in the old work songs of the plantations. Ward called the group The Dominoes and they recorded their first song, "Sixty Minute Man."

It was a sensation, and went straight to number one in all the new rhythm and blues sales charts. Suddenly, scores of other groups discovered that gospel with rhythm and blues was a treasure house. Gospel passion—real or phony —spiced with a sufficient touch of the blues to liven up the lyrics, was a device to coin gold. Some groups had absurd animal and bird names: the Spaniels, the Flamingoes, the Penguins, as well as the Moonglows, the Clovers, and the Midnighters. The biggest was not the Dominoes, but the group that later acquired Clyde McPhatter, the Drifters. They sang "Money, Money," and they meant it.

The "gospel" sound, overlaid with secular lyrics, provided a neat alternative to the apparently uncouth, and certainly unacceptable, moaning of such as Howlin' Wolf. Although removed from the church, they acquired a veneer of sanctimonious respectability. Spontaneity was abandoned to scrupulous planning. The new dream was not just escape from the ghetto, but escape with elegance and sophistication. Reality, an unsavory blend of poverty, illiteracy, oppression, and all the stigmata of a shameful and shaming past, was forgotten. The new music harkened from a never-never land beyond the clouds where blackness was unknown. As if to prove it, these new apostles dekinked their hair, plucked their eyebrows, dressed in shiny suits, and strutted like wind-up dolls. Their dance routines were straight out of white vaudeville.

They resurrected "Red Sails in the Sunset" and "Smoke Gets in Your Eyes," smooch songs of purest whiteness. They became symbols of teen romance, viz., "Sincerely." They spouted nonsensical dance tunes like "Nip, Sip." Compared with Eddie Fisher or Perry Como, of course, these groups still sounded freaky. But, unlike T-Bone Walker or Illinois Jacquet, they represented no real danger. The white girl from Scarsdale was safe.

Just as young blacks were anxious to seem chic, young whites were eager to seem a little more daring than their parents. In 1953, a gospel-based group recording for a small independent label answered both needs. With Sonny Til singing tenor, the Orioles had their biggest hit, "Crying in the Chapel." The song was borrowed from country music; its sentiments were purest Tin Pan Alley. But the group was black and so was their style. Others who had been successful in the white pop charts, including the Mills Brothers, Nat "King" Cole, and the Ink Spots, had masked their blackness and offered easy listening. "Crying in the Chapel" abandoned subterfuge. For all its smoothness, the sound was unmistakably tough and black. By all the accepted rules of the white record market, the song should have made no waves. But it sold over a million copies. Young whites were hooked.

For a while, the major record companies lacked the nerve (or the inclination) to sign up and promote original black artists, and instead, packaged a dreary succession of white imitations. Jerry Wexler, whose Atlantic Records was still small but growing, says: "Many black artists were disgusted at the way the music they had originated was merchandised by the major companies. Some of us felt the same. We had a good, albeit parochial, sale with our real rhythm and blues, but the bigger companies would get a

vast sale simply by copying our material with white artists. The word is 'cover,' but the truth is that they were copying our songs. They would get a Patti Page or the Fontaines and take a song from our Ivory Joe Hunter or Ruth Brown, record it with a white studio band, and rush around to a white radio station and immediately put it on the air. Their sales would be huge. We were restricted, meanwhile, to the black radio stations because white stations wouldn't play a black record. They'd say to us: 'Bring us a white cover.' But, of course, we didn't have any white artists."

The white record market tried to disinfect the music. The lyrics were cleaned up and the beat toned down. "Roll With Me, Henry," became "Dance With Me, Henry" in its cover version. But white youth wanted more. Most white music was aimed at their parents: crooners, big bands, romantic ballads, the occasional novelty songs. As time passed, new names would

The blues become gospel. *Top left:* one of the many small clubs that still flourish on the West and South Sides of Chicago. In places like these, the first hint of gospel was heard through the raucous noise of urban blues. But it needed white record executives like Jerry Wexler *(above)* to develop what was essentially a black sound. Wexler's Atlantic Records established its reputation by recording urban bluesmen in the 1950s, but the sound was more immediately exploited by black groups themselves such as the Miracles *(center left)* and the Platters *(bottom left).*

emerge—Perry Como, Eddie Fisher, Dean Martin, Vic Damone—but none was much different from Bing Crosby, and he was prewar. Only one gave a hint of the pandemonium just around the corner: the Million Dollar Teardrop, the self-styled Nabob of Sob, Johnnie Ray.

A frail and tormented youth from rural Oregon, he said he had been tossed out of a blanket at ten onto his skull. This had turned him from a sunny, gregarious youth into a solitary introvert, racked with psychic twitches. The accident had also left him nearly deaf. To revive his spirit, Ray took up singing. But the strain of performing seemed to tax him beyond his emotional limit: every time he appeared on stage, he ended up in tears.

If it was a gimmick, it worked. People flocked to see if the teardrops were real. With hearing aid dangling, Ray staggered and gasped, choked on his words, and beat his chest; he fell forward on his knees, appeared to strangle himself with

passion, and wept—until the audience was satisfied. That is what his public required, he says today, so that is what he did.

His audience was female: housewives, matrons, schoolgirls. His material consisted mostly of conventional droopy ballads. But, with more than a squint at the pampered gigolos of rhythm and blues, he revived the concept of performance. To the white audience he introduced excess. His act had all the swagger of rhythm and blues, but none of its driving musical ambitions. Although clumsy and tuneless by comparison, it was purest gospel in format. His commercial success dispelled the music industry's fear that its public would faint away at any hint of indelicacy. Ray earned a fortune proving them wrong: he was screamed at and mobbed and had his clothes ripped from him. All, as he admits, without a voice: "I've got no talent, still sing flat as a table. I'm a sort of human spaniel. People come to see what I'm

like. I make them feel, I exhaust them, I destroy them.

"I didn't want to be a singer," Ray told me. "I wanted to be an actor, and the only way I could stay in touch with the business was by bluffing. Which is what I'm still doing, twenty years later." The story of his biggest hit? "A lot of people get confused because they think I wrote 'Cry,' but I didn't. It was written by a black man by the name of Churchill Coleman, who was a songwriter from Pittsburgh, Pennsylvania. The way I recorded it and the way people heard it on stage, however, was not the way he wrote it. We improvised in the studio when we first recorded it, and the results were not what he had had in mind."

At the time, of course, Coleman kept his mouth shut. He needed the money. But, try as it might, the industry could not fend off the inevitable. As early as 1952, Cleveland disc jockey Alan Freed saw that imitations only increased a hunger for the real thing. In a downtown record store, he watched a crowd of white teenagers dancing wildly to black records. He realized that something new and powerful was brewing and began to feature rhythm and blues songs on his radio shows. But he carefully avoided describing the sound as rhythm and blues, which had become as much of a signal as "race music" had been. Instead, he called it rock and roll.

Freed's progress was astonishing. Within

Left: in the early sixties, the Supremes—formerly the Primettes—established Berry Gordy and Motown. From right to left, Diana Ross, Mary Wilson (still performing as a Supreme, but with two different partners), and Cindy Birdsong, who replaced the third original Supreme, Florence Ballard, after a dispute in 1967. Ballard died, destitute, in Detroit in 1975. This photograph was released shortly before Diana Ross became a solo performer. Their first ten records were failures; their next twelve, Number One hits. *Top right:* Aretha Franklin, daughter of a leading Detroit minister, was discovered by John Hammond and nurtured by Jerry Wexler. She made a succession of gospel-influenced rhythm and blues records during the early sixties, but moved toward her own version of gospel in the seventies. She told me: "The church, without a doubt, has been and still is my route. Some of the finest people in the entertaining business have come out of the church." *Bottom right:* Lightnin' Hopkins, born in Texas, 1912, a private but ubiquitous eminence of blues for forty years.

weeks of instituting his new format, he became the top DJ in Cleveland. Then he was bought up by WINS, one of the larger New York stations, where his audience figures soon outdistanced those of all competitors. Even though the performers were black, the great majority of the audience was white. The atmosphere at live shows he produced was, by his description, delirious. At one — in an outdoor stadium where the crowd topped thirty thousand — rioting broke out and the police made a charge. Rock and roll was on its way.

Rock and roll was a unique catch phrase, the most exciting password white youth had yet found. But the music itself lacked form and identity. Above all, it lacked a white leader. A small, independent record company called Essex (hitherto obscure) discovered a former country singer (even more obscure) who had dabbled in rhythm and blues. Bill Haley made a record for Essex and called it "Crazy Man Crazy."

Haley was a clod. By any black standard, he was amateurish and febrile. To the white world, however, he was a bombshell. Nothing so frenzied, so juvenile, or so shameless had ever been unleashed. To the young, he was a call to arms.

Top left: Johnnie Ray, heavily influenced by gospel and, in his heyday, anything but private. *Above:* two faces of James Brown, gospel singer and rocker. *Bottom left:* Paul Butterfield, born in Chicago in 1941, one of the few white blues players to enjoy the consistent approval of black performers. *Facing page, top left:* Sam Cooke began with the gospel group, the Soul Stirrers, and became one of the first black singers to succeed with a white rock and roll audience. He was shot to death in a Los Angeles motel in 1964. *Top center:* Illinois Jacquet, who progressed from blues performances in Kansas City through swing with Count Basie and Lionel Hampton to modern jazz during the 1960s. *Bottom left:* McKinley Morganfield Waters, born in Rolling

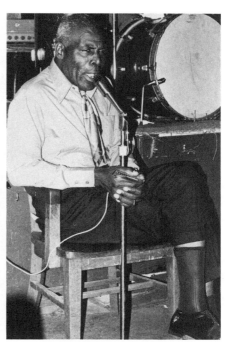

Fork, Mississippi, 1915. Muddy Waters says: "All my life I was having trouble with women . . . I've done a lot of writing about women. Then, after I quit having trouble with them, I could feel in my heart that somebody would always have trouble with them, so I kept writing those blues." One man who was always having trouble was Chester Arthur Burnett *(top right)*, born in Aberdeen, Mississippi, 1910, shown here shortly before he died, but still unmistakably Howlin' Wolf. Until his death "the Wolf" maintained his connections with the Mississippi farmland, where he spent the first forty years of his life, and with the west side of Chicago, which he later made his home. More than anyone else, Howlin' Wolf preserved the feeling of the blues for half a century. *Bottom right:* Bo Diddley, born in McComb, Mississippi, 1928, a juvenile violinist from the South Side of Chicago who became a rock star by way of the blues. "I didn't see no black violinist is why I stopped playing it, but it gave me an edge on some of the others." Of his young days playing guitar on Chicago street corners, Bo told me: "If you couldn't play like Muddy Waters, you couldn't get no gig, because Muddy had got Chicago sewn up." Bo Diddley, who lives near Albuquerque, New Mexico, said: "I'm here now because I stayed home most of the time then."

And they bought him, straight up the charts. The major recording companies were forced to give ground. In 1954 Decca bought out Haley's contract from Essex and let him record two songs: "Shake, Rattle, and Roll" and "Rock Around the Clock." Both stank of sweat and sex. Cleanliness seemed a lost cause.

Judged as rhythm and blues, the results were wretched. "Shake, Rattle, and Roll" was already a hit for black Joe Turner, who had set its action in bed. Haley moved it into the kitchen, steadied the beat, and drained the lyrics. But, compared to Rosemary Clooney or Teresa Brewer (his immediate competitors for the white market), Haley was the roughest of the rough. Youth decided he was their Deliverer, and mobbed him wherever he went. Within a year, Bill Haley and His Comets had sold almost five million records. The moral was inescapable: if performers like Haley or Johnnie Ray could create such a stir, what would happen if someone less inhibited emerged?

Perhaps it was no accident that Memphis, which earlier had given purpose and direction to the blues, should now figure so prominently in the triumph of rhythm and blues. During the late forties, a discerning control engineer called Sam Phillips had been recording big bands in a local hotel, the Peabody. He had found the work, and the music, boring. "They were great

Bill Haley moved Joe Turner's hit into the kitchen, steadied the beat, drained the lyrics.

in a way," he says. "But I didn't see too much creativity in them. I had been born and raised on a farm in the South, in Alabama, and I had lived closely with the black man and his music. I was never a musician myself, but I always had a great interest in their music. I enjoyed their rhythms, their abandon, and their love of life as expressed in their songs. I decided to open a small recording studio here in Memphis. I knew that some black musicians went to New York or Chicago, but most couldn't afford to get that far and there was no place locally for them to record their sound. I opened up at 706 Union Avenue. Pretty soon, the word got round that a black man, or a white man, could go there to be recorded and not get ripped off.

"It wasn't long before B. B. King, Roscoe Gordon, Rufus Thomas, and others like them were in the studio. Then the word spread further and musicians began to come from Mississippi and Arkansas, musicians like Howlin' Wolf, Jackie Brenston, and Ike Turner. As I recorded them, I leased out the masters to various independent record companies and got some enthusiastic responses. But I was not really satisfied. I was convinced that there was more to be done.

"You see, I had heard this sound—in my head and in my heart—and I was determined that others should hear it, too. I hate imitations. But, having grown up in close proximity to the black man, I thoroughly believed that a white man, a Southern white man, could approximate the same sound and feeling. There was still a lot of hatred between the races in the South, but music was the one area where black and white were closer than people realized. The young whites loved the black music they got to hear. So I felt that if only I could find a white artist who could put the same feel, the same touch and spontaneity into his songs, who could find this total abandon of the black artists in himself, then I would have the opportunity, the means by which to give others the sound I had heard."

And in walked Elvis Presley.

Top left: blind from the age of seven, a fan of boogie-woogie, the Grand Ole Opry, Nat King Cole, Big Boy Crudup, Big Joe Turner, and the ever-present Muddy Waters; later influenced by Billy Eckstine and Dizzy Gillespie: from this mélange came Ray Charles, who can say with no offense, "I never wanted to be what we call famous, but I've always wanted to be great." *Top right:* at the 1969 Ann Arbor Blues Festival, left to right: B. B. King; Big Mama Willie Mae Thornton (in hat), original performer of the Leiber and Stoller song "Hound Dog"; Junior Wells; Roosevelt Sykes. *Bottom right:* Junior Wells, B. B. King, Bobby Bland, and Buddy Guy. A curiosity of the blues scene is that such performers play night after night to audiences of casual blacks plus a few enthusiastic whites in the dingy clubs of Chicago; the next evening might find them, as here, in New York's Avery Fisher Hall. Their tours of Japan, Europe, or Africa fill football stadiums.

10
Making Moonshine

Elvis Aaron Presley was, by his own description, a country "Southern gentleman." He was born in 1935 near Tupelo, Mississippi, a shantytown sixty miles southeast of Memphis. His parents were a popular local gospel duo. But when he launched himself on a career of unprecedented vulgarity, Elvis billed himself as the "Hilly Billy Cat." "Ain't nothing but a houn' dog . . ."

The hillbilly music he copied was broadcast by a growing number of powerful radio stations that had opened up throughout the South in the twenties and thirties. The nearest country station was just over a hundred miles to the northwest, in Nashville, Tennessee. In the early thirties, annual radio sales throughout the United States totaled almost one billion dollars. Admittedly,

Two Rockingham County, North Carolina, entertainers, c.1860.

the smallest percentage of radio ownership was in the South, where a large low-income population reduced the average. But by the year of Presley's birth, every third home in the country owned a radio.

From the first, regional musicians had been firm favorites with the listeners; WBAP in Fort Worth, for instance, had featured an hour and a half of square-dance music on its opening night, directed by an old-time fiddler and Confederate veteran, Captain M. J. Bonner. The program had caused an extraordinary audience response; the station was inundated with phone calls, mail, and telegrams demanding more. Less than three years later, WSM, operating out of Nashville, had followed a similar course. And on November 28, 1925, after a genteel network show entitled *Musical Appreciation Hour,* WSM station director George D. Hay announced: "You've just been listening to a program of Grand Opry Music. And now, you're going to hear some Grand *Ole* Opry music." Then an eighty-year-old fiddler,

Uncle Jimmy Thompson, and his niece, piano player Mrs. Eva Thompson Jones, performed in front of a second-hand carbon microphone for over an hour. Hay asked if the old fiddler was getting tired. "Why shucks," Thompson replied, "a man don't get warmed up in an hour. I just won an eight-day fiddling contest down in Dallas, Texas, and here's my blue ribbon to prove it." He claimed to know a thousand tunes, and seemed determined to play them all. Before radio, no one outside the

rural areas of its origin knew that music like this existed. And very few comprehended the extent of its survival.

"Survival" is perhaps the appropriate word when one considers what happened to every other form of America's music. In the South, where life itself was a perpetual struggle, innovation was avoided and outsiders despised. Only the family, the church, and the village community provided strength and hope. While the North had become increasingly obsessed with progress and modernity, the South had remained defiantly, unshakably archaic. Its music had been preserved and cherished long after it had been forgotten elsewhere. The old hymns, reels, and ballads had been handed down through generations, as though inscribed on tablets. George Hay recalled that within weeks of Uncle Jimmy Thompson's debut, "we were beseiged with other fiddlers, banjo pickers,

Above, top: country hoedown in Denison, Texas, at the turn of the century. *Above:* fiddlin', country-style. *Right:* the Original Carter Family. Alvin Pleasant Carter, his wife, Sara, autoharp, and his sister-in-law, Maybelle, guitar. Sara and A.P. were married in June 1915; they divorced in 1936, but continued performing together until the early 1940s. Maybelle became known as Mother Maybelle and organized, with her daughters, a second generation of performing Carters. June Carter married Johnny Cash, and now works as part of the Johnny Cash Road Show.

guitar players, and a lady who played an old zither.''

The earliest white settlers on the East Coast of America had entertained themselves with the songs they brought from England, Scotland,

Wales, and Ireland. Later, traveling south and west, they had discovered the remote valleys and tree-clad hills of the Appalachians and the Ozarks. Reminded of home, they stopped in west Kentucky and Tennessee, and in northeast Arkansas. For generations, little disturbed them. There were no roads, just rough wagon trails and difficult rivers. In Stone County, Arkansas, there were no paved roads until the fifties. Whole communities were shut off. And the songs they performed were those their fathers and forefathers had sung.

When the hill settlers gathered of an evening to share a little music, they did not repeat the old British ballads word for word. They adapted

The first and most famous. Eck Robertson (*upper left*) born in Amarillo, Texas, in the 1880s, was among the first singers to perform in full western costume; almost certainly, he was the first to record. Later, he won a fiddlers' contest in Idaho in 1962. *Right:* Jimmie Rodgers (shown with Will Rogers). *Lower left:* Rodgers with the Carter Family. Even though the Carters made their first records for Ralph Peer on the same weekend as Rodgers in August 1927, there is no evidence that they met. Certainly, Rodgers' life-style was scarcely compatible with the Carters' respectable image.

them to tell of the old pioneer days in America, often forgetting where the songs had originated. Jean Ritchie, who has spent a lifetime studying the dulcimer and collecting old songs in the southern Appalachians where she was born, says: "Not too many years ago, I was playing 'Barbara Allen,' one of the earliest British ballads. An old man who came from the next county was listening and said to me: 'Well, I knew those folks in your song. They lived right over the hill from me.'" Local names were substituted for the original names in the ballads; the songs took on a new life; the music became as American as its settlers.

The instruments were primitive, sometimes no more than approximations of instruments left behind in the old country. The dulcimer, quite unlike its medieval counterpart of the same name, was merely a box with strings tuned to resemble the drone of a bagpipe. The single-stringed bow, placed against the performer's mouth as a sounding box with the string plucked by a feather, was still common in the Smoky Mountains at the end of the nineteenth century. The banjo—often simply hide stretched over a gourd, with horsehair for strings—and the fiddle completed the family; the guitar was almost unknown. The fiddle provided melody and rhythm, one player beating on the fiddle strings with sticks as another sawed away with the bow. The tuning was equally straightforward, again an approximation to the sound of bagpipes, although various methods of tuning helped preserve the isolation. In Oklahoma Territory, for instance, a minor-key tuning known as Cherokee was popular among fiddlers. If these same fiddlers traveled to the Ozarks, however, no one could play with them; there, the tuning was different.

The content of the songs matched the lives of the singers, wherein self-sufficiency was a necessity and death the only certainty. In the conclusion to his authoritative survey of commercial country music, (Country Music, U.S.A.) Bill C. Malone writes that in order to preserve the varying styles that are today called country music, "One must also preserve the culture that gave rise to them, a society characterized by cul-

tural isolation, racism, poverty, ignorance and religious fundamentalism." "Cousin" Minnie Pearl, otherwise Sarah Ophelia Colley Cannon and a star comedienne of the Grand Ole Opry for thirty-five years, told me: "Country music deals with everyday problems that most people can identify with. Some of it is about beer halls and broken homes and divorces, some of it about ordinary, everyday occurrences. When people hear that music, they get a feeling that they belong to the music and the music belongs to them."

Music in the hills was a community affair— front porch gatherings, dances, and picnics— and until the Civil War the community was private. Then, into this society swaggered the medicine show, the greatest, most exciting entertainment that rural America had ever known. From 1870 until World War I, every village and hamlet of rural America was visited by quacks touting miracle cures for everything from bunions to impotence. Between the sales talk, they offered variety acts from freaks to black-faced minstrels. Music was a sure way to draw a crowd, so they hired musicians.

Being paid to make music was particularly appealing to the hill farmers, and before long, musicians from the countryside were swarming all over the towns. They discovered that politicians would pay to liven up political rallies, society gatherings needed music for dancing, and that playing on the sidewalks after a Saturday night get-together could be profitable. The music lacked a name; it was just music— Southern, white, and rural. Its performer, according to a writer for the *New York Journal* in 1900, was a "free and untrammelled white citizen. . . . A hillbilly . . . who has no means to speak of, dresses as he can, talks as he pleases, drinks whisky when he gets it and fires off his revolver as the fancy takes him."

Tainted by city life, the music embraced heartache and worship, blood and lust, love and revenge—all seen through a tearful mist, a memory of the faithful dog waiting at the homestead gate with a comely, grieving mother at the supper table. Faithful to its past, the music bore witness to sin confessed, drunkenness cured,

morality upheld, penance exacted. Death—usually early and undeserved—awaited. It was as homemade and potent a mixture as the moonshine whisky that lubricated it.

Radio also broke down rural isolation. Like their predecessors, the medicine men, the advertisers who bought air time called on the musicians from the hills to fill the space between commercials. Thus, the hundreds of local radio stations set up all over the Southern states in the twenties and thirties brought the hillbilly musicians into contact with an audience outside their immediate neighborhoods. They were paid little, and were hired and fired indiscriminately. But a radio job brought a following, and performers like fiddler Eck Robertson from Texas, banjo player Charlie Poole from North Carolina, and the Skillet Lickers group from Georgia built up steady reputations in the South. Eck Robertson, with characteristic nerve, made the very first hillbilly recording by the simple expedient of traveling to New York, marching into the Victor Talking Machine Company's offices, and demanding to cut a record. His version of "Arkansas Traveller" sold a few copies, and that was that. It was not until Ralph Peer, a talent scout for OKeh Records who had earlier recorded blues singer Mamie Smith, was persuaded to venture into Atlanta that the business of recording white rural music really began.

Fiddlin' John Carson, already past fifty, was the man chosen in June 1923 for this experiment. A house painter by day and a moonshiner by night, Carson performed two of his songs in a rented loft on Atlanta's Nassau Street for a shocked Peer, who described Carson's voice as "pluperfect awful." Appalled as well by the simple-mindedness of Carson's songs ("The Little Old Log Cabin in the Lane" and "The Old Hen Cackled and the Rooster's Gonna Crow"), the man from the North could not bring himself to give them a catalogue number. He refused to allow the five hundred copies that were manufactured to be circulated outside the immediate vicinity of Atlanta. Within a month, however, Peer had to make another five hundred. By the end of the year, the record had sold so many copies that Carson was rushed to New York to get his signature on a contract. "Looks like I'll have to quit making moonshine," Carson said at the time, "and start making records."

Thereafter, the pattern was familiar. The major companies would roam the South, rounding up every musician they could find. Recordings were ad hoc, and since the Northern talent scouts and engineers had no idea what they were recording—and didn't like it anyway—they would record anybody who turned up with a banjo or a fiddle in his hand. The results were mostly crass, but modest sales were achieved in the South and that was sufficient. North of the Mason-Dixon Line, the music was still considered illiterate and uncouth. It even lacked a name until, one day, a motley string band (led by Al Hopkins) was recording for Ralph Peer. They had straggled up from North Carolina and Virginia to the OKeh studios in New York, hop-

The Solemn Old Judge, his performers, his audience, and a former Opry home. *Top left:* when "Judge" George Dewey Hay was a reporter in Memphis, he scooped the world reporting the death of President Harding in 1923. The next year he moved to Chicago as chief announcer for WLS, where he started a show called the *Barn Dance.* Soon, *Radio Digest* pronounced him the top U.S. announcer. Nashville called with a new 1000-watt station, WSM, where Hay was made director and instituted another *Barn Dance*, which soon became the Grand Ole Opry. *Top center:* Opry comedienne Minnie Pearl whooping it up with Roy Acuff, the man who has made the aggrandisement of the Opry his life work. Acuff was prevented by sunstroke susceptibility from signing a contract with the New York Giants. With the Rose family, he has become principal architect of the Nashville/Opry supremacy in commercial country music. *Top right:* an early Opry program. *Center left:* Uncle Dave Macon of Smart Station, Tennessee, with his son Dorris. Macon was a country boy, but his father's Nashville hotel edged him toward entertainment. When he wasn't performing solo or with his son, he fronted the Fruit Jar Drinkers' Band. *Bottom:* the Audience. A Texan farmer and his wife riveted by radio in the mid-1930s. *Center:* the Ryman Auditorium, the longest surviving (1941–1972) of the Grand Ole Opry's homes, which have also included various studios at WSM, the Hillsboro Theatre, the War Memorial Building, and the East Nashville Tabernacle. The present home, a glass and concrete palace, nestles in Opryland U.S.A., an amusement park just outside Nashville.

ing to make their fortunes. When the session was over, Peer asked the group's name: "Call us anything," Hopkins is said to have told him. "We're nothing but a bunch of hillbillies anyway." So Peer, the careful businessman, wrote them down as "The Hill Billies."

Among the rubbish, there were a few excellent recordings. Some of the more talented hillbilly artists chose to record traditional songs rather than compositions of their own; "Barbara Allen," "Cumberland Gap," and assorted British ballads appeared time and again, always sentimentalized and always smeared with godliness. A failing popular singer called Vernon Dalhart sketched out the shape of things to come. To begin with, his name was not Vernon Dalhart. Those were the names of two towns from his native state of Texas; he had adopted them for his career as an operetta tenor in New York before World War I. His real name was Marion Try Slaughter, although he had already recorded under a range of pseudonyms. Coming

Above: the Washboard Wonders, November 1936, and an extreme sampling of country music instruments. *Right:* from *Radio Digest,* 1926, showing the group who created the name Hill Billies.

from Jefferson, Texas, he did not have the qualifications to style himself a hillbilly. But he persuaded Victor to let him re-record two old ballads cut earlier by Henry Whitter, one a standard called "The Wreck of the Old 97"—a tale of death on the Southern Railway—the other a sad story entitled "The Prisoner's Song"—written, he insisted, by his cousin (it was untrue) with new music by a Victor executive. It included the immortal lines: "If I had the wings of an angel/over these prison walls I would fly."

The sales were beyond anyone's imagination. Dalhart gave Victor its greatest wax recording triumph so far; almost six million copies were issued within two years. He stuck to his name and now only recorded "hillbilly" songs. By the end of the twenties, Dalhart was the best known and most successful of the new hillbillies. But whereas the genuine country artists glorified their hickness, giving themselves names like the Hoss-Hair Pullers, the Cornshuckers, and the Tar Heels, pseudo-hillbilly singers such as Dalhart recognized that if professional techniques were applied to hillbilly music, a fortune was in the offing. Dalhart was bland, slick, and self-conscious. Like countless stars who followed him, he saw his audience from a distance and made a killing. To affect countryness and wheedle the dollars from a naïve and God-fearing hill folk, he roughened his voice, learned how to sing through his nose, and produced a sob that went straight to the hearts of millions.

With the success of "The Prisoner's Song," disaster became a prerequisite for success. Song writers invented train wrecks, exploding coal mines, collapsing mothers, and murdered infants. Amid the carnage, God peered down, beneficent but impassive, beckoning the sufferers to a better world. The market place was inundated with Death.

And then came the Depression. Record sales slipped. Radio, by now widespread, assumed even greater importance. As William Ivey, director of the Country Music Foundation, asserts: "It was very important for a budding country artist to establish his career by using radio. If he could get on a radio show, it meant

"Hill Billies" Capture WRC

Boys from Blue Ridge Mountains Take Washington With Guitars, Fiddles and Banjos; Open New Line of American Airs

MODERN improvements make slow progress in the hill country of the South. During the World war it was discovered that some of the more remote communities were living much as they did a century ago.

But Radio has taken hold of the primitive inhabitants with amazing alacrity. It's effect on the development of their education and communication with the outer world promises benefits untold. They are learning a new language. They are discovering America as it is today. To some who were born and have grown old within a few miles of the homes of their fathers it is a revelation. They scarcely associate it as being in reality a part of their own world. They do not all have receiving sets but there is one in the general store and they come from far and near to hear the concerts. The storekeeper in many instances has made it possible for individual families to own their own receiving sets.

A few weeks ago Radio Station WRC at Washington, D. C., broadcast a concert by an organization called "The Hill Billies." The response was astounding.

Letters and post cards arrived from the mountains of Tennessee, from the hills of Kentucky and the Carolinas and the Blue Ridge counties of Maryland and Virginia. Phone calls, local and long distance, demanded favorite numbers, and repeats, and what not.

* * *

A VOICE with a distinct Georgia drawl asked that they play "Long Eared Mule," and added the significant remark: "You-all caint fool me, ah know where them boys come from. They's Hill Billies for suah. They ain't nobody kin play that music 'thout they is bawn in the hills and brung up thar."

And he was right. The Hill Billies are really boys from the ranges that skirt the east coast states. They are six keen-eyed, ruddy-cheeked youths who have captured the

rhythms of the hills, and who, with fiddles and other stringed instruments, present the classics of the country entertainments.

There isn't a bar of jazz in the Hill Billy music. There isn't a note of weird modern harmony or anti-harmony, nor is there a single skip-stop syncopation. And yet the Hill Billy music, with its "Sally-Ann" rhythm and its "Cinday" swing, starts feet to tapping unrestrainedly and unashamed. It is the folk music of America, to which the backwoods youth and the farmer boys "hoe it down" on rough-plank dance floors.

The Hopkins boys, the nucleus of the organization, form a vocal quartet, which, although of debatable value as to timbre of voices and blending of tone, is of indisputable predominance in volume and exactness of harmony. All four are natural baritones, but somebody has to sing tenor and somebody has to growl bass, and that's that. Joe Hopkins, now first tenor, until recently sang deep bass, but had to change because Elmer, who had been first tenor, contracted a cold and couldn't carry higher than baritone. When they "cut loose," as they say, one is reminded of their native habitat, and feels that "the strength of the hills is theirs also." WRC experimented with transmission for some time, and finally decided that the only way to keep them from "blasting" the microphone was to put them outdoors and hide the mike in a closet.

* * *

THOSE Hopkins boys, Al, Elmer, John and Joe, come from down Ash county way in No'th Ca'lina. For several years they have been "tank-towning" the South, playing for church and fraternal entertainments and dances, with Elvis Alderman (of Carroll county, Vi'ginia, suh) fiddling along with them. Carroll, if you must know, is the county in which the famous Allen gang, feudists extraordinary, lives and has its being, and takes occasional pot-shots at unsociable neighbors.

Below is the famous gang of Hill Billies who took nation's capital by storm. They are, from the left: A. E. Alderman of Carroll county, Virginia; Al, John and Joe Hopkins of "No'th Ca'lina," and "Fox-Hunt" Charlie Bowman of Tennessee. Every one of 'em from the "mountings" and born with the lingo.

Behold here a real Hill Billy, "Fox-Hunt" Charlie Bowman (above) who lives in a log cabin back in the hills ten miles from Mountain City, Tenn. Charlie came to town for a fiddlers' contest and the Hopkins boys from North Carolina were so pleased with his performance they induced him to join the Hill Billies gang.

he could promote his next personal appearance every week and promote any record he might have made. Live radio was vital." The successful radio shows brought comfort—and hope. They sought to re-create the happiness of the old mountain communities, and, in particular, the Saturday night square dance beloved of village life. The first to make any impact in the twenties had been the WLS *National Barn Dance* broadcast from Chicago, sponsored by what was then the World's Largest Store, Sears, Roebuck & Co. The *National Barn Dance* was used to promote artists published by and contracted to Sears, which sold records along with household goods. It broadcast comedians, mimics, Hawaiian groups with their twangy guitars, country dance callers, fiddlers, and any other appropriately bucolic entertainment, including hillbilly singers—among them Bradley Kincaid, the "Kentucky Mountain Boy" with his "Houn' Dog" guitar.

Its first announcer was George Dewey Hay, previously a news reporter on a local paper. Visiting a country hoedown, the idea had occurred to him of producing the same mixture for radio. Having instituted the *Barn Dance*, he was soon tempted away to Nashville where he styled himself the Solemn Old Judge. "He was a wonderful gentleman," Ernest Tubb, one of the Opry's biggest stars, remembers, "and we all loved him very much. We miss him still. He'd come out and blow an old steamboat whistle and yell out: 'Let her go boys, let her go!' " Minnie Pearl has similar memories. "He used to say that he built the Opry on brotherly love," she says. "The first night I went on, I was frightened and nervous and he said: 'Don't worry. Just love 'em, and they'll love you right back.' "

The Opry was no different in format from its rivals—the Louisiana Hay Ride from Shreveport and, later, the Big D Jamboree from Dallas and the Town Hall Party from Los Angeles—but the Opry took itself more seriously. George Hay made it clear that nothing new was acceptable until it had received the Opry's imprimatur. Yet the Opry's popular success was mostly due to the performer who dominated the show for the first fifteen years of its existence, Uncle Dave Macon. The owner-operator of a mighty haulage company—the Macon Midway Mule and Wagon Transportation Company in Readyville, Tennessee—he was an absolute natural as an entertainer. Before the Opry, he played with his son Dorris for free at local dances; he was said to have been surprised when his joking demand for fifteen dollars after a party performance was paid on the spot. His appearance was striking. He was fat and whiskery, often wore a black suit complete with loud tie, high wing collar, and black felt hat. He could have been a hillbilly dressed in his Sunday best, or a country preacher on his day off. He always carried a small black bag in which there was (he said) a Bible and a pint of Jack Daniel's.

Macon did not join the Opry until he was fifty-six, but proceeded to play there with all the gusto that had characterized his private shows. On occasion, he had to be restrained from doing his whole show for fellow hotel guests lest they get free what they had already bought tickets for. A Hollywood record producer in the thirties, sent to Nashville for a view of this phenomenon, said: "I've never met a more natural man in my life. He prays at the right time and cusses at the right time and his jokes are as cute as the dickens. He kicks up his heels, roars like a branded steer, and they call him the Dixie Dewdrop."

There were some who viewed the Opry (correctly, so it turned out) as intent on nothing but the commercialization of a relatively pure Anglo-Saxon folk song tradition, represented most influentially by the Carter Family. They never appeared on the Opry, although they did perform later on some of the powerful Mexican border stations. They, too, prayed at the right time; some said they prayed all the time. Certainly, their music smelled of gospel. They were of the strictest Christian upbringing, from Poor Valley, Virginia. Their family had lived in the same spot since the eighteenth century. Alvin Pleasant (A.P.) Carter, his wife Sara, and his sister-in-law Maybelle Addington Carter were all accomplished instrumentalists. They did much to preserve traditional songs throughout the "golden age" of hillbilly music (between the birth of the Grand Ole Opry and World War II) and became a rallying point for purity. They were devout, stern, noble, and the epitome of Southern propriety. They were also sober, unrelievedly worthy—and cunning.

For years, they had performed at church socials and schoolhouses before anyone bothered to record them. A.P., who sported dignified waistcoats, sang bass. (His father had considered the fiddle a "devil's instrument.") Sara played the autoharp and sang lead. Musically, the real talent was Maybelle, whose complex melodic style gave the group its distinctive sound and helped promote the guitar as hillbilly's dominant instrument. They rarely toured far from home, especially after Ralph Peer, now working for the Victor Talking Machine Company, had introduced them to the ease of recording on August 1, 1927, in Bristol, on the Tennessee–Virginia border. According to Sara, they cut over three hundred songs during the next ten years and were among the first to use the new electrical processes by which sound reproduction was considerably improved. A.P. was also among the first to secure copyrights for his music. He copyrighted "Wabash Cannonball," which he did not write; "I'll Be All Smiles Tonight," which he did not write;

After Jimmie Rodgers, the city and its pursuit of money and thrills became an essential part of the music.

"Wildwood Flower," which he took from a nineteenth-century parlor tune called "The Pale Amaranthus," plus several other traditional melodies. Hitherto in the public domain, these songs were now owned—and, admittedly, perpetuated—by A. P. Carter. Folk singers such as Huddie (Leadbelly) Ledbetter and Woody Guthrie acknowledged their debt to a group that preserved for a while what might otherwise have been lost.

The same weekend that the Carter Family performed for Ralph Peer, an erstwhile blackface entertainer and city detective made his way to Bristol in response to Peer's advertisement for talent. The group of musicians with whom he had been working arrived before him, decided they would audition on their own, and went on to make a modest success as the Tenneva Ramblers; the twenty-nine-year-old Jim-

Left: Hank Snow, born in Nova Scotia, Canada, 1914, proved that country music was not an exclusive preserve of the southern states of the U.S.A. *Right:* the Monroe Brothers in 1936. Bill (right) and Charlie (left) played together from the mid-1920s until after World War II, when Charlie retired to his farm in Kentucky. Amid conflicting claims about the origins of "Bluegrass," there is general agreement that Bill Monroe has done most to perpetuate not only the style but the principle. He can also lay claim to the invention of the name (related to the bluegrass of his home state).

mie Rodgers was forced to sing on his own in an abandoned warehouse. The resulting record brought him a royalty check for twenty dollars.

Victor thought Rodgers worth recording again, however, and invited him to Camden, New Jersey, near the end of the year. He took with him one of his own songs, "T for Texas." In form, it resembled the blues; in style, it was not dissimilar from most hillbilly music. But at the end of its third line, Rodgers raised his voice to a higher octave and began to yodel. The sound was to make him the most renowned hillbilly star of his generation.

Ernest Tubb told me: "I just wanted to sing like Jimmie Rodgers. He was my idol. He was Hank Snow's idol and Bob Wills' idol. In fact, if you checked with most country singers of the past forty-five years or so, I'd say eighty percent of them were inspired directly or indirectly by Jimmie Rodgers." It may sound like an extravagant claim for a man whose career lasted less than six years, who—apart from his yodel—had a dreary voice and poor guitar technique. But Rodgers transformed hillbilly music from a rural, despised, quasi-folk entertainment into what it is today. He refused to join in the

Left: Jimmy Driftwood, born 1907, singer, fiddler, guitarist, banjoist, leaf-and-bow player, and folklorist, drives an ox-cart of rural musicians including, second from right, Bookmiller Shannon, one of Arkansas' finest banjoists. Driftwood (real name Morris) is best known for his song "Battle of New Orleans," but his achievement has been the preservation of rural music of early American settlers. *Right:* Roy Acuff (second from right) in his earliest days at WSM.

charade that the South was as pure and righteous as before. The traditions of homestead, village, and chapel existed mostly as memory, while the real world went on in bars and flophouses, down by the railroad tracks, outside the factory gates. After Jimmie Rodgers, the city and its pursuit of money and thrills became an essential part of the music.

Although his influence was colossal, Rodgers' life was vile—a saga of trauma, sickness, betrayal, and loss. He was born in 1897, in Meridian, Mississippi. His father worked on the railroad; his mother died while he was still an infant. Throughout his childhood, he was shunted from one set of relatives to another, too sickly for school. When he reached fourteen, he followed his father into the railroads and became a brakeman.

He was frequently too ill for train work, so he learned the banjo and guitar to make extra money playing at dances. In 1920, he got married. Within days he collapsed with double pneumonia. A few years later, having fathered a couple of daughters, he found a brakeman's wage insufficient to feed his family. So in 1924 he blacked his face and joined a medicine show, picking his banjo through Kentucky and Tennessee. But when Christmas came, he was broke. He pawned his banjo to raise the fare back home—in time for his younger daughter's funeral.

Again he collapsed, now with tuberculosis. He spent three months in a sanitarium, and when he recovered, left home and formed a dance trio—working at schoolhouses, beer joints, roadhouses, barns, anywhere they would take him. He threw away his money before he'd earned it, and was always being conned or stranded. He was a hustler's dream. He played "the sticks, the tanks, the jerk-waters, the turkeys," slept rough, jumped the freight trains, and lived like a hobo. His lungs got worse. He was thrown into jail for vagrancy.

His meeting with Ralph Peer changed little, except that after recording "T for Texas" he was soon earning two thousand dollars a month. Yet he was often broke and in debt, always being conned. He did pop songs and cowboy songs, watered-down blues, hobo and railroad ballads; was backed by country fiddlers, Hawaiian guitarists, ukuleles and musical saws, Palm Court strings, whistlers, on one occasion by Louis Armstrong and Earl Hines. Nor was his yodel original; singers had recorded it before him. It had been a standard vaudeville turn since the 1870s, when various Swiss groups touring the Midwest had popularized it.

Without a trace of affectation, however, Rodgers pulled all these elements together into a sound that was unique. He recorded over a hundred different numbers at the rate of two a month, the style remaining constant throughout. He took the silliest jingle and made it sound as if it came from the depths of his suffering. In his songs, he drank, gambled, was ensnared by scarlet ladies, and bummed the freights. Yet he yearned for a cottage in the hills, entwined with roses and perfumed memories. He sinned and was sinned against, and he never forgot his mother.

His art lay in simplicity, in transparent honesty. Nothing he sang was faked. No matter how sentimental his songs, he believed every word and carried his audience along with an effortless informality. After all, he was one of their own. His wife, Carrie, wrote of him later in *My Husband Jimmie Rodgers*:

The poverty-stricken, gripped by sickness and troubles almost more than they could endure, knew that here was a fellow who understood, who had "been

there." Far, lonely cabins on Western plains, on the high ranges, in distant forests; isolated dwellers in such places knew that this boy knew them too. Army men, hard-boiled, grim-faced he-men, scoff and wise-crack as they might, knew deep in their hearts a genuine liking. . . . He talked the language of all of them. Sweethearts—mothers—fathers—hoboes—husbands and wives—even cops! For each, some gift of cheer, of sympathy, of broad or tender humor. Jimmie Rodgers reached them, every one with his sobbing, lonesome yodels.

For the burgeoning hillbilly industry, Rodgers' life became the blueprint for stardom. Success brought the usual rewards; he juggled his debts in Kerrville, Texas, where he built a fifty-thousand-dollar mansion, the "Blue Yodelers' Paradise." He bought fancy suits and a fleet of cars, traveled with retainers and hangers-on to whom he would hand out fifty-dollar bills for the asking. But his health grew steadily worse. Constant tours and recording sessions exhausted him. His medical bills seemed endless, and eventually he was forced to sell Yodelers' Paradise. By 1933, it was obvious he was dying. In May, he journeyed from Texas to New York for one last recording session in order to leave some provision for his family. He was so weak that a cot had to be set up in the studio for him to rest on between takes. Two days later, he asked to be taken to Coney Island, but, halfway through the outing, he collapsed and was rushed back to his hotel, the Taft. He died the same night, alone in an alien city. Some of his recordings were withdrawn, "on account of you could hear him dying," his friend Bennie Hess said. He was only thirty-five years old.

If Rodgers brought to hillbilly music a taste of reality, he also pushed it down a trail of fantasy that was unashamedly romantic. For his health, he had moved to the dry plains of central Texas, where he had been able to indulge a lifelong passion (which he shared with many young Americans) for the West. Rodgers collected cowboy boots, ten-gallon hats, spurs, saddles, and handguns. He delighted in posing for photographs in full cowboy regalia, and recorded a stream of western-oriented songs. He

was not the first singer to do so; real cowboys like Carl T. Sprague and Jules Verne Allen had enjoyed regular sales for over ten years and had even indulged in an occasional yodel. But it was Rodgers who showed the way to this blend of country and western.

Before long, he had inspired posses of imitators. One young man, who had been imitating Rodgers for years on the WLS *National Barn Dance* and now billed himself as "Oklahoma's Singing Cowboy," traveled to Hollywood the year after Rodgers' death hoping for a part in one of the new series of musical western adventure movies starring Ken Maynard. Maynard sang in his movies, but had made little impact. As yet, neither had his new supporting actor, Gene Autry, who once painted a sign on his dressing room door, stating that he was "America's Biggest Flop."

After Autry's first film, however, the fan response was sensational; his second picture—*The Phantom Empire*—made him a star. Within months, singing cowboys were swarming all over the movie lots; the Riders of the Purple Sage, the Lone Star Cowboys, the Cowboy Ramblers, all provided for by the herd of song writers newly arrived from Tin Pan Alley. Autry himself was a poor actor and routine musician, but he had a good set of teeth, a happy enough personality, and could ride a horse and be relied upon to keep squalid reality out of his movies. He signified adventure, freedom, and opportu-

Top: Roy Rogers. Rogers was happy to play co-lead with an animal. Trigger, "mounted," now dominates the Roy Rogers Museum in Apple Valley, California. *Bottom left:* the first of Hollywood's singing cowboys, Gene Autry, came out of the *Louisiana Hayride. Bottom right:* Autry with his boot collection. He also owns a radio station and a baseball team, the California Angels. *Center:* Webb Pierce by his swimming pool in Nashville. Born near West Monroe, Louisiana, Pierce achieved a considerable following in his home state before moving to Nashville. In 1952–1953 he gained the first of many awards: *Ranch and Farm* magazine's award as top folk singer, and the Juke Box Operators' Award as Number One singer. *Bottom center:* Bob Wills. Although born in Hall County, Texas, Wills was more at home on stage than on a horse. Shown here with English-born Arthur Satherley, who worked briefly with Edison in pioneer recording developments before going on the road for more than forty years as a scout.

nity. It happened to be just the right tonic for an America belabored by economic troubles.

The Slye Brothers, and their cousin Leonard, came from Duck Run, Ohio. With their parents, they had trekked from the Dust Bowl to California in search of work. Leonard—later, Roy Rogers—had worked variously as a trucker and migratory peach picker before he sang (with two friends) on an amateur hour run by one of Warner Brothers' Los Angeles radio stations. They performed a song called "The Last Roundup," which so impressed the men from Warners that they put all three on staff at thirty-five dollars a week—"more money than we'd ever dreamed of," Rogers says today. The group changed their name, in appropriate western fashion, to the Sons of the Pioneers; more than forty years later, the group—albeit with different personnel—is still playing. "We did a lot of riding and singing as the Sons of the Pioneers as background in some of Gene Autry's pictures," Rogers told me. "Then, since they wanted to start another Singing Cowboy, they auditioned about seventeen other guys and me. I got the job and made my first picture in January 1938.

"The early stories of winning the West were exciting," Rogers continues, "especially for children. The stories were built around the cowboys and the heroic things they did, the hardships they had to suffer, and the outlaws they had to beat. Yes, it was a romance." Later, when his producer saw the musical *Oklahoma!* in New York, Rogers was launched into an endless series of wholesome movies that had no more flavor of the South or the West than Mickey Mouse. But realism was not their intent. "We made features about Oklahoma, about Wyoming, about Idaho, and about Utah," Rogers says. "And then we started making television films. Usually one every five days."

The process was familiar. The films, and the songs they contained, filched a folk art, rendering it painless and profitable. They cleaned up the hillbilly and made him a cowboy; instead of a hick joke, he became a mythic ideal. The truth was lost, but money was coined. The music, a

white music, was wasted, and from there on, the story of commercial hillbilly music—or "country and western," as it became known—is all downhill.

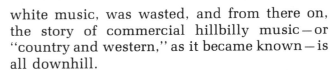

Upper left: Lester Flatt (right) played for some years with Bill Monroe's Bluegrass Boys, but then formed a duo with fellow-member Earl Scruggs (left) in 1948. The pair had a substantial following in both country and folk music audiences; they split in 1969. *Lower left:* Bill Monroe and his Bluegrass Boys playing in Chicago. *Upper center:* Loretta Lynn, from Butcher's Hollow, Kentucky, was described in a *Newsweek* cover story as a girl who couldn't read well enough to pass the written test for a driver's license. She came to prominence during the 1960s and now owns three publishing companies, a chain of clothing stores, and a talent agency. *Upper right:* Merle Haggard, born in Bakersfield, California, acknowledged his family roots in Richard Nixon's favorite song. "Okie from Muskogee," which dwells at some length on the homespun virtues of American country life. *Lower right:* the Everly Brothers, with Wesley Rose, in 1957. Don and Phil were part of their parents' radio show from the age of 8 and 6 respectively, on station KMA in Shenandoah, Iowa. Their commercial success, however, came not from country music but from ballads like "Bye-bye Love" in 1957, published by the house of Acuff-Rose.

As a result of the cowboy craze, the center of country music shifted away from Arkansas, Kentucky, and Tennessee to the Southwest where, since the early thirties, a chain of powerful radio stations had flourished along the Mexican border. Mexico had been irritated with a bilateral decision on the part of the United States and Canada to divide up the entire longwave radio band between them. Mexican law had been changed, accordingly, to allow its stations a much stronger wattage than was permitted in the United States. American salesmen were delighted, and in 1930, a quack named J. R. Brinkley opened station XER as a medium for plugging his goat-gland operation by which lost potency could be restored. The station blasted out five hundred thousand watts and could be heard all over America. And what America heard was a deluge of medicinal cures interspersed with music.

Radio sponsors formed bands to promote their products—among them Garret Snuff,

Royal Crown Cola, and Crazy Water Crystals. There were cowboy songs and jazz from Louisiana; Spanish music from Mexico, black country blues from northern Mississippi, gospel from Oklahoma, and ballads from Tennessee—most of it meant for dancing. "Imagine a Saturday night dance hall in Norman, or Muskogee, Oklahoma," remembered J. R. Goddard, a critic from New York. "There might be twelve hundred people jammed into the hall, some of whom drove one hundred fifty miles for the dance. Some were hard-shell Baptists, oil workers, and mule farmers. They were just coming out of the Depression, out of the worst kind of rural isolation, just beginning to get electricity in their homes."

The popularity of this sound gave birth in the late thirties to yet another brand of "country" music. Since the most commercial music of the time was called swing, this latest package became known as western swing; most successful of the new bands was Bob Wills and his Light Crust Doughboys, later called the Texas Playboys. "Wills dressed conservatively in a starched white shirt," Goddard recalled, "but always wore a hundred-dollar pair of boots and a hundred-dollar cowboy hat. He had bought a bus to take his band around, a bus with a big longhorn steer head on the front. The people had never seen anything quite like that. Wills could provide visual style as well as musical style. He was a sort of folk hero, but a reachable hero who gave these people something to live up to and look up to."

The Grand Ole Opry had never seen anything like Wills. Minnie Pearl says: "It was the first time we'd seen somebody pull up in a great big bus—everybody has a bus now, but Bob Wills was the first. And when he came on the Opry, it was the first time that a band had appeared on our stage in full western wardrobe with amplified instruments and twin fiddles. And I remember Roy Acuff, one of our most respected Opry stars, said to me: 'They're spoiling the Opry—putting on those amplified instruments here.' But the people got a kick out of it, especially when Wills and his singer, Tommy Duncan, performed 'San Antonio Rose.' "

The amplified instruments that worried Acuff were to have a lasting effect. They had first come to prominence in the dive bars known as honky-tonks, which had sprung up throughout the shantytowns of the Southwest during the oil boom of the thirties. Weekdays, they used jukeboxes for music. But on weekends, a live band would be crammed in; the bands found amplification essential to be heard above the din. The music they played matched the brawling and boozing that filled these shacks. "Stompin' at the Honky Tonk" was more appropriate, it was felt, than "Poor Old Mother at Home."

World War II accelerated these changes. Until 1941, hillbilly, rural, western, or honky-tonk music scarcely penetrated the North. The artists recorded mostly in the South, and although cowboy movies were shown all over America, the commercial effect of country music was relatively small. The war opened the final breach. Two major disputes in the music industry had already prepared the way: the row between ASCAP and the broadcasting companies, which smashed the monopoly of Tin Pan Alley, allowing in BMI and its new catalogue of hillbilly music; and the strike by the American Federation of Musicians, which led the recording companies to consider more favorably those musicians who were not controlled by the union—among them, the hillbillies. Roy Acuff and songwriter Fred Rose decided it was an opportune moment to set up their own publishing house, devoted exclusively to country music—not in New York, but in Nashville.

As America entered the war, conscription yanked tens of thousands out of their Southern homes and scattered them throughout the Union. The sound of guitar picking and Southern accents spread. By 1945, hillbillies were everywhere. A popularity contest for the world's greatest singer run by the Armed Forces Network in Munich pulled thirty-seven hundred votes. Roy Acuff won with six hundred votes more than Frank Sinatra. He was a national symbol. The son of a Baptist preacher, he was by his own admission a second-rate country fiddler and exponent of the yo-yo. Yet his song "The Great Speckled Bird" (the title is a phrase from *Jeremiah*, Chapter 12) summed up everything that Americans were fighting for—mother, home, and God. As the Japanese launched their attack on Okinawa (so the Nashville version of the story goes), they had been tutored in the ultimate anti-American battle cry: "To hell with Roosevelt, to hell with Babe Ruth, to hell with Roy Acuff!"

Acuff did not go to hell; he went home to Nashville. Even though Acuff was breaking all records at his concert performances, even though Nashville was plagued with publishing houses competing with Acuff-Rose, even though the Opry Show was steadily increasing in popularity, the city itself remained unaware of the gold mine. Ernest Tubb says, perhaps with hyperbole: "When I first joined the Opry in 1943, Roy was the biggest artist in country. But there were no stores that featured country music records. In fact, if you went into any one of the big stores and asked for a country record, they would laugh at you. They only sold 'pop' music, meaning the music from New York." So Tubb started his own record shop.

Nashville was learning fast. Hillbilly music now had a national audience, so Nashville would give the nation what it wanted. Country music had been a business for twenty years, but its organization was haphazard. Now, the age of innocence was over. Tin Pan Alley was reborn—with a Southern accent and a pair of cowboy boots. Hits were manufactured by the dozen. Lyrics were pruned of references to the South, rural living, or anything distasteful. Following the trauma of war, America wanted a music that twanged and twittered in a style that slipped down easily. In such an atmosphere, the term "hillbilly" seemed uncouth. Respect was measured by the length of a Cadillac, the depth and shape of a swimming pool, the number of cowboy suits a man owned. The approved term was "country and western," or just "country."

Those who struggled to keep the music pure, to prevent its becoming merely a relic of vaudeville and the minstrel shows, were the exceptions that proved the rule. Bill Monroe, who had brought mandolin and banjo picking to a new level of musical accomplishment with the form he called "bluegrass," gradually cut himself off from the Opry circus. "I put in the music what I wanted to have in it," Monroe told me. "You'll find Scots bagpipes in it and Methodist holiness singing in it. I wouldn't play it if it wasn't pure. Bluegrass is the most cleanest music in the world. There's no sex in it and no filth in it." Another was Hiram "Hank" Williams. Ernest Tubb says: "Williams grew up listening to Jimmie Rodgers' records and Jimmie was his favorite. Roy Acuff was also an inspiration. Then I came along, and he told me: 'I started singing your songs. I liked Roy Acuff and I liked you, but finally I found a place right between you all." The place he found earned him a notoriety that overshadowed even Acuff's. He seemed hillbilly incarnate. At the height of his fame, he always looked and sounded like an archetypal farm boy dressed up for a night on the town, the epitome of all that country music had been. He was also, in his cowboy hat, fancy clothes, and extravagant living, the model that all those who followed sought to emulate.

Williams was born in 1923, in a two-room log cabin outside Mount Olive, Alabama. He grew up solitary and wild. When he was seven, his mother gave him a three-dollar guitar. After that, he spent most of his time in town, shining shoes, selling peanuts, and learning the blues from a black street singer called Teetot. By his mid-teens, he had left home and formed a band—the Drifting Cowboys—that played local dances and county fairs. He had a one-day stint with a Texas rodeo, which landed him in the hospital with a mangled back. He joined a medicine show and met his future wife, Audrey, who became his manager. Already he was drinking heavily, shooting up hotel rooms, falling down on stage. But he managed to carve out a devoted following around Montgomery; in 1948 he signed for Acuff-Rose and cut his first records.

He wrote in a bewildering range of styles,

Hank Williams, Jimmie Rodgers' successor as the most charismatic figure in country music. Like Rodgers, he achieved that status in just six years (1947–1953). His first of several hits during 1952 was "I'll Never Get Out Of This World Alive." He died on New Year's Day, 1953.

from love tragedies to hymns, comedies to sentimental monologues, honky-tonk rowdyisms to homespun philosophies. But even in his most upbeat moods, his voice was tinged with melancholia. "Sincerity?" he said. "You've got to know a lot about hard work. You've got to have smelled a lot of mule manure before you can sing like a hillbilly." Dozens of his songs developed into standards. His earnings were astronomical, his fan following fanatical, his status almost godlike. But none of it brought him repose. He drank harder than ever, spent several periods in a sanitarium, fought unremittingly with his wife. Like Jimmie Rodgers, he threw his money around like confetti. "Trying to cope with him was like riding a tiger," Minnie Pearl says. "You couldn't ride it and you couldn't get off. He was not prepared for the sudden fame or money. Money was a big pressure on him. Yet Hank was just as authentic as rain. A rough sack of bones who could tackle a buzz saw."

By 1952, his marriage had broken up and his drinking was hopelessly out of control. The Opry fired him for chronic drunkenness, but his records sold as strongly as ever. Always lean, he was now a walking cadaver, with gutted cheeks and canceled eyes. He coughed up blood as he sang. And on New Year's Day 1953, while driving to a show in Canton, Ohio, he died — in the back seat of one of his five Cadillacs. He was twenty-nine. At his funeral in Montgomery, Acuff, Tubb, and other Opry stars sang in his memory. It was, said Tubb, the "greatest emotional orgy the town had seen." As an epitaph, Tubb recorded a song called "Hank, It Will Never Be the Same Without You." And it wasn't.

By the late fifties, the country music industry decided the time had come to put a seal on its respectability. The Opry radio show attracted a regular audience of ten million; by 1960, over seven and a half million had attended its live broadcasts. "They had built a small empire in Nashville," William Ivey explains, "a very successful segment of the commercial recording scene. Yet country music was still put down as being unsophisticated and simple. People said: 'Damn it, if they don't like us, we're going to put together a museum and a library and show the world just what is good and useful about this music.'" So they did. Modeled on the Baseball Hall of Fame in upstate New York, Nashville constructed a temple to enshrine its heroes forever. It was, says Ivey, its present director, "justifiable defensiveness." A one-thousand-dollar contribution to the museum earned the right to

have your name trodden on by tourists in the gold-lettered "Walkway of the Stars." Within, one could see Merle Haggard's pardon from the governor of California, Tex Ritter's cowboy hat, Uncle Dave Macon's curiously bloodstained banjo.

In 1974, the Opry moved from its old Union Chapel in downtown Nashville, complete with 1897 Confederate Gallery, to a glass-and-concrete forty-million-dollar palace called Opryland, "Home of American Music." Before the Friday and Saturday night six-hour broadcasts, you can enjoy a ride aboard the Wabash Cannonball, eat Oprydogs, visit the Chuck Wagon and the Opry Record Shop, or pass through the Acuff Museum and the Country

Far left: Johnny Cash and Carl Perkins. Both achieved their first success out of the Sam Phillips/Sun Records stable. Phillips sold Elvis Presley, thus raising the money needed to promote rocker Perkins. Cash, an honorary inmate of the various jails where he has taken his show, compensated for his hard upbringing by developing into one of the most commercially successful country singers. Marrying into the Carter Family helped. *Left:* Charlie Pride, from Sledge, Mississippi, and the only black member of the Grand Ole Opry. *Above:* Opryland U.S.A. pushes out the boat.

Store. Then, to the sound of Bill Anderson or Dolly Parton or Tammy Wynette or Loretta Lynn, you can trip down a memory lane tinkling with happiness. No expense has been spared in their sequined costumes, no emotion untouched by their concerned sincerity; their instruments sing, their voices swoon, and all is well with the world. And what better way to end the evening than by staying on in the auditorium for Grand Ole Gospel Time in which the Reverend Bob Harrington or singer Hank Snow's son, the Reverend Jimmy Snow, will invite you to declare yourself for God. As Harrington says, good is country and country is good. "Country music is all geared to God."

Afterward, there's still a chance to rush back downtown to the Ernest Tubb Record Shop for his Midnight Jamboree Radio Program—you can always buy a few more records as you leave. "People come up to me and mention a song that's meant something in their lives," Tubb told me. "Usually, it's been good and has kept them from making a mistake. Yes, this is *real* American music." Well, at least, it was. Until Nashville strangled it.

Go Down, Moses!

Woodrow Wilson Guthrie was born in Oklahoma in 1912. He grew up in a community ravaged by exploitation and poverty, but escaped to Los Angeles, where he eventually got a job with a radio station. As other Okie victims of the dust storms shuffled into California, however, Guthrie became profoundly distressed by their condition. So, using traditional melodies from Oklahoma and Texas, he began to write songs expressing their plight and his anger at a haphazard political system that had caused so much misery. Before long, he found himself being used by every liberal cause in need of a spokesman, as if an entire generation had suddenly awakened to the fact that music, especially song, is among the most effective weapons of propaganda known to man. From the coal

Joan Baez at an antiwar demonstration in Trafalgar Square, London. Donovan is below her left arm; Vanessa Redgrave is seated behind her.

mines of Kentucky to the ports of the Mississippi, the white man discovered he had his own blues, as eloquent and as subtle as any the black man possessed, although buried hitherto beneath a mountain of musical garbage.

Guthrie traveled to New York, invited there by an intellectual elite that yearned to have its own expression of a social conscience not dependent on black inspiration. Probably it wasn't any feeling of guilt toward the black man that prompted their immediate acceptance of the white Woody Guthrie, but this must have crossed some minds. It is argued that Guthrie's migration to New York cut him off from the folk who had spawned both him and his music. Previously, he had been content to describe himself as a hillbilly singer; now, that description no longer seemed worthy of his role. Yet, by 1940, when he organized a folk-singing group called the Almanac Singers, he had clearly unearthed a vein of discontent far more universal than the local concerns of dispossessed Okies. A fellow member of the original group, Pete Seeger, says they traveled for several years offering songs "of, by, and for the people, not from Broadway and Hollywood for the profit of Broadway and Hollywood." The music industry was perplexed. "They used to say to us: 'Don't you want to make money? Don't you want to get a hit? If only you would change your song a little bit.' What they didn't realize was that there were tens of thousands of musicians like us who were going to continue to make the music we wanted whether or not we got accepted by the industry or the media."

Seeger remembered that when he was sixteen his father took him to a square dance festival in North Carolina. "Up till then, I had not realized how much music could grow up out of old traditions. I had thought that folk music was something old, back in the library, and pop music was new—it was something you could hear on the radio. All of a sudden I realized that was a phony distinction. Millions of people were making music which grew out of the old traditions, mostly making up new words to fit old tunes. New words to fit new circumstances. This is what I call the folk process." For once, musicians acknowledged their sources. Guthrie used the melody of the Carter Family's "Wildwood Flower" for his song *"The Reuben James"*; the tune for "This Land Is Your Land" was taken from a traditional melody, "Little Darling, Pal of Mine."

Then, like Guthrie, Seeger began to under-

Top left: Josh White spent several years as the eyes of numerous blind singers, including Willie Johnson, Blind Lemon Jefferson, and Joel Taggart, all of whom taught him their songs and styles. After an accident which temporarily paralyzed one of his hands, White managed to get a part in a Broadway show, playing Blind Lemon Jefferson to Paul Robeson in the title role of John Henry in 1932. White also played the White House for President Roosevelt, as well as Café Society for Barney Josephson. *Top center:* Mother Maybelle Carter as folk musician at a Chicago festival in the mid-1960s. *Top right:* the Weavers, whose success was in proportion to the enthusiasm with which they were blacklisted. The group was formed in 1948 by Pete Seeger (left), disbanded in 1952, and reformed in 1955. They disbanded permanently in 1963, just as the commercial "folk" boom was beginning—that is, just as Tin Pan Alley had discovered folk had an audience; but Joan Baez, for one, would not appear on ABC's *Hootenanny* unless the blacklisted Seeger was admitted. *Bottom:* "Leadbelly"—born Huddie Ledbetter near Mooringsport, Louisiana, in 1885. Although relatively unknown until he was 50 years old, Leadbelly broke through to prominence when John Lomax, the folk song collector, heard him in the Louisiana State Penitentiary in 1932. He enjoyed a minor career until his death in 1949.

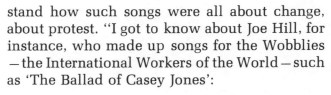

stand how such songs were all about change, about protest. "I got to know about Joe Hill, for instance, who made up songs for the Wobblies — the International Workers of the World — such as 'The Ballad of Casey Jones':

> 'The workers on the SP line
> The strike sent out a call
> Casey Jones the engineer
> He wouldn't strike at all.' ''

Seeger realized that Joe Hill was just one of hundreds of song writers who hardly ever got a hearing on the radio or on records because the music they wrote had a purpose other than making money. There was Aunt Mollie Jackson, a Kentucky miner's wife who sang of the injustice of mining. There were Lee Hays and Millard Lampell, fellow members of the Almanac Singers. All believed that popular song could be useful, and to the living. After all, protest music has always been popular, because there has always been something to protest about. But the exact popularity of that music has been hard to measure. By its nature, the music has been clandestine. It tends to be quiet when anyone in authority is listening — one reason, unconscious

perhaps, why so many songs of protest are set to familiar tunes: the singer can slip back into the "authentic" lyrics when danger calls. Almost without exception, the songs that have summoned troops to the flag at the beginning of a war have later been adapted with words saying they want to go home. Battle hymns have become protest songs. But then, protest songs have always been battle hymns. "Often," Seeger told me, "it mattered little what you sang. The fact that you were singing at all was enough to turn people off." The only songs that were per-

Upper left: Woody Guthrie, holding bass, in unfamiliar guise as a musical cowboy with the String Band in Pampa, Texas, in the early 1930s. During the 1940s he joined Pete Seeger and others in the Almanac Singers (lower left, Guthrie on left). During his long and terminal illness in the 1960s, his bed was a place of pilgrimage for numerous folk singers, including Bob Dylan. He died in October 1967. Above: Guthrie with Pete Seeger, Freddy Hellerman of the Weavers, and Jean Ritchie, the foremost exponent of the Appalachian dulcimer. Ritchie, born Viper, Kentucky, in 1922, was the youngest of fourteen children of a noted musical family. Her achievement has been the preservation and development of early forms of settler music. Right: Arlo Guthrie, Woody's son. His expository style is taken from his father, but fashioned entirely by his own invention.

mitted, it seems, were those that rallied the troops—which is how it had always been.

Since America gained independence, she has fought eight wars against other nations. Of these, she has won six, tied one (Korea), and lost one (Vietnam). Each produced a bumper crop of war songs, both for and against, but overwhelmingly for. Not until Vietnam, the longest and least rewarding war in American history, did the songs against war outnumber those in favor. Previously it had been in the interests of propagandists, governments, and song writers to send the boys off with a song in their hearts; there was nothing like a good martial display with cheerful music to thrill the blood. In eighteenth-century England, the sight of well-drilled soldiers parading in their bright red and white uniforms, flags flying, drums beating, and fifes shrieking the Duke of Marlborough's own recruiting song, "Over the Hills and Far Away," had moved many to take the bounty and march away to their death. During the Napoleonic wars, one Charles Dibdin had written so many stirring songs for his productions at Sadler's Wells that a grateful British government had given him a pension for his "services to recruiting." The chauvinist song is guaranteed box office in the early days of any war. Later, if defeat seems imminent, the patriotic ditty—whether made for the troops or for home consumption—encourages defiance, heroism, bravery, and all those admirable qualities that war engenders. "War is a delight," noted Erasmus, "to those who have no experience of it."

Traditionally, the common soldier hates war, hates the lies that get him into it, and hates the lies that keep him there. Songs have always been his only relief. They have enabled him to curse the appalling living conditions, the poor food, the unnecessary punishments, and the class structure that oppresses him, all without danger of being thought mutinous. A bowman engaged to fight at the Battle of Crécy in 1346 had been paid sixpence a day for his effort. An infantryman in King George's army in 1776 was paid exactly the same. There were no barracks to house the King's soldiers in the colonies, so Americans were forced to billet troops in their houses. Small towns dreaded the arrival of the King's regiment, full of drunken troops. Homes were wrecked and tavern bills often settled by the direct expedient of "leg bail"—marching away:

How happy the soldier who lives on his pay
And spends half-a-crown out of sixpence a day;
Yet fears neither justices, warrants or bums,
And pays all his debts with a roll of his drums.

At home in Britain, barrack-room conditions were repulsive: twelve soldiers were packed into each room, two to a bed; the bathtub by day was used as the urinal at night. The newest recruit was expected to empty the filth every morning, refilling the tub with the day's ration of water. Barrack mortality was high; the British government voted money for bounties to encourage recruits, and then killed them off at twice the civilian rate before they even saw the enemy. Soldiers could live with their wives, but the only privacy a man could expect was a blanket draped between his bed and the next:

Oh say, bonnie lass, will you lie in a barrack
An' marry a soger, and carry his wallet?

When it was time to fight, the soldiers drew lots to decide who could take their wives. Only six wives were allowed to each company of forty men:

I'm lonesome since I cross the hill
And o'er the more and valley.
Such heavy thoughts my heart do fill
Since parting with my Sally.

God Blessed America

This Land Was made For you & me

This land is your land, this land is my land
From California to the New York Island,
From the Redwood Forest, to the Gulf stream waters,
      God blessed America for me.

As I went walking that ribbon of highway
And saw above me that endless Skyway,
And saw below me the golden valley, I said:
      God blessed America for me.

I roamed and rambled, and followed my footsteps
To the sparkling sands of her diamond deserts,
And all around me, a voice was sounding:
      God blessed America for me.

Was a big high wall there that tried to stop me
A sign was painted said: Private Property.
But on the back side it didn't say nothing —
      God blessed America for me.

When the sun come shining, then I was strolling
In wheat fields waving, and dust clouds rolling;
The voice was chanting as the fog was lifting:
      God blessed America for me.

One bright sunny morning in the shadow of the steeple
By the Relief office I saw my people —
As they stood hungry, I stood there wondering if
      God blessed America for me.

                    * All you can write is
                      what you see.

original copy
of this song

                              Woody G.
                              N.Y., N.Y., N.Y.
                              Feb. 23, 1940
                              43rd st & 6th Ave,
                              Hanover House

The music was not the product of some jangling factory on Forty-second Street. Any melody, secular or sacred, pop or traditional, was good enough; the melody of the "Battle Hymn of the Republic," originally a Methodist hymn, was used for at least sixty sets of words. Occasionally a tune was put to contradictory uses. The dirge written in 1745 to stir the English against the advancing armies of Bonnie Prince Charlie was used during the 1776 Revolution to stir the Americans against the British. Later, the same melody was used as the British National Anthem; later still, for America's "My Country 'Tis of Thee." The words of the "Star-Spangled Banner" are set to a traditional English drinking song.

Many of the British soldiers' songs were collected around 1860 in a volume entitled *Broadside Ballads*. There is no proof that any come from the field; more likely, they were written by balladeers called "penny pot poets" who loitered in alehouses until called upon by a drunken clientele to improvise a set of verses on the latest item of news from the front. While a fiddler or flutist played a popular melody into his ear, this "poet" would versify a ballad illustrating the horrors and disappointments of war.

When news was scarce, the verses concentrated on hard times at home. Ex-servicemen with permits to beg supplied the balladeers with their subject matter. Others took material from soldiers' letters. Others copied William Russell's Crimean dispatches to the London *Times*. These, written in the first person, gave the impression that the singer had seen and suffered the privations Russell described.

Without these songs, it is doubtful whether the civilian population would have had any grasp of what was going on; all that most citizens knew of war in a distant country was a battle lost or a battle won. The rosy yarns of the recruiting parties were usually sneered at. Only the limbless and mutilated campaigners who returned home to shock their wives and families bore witness to the realities:

> *Oh cruel was the engagement*
> *In which my true love fought*

And cruel was the cannon ball
That knocked his right eye out.

The introduction of the electric telegraph brought the truth a little nearer home: the public learned that hundreds in the British Army had died of cholera before reaching the Crimea; that the soldiers laying siege to Sebastopol in the winter of 1854–1855 were dying where they lay in the trenches—from cold:

> *All you who live at home at ease*
> *And sleep on beds of down,*
> *Pray think of our brave soldiers*
> *Who lie frozen on the ground.*

In America, the pattern of development had been similar, with the same bizarre interchange of melodies. The definitive Southern anthem was originally a Northern song. Written by a

Left: the original manuscript of "This Land Is Your Land," written by Woody Guthrie in 1940. *Above:* anticommunist vigilantes who broke up a Paul Robeson concert in Peekskill, New York, in 1949. Cars were overturned, scores of people injured.

Cheering the troops. *Top:* "Forces Favourite" Vera Lynn presenting a mobile canteen to British troops in June 1942. *Center:* Marlene Dietrich, who had the curious distinction of being the most popular singer of opposing armies: "Lilli Marlene" was a favorite song of both Rommel's and Montgomery's armies in the North African desert campaign of 1943. *Bottom:* Artie Shaw in the South Pacific, August 1943. *Facing page:* Gracie Fields, who was later to purchase most of the island of Capri, entertaining Scottish shipbuilders in 1941 on the home front.

member of Bryant's Nigger Minstrels, the tune of "Dixie" had begun life on the New York stage as a "walk-around," or finale. Although it became the official Southern battle hymn in 1861, it continued to be used in the North (with suitable lyrics) until 1863. "The happy land of Dixie" was replaced by the line "Our Union shall not sever." The Civil War, the bloodiest engagement of the nineteenth century, was also its most tuneful. During its first year alone (1861), more than two thousand songs were published, commemorating each battle in great detail. "All the phases through which this dreadful struggle has gone," noted the *New York Weekly Review*, "are duly represented in the songs. . . . There is not an event, whether political or on the battle field, which does not find its echo in this." Nursery rhymes were conscripted. Referring to the 1860 Democratic Presidential nominee Stephen A. Douglas, a popular refrain went:

> *Sing a song of Charleston!*
> *Bottle full of Rye!*
> *All the Douglas delegates*
> *Knocked into pi!*

A group of captured Confederate officers, paroled to attend a Victory Ball, asked to hear some of the Northern marches. At the end, one said: "If we'd had marches like yours, we'd have licked the boots off you." No doubt they remembered General Sherman "Marching Through Georgia," burning and looting the Southern countryside as he went.

> *. . . a thoroughfare for freedom and her train*
> *Sixty miles in latitude*
> *Three hundred to the main.*

Death was admirable, especially when the soldier's last thoughts were of his mother — "the source of all that is pure and good in this world," the *New York Weekly Review* observed:

> *Tell my mother I die happy*
> *That for me she must not weep,*
> *Tell her how I longed to kiss her,*
> *Ere I sank in death to sleep.*

These were "the last words of Lieutenant

Crosby, who was killed in his battery at Salem Heights, May 2nd 1863''; at least, so the song's publisher assured his public, which could obtain this and nine other illustrated songs ''on Notepaper, mailed to any address on receipt of 50 cents.''

Above, top left: Burl Ives—Cap'n Andy in *Show Boat*, singin' cowboy in *Smoky*, almost a teacher, occasionally a professional football player, author of *Wayfaring Stranger's Notebook*, he also found time to become a folksinger, as well as Big Daddy in Tennessee Williams' *Cat on a Hot Tin Roof*. *Above, top right:* Chad Mitchell of the Mitchell Trio, who was famous momentarily during the early sixties. He was replaced in 1962 by an unknown named John Denver. *Above:* Peter Yarrow, Paul Stookey, and Mary Travers, who achieved fame at the same time as Mitchell, but managed to avoid relegation. Some of their greatest successes came with sweet versions of Bob Dylan's songs; one was a sub-drug song, ''Puff the Magic Dragon.'' *Facing page:* Baez and Dylan.

Support for the war, however, was not universal. When Abraham Lincoln had difficulty finding volunteers in the North to fight the Civil War, sixteen composers offered different tunes for John Sloan Gibbon's recruiting lyric: ''We Are Coming, Father Abraham, Three Hundred Thousand More.'' None of them worked and Abraham Lincoln became the father of the draft.

Throughout the second half of the nineteenth century, while most European nations were grabbing every fragment of colonial territory they could lay hands on, patriotic fervor was de rigueur. German and British politicians, sitting comfortably at home, had drawn lines on rough maps of continents still unexplored and then dispatched troops to secure the territory.

The music halls gave this imperial fever its name. First used at the Pavilion in London in 1878, when Britain was considering declaring war on Russia, a word rapidly acquired universal popularity:

We don't want to fight, but by Jingo if we do
We've got the ships, we've got the men
And we've got the money too.

By 1914, ''jingo'' was applied to anyone clamoring for war. Music hall artists competed furiously to become the singer whose jingo song would be the hit of the war, even if it had failed to provoke its outbreak. In the best music hall tradition, the songs were of such banality that it remains a wonder why every man in the audience did not immediately join the army to escape the music. One performer, dressed in the uniform of a British naval officer and standing beneath a giant Union Jack flag, sang:

''Cricket for the time must end
This is the wicket we must defend.''

And Phyllis Dare, among the more notable music hall dames who weighed in, took the title of her famous recruiting song from the poster picture of Lord Kitchener who waggled his finger and said: ''Your King and Country Need You.'' Originally a recruiting slogan of 1779 for the war against the Americans, ''Your King and Country Need You'' was copied for display in America when the United States declared war

on Germany in 1917. Lord Kitchener was replaced by Uncle Sam, who was more personal: "I want *you*."

There was, however, a growing disillusion with the idea that popular song was a useful or proper medium for chauvinistic propaganda.

> *When this lousy war is over*
> *Oh, how happy I shall be.*
> *I shall kiss the sergeant-major,*
> *No more soldiering for me.*

was sung to the old English hymn tune: "I Have a Friend in Jesus." Nonetheless, for the most part, radio and newspapers avoided songs which suggested protest. And by World War II, for instance, one of the most popular singers in England was Vera Lynn, lately honored by the British Queen as Dame Vera. "I still get thousands of letters just thanking me for helping during the troublesome times with my songs," she told me, "and for keeping their morale up and thinking that there were better times ahead." She succeeded magnificently. "We're a very unsentimental age now. But during the war, it wasn't so. Sentiment was needed. If anybody goes away and leaves you, you must feel sentimental when you think about them and wish they were back home with you." "We'll meet again, don't know where, don't know when," she sang, "But I know we'll meet again, Some sunny day."

The tradition that Woody Guthrie inherited, therefore, was complex and old. By its use of popular melodies, war and protest song had done as much to preserve folk music as any outpost of fiddlers in Arkansas. And as the Nashville machine gathered momentum, Guthrie and his friends nourished the hope that the essential spirit of this music would survive. His determination to safeguard that tradition grew as he began to realize that the white popular music industry did not accept and did not wish to accept any part of its heritage that questioned

The civil rights movement and the escalation of the Vietnam War finally catapulted the protest song into the front line of public awareness.

the industry's, and the nation's, economic ambitions.

"We have a very useful phrase in the American Constitution," Pete Seeger says, "called the First Amendment—the right to freedom of speech. But what it boils down to in modern America is that you have freedom of speech as long as you only want to speak to a few friends. If you want to get on prime-time TV, on the other hand, you'd better have a lot of money. Because the people who control the media, whether television, radio, newspapers, or records, are kind of particular about what gets out to the millions.

"After World War II," Seeger continues, "I was involved in trying to elect Henry Wallace to the Presidency. Maybe I was right and maybe I was wrong. But a month after the election, I was sitting waiting to sing some children's songs in the lobby of a TV network. A man came through and looked rather strangely at me and five minutes later the program director came out and said: 'I'm sorry, Mr. Seeger, we've had to

change the script and we don't have room for you on the program.' I found out later that the man who had come through was the head of the station. He'd gone to his director and said: 'Don't you know who that is? That's the commie bastard who was digging for Wallace. Get him out of here.' "

In 1950, Seeger was preparing to do a nationwide weekly show with his group, the Weavers, who were at the time achieving some commercial success with a Leadbelly song they had recorded, "Goodnight Irene." A professional blacklisting outfit called AWARE, Inc., objected and succeeded in having the contract for the show torn up. "We were all set to go ahead, but the sponsoring company wasn't. Van Camp's Beans decided that we couldn't sell their beans any more—for people to fart by. And I couldn't get a TV network appearance for another seventeen years."

In the early sixties, when the music of Guthrie, Seeger, and others spawned a number of untainted performers and began to attract a large crowd, the media and the music industry

realized it was missing out on a few more dollars. The folk boom brought a number of artists like Peter, Paul, and Mary, the Kingston Trio, and the Tarriers into pop music prominence. ABC television devised a show called *Hootenanny*—the popular name for a folk music gathering—and then ensured it bore no relation to folk music as Seeger and others had come to understand it. "ABC's version of *Hootenanny*," Seeger told me, "was a bunch of white college kids all clapping inanely, no matter what song was sung, big smiles all over, and never a hint of controversy or protest. In the six months the show was on, it almost ruined the word 'hootenanny.' I was pleased when they moved on to make money out of something else."

For a while, the civil rights movement and the subsequent escalation of the Vietnam War catapulted the protest song into the front line of public awareness. "There was Vietnam War resistance, draft resistance, and tax resistance," Joan Baez says. "There was the civil rights movement, there were antiwar demonstrations, there were returned GIs against the war to support." Never had America been affronted by so much criticism from within. But its music was still controlled by the media. Woody Guthrie always believed that it was only the second-rate

Four manifestations of apparent folk roots. *Facing page:* Odetta, born in Birmingham, Alabama, December 31, 1930, started out as a classical musician. *Top left:* Miriam Makeba, born in South Africa. *Center:* Buffy Sainte-Marie, a Cree Indian. *Right:* Janis Ian, a Jewish girl from New York.

songs, whether white or black, that got on the radio. Pete Seeger agrees. "There was a song by Country Joe McDonald that would surely have been number one in 1970 if it had not been pushed aside by the media. Later, it slipped in front of the public when the Woodstock Festival film was released:

'Come on all of you big strong men
Uncle Sam need your help again
Got himself in a terrible jam
Way down yonder in Vietnam.
Put down your books, pick up a gun
We're going to have a whole lot of fun.
It's one, two, three, what are we fighting for?
Don't ask me, I don't give a damn,
Next stop is Vietnam.
Be the first one on the block
To bring your boy home in a box.' "

In 1971, Paul McCartney wrote a song, "Give Ireland Back to the Irish," which was banned altogether by the BBC.

Without question, the most important figure in the protest renaissance of the 1960s was Bob Dylan. Like his idol Woody Guthrie, Dylan believed he was "trying to be a singer without a dictionary, and a poet not bound with shelves of books." He had a voice caught in barbed wire,

he looked like a cross between Harpo Marx and the younger Beethoven. "What I do," he said, "is write songs and sing them and perform them. Anything else trying to get on top of it, making something out of it which it isn't first, brings me down." Yet his song "A Hard Rain's A-Gonna Fall" was about, or at least inspired by, the 1962 Cuban Missile confrontation; the "Ballad of Hollis Brown" commemorated a particularly bloody killing of a Dakota dirt farmer; "Oxford Town" concerned the ordeal of James Meredith; his recent return to activist singing, "Hurricane," is about a black prize fighter wrongly jailed (so it is claimed) for murder.

Dylan's protest songs are full of savage melancholy, flinty and drawling. Their subject matter is intolerance and the loss of liberty. The commercial show-biz atmosphere was never for him: "Fat guys chewing cigars, carrying around gold records, selling songs, selling talent, selling an image. I never hung out there." Such a sentiment is difficult to reconcile with the fact that Dylan was born Robert Zimmerman, of German-Jewish origin, the son of a cigar-smoking appliance dealer in Hibbing, Minnesota. He sings with a Southwestern accent, but he speaks without it.

Even so, his lyrics have brought eloquence to

an age that has little, dignity to a generation that tends to forget its meaning, and a terrible honesty to a society which prefers deceit. A prophet of reasoned defiance, he works in a medium where such an attitude had been virtually unknown among whites, though it is now seen as a cornerstone of future musical development. Like other folk artists, he steals from the past to revitalize the present. His debt to black music and to the blues in particular is often unacknowledged and damaging to both. But as a lyricist, his example stands as a warning to those who "go mistaking Paradise for that home across

Far left: the Kingston Trio, clean and good, personified the packaging of folk. *Center left:* Country Joe McDonald, born of a left-wing family, merged the substance of protest music with the style of rock. *Near left:* Canadian poet-song-writer-novelist-singer Leonard Cohen. *Above left:* Bob Dylan before he shocked the audience at the Newport Festival with his electric guitar. *Above right:* Leon Rosselson, doyen of the English folk revival during the 1960s. Latter-day American troubadours, from Dylan to Paul Simon, took sustenance—not to mention melodies, such as Dylan's "Girl from the North Country"—from the innumerable folk clubs assembled in the upstairs rooms of English pubs. Simon sang all over England for £10 a night at gatherings which preserved a tradition that countless others stole from in the late sixties and the seventies.

the road."

"There are a lot of wonderful musicians who go unrecognized and unpaid," Seeger says. "I long ago decided there wasn't any sense in making money. The U.S. government simply takes it away to build more things to drop bombs out of. And it doesn't do to withhold taxes. Joan Baez tried that. The tax collector just comes right into the ticket office, and when people pay for a concert, he just puts the money into *his* bag. So the only thing to do is to sing for free. Now I only perform for money about six times a year."

"People expect the revolution to happen overnight," Joan Baez adds. "And when it doesn't, they go home to make organic honey or start throwing bombs and lose their sense of perspective." The folk singer is one who acknowledges that the folk process is without end:

How many times must a man look up
Before he can see the sky?
Yes, an' how many ears must one man have
Before he can hear people cry?

Today, says Baez, "we have been trained to be impotent."

CinemaScope
MIDDLETON
Elvis Presley
DON'T BE CRUEL
NOT CROSS
DEPT.

Hail! Hail! Rock 'n' Roll!

"**S**o I was in the studio one afternoon at 706 Union—a very good address, believe me," Sam Phillips remembers, "when a young man passed by. In those days, we had a store-front glass type building for a studio. I noticed this young man going back and forth while I was in the control room doing some editing. Finally, he came in, with his box. His guitar, you'd call it. Very timid, he was. You could tell from the way he was moving around. Very nervous. He told my secretary, Marion Keisker—there were only two of us in those days—that he wanted to cut a record for his mother's birthday. She came back and asked me if we could take him. I said: 'Well, I really don't have the time, but if tomorrow is his mother's birthday, we'd better take him.' So she sent him back and he in-

Elvis Presley fans waiting in line for his first film, *Love Me Tender*.

Ronnie and the Hi-Lites.

troduced himself. And I asked him: 'What do you do?' He said: 'Well, I can't sing very well, but I'd like to try. As the old saying goes, my momma says I can.' And I said: 'Well, fine. Get in there and let's go.' "

It's a familiar story. Sam Phillips has told it many times. But with Elvis Presley, the fact has always been more unusual than the fiction.

His family was poor, his father a casual laborer and occasional gospel singer. The Presleys were devout, and frequently attended the First Assembly Church of God. Elvis had had a twin, Jesse, who died at birth; consequently, his mother had pampered Elvis. He was granted any treat they could possibly afford, even if that meant his parents didn't eat. When he was seven, his mother had saved up and bought him a guitar—for twelve dollars and ninety-five cents. His mother always enjoyed hearing him sing sad songs like "Old Shep," which made her cry. But his early efforts were not particularly successful: when Mrs. Presley entered him in a local talent contest at a country fair, he came in second. He was a solitary child, with a preference for hiding in his bedroom rather than playing with other children.

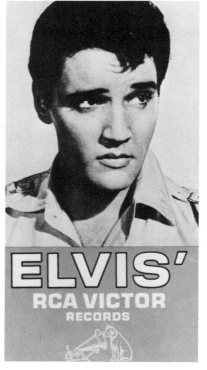

The Presleys decided to try to improve their lot by moving to Memphis, the nearest big town and commercial center. Nonetheless, Presley Senior could only manage part-time work and the family was forced to live in a slum tenement in the middle of a black ghetto. Presley Junior worked as a movie usher after school, and later as a truck driver for forty-one dollars a week, before, in the summer of 1953, he cut two songs in Sam Phillips' studio at a cost of four dollars.

Both songs were sweet and slow: "My Happiness," an old Ink Spots number, plus a gloomy country recitation called "That's When Your Heartaches Begin." Phillips was intrigued. "He was singing like Bill Kinney of the Ink Spots," Phillips told me. "Not that Bill Kinney or the Ink Spots were especially black or white. But I noted a certain quality in Elvis' voice, and I guessed he had a feel for black music. I thought his voice unique, but I didn't know whether it was commercial."

Phillips decided to look for material that might suit Elvis better. A recording date soon after in the Nashville Maximum Security Prison with a group called the Prisonnaires unearthed an attractive song entitled "Without Love," written by a white prisoner. "So I had my secretary call Elvis," Phillips continued, "to see if he would like to come by and go over the song. Now before she'd hung up, he was in the studio. And I wondered how on earth he had got over so fast, even in an automobile, because he lived over a mile away. He said: 'Mr. Phillips, I ran.' "

The session was not a success. Phillips realized that Presley did not have the experience necessary to make the song persuasive. But he tried again. He called up two session men, Scotty Moore and Bill Black, and asked them to meet Elvis and work with him on any material they could. Phillips also recommended the occasional studio run-through to check progress.

For six months, there was none. Elvis seemed unable to settle on any particular style. "The trouble was," Phillips says, "Elvis had absorbed just too much music." One day he would sound like the slickest product of Nashville; next day he was a white crooner parodying love songs from Hollywood. Sometimes he might easily have been singing with a black street band,

Right: Elvis Presley performing before 26,000 fans in Dallas, Texas, November 1956.

busking the blues. Other times he was still in church, singing hymns. Often he was louder than the loudest rhythm and blues merchant from Chicago. Elvis appeared to have taken it all in like a vacuum cleaner.

Still, Sam Phillips persisted. "He wanted to put it all together and make it grow," another of his protégés, Conway Twitty (born Harold Jenkins), recalls. "He knew what he wanted to hear, and everybody that walked into his studio —no matter what kind of music you sang—he'd push you in a certain direction, toward something that he wanted to hear." But Elvis would not respond.

By his own admission, Phillips was ready to give up. As a last resort, Elvis asked if they could try out a version of an Arthur "Big Boy" Crudup song recorded ten years earlier. Scotty

Above: Elvis, one-time supporting act to Liberace at Las Vegas, returns as honored guest, November 1956. *Right:* Pat Boone, edged uncomfortably into rock and roll by the Presley explosion, arrives in Los Angeles with his family, late fifties. In his arms, the children who grew up to be part of his family show during the early seventies. *Facing page, top:* Fabian Forte, a star at 15, over the hill at 17. *Bottom left:* Bobby Vinton, or is it Bobby Vee? or Bobby Rydell? or Bobby Darin? *Bottom right:* Leslie Gore, from Tenafly, New Jersey, spoke for every co-ed's dream when she sang "It's My Party" in 1963.

Moore remembers: "The microphones were dead. So Elvis relaxed. He forgot about correcting the sound, picked up his guitar, and started banging on it. Bill Black started beating on his bass and I joined in—just making a bunch of racket, we thought. The control room door was open and when we were halfway through the thing, Sam came running in and said: 'What in the devil are you doing?' We said: 'We don't know.' He said: 'Well, find out real quick and don't lose it. Run through it again and let's put it on tape.'" The song was "That's Alright, Mama."

"I asked Elvis why in hell he hadn't suggested doing this song before," Phillips says, "and he told me it hadn't occurred to him. Well, we had to have something to put on the back of the record so he ripped into 'Old Blue Moon of Kentucky' by Bill Monroe. And I said to myself, 'I don't believe this, we're about to put out a pure white country song back to back with a real black man's song.'

"We put the record out and we got from ridiculous comments to more ridiculous comments. I played the blues side to a black radio station man and he said: 'This boy is a country rooster

crowing who shouldn't be allowed to sing after the sun comes up in the morning.' So I took the country side to a white radio station and the announcer said: 'Sam, if I play this, they'll run me out of town. I've got to play pure and simple white country music.' "

Eventually, "That's Alright, Mama" sold quite well, but only in Memphis. After a struggle, it was on top of the local charts. But Elvis' shyness made the all-important personal appearances a torture to contemplate. Sam Phillips worked hard. The first public appearance was at a small night club in East Memphis — Elvis was "scared to death." Phillips tried again. "I put him on a show at Overton Park in Memphis with Slim Whitman, who was probably one of the hottest country acts of the time. When I got there, Elvis grabbed me. He was sweaty and shaking all over. I just had to psych him up. I told him: 'Elvis, you are going to be fine.' Then he got a thunderous ovation after his first selection, and we didn't have too many problems with him after that."

Phillips got Elvis onto the *Louisiana Hayride* radio show and then into the Grand Ole Opry. He played bars and country fairs and school-

houses and cut some more records. The rumors spread, albeit slowly, as far as Cleveland, Ohio. Pat Boone, then a popular crooner with songs in the national hit parade, had agreed to do a high school show as a favor to disc jockey Bill Ran-

dall. When he arrived, Boone told me: "Bill came over and said: 'There's a new fellow supporting you tonight. He's going to be a very big star.' I said: 'Oh, really? Anyone I know?' Bill said: 'I doubt it. His name is Elvis Presley.' I knew the name all right. I'd seen it on some country juke boxes, so I knew he was a hillbilly singer. So I smiled to myself and thought: A hillbilly? With a name like Elvis Presley? How can he ever be a star? But when Presley came on and started twitching and the kids started going crazy, I was glad I had a big hit record going for me because I had to follow him."

Even so, selling Elvis to a wider market proved an uphill struggle. "When we started going out on tour," one of Elvis' colleagues at the Phillips studio, Carl Perkins, says, "we would take with us a truckload of records. We were our own promotion men. We would go into town and head for the nearest disc jockey." The music itself was not as popular as legend

Top: out of country into rock. Left: the Everly Brothers in 1960. Right: Gene Vincent and the Blue Caps; Vincent, real name Vincent Eugene Craddock, died of bleeding ulcers in 1971 after spending seven fruitless years in England, where earlier he had enjoyed his greatest success. Below: the Coasters, Mark II, a group formed in 1956 by songwriters Lieber and Stoller out of the fragments of a group known as the Robins. The Coasters' personnel and numbers changed several times; their specialty was comedy.

has subsequently encouraged us to believe. Conway Twitty recalls an early visit he made to Canada. "When we showed up at this club where we had a two-week booking, we had on black pants and black shirts with white belts, white shoes, and white ties. And the guy who owned the club took one look and said: 'What have we got here?' Anyway, opening night we got on stage and cut loose and the guy nearly went out of his mind. He said: 'My God, turn that thing down, turn it down.' So we did, and the audience began to leave. I told the boys in the band: 'To hell with it. Just turn the music back up.' Then the bartenders left. Next night we played to an empty house."

Sam Phillips now says he has no idea how word got around that he was thinking of selling Elvis Presley's contract—but he was. Carl Perkins' style was similar to that of Elvis, and it was against Phillips' policy to have two artists with the same style. Anyway, he needed the money to promote his new boy. "I was poor then, and still am," he says. The twenty months he had spent producing Elvis Presley had been expensive. Presley's contract was still good for over two years, so Phillips called Colonel Tom Parker, a well-known Southern showman, whom he suspected of propagating the rumor that Elvis was for sale. Parker, in his New York hotel, claimed total innocence. But, at the end of the conversation, he asked: "By the way, *are* you selling Presley?" "I'll talk to anybody about any business proposition," Phillips replied.

Parker said: "We'll be in Memphis tonight."

The Colonel was a hustler. He had started out in carnivals and fairs peddling hot dogs and lemonade. Later, he had developed his own act —dancing chickens. After chickens, he turned to humans and became one of Nashville's sharpest entrepreneurs. He managed Hank Snow and Eddy Arnold, two of the biggest country stars of the early fifties, and began to challenge the Opry in his promotion of road shows. To Parker, rock and roll meant dollars. While Presley had been establishing his reputation in the South, the storm heralded by Haley's "Rock Around the Clock" had broken in the North. Tin Pan Alley had not the faintest notion of what was going on; but if the kids liked this preposterous noise, then it was the industry's clear duty to feed them all they could swallow.

The record companies began signing up "rock" singers by the gross on the theory that Bill Haley might turn out to be John the Baptist, and someone bigger, better, and even more profitable might come along. Colonel Parker arranged for this blessing to fall on RCA Victor. Sam Phillips and his Sun Records sold Elvis Presley for what was then an enormous sum, thirty-five thousand dollars. RCA also picked up a six-thousand-dollar royalty check owed Elvis. In January 1956, Elvis cut his first record for RCA. Within a month, it rocketed to number one on all known charts. It stayed there for eight weeks and eventually sold three million copies around the world. It was "Heart-break Hotel."

Elvis' style was impossible to define. He sang country, gospel, rhythm and blues, and pop — all mixed into one. His voice changed continually; he used a different tone for almost every song. The only constants were sex and excitement. ("We never sold no sex or sideburns," Bill Haley claims. "If we wanted to sell sex or sideburns, we'd have dressed differently.") The only god was sensation. As he gained in confidence, Presley's appearances became even more cathartic than his records—especially the guest spots he did on network TV shows like those of Ed Sullivan and Steve Allen. He came on leering and twitching, his hair all down in his eyes, his grin lopsided. The moment the music started, he went berserk. Spasms rocked his body as if it had been plugged into the same electrical source as his guitar. His hips began to grind, his legs vibrated like power drills. He pouted and humped and walked as if he were sneering with his legs. Onstage, he bounced like a jeep driver crossing a plowed field. On TV, sponsors would allow Presley to be shown only from the waist up.

Critics loathed him; preachers called him sinful; in Miami, he was charged with obscenity; in San Diego, the city fathers voted to ban him altogether unless he omitted from his act all "vulgar movement." A Baptist pastor in Des Moines declared him "morally insane." According to the East German Communist paper *Young World*, Elvis Presley was a "weapon of the American psychological war aimed at infecting a part of the population with a new philosophical outlook of inhumanity . . . to destroy anything that is beautiful, in order to prepare for war."

In fact, nobody was certain how to describe Elvis—as a country singer, a bluesman, or simply a freak. But nothing made the slightest difference. As far as the young were concerned, Elvis was everything they had yearned for, albeit subliminally: sex, rage, independence, arrogance. And infinite energy. "It was about the time when the kids decided: 'I don't want Mom and Dad to buy my clothes. Give me that dollar and I'll buy my own leather cap,' " Carl Perkins says. "And it was the same with the music." They were of a generation that had not participated in the war, had not experienced the triumphant idealism of bringing peace on earth. The atmosphere in the mid-fifties smacked of disillusion. Youth went sour on everything associated with the past and they wanted a music to express this feeling—"the passion of a moment that was meaningless," as Phillips put it. Elvis was theirs, private teen property. No outsider, no interfering adult could penetrate his mysteries.

Guided by the Colonel, Presley became a one-man industry. Within two years he grossed a hundred million dollars. He made four smash-hit movies. For a personal appearance, he drew twenty-five thousand dollars a night—twice the previous record. There were Elvis Presley blue jeans, Elvis Presley T-shirts, Elvis Presley hairbrushes and plush hound dogs, ballpoint pens, bermuda shorts, bobbysox, and bubblegum. Diaries, buttons, badges, pins, fluorescent socks, lipstick, toilet paper—altogether more than fifty products, worth millions of dollars. When he wanted a yacht, he bought not any old yacht, but the Presidential yacht *Potomac*, on which Churchill and Roosevelt had drawn up the Atlantic Charter. A TV network offered Presley fifty thousand dollars for a single show. "That's fine for me," said the Colonel. "Now, how about my boy?" "I don't aim to let this fame business get me," Presley said in a rare interview. "God gave me a voice. If I turned against God, I'd be finished." The spirit of country music lived on.

"I was leaving the studio one evening," Jack Good, a British television producer who pioneered rock on TV in America and Britain, says, "when the head of BBC Light Entertainment asked me how long rock and roll would last. Boldly, I replied that it could go on forever. He said: 'More likely to be three months at the outside.' That was 1957. I met him again at the Beatles' Carnegie Hall Concert in 1965 and asked him again how long he gave rock and roll. He had to admit that he couldn't see any end of it, although he wished he could. He's dead now. It lasted longer than he did."

Rock and roll had no connection with the musical heritage of Europe. European jazz had always been derivative and imitative of American styles; in no way had the music developed out of anything peculiarly British or even European. The bands just churned out their version of American music. It had always been so, and virtually the same happened with rock and roll. In fact, it was worse. British "rock" bands despised what they were playing.

The first rock group to appear in Britain, for instance, was led by a drummer, Tony Crombie. It was a pick-up band and included several eminent British jazz players. They managed to get top billing at the London Palladium, the temple of British music hall. But while British youths were buying up every American rock and roll record they could find, British musicians were openly contemptuous of the music they were being asked to play. Jack Good says: "They went through the motions of doing a Bill Haley, but it was a revolting display with no guts at all. I'm sure they felt this was just a bandwagon which would soon run out of gas."

Would-be British rock and roll singers were musically stranded; there were no bands to back them with any conviction. The first "breakthrough" was Tommy Steele (born Hicks), whose band included an excellent guitarist named Roy Plummer. Tommy Steele's first concert was a shambles. When he shouted at his bewildered audience: "Rock with the Cavemen!" he hadn't a clue to what he was doing or why. And Roy Plummer seemed to think that a rock solo consisted of playing

Gospel glitter: the Bird Groups. The generic terms came from the early popularity of such groups as the Penguins, Orioles, Pelicans, etc. Personnel changes occurred so frequently that personal identification became irrelevant—all that was required, it seemed, was a glossy publicity shot and a little reasonably close harmony. *Top, from left to right*: the Fiestas; the 5 Satins; the 5 Royales. *Center*: the Mellow Kings, whose black arranger, Dick Levister, successfully made them sound like a black group; the Schoolboys, who disbanded after their only hit, "Shirley," in 1957, presumably because their voices broke; the Solitaires. *Bottom*: the Pastels; the Willows; the Delroys.

twenty-four bars of the same note. The performance was bad not because the musicians were bad, but because (according to Good) they thought the music they were playing was rubbish and what they were expected to play was rubbish—and so they did.

British pop music had made a limited contribution, however, with a style called skiffle. The English equivalent of American jug band music in the thirties, skiffle had emerged from under the wing of traditional or New Orleans jazz, in particular from a band led by Chris Barber and featuring Lonnie Donegan. Born in Glasgow of Irish extraction but brought up in the East End of London, Donegan was the first original performer in English pop music of the fifties. His sound was his own creation and first received attention through a track on a Chris Barber album called *Rock Island Line*. The title song achieved a considerable success as a single, and before long skiffle groups had appeared all over Britain. Like the American jug band music they imitated, skiffle was easy to play.

"The name 'skiffle' came from Chicago," Donegan says. "It was music people would play for rent parties. Impoverished neighbors would get together and hold a party. They'd have a whoop-up with home-made wine and then play bits of music with a broomstick or a washboard

---

Little Richard, born Richard Penniman in 1932, came to stardom from washing dishes in the Greyhound bus station at Macon, Georgia. Between 1955 and 1957 he released a string of hits, until he was persuaded that the launching of the Russian *Sputnik* was a sign he should forsake rock and roll for the ministry. Several years later he forsook the ministry for Golden Oldies. Jimi Hendrix once toured with him as a sideman.

Little Richard threw all his diamond rings over Sydney Bridge in Australia, entered a seminary, and became a preacher.

—anything that was handy. Then they'd pass the hat around to collect for the rent." Skiffle consisted of just three chords, and anyone could play a washboard or a tub bass. "What's more," Donegan reminded me, "it was very difficult to buy an acoustic guitar in England at that time. And banjos were impossible, unless you were lucky enough to find one in a second-hand shop." "Rock Island Line" sold over a quarter-million copies. Donegan had agreed to union scale for his performance: three pounds, ten shillings—then eleven dollars. He received no royalty.

Skiffle apart, the British pop scene at this time (1956) was inane. Donegan himself expressed total contempt for rock and roll and developed an obsession against the man who seemed to represent all that was contrived about the new music, Tommy Steele. Steele became the butt of endless sarcastic remarks by Donegan. Once, during a television show on which they both were appearing, Donegan snarled one of his typical antirock, anti–Tommy Steele remarks and then began to sing his own "Bring a Little Water"—whereupon Steele appeared with a bucket of water and threw it all over Donegan.

Steele soon aquired his own Colonel Parker in the form of two Tin Pan Alley salesmen, John Kennedy and Larry Parnes. Their problem was acute. Although the sound of American rock and roll had already crossed the Atlantic via such Bill Haley films as *Rock Around the Clock*, its exposure in Britain was limited. On radio and television, it was nonexistent. The BBC maintained its monopoly over sound broadcasting, and had no intention of allowing such cacophony, either on record or in live performance, to pollute the airwaves. The only alternative was Radio Luxembourg, which transmitted an English-language service from the far side of the English Channel. Surprisingly, Luxembourg was slow to realize that rock and roll was the one element that, since the BBC had chosen to ignore it, might prove to be its own commercial salvation. There was no sense, as there was at American radio stations, that if rock and roll attracted an audience, then it was good business to play it.

The only outlet for these new sounds was through the old music hall circuit. For the bookers, rock and roll was merely the latest novelty act, which, if it managed to arouse sufficient interest, would bring new people into the halls. The rest of the evening's entertainment was unchanged: stand-up comics, jugglers, animal acts, dancers, singers, and a pit band. The pit bands, incidentally, were offended when asked not to play for rock and roll acts. The idea of a man coming on stage with his *own* band was thought very odd.

This bizarre meeting between music hall and the English imitators of American rock and roll had two important consequences: the early British rock public was obliged to sit through a whole gamut of traditional British variety acts in order to see their idols; and the early British rock star found himself performing alongside comedians and singers thoroughly versed in the whole gamut of British stage skills. Tommy Steele, for instance, sometimes performed after two clever young British comedians, Mike and Bernie Winters; they helped him understand that there was more to an appearance on stage than singing and shouting at the audience. He began to interest himself in matters of presentation and stage discipline. As a result, his act acquired polish. His music may have been abysmal but, theatrically, he learned his job well.

In America, the world of rock and roll centered on the recording and publishing industries. Personal appearances were considered publicity: they helped sell records, which was what mattered. The new rock stars would tour in packs; the big star merely closed the second half of a musical roadshow, which might consist of as many as a dozen other acts. The new rock managers, like Colonel Parker, had previously deployed their talents operating country and western acts; on the East Coast, the promoters were men whose experience was in dance halls and night clubs. None of them had had any contact with theater.

In Britain, on the other hand, theater was everything. The agents who sold the rock acts were almost exclusively theatrical agents. And when British television eventually discovered rock music (some would doubt whether it has done so even now), the music hall training proved crucial. In fact, rock and roll arrived on British television by mistake. In the mid-fifties, there was a touching agreement between the two television companies (BBC and Independent) known as the "Toddlers' Truce." They agreed not to broadcast any programs between six and seven in the evening, so that children could be put to bed without bullying their parents to let them stay up and watch television. This noble gesture was soon broken by the Independent commercial station, which began to broadcast—among other programs—the *Jack Jackson Record Show*. It proved immensely popular, so the BBC decided that with the truce now broken, they, too, would fill up the twilight hour. "They would broadcast a program for young people," Jack Good says, "or 'adolescents,' as they called them—the word 'teen-ager' just wasn't used in polite society. The program would show items the BBC decided were interesting to young people—mountaineering for boys and 'how much make-up—if any—should I use?' for girls. The BBC also decided to make me its co-producer, principally because I was the youngest person in the building at the time."

Good had already seen the first Bill Haley film and, "like Paul on the road to Damascus, became a convert." To this day, he is not sure whether he was more excited by the music or by the scenes of young people in what seemed "postures of wild abandon." He decided for the kids and politely asked his superiors at the BBC if — for the first time — he could have teen-agers move about and dance freely in the studio, sometimes in front of the camera. Certainly not, said the BBC. Teen-agers would "break up the cameras." Anyway, the British public wouldn't put up with "that sort of person 'bopping' around the floor."

Good was determined not to be overruled and had a set constructed for the show that looked harmless and was approved by management. What the designs failed to show, however, was that each segment of the set had wheels. During rehearsals, the entire set was quickly moved around so that the audience for the show was in front of the cameras as Good had planned. The show, which was called *6.5 Special*, was a riot. All those who loathed rock and roll were switching on to see what horrors might appear next. "They tried to stop it, of course," Good says. "The head of Light Entertainment came up to the control room in the middle of one show and said: 'You can't do this!' I said: 'I'm doing it. Cut to camera five.'"

Rock acts, in the early days, were brief. So Good and his team toured London's coffee bars and night clubs looking for more and more to fill up the show. The word spread, and soon every stripling who could play three chords clamored for an audition. Terry Dene, the first major Presley impersonator in Britain, succeeded. "He was found in a coffee bar by one Hyman Zahl, a variety agent," Jack Good remembers, "and for the first time in my life I saw a guitar amplifier that was larger than eighteen inches square. Dene lacked a group, although every rock singer had a support band with a name not unconnected with their leader. So Terry Dene was backed by the 'Dene-Agers' — who, incidentally, looked anything but 'Dene-Agers.' Nonetheless, here was an artist conscientiously doing the job of impersonating Elvis. I signed him up — immediately."

Within weeks of his first appearance on *6.5 Special*, Dene was touring the music halls as top of the bill. Unfortunately, however, he was soon in trouble and arrested for throwing bricks at street lights. Before long, he was conscripted

into the army, where he cracked up. Later he got a release. It was all a little theatrical, as was the Two I's coffee bar in London's Soho — allegedly the place where Tommy Steele was first "noticed." Run by one Paul Lincoln, otherwise celebrated as a black-masked wrestler called Dr. Death, it was decorated with giant photographs and autographs all over the walls, including those of Lincoln's pet discovery, Wee Willie Harris. Harris was a plain, pale young man who played jazz-cum-rock. Lincoln persuaded him to grow his hair long and color it bright orange. Thus, in 1957, Harris became the first long-haired rocker. He acquired a red jacket, which had belonged to a rock star who had died, and wanted to have sewn across it in large letters "Wee Willie Harris" — an idea straight out of wrestling. Jack Good was stunned and determined to put "this ugly little fellow" on his show as often as he could. His appearance led to questions being asked in the House of Parliament about whether the decadence of modern teen-agers was actually being promoted by the BBC.

It has to be remembered that Harris, Tommy Steele, Terry Dene, and the rest were insignificant musically. Most were incapable of making a record with anything like the power or guts of a Haley let alone an Elvis Presley. But, in Bri-

Left: Dick Clark, the perpetually young maestro of *American Bandstand*. *Right*: Jack Good, who stage-managed the introduction of rock on British TV.

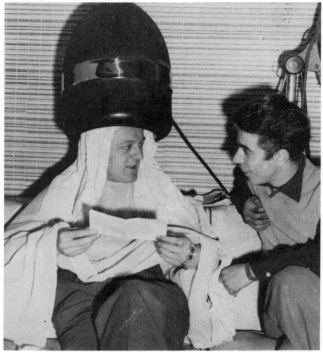

tain they were stars. They had been seen on television and proved themselves good to watch. Their stage presentation, moreover, was far in advance of anything in America. Because Presley and his cohorts never visited Britain, their songs were reckoned fair game by the British. Terry Dene sang "All Shook Up," and British youth loved it.

In America, on the other hand, those artists who made the best early rock records were—with only a few obvious exceptions—dull performers and not particularly attractive. Buddy Holly had broken teeth and wire glasses. Haley was fat and middle-aged. Yet the musical image they all succeeded in conveying was quite different. Gene Vincent sounded like a Southern razor boy who could slit a man from ear to ear without flinching an eyelid or missing a beat of "Beebopalula." But when Good persuaded him over to Britain, where Vincent was greeted at the airport by a hysterical crowd of fans, he was appalled. As the airplane door opened, down the steps came a quiet, polite Southerner who bowed to Good and said: "I'm mighty pleased to meet you, suh, and mighty proud to be in this wunnerful country of yours." Good remembers thinking: Oh dear, this won't do—the British public isn't ready for a shock like this. Mr. Vincent is going to have to change his image.

"Fortunately," says Good, "Vincent suffered from a bad leg—having fallen off a motorbike—and wore leg irons. This gave me the clue. As he limped, I saw that he must become a Richard III figure, dressed entirely in black, including black gloves. He must hunch his shoulders and lurch in sinister fashion toward the camera before singing. I arranged on his first television appearance for him to walk down several flights of stairs so that his limp would be emphasized. I also gave him a medallion to wear around his neck to make him look more Shakespearean. When I saw him gingerly trying to negotiate the steps, I had to run round the back of the set and shout: 'Limp, you bugger, limp!' "

Eventually, Good left the BBC and joined the rival commercial television station. His new

Top: British rocker Wee Willie Harris getting his orange hair fixed. *Below:* Selection of British fan magazines.

program carried theatricality to extreme lengths. The stage was designed in classical style with a band on each side, rostra at the back for singers and dancers, and a central microphone for the star. No song lasted more than two minutes and each was rehearsed shot by shot with meticulous close-up attention to catch all the carefully manufactured mean looks. The lighting—hard white lights cutting through a black limbo—was taken direct from the French National Theater.

Against such a background, Good launched a young man named Harry Webb who became known, and loved, as Cliff Richard. Good told him to curl his lip and wear outrageous clothes. On screen, it looked as though Cliff was giving a completely spontaneous performance, which the cameramen were lucky to capture. In fact, the performance was the result of endless rehearsal. There was one particular movement for which Cliff became renowned: he would grab his left upper arm with his right hand and display an anguished look of realization. This was achieved, Good explains, by suggesting to him that he was being awakened from an anaesthetic by the sharp jab in his left arm of a hypodermic syringe.

Jack Good journeyed to America for the first time in 1959. What he discovered shocked him considerably. On television, rock and roll was the property of a daily broadcast called *American Bandstand*, run by Dick Clark. Clark was a pleasant young man who looked as if he drank lots of milk and took plenty of exercise. Artists were being cultivated who would conform to the traditional pop styles of the past —Bobby Darin liked appearing in black mohair, Bobby Rydell crooned and winked and smiled. Each performed a little dance to conclude his act, in a style meant to indicate easy sophistication. The show, which was liberally interspersed with ads for lotions to improve the complexion, was "littered with callow youths who jumped around in a semistupefied condition as if to indicate excitement," Good says.

Originally, rock and roll had been rebellion. Was it possible that in only four years the promise of Elvis Presley had been dissipated? Admittedly, there had been strong attempts to contain its threat by local law enforcement and by social pressures. But when both these ploys failed, an effort was made to tame the beast. Singers were persuaded into tuxedos and placed in front of sixteen-piece bands with comfortable and familiar voicings; the singers suffered from a conflict between the rebellion the music had represented and conformity the promoters demanded. And the villain was none other than Elvis Presley.

Presley had never reconciled himself to the Frankenstein he had unleashed. His painful shyness had developed into an obsessive need for protection, instantly supplied by the ever-watchful Colonel Parker. It was he who had organized the quite astonishing display that occurred when Elvis was drafted; Parker had made it seem a voluntary spiritual retreat—amidst, of course, multitudes of cameramen and journalists. Elvis the Monster had become Elvis the All-American Boy. Deftly programmed by Parker, he had refused a commission and never rose above the rank of sergeant. He had done everything he was told and everything that middle-aged middle America would appreciate. "I shall consider it," said Parker, "my patriotic duty to keep Elvis in the ninety percent tax bracket." All of which was totally against everything that rebellious, antiestablishment rock and roll had seemed to represent. The head of Elvis' local draft board, Millyon Bowyers, ignored the distraught fans who demanded Presley's release after pointing out that the Army had not conscripted Beethoven. "That," replied Bowyers, "was because Beethoven was not American."

When Elvis emerged after twenty months of dutiful boot polishing, he was changed. He had become a pleasant young man, slightly overweight, who smiled a lot. His records, although they still sold well, were gutless. His films were uninspiring. Whereas a film such as *King Creole* had fostered the hope that Elvis might be another James Dean or even Marlon Brando, his new movies, like *Blue Hawaii*, were effete. He no longer toured, no longer made public appearances of any kind. He shut himself away in

his various mansions with a few hired retainers who became known as the Memphis Mafia: half friends, half servants, to play touch football with him or find him girls or fetch him cold drinks. From time to time, his golden Cadillac would be sent out on tour across America. His followers flocked to see it, to touch it, the empty symbol of a revolution contained.

As a person, Elvis remained a mystery. He possessed two trunks of jewelry and more than a hundred teddy bears. Onstage, he was a Southern potentate; at home, he slouched around in jeans and an old leather jacket. In the best traditions of country, he loved his mother. He could not sleep, so he said, unless they'd talked on the phone. But if anyone threw a punch at him or called him names, he'd beat him to a pulp and would have to be dragged away before he killed. He was aloof, unreachable. Yet he always addressed strangers as "sir" or "ma'am." He could be courteous, abrupt, straightforward, unguessable; nobody was close to him, not even the woman he married in a hotel called The Aladdin. (They divorced, unhappily, after a few years.) He was generous and considerate, yet utterly cold. When he wished to relax, he sang hymns or rode his motorcycle. He loved comics, practical jokes, and furry toys, but he also carried a gun. His favorite treat had always been a banana-and-peanut-butter sandwich, prepared by his mother, last thing before he went to bed. In his public battle against society, Elvis Presley—thanks to the Colonel—had lost.

Those he inspired were deserted, leaderless. Coincidentally, Little Richard threw his diamond rings off a bridge in Australia, entered a seminary, and became a preacher. Eddie Cochran drove into a lamp-post after a show in England; Chuck Willis sang: "Ain't Gonna Hang Up My Rock and Roll Shoes," and died.

Others just faded away. Chuck Berry, an early rock star whose appeal was mostly to black audiences, was thrown into prison; years later, he resuscitated himself as a throwback in rock revival shows. Conway Twitty, who started off with the full Sam Phillips treatment and made hit after hit, quit. He says today: "I thought: If I

Left: Diana Ross, going it alone. *Above, top:* Carole King. Her marriage to Gerry Goffin coincided with their eminence as a rock and roll song-writing team. Later, divorced, she became known as a performer. *Above:* the Crystals, manufactured by Phil Spector, in 1962.

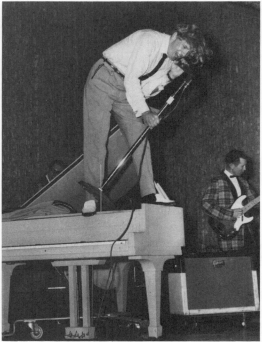

can do this well at something I consider my second best, I believe I can do a whole lot better at something I consider my best." Country was Conway's best, and that is where he returned. Duane Eddy, who appealed equally to boys and girls and would not resort to bumps and grinds, was despised by his audiences as weak, and went into music publishing. Carl Perkins, who wrote and recorded "Blue Suede Shoes" (also one of Presley's greatest hits), broke his neck in a car accident, went bald, found God, and joined the Johnny Cash Road Show.

There was, perhaps, only one figure who never abandoned early rock: another member of the Assembly Church of God, Jerry Lee Lewis. Sam Phillips had discovered him also. "Jerry can do so many things so well," Phillips says, "from country gospel to real black spiritual, from some of the greatest blues you'll ever hear, to rock and roll. If you're a dyed-in-the-wool hater of rock and roll, and especially of Jerry Lee Lewis, you're still going to find something. If you're in that audience, Jerry is just gonna get a hold of you."

But the rock world abandoned Jerry Lee. On a tour of England in 1958, it was discovered he had brought with him a thirteen-year-old wife who was also his cousin. The sensibilities of British rockers were affronted. What might be acceptable in Louisiana could wreck a man in London. At a concert in the East End, a large audience of rockers booed him. He stopped playing, glared defiantly at the audience, combed his locks, and then continued. But the British public hated him, and the British Home Office had him thrown out. Word got back to America. He was disgraced; unlike conscript Elvis, Jerry Lee Lewis was not every mother's son, was no promoter's friend. He says

On a tour of England in 1959, Jerry Lee Lewis had brought with him a thirteen-year-old wife who was also his cousin.

today: "I just kept on working, playing my piano, singing, working, and traveling. I guess me and my manager Cecil Harrelson have driven maybe a few million miles since then, working and trying to make it back." For him, rock and roll had been "like a bush fire which had got very hot and burnt itself out in the process."

It was the music industry that rescued rock. If the likes of Jerry Lee Lewis were no longer acceptable, then others—lads who would be more amenable, who wouldn't object to being "guided" by their business advisors—would have to be found to replace them because rock and roll had become a major industry. One callow youth with handsome features, Fabian Forte, was given the nickname "The Tiger" and set upon America. At sixteen, he was conquering all—appearing on the *Perry Como Show*, the *Dinah Shore Show*, the *Ed Sullivan Show*, in his mohair suit, skipping around songs with a range of three tones. Some said that his records were created from hundreds of pieces of tape that contained the occasional right note.

"We, on the other hand, kept cutting rock records," Jerry Lee told me, "though nobody would play them. They let rock and roll down in the sixties. Elvis started singing like Bing Crosby. Don't get me wrong, I love Elvis and he's a great talent, but I think he let us down. All you could hear was Bobby—Bobby Vee, Bobby Vinton, Bobby Denton, Bobby Rydell, Bobby Darin. There was nothing but Bobbies on the radio."

Elvis was simply an image, a godlike memory, from long ago and far away. In his time, he had cut loose a whole generation. He had united white and black. He had brought sex into the open and demonstrated the possible. When he ended his seclusion in the late sixties, although his presence seemed as mesmeric as ever, his performing home was Las Vegas.

"Thank God for the Beatles," Jerry Lee Lewis says. "They showed us a trick or two. Cut them down like wheat before the sickle."

Top left: Bill Haley and the Comets. William John Clifton Haley, Jr., later retired to New Mexico. *Top right:* Jerry Lee Lewis was banned because of his "child-bride" marriage in 1958, but kept on rocking. *Bottom:* Elvis Presley, on the other hand, went to Las Vegas.

13

Mighty Good

One weekend in June 1967, a hundred thousand orchids were flown from Hawaii and scattered over a field near Monterey, California, among crowds that had gathered for a weekend of music. From the stage, flanked by what seemed at the time incredible banks of loudspeakers, roared a sound that was to echo round the world. Eleven hundred of the world's "communicators" were there, newspaper and magazine journalists, critics, photographers, television and radio reporters. Although few realized it then, the event marked the climax of seventy years of popular music, and the beginning of its end. Within a very few years, the hopes and aspirations that had goaded this music into immense achievements were dissipated and destroyed. Thereafter, the cost of popular approval was too great for individual acceptance.

The Beatles at Shea Stadium, New York, September 16, 1965.

Maharishi Mahesh Yogi.

Monterey began, like other towering extravaganzas, in Hollywood. It was the idea of a moneyed dilettante named Alan Pariser, who brought it to a dashing, if disorganized, entrepreneur named Ben Shapiro. Together, they took the idea to former Beatles publicist, Derek Taylor. Taylor says: "I didn't believe a word of it. 'We'll get the Beatles, we'll get everyone,' they said. In a way, they did."

Festivals were hardly an original concept; but then, hardly anything in rock was original. Everything else had festivals—opera, ballet, folk, jazz, wine, and cheese—some even at Monterey. But for rock, there were obstacles. "The local people of Monterey," Derek Taylor continues, "were cold, hard bastards. They behaved like monsters and made life hell. I sensed that Monterey was very unpleasant, politically. Not corrupt in a big-city way—it was too small for that. But I always felt that in a spiteful, local way, money and jobs and power were changing hands under the counter. There were too many dainty fingers in the till."

There were endless, yawning meetings with local officials. "At the end," Taylor remembers, "the mayor—a disagreeable lady who, it seemed to me, had done her lower-than-level best to stop us—came to our final press conference to thank us for being so beautiful. And, by God, we *had* been beautiful. Once the festival started, the associations began to be made, the police were won around. But you can't take that sort of middle-class authority and turn him or her into a convert. The local police chief accepted a leather-and-glass bead necklace from me. We had our festival—but he and others made sure we never had another."

Those who never made it knew they had missed something. Chuck Berry had been invited, but said he "didn't do nothing for char-

ity" (the other performers were all donating their services to the great event). John Phillips of the Mamas and Papas, who had joined the organizing team, had tried to persuade him. He told Berry: "We're paying first-class flights." "That's okay, man, that's fine, man," Berry replied, "I don't need no free flights. I got my own arrangements with TWA, man." The Who, Eric Burdon, Country Joe McDonald, and the Byrds were there. Roger McGuinn of the Byrds remembers: "Everyone had flowers on their motorcycles. It was a beautiful sight. It was the first time that all the pop groups had gotten together in one place to see each other personally and discuss their views on music and everything else."

Clive Davis, newly appointed chief recording executive of Columbia Records, went to Monterey and was overwhelmed. "It was the first time that artists could just come up on stage in an endless stream and play for thousands of young people," he told me. "I realized that this was the time for me to step forward and make my creative mark and sign up some of these

From the Liverpool Cavern *(above, left)*, since redeveloped, to Carnegie Hall *(above, right)*, unchanged in decades, where America put a Seal of Approval on the Beatles. By 1968 Beatles records had grossed a total £70 million, the greater part coming in foreign currency. *Facing page:* the magical mystery tour. Brian Epstein and George Martin *(top right)* were the conductors. *Bottom:* the Beatles in the Cavern, at the beginning of the trip.

The HESWALL JAZZ CLUB

present their ★ ★ ★
★ ALL ★ STAR ★ BILL
★ Starring
THE BEATLES

★ Mersey Beat Poll Winners!
★ Polydor Recording Artists!
★ Prior to European Tour!

★ plus
The Pasadena Jazzmen
Firm Favourites!

plus ★
'Top Twenty' Records

at Barnston Women's Institute
on Saturday March 24th, 1962
7-30 p.m. — 11-15 p.m.

7/6 ADMISSION **7/6**
Strictly by TICKETS ONLY

BEATLE STREET
Liverpool Four

N° 463

CIVIC RECEPTION FOR
"THE BEATLES"
FRIDAY, 10TH JULY, 1964
FROM 7·0 P.M. TO 8·0 P.M.

ADMIT ONE PERSON

THE BEATLES' ROUTE

ARRIVE ODEON 8·40 P.M.

ARRIVE TOWN HALL 6·30 P.M. LEAVE 8·30 P.M.

ARRIVE AIRPORT 5·15 P.M. LEAVE 6 P.M.

wonderful new stars." Jimi Hendrix was there, so was Janis Joplin. Brian Jones of the Rolling Stones sat in the audience. And although the Beatles were absent, the festival was so heady a rumor grew that they *were* there. Derek Taylor: "It grew with such power and so steadily that, come the final night, I could deny it no longer. Instead, I white-lied. I announced that it was known three of them were on the field, 'disguised as hippies.' Which three, the press asked. 'We have no way of knowing,' I replied. It never occurred to anybody that if we didn't know which three, how could we know any of them were there?"

In a sense, they were there because without them the sixties and the whole of popular music would have been different; there would have been no Monterey. In fact, the Beatles were in a recording studio seven thousand miles away. That very same weekend, they were completing what came to be recognized as their masterwork—*Sergeant Pepper's Lonely Hearts Club Band.* The origins and development of that single piece of music (actually a song cycle comprising twelve quite separate songs) accurately measured what popular music had become.

The group that was to be described as "bigger than Jesus Christ" had first come to public attention in 1962 with a minor success in England called "Love Me Do." Subsequently, as Derek Taylor said in 1967, it became the "longest running saga since World War II—except that with the Beatles, nobody died." More words have been lavished on that saga than on any other comparable story in popular music history, including that of Elvis. It had begun, straightforwardly enough, in Liverpool. Like many ports, Liverpool was a musical city. The music arrived with the seamen, who took it to the music halls and dives where they went for entertainment. "My dad used to work the lights in the local music halls," Paul McCartney told me. "He actually burnt bits of lime for the limelights. He also used to bring home the programs from the first house so that my Aunt Millie could iron them out in time for him to resell at the second house. The following day,

he would play on the piano all the tunes he had heard in the halls. It was music from everywhere. In Liverpool, you'd know about Chuck Berry

Left: the Beatles in action at a New York charity show. *Above, top:* the Beatles in suspended animation at Madame Tussaud's Waxworks in London. *Above:* Paul and John. The most popular Lennon-McCartney song, "Yesterday," has been recorded by 119 different artists.

and Big Bill Broonzy and the other blues and rock and roll guitarists long before most people in America had heard of them. Liverpool was also called the capital of Ireland, because we had lots of Irish folk living there. And then, there were the songs from the Broadway shows, which the sailors wanted to hear. Put the whole lot together and you'll find my influences: from Fred Astaire to Little Richard. It's quite a way."

Although the British working class was financially more secure in the late fifties than its American equivalent, the same oppressive social conditions prevailed. Inside the ghetto — whether the black ghetto in America or the working-class neighborhoods in England — only three escape routes seemed possible: sport, the army, and music. The British Communist newspaper *The Daily Worker* was to describe the sound the Beatles inspired as: "The voice of 80,000 crumbling houses and 30,000 people on the dole." In fact, only Ringo was of working-class origin; the others were middle class. Yet, as Allan Williams — who "discovered" the Beatles while operating a collection of Liverpool cafés and music clubs — says: "No matter what street you went into in the south end of Liverpool, or any working-class area, there would be a bunch of kids practicing in someone's basement or driving someone mad on the street. It was mostly English skiffle music or American washboard blues. The kids had found a way of releasing their violence. Instead of going out to kick people to death, they started to beat up a drum."

Of the early Beatles — called variously the Quarrymen, Wump and the Werbles, the Rainbows, John and the Moondogs, and the Silver Beatles — Williams remembers: "They were scruffy, very scruffy. There was also some trouble over furniture they had burnt for heat in one of their lodgings, they were so poor. I think

Paul McCartney: "We started off by imitating Elvis, Buddy Holly, Chuck Berry, Carl Perkins, Gene Vincent, The Coasters, the Drifters — we just copied what they did."

they got their art school grants stopped for that. We used to sell jam butties [Liverpool slang for jam or jelly sandwiches], and if we made them with toast we'd charge an extra penny for the jam. Now, whenever they went out on an engagement, they would have to pay the driver who'd taken them, so they'd have a big argument over whether they could afford to have jam on their toast. Once I sent them up to Scotland for a promotion. The local promoter took one look at them and phoned me up saying: 'What the hell have you sent me?' They used to wear American-style baseball shoes and black trousers and terrible black sweaters. And their amplifiers were like tiny little suitcases." In the early days, the line-up was John Lennon and his art school friend Stuart Sutcliffe, their friend Paul McCartney, and his friend George Harrison, plus a succession of drummers. "We started off by imitating Elvis, Buddy Holly, Chuck Berry, Carl Perkins, Gene Vincent [whom they later invited to one of the Liverpool clubs in which they performed, the Cavern], the Coasters, the Drifters — we just copied what they did," McCartney says. "John and I used to sag off school and go to my house or to his house, and just start trying to write songs like theirs. We'd put a Buddy Holly record on, and then after we'd listened to it several times, we'd sit around with our guitars and then try and write something like him. The people we copied were all American, of course, because there was no one good British. There still isn't. I'd much rather have an American colored group singing one of our songs than us. 'Cause they do it better." As a group, they began to play with wild abandon, sometimes to the accompaniment of frenetic fights. "Things really got out of hand in the first few years we played," McCartney added. "There'd be a hundred lads from one gang and a hundred lads from another on opposite sides of the ballroom. Then someone would ask a girl from the other mob to dance — and then the bottles would start flying.

Top: the Beatles inspire collapse at San Francisco's Cow Palace, September 1965. *Bottom:* at ease in Nassau.

That was the lunacy. In fact, the violence got less as we got bigger and bigger audiences. People complain nowadays about groups inciting the crowds—but that's what everyone has always done."

Williams got them a job in the north German port of Hamburg, at a club called the Indra, just off the Reeperbahn brothel district. Their routine was staggering. For six months, six nights a week—occasionally Sundays as well, because they could get overtime pay—the Beatles played almost nonstop from seven o'clock in the evening until three o'clock the following morning. "They'd lose all count of time," Allan Williams says. "Everything was pitch black in the club and they'd stagger out to discover it was nine o'clock in the morning. To keep up with that sort of pressure, it was inevitable that they went on to pep pills and other sorts of drugs. At that time, Hamburg was the vice

center of Europe. You name it, and that was Hamburg. They were thrust in at the deep end. Although Liverpool was also a seaport, there was none of the vice or the strip clubs and the donkey business of Hamburg. And they were there while they were only teen-agers. Of course, all the prostitutes used to make a big play for them. The transvestites used to try to get them into bed. Naturally, this turned them into old men in their minds."

"When you're in Hamburg and you're only eighteen years old," McCartney told me, "and you've never been abroad in your life, and you've got a bit of money in your pocket, and you go out on your night off, and you end up still out the next morning, you do some looney things. But the legend grows, the myth of 'I remember them, they were the tough days.' But it wasn't much different from now. There was a little more lunacy then, that's all. Quite a bit more lunacy. But it was only good, clean fun. Good dirty fun, actually."

Progress in England, however, was slow. When the Beatles returned from Hamburg in 1960—minus Stuart Sutcliffe, who had left the group and died soon after of a brain tumor—they could find nowhere to play. Larry Parnes, who had helped Cliff Richard on his way, turned them down. Eventually, according to Williams, a promoter agreed to slot them into a

Left: John Phillips of the Mamas and Papas, born in Parris Island, South Carolina, was a basketball and track hero at school, and later formed a group known as the Smoothies with Scott McKenzie. McKenzie went on to make the golden hit of flower power, "If You're Going to San Francisco," while Phillips (at right) became Papa John of the Mamas and Papas. *Right:* Simon and Garfunkel. To their surprise, they created a new line in clean-cut college music (the pair had already split up when their song "Sounds of Silence" became a hit).

Christmas variety show for a fee of six pounds (then barely four dollars each). But when they started to play, looking scruffier than ever in the black leather suits they had acquired in Hamburg, there was a stampede. The promoter went backstage, got out his diary, and booked them for three months at ten pounds a night.

Another visit to Hamburg—this time to the prestigious Kaiserkeller—consolidated the Beatles' expertise, although it did nothing to improve their financial condition. Back in Liverpool, they began at a local rock and roll club called the Cavern for the massive fee of three pounds fifteen shillings per night (about two dollars per man). Meanwhile, a young Liverpool shopkeeper named Brian Epstein, head of the record department in one of his family's furniture and electrical goods stores, noticed that demand for a particular record seemed excessive, particularly since he had never heard of the musicians on the disc. (The record was "My Bonnie," sung by Tony Sheridan, backed by the Beatles.) To his surprise, Epstein discovered the group came from Liverpool and was playing at the Cavern. He decided on a visit; apparently he was unimpressed and noted on his calendar: "November 9, '61. Dark, damp and smelly. I regretted my decision immediately, the noise was deafening." Later, however, he played the record to his parents, insisting that they "don't pay any attention to that singer, just listen to his backing group." And when he finally met the Beatles, he came home and told his parents: "I want to manage those four boys. It wouldn't take me more than two half-days a week."

Epstein's mother says: "Brian wanted to do things which, all that time ago, seemed rather strange when we had a family business for him to go into. He wanted to be an actor and managed to get into RADA [the Royal Academy of Dramatic Art], but he gave it up after a year. He didn't like the life and he didn't fancy having to spend years in all those repertory companies. So he came back, joined my husband and his brother Clive, and took over all our record departments. Then, when he began to manage the Beatles, he asked us to go and see them. They were playing in Southport, he told us. He

was very insistent that we should go. I'd never been to a rock and roll concert before and I asked him what I should wear. He said: 'Look young.'"

"The Beatles chose him because he could offer them order and clarity instead of disorder," Derek Taylor says. "It was the difference between having to line up in a cafeteria and being shown to your reserved seat in a restaurant, knowing that someone would take care of you and that the meal would be all right. Brian gave them confidence. He took the weight away." Epstein's mother believes they liked Brian because he could show them a kind of life they were not used to—a more comfortable life. "They thought of him as a father figure. I'm sure they were extraordinarily fond of Brian. His honesty appealed to them, and the fact that he was very sure they were going to reach the top."

They did, of course, reach the top, and in a manner achieved by no one before or since. They were unique: they tore the hackneyed pants off pop music like frenzied lovers. They "turned on millions of adolescents to what had been hurting all the time . . . but the young never did want it raw, so they absorbed it through the Beatle filter." They served as the introduction to, and the popularizers of, a whole new world of creative adventure. They traveled only a few miles beyond the avant-garde, consolidating gains and making new ideas acceptable. "They had the capacity of very attractive children for getting away with it," Derek Taylor continues. "They said: 'We're more popular than Jesus,' tried LSD and admitted it, signed the 'Legalize Marijuana' petition—two of them were fined for smoking it—and followed the Maharishi. Yet people still smiled when they saw them."

Individually, the Beatles' memories are notoriously unreliable—which is understandable since so much happened in a comparatively short time. Between 1962, the year of "Love Me Do," and 1967, the year of Epstein's death, their 230 songs, written at the rate of almost one a week, sold over 200 million records —and that does not include cover versions by other performers: "Yesterday" (among them-

selves they called it "Scrambled Eggs") had 2000 different recordings. Their earnings were incalculable. The ballet critic for *The Sunday Times* thought they were the greatest composers since Beethoven; others mentioned Schubert; Leonard Bernstein cited Schumann. *Newsweek* compared their lyrics to T. S. Eliot's; the English critic Cyril Connolly offered Joyce. Their song cycle *Sergeant Pepper* was described as the "great contemporary Bible"; the Reverend Ronald Gibbons wanted the Beatles to make a tape recording of "O, Come All Ye Faithful, Yeah, Yeah, Yeah," because, he said, "the Beatles cult can be the very shot in the arm that the Church needs today." The Reverend David Noebel felt differently. "You listen to this, Christians!" he told a Baptist congregation in Claremont, California. "These Beatles are completely anti-Christ. They are preparing our teen-agers for riot and ultimate revolution against our Christian Republic." Billy Graham said: "The Beatles? They're a passing phase, symptoms of the uncertainty of the times and the confusion about us."

"We never planned anything," Paul says. "I *still* don't know what *Sergeant Pepper* was about. We always thought of ourselves as just happy little song writers, just playing in a rock group. Unfortunately, it gets more important than that after you've been over to America, and got knighted."

From American rock and roll they absorbed via Elvis a musical language now comprising elements of country, rhythm and blues, and gospel. From latter-day gospel performers such as the Drifters they took the notion of a group. Chuck Berry, Jerry Lee Lewis, and Tommy Steele had been performers with backing musicians. But the Drifters, the Dominoes, and the Coasters, although vocalists and not instrumentalists, were "groups"; that is, each singer was an essential and equal member of the whole. And from the British music hall tradition, the Beatles acquired the art of stage presentation. No doubt these influences were unconscious, but each needed the other. The

The English counter-revolution. *Top:* the Who; and *bottom, from left to right:* the Yardbirds; Manfred Mann (at piano); Eric Clapton of Cream.

combustion that resulted caused sparks that set the youth of the world ablaze with energy. Within a year of "Love Me Do," there were over 350 groups in Liverpool alone. "The Beatles' method was music—and that was fine," Lonnie Donegan says. "Had they known what the aftermath would be, I wonder whether they would have done it the same way. I admire their musical integrity, but, at the time, I was resentful of the change. The whole of conventional show business had the same resentment. Pop groups were closing the theaters and putting everybody out of work. A strange bedlam was taking over which had nothing to do with anything we had previously known."

George Martin, a record producer with EMI, remembers how it started for him. "I was looking for something new. I didn't know what I was looking for. Then Epstein walked into a recording company to get some lacquers cut of some of the Beatles tapes. The engineer thought they were interesting and telephoned a colleague of mine in the publishing branch. He called me and said: 'This guy has been round every record company in London—and he's getting nowhere. Will you see him?' So I did. And when I listened to the tapes, I understood why everyone had turned them down—they were awful. But I asked Epstein to send the boys down for a test. When I met them, I thought they were great. I didn't think their songs were very good. But I offered them a contract." The Beatles went to Hamburg again, on their third "European tour."

Martin thought they would make out as recording artists, but not as hit writers. The songs they had produced were elementary, and on their first recording date at EMI (September 11, 1962), Martin replaced Ringo Starr with a session drummer and left the fourth Beatle with a tambourine to rattle. Success, however, was like a hothouse. "It forced them up in a beautiful way," Martin says. "They were very quick learners. And they were always wanting to experiment, always asking questions. We used a string quartet, for example, very early in their recording lives. I would suggest using a piccolo, or a trumpet, or a cor anglais. They would say: 'What's a cor anglais?' And I would demonstrate how it sounded and they'd say: 'Great. Let's try that.' They were fascinated by the techniques of orchestral players, and slightly confused sometimes. I remember on one occasion I was using a saxophone section in the studio and I was asking John what notes he wanted for the riff in the backing. He sketched it for me on the guitar and I transcribed the notes for the sax section. But he said: 'You're giving them the wrong notes. You said A flat and it's really F.' So I explained that I had to give them an A flat for his F. John said: 'How's that?' I said: 'Because your F is their A flat. He just said: 'That's bloody stupid.' He was quite right, of course."

Lennon said later: "George Martin helped us develop a language to talk with musicians. Because I'm shy, I didn't go much for musicians. I didn't like having to go and see twenty guys sitting there and try to tell them what to do. Martin translated for us." Martin explains how this translation worked. "John said to me: 'I've got a song called 'Being for the Benefit of Mr. Kite' and I want it to sound like a whirligig, fairground noise.' So we organized two electric organs, one for each of us. Then I overdubbed a swirling, chromatic run at half-speed. That is, slowing the tape down to half-speed and then speeding it up again so that eventually it is played at twice normal speed. Next I got dozens of old steam organ tapes, playing everything from Sousa Marches to the Liberty Bell. I cut the tapes into fifteen-inch lengths and told the engineer to throw them all up in the air, which he did. Then I told him to pick them all up and stick them back together again, which he did. Finally, we reshuffled them a bit until we had a tape which had no musical shape and was nonsense. But it *was* the sound of a steam organ. I laced that into the vocal track and created a floating, fairground sound. And that's how 'Mr. Kite' was done. Like a huge jigsaw puzzle. There was nothing clever about it. It was merely developing new ideas by means of modern techniques."

The Beatles became an abstraction, like Christmas. They belonged to the world. "They represented hope, optimism, lack of pretension, that anyone *can* do it, whatever their back-

ground," Derek Taylor says. "Their capacity for survival impressed people. Their collective charm was powerful and they just seemed unstoppable." "Paul and I wanted to be bigger than Elvis," Lennon said. "Because Elvis was the thing—whatever people say, he was it." "A fellow once said to me: 'I remember you, Ringo,' " Paul McCartney says. "So I said: 'Remember when I was drumming?' He said: 'Ah, you were great then, too.' Well, I don't remember it, but *he* remembers it, so maybe it was true." The myth had become more real than the reality.

Murray Kaufman—Murray the K, New York disc jockey—remembers getting a record called "She Loves You" in October 1963. "I played it on a record contest I used to run and it came in third. I went on playing it for a few weeks but nothing happened, so I dropped it and went off to Miami for Christmas. Suddenly, listening to the radio there, every other record was by the Beatles. I got a call from my program director saying: 'You've got to come back, the Beatles are coming.' I said: 'Get yourself an exterminator.' But he put it in no uncertain terms that I was to cut my vacation short and get to the airport and meet them. I did. It was pandemonium."

It happened that the Beatles knew of Murray the K from record albums for which he had written the sleeve notes. They invited him to join their tour—he shared a room with George Harrison—where he acquired a close view of Beatlemania, American style. "It was absolutely unreal, almost getting crushed to death at Union Station. They were quite different from our old familiar superstars like Sinatra. They didn't take themselves seriously and looked to the crowd, more or less, for their own entertainment."

Musically, they were a traumatic shock to America. Their love of black rhythm and blues, which they had first heard as youngsters in Liverpool, was immediately evident in their music. A whole generation began to ask itself why it had ignored this music for so long. The promise of Elvis was revived, but this time by a group of rough, rug-headed bumpkins who, being British, neatly turned out, expert stage performers, and socially acceptable, dictated their own terms. Murray the K recalls: "They wanted some records by a folk singer I'd not heard of. I got hold of a few and played them. I might never have heard of this strictly folk musician if the Beatles hadn't made me aware of him. He was Bob Dylan."

The Beatles also had a startling effect on American dress and attitude. They were invited to a party given by David Ormsby Gore, then British Ambassador to the United States. They hated it, and it showed. "They thought he was great," Kaufman remembers, "but they hated all those society ladies. They were utterly different from any other musical, or even movie, stars that America had ever seen." They related instantly to young people and thereby galvanized the discontent experienced by many in the aftermath of Kennedy.

What the Beatles had taken from America, and particularly black America, they now repaid a dozenfold by their example. In a Los Angeles folk club called the Troubadour, for example, Jim (later he would call himself Roger) McGuinn was trying to put a "Mersey beat" into his songs. McGuinn told me: "The folk freaks didn't think much of it. They just didn't understand where I was coming from with that sound." McGuinn had seen the early Beatles film *A Hard Day's Night* and entirely changed his view of what was possible in popular music. Before long, he was joined by Gene Clark and David Crosby and then by Michael Clarke. All they possessed was a twenty-five dollar Japanese guitar and a bunch of cardboard boxes on which Michael Clarke learned to play the drums. Later, Chris Hillman joined them from bluegrass and for eight months they rehearsed. Finally, they recorded a song by Bob Dylan, produced by Doris Day's son Terry Melcher. *Mr. Tambourine Man*, as sung by the Byrds, went to number one in almost every chart throughout the world and inspired a multitude of folk-rock songs that looked for a while as if they might revitalize with electric sounds the folk tradition being squandered by Nashville.

"The Byrds' audience were the first really strange group of people I had seen," Derek

Sounds from the North Country (of England). *Top:* Gerry Marsden and the Pacemakers, performing in the Cavern; *center:* Freddie and the Dreamers, a more esoteric version of the "Mersey" sound; *bottom:* the Animals, featuring Eric Burdon (center).

Taylor remembers. "Bohemians, poets, afternoon alcoholics who declaimed on politics and art. Yet they were preaching nothing at all; they reeked of a strange oil called patchouli, and the girls wore long dresses from past generations. They danced alone, half demented, it seemed, smiling to themselves. They were the first full-time freaks. They wanted to be outcasts. And they were, because they wanted to be."

Among the Byrds' friends was actor Peter Fonda, who asked them to play at his sister Jane's birthday party. And they did. Henry Fonda was not unpleased, although, as McGuinn recalled later, he *did* ask them whether they really had to play quite so loud. "What they hadn't bargained for," Derek Taylor says, "was that anywhere the Byrds went, Byrds' followers were sure to flock." Uninvited, the Byrd freaks lurched into the Malibu beach house belonging to Henry Fonda that was used for the party. Taylor was appalled to see them dancing at Fonda, pinning him to the wall, and went over to their manager Jim Dickson and said: "Look, they're gate crashers. And look what they're doing to Fonda!" "Doing?" said Dickson. "Doing? This is Hollywood! They've *made* this party. Don't you realize what all this means to these people? They *want* this madness, they've seen nothing like it since the thirties. This is the beginning, this is where the worlds meet again."

California had always been the promised land. California was as far west as a man could go, and America knew all about going west. In 1905, a man named Love moved to California to escape economic servitude in Louisiana. California was where the Okies went during the Depression. A family named Wilson had been among the first. Like thousands of others, they hoped for a place where the climate was gentler and where getting a job might be easier. When they arrived on the Coast, they slept on the beach. Even when the Love and Wilson families became prosperous and moved to comfortable middle-class houses, they retained their fondness for the beach. Eighty percent of *all* Californians live within fifty miles of the beach.

The families combined in marriage; their children grew up together. Although the children had an easier life than their parents—they had cars and they had money to spend on their girls—the beach with its giant rollers and surfing still exerted a powerful fascination. At night the families would gather to share music. Two of the girls played harp, and all of them had piano lessons. Together, they sang of the Cali-

Left: building the Woodstock generation. *Above, top*: Murray "the K" Kaufman, New York disc jockey who promoted post-Beatles British music in America. *Above*: Bill Graham, born in Berlin, 1931, and a refugee to the U.S.A., in his San Francisco office, complete with gold telephone. "I would talk to a lot of the kids; and what it amounted to was they wanted to live very fast, die very young, and have a good-looking corpse."

stars, we just sang because we loved it." Carl Wilson, youngest of the brothers, adds: "The beach was a social place. *Everybody* went there for surfing and just to hang out. And it was the people and their experiences that led to the music that Brian created and we sang. When we were teen-agers, our father would drive us to the crest of a ridge overlooking the ocean and, pointing to the beach which had once been his home, he would say: 'Look at that. Isn't that mighty good? Well, make the most of it, because now you have to go back and work.'" "Our music expressed a desire for life," Mike Love says, "the joy of being."

The Beach Boys had been successful before the Beatles arrived in America. But it was the Beatles who encouraged them to break out of their Coke-soaked surfing image and grow their hair. They were managed by the Wilsons' father, Murray, a scarlet-faced despot who had called their publishing company Sea of Tunes. By all accounts, he managed them remarkably well until the mountain of millions became too steep to leave with less-than-reliable show business lawyers and accountants. "One afternoon," Derek Taylor says, "he had burst into my office on Sunset Boulevard — and I'm not using the word 'burst' lightly. His first words were: 'I'm Murray Wilson,' which I knew, followed by the question: 'Am I coming on too strong?' He was. He always did."

The reason for his visit was to discuss plans for a larger-than-life stained-glass window for his house showing "the boys" standing tall under the California sun, gazing "into the Pacific — into the Sea of Tunes." He needed pictures, he said. Taylor had dozens, but they were all recent, showing them out of their uniform of striped shirts and white pants, on which they had based their performance image and which they were close to discarding for ever. Murray hurled the new pictures all over Taylor's desk and bellowed: "They've all got long hair! I can't use all this long-haired stuff. Where are my boys the way they used to be?" "Life had always been exciting with Murray," Carl Wilson remembers.

The Beatles toured America in 1964, 1965,

fornia they loved. Eventually, the boys — Carl, Dennis, and Brian Wilson, and Mike Love — decided to start a singing group. It was not intended as a commercial venture; it was simply an expression of the way they lived. It seemed natural they should call themselves the Beach Boys; that is exactly what they were.

"We used to go over to each other's houses and just sing round the piano," Mike Love says. "We didn't have any grand desires to be rock

and 1966. Just as more familiar voices, like those of the Beach Boys, began to show the changes wrought by the Beatles, so other new voices began to be heard. The Grateful Dead began in 1965. So did Big Brother and the Holding Company, with its lead singer Janis Joplin. Perhaps most important of all, an entrepreneur named Bill Graham opened the first auditorium specifically for rock and roll (or rock, as it had become known) on Geary and Fillmore Streets in San Francisco. "I had no connection whatsoever with rock before 1965," Graham says. "I was a Latin music fan. But once, when I was with a radical theater group, we did a benefit show with some of the groups. The benefit was a success, and more and more it seemed to me that the kids wanted to escape society as it was and come into a bunker with soft lights and loud music. Music was the scenario. Music even became part of love-making. People would say: 'Hey! That's great for balling.' Ten years before, only about two percent of the population might tell each other what made them fuck better. Now music was part of that exchange. The long-haired and the extroverted and the liberated could just swan in and do their thing. But what about the others? What about the guy who was straight, who came to the Fillmore for the first time in his suit or his Saturday pants? I was concerned about *these* people. So, if there was a light show, we'd have posters in the hallway explaining it. I wanted to tell people about the groups.

"What we wanted to do was encourage people to let their insides out a little. When I was younger and went to ballrooms, it was always very light and everybody could see everybody else. But for an introverted guy, it can often be very difficult knowing how to behave in a public place. So we kept the lights low and the atmosphere relaxed. And it would happen a thousand times that, because a guy would feel that he was not being watched, he would begin to move a little, and maybe his Saturday night date woud move a little. So the second time he'd wear sneakers, and maybe the fourteenth time he'd open his shirt and just have a good time. He was snatching—ever so gently—at a new

Facing page: before and after. *Top:* early Byrds, 1966, Jim (now Roger) McGuinn at left, David Crosby next to him. *Bottom:* later Byrds. McGuinn: "We felt our best shot was to interpret Bob Dylan and Pete Seeger and just stick a few of our own songs in there and hope they would be of the same quality." He told me: "I wrote 'So You Wanna Be a Rock and Roll Star?' with Chris Hillman; it was a bitter kind of song—we were just falling off then. Every group has a two-year chance to get on top. If they're very lucky or very clever, they can stick together like the Rolling Stones or the Beach Boys. Generally a group only has a couple of years. We used our time, and cracked up." *Above top:* the Beach Boys the way their fathers liked them. Left to right, Al Jardine, Mike Love, Carl Wilson, Brian Wilson, Dennis Wilson. Mike Love told me: "It was kind of all very innocent in the beginning. We didn't have any grand design to be rock stars—that wasn't a clearly defined goal for anyone in those days. We just sang along with Chuck Berry and Elvis songs then." *Above:* what became of the Beach Boys.

life-style. Music should be free. Flowers in the streets. Trees blossoming all over. Power to the people.''

Graham began to organize free open-air concerts in Golden Gate Park. Ten or fifteen thousand people would show up. ''One time I had my son on my shoulder, he was two years old,'' he recalls. ''I walked into the park, like I did every Sunday. There was no sign saying 'Bill Graham Presents.' It was just there—part of our contribution. And it then hit me that I knew every face that was there. They were always there,

every Sunday. So I started talking to them: 'Hi, what do you do?' And they would say: 'Hey, man, wait for Sundays, baby.' 'What do *you* do?' 'This is far out, man.' 'What do *you* do?' 'I panhandle, man.' And I realized that for sixty or seventy percent of them this was their life.''

Within the Fillmore Auditorium, according to Graham, there were also moments of magic. Aretha Franklin and Ray Charles came there; Graham, for once, turned *up* the house lights. ''For the first time in my career I actually saw an audience of equal black and white. They

sweated together, armpit to armpit, and everybody liked each other, and went out together at the end." Then there were Thanksgiving dinners; the Fillmore staff printed three thousand tickets for the regular customers, and on Thanksgiving night the theater would open for a mighty party. There was a strange but undeniable feeling of unity and purpose.

In 1966, the Byrds toured England — heralded, to their own embarrassment, as "America's answer to the Beatles." They asked to meet the Beatles, and the Beatles declared them to be the best American band there was, so they must have been. Confusingly, McGuinn says: "I grew my hair to copy the Beatles, but also to express myself. I didn't want to be put in a mold and squared off and shipped out like something that was made in a factory. It was a rebellion, but using commercial means. We all wanted to break down the established structure of society."

Soon, the Beatles met the Beach Boys. Elvis Presley acknowledged what was happening and, not fearing for his crown, became the Beatles' friend, exchanging gifts and meeting them. It was, in that immortal phrase, all coming together. It was no longer surprising to find poets like Allen Ginsberg backstage at a rock concert, to see novelist Norman Mailer at ringside when the Byrds did a show at the Village Gate in New York. Music had acquired a message, and a mystique. The Mamas and the Papas and the Lovin' Spoonful went west from New York and bathed in the sweet smells and sounds of San Francisco. Donovan and the Animals came from Britain and fell into the same ethereal pit. "It happened in San Francisco. It happened all right, didn't it?" John Lennon told an interviewer. "I loved it. We were all kings then. We created something there. We didn't know what we were doing, but we were all talking, blabbing over coffee, like they must have done

The all-pervasive effect of the Beatles even got the Rolling Stones into uniform. Bill Wyman, bass player, second from left, told me how those uniforms were worn twice, once for a TV show and once for this photograph. Then they were thrown away and the Rolling Stones got on with the serious business of being a youth revolution.

in Paris, talking about paintings. Me and Eric Burdon and the others would be up all night and day talking about music, playing records and arguing and getting drunk. It's beautiful history."

The summer of 1967 was particularly beautiful. The Beatles recorded "All You Need Is Love," God was in His heaven with Mammon salivating around every California palm tree. No governments had fallen, no churches collapsed. But, among the young, a ludicrous, joyful hope persisted. There were dreams a-plenty. As Donovan said to me at the time: "What pop does is make me very rich. As a result, I've got big dreams. I see all the writers together again, and all the film makers together. All beautiful things. Controlling the whole market, all the markets, with all the art. Just how you'd imagine if you sat down, how you'd really like it. That's how we're gonna make it. Like Greece, the Parthenon. All the great minds of the world sitting up on top of the world working it out. And painters and musicians and everybody can come from all over the world with their dreams. And we will say: 'Yes, you can do that dream. Here's so much, do it.' Pop music is the beginning. Because pop music is changing the scene anyway. Fashion will change, architecture, everything. Because we want it a certain way, and we're gonna have it." At Monterey, that seemed a possibility.

Admittedly, the Beatles had stopped touring; what with all the screaming, it became impossible to hear or be heard. But they consoled themselves with a trip to India and a guru who giggled, the Maharishi. As Lennon said, they came back rested; Ringo said it "was just like Butlins." Admittedly, their relationship with Epstein had suffered a few knocks. His brother, Clive Epstein, says: "It was inevitable people would find out that things done for the boys in the early years, however well-meaning the intentions, were not always done for the best. I don't mind admitting I've found out since that we could have done better deals for them. But you've got to remember that we were all new to show business."

Some evidence now suggests that Brian Ep-

stein was not a good businessman. NEMS Enterprises, his company, had gotten out of control and Epstein was already looking for someone to take over part of his business responsibilities. The Beatles began to feel they had outgrown him. Lennon was to say later: "Brian put us in suits and all that, and we made it very, very big. But we sold out, you know. The music was dead before we even went on our first theater tour of Britain." "The Beatles didn't treat Brian badly, not to my knowledge," Derek Taylor says. "The last time I saw them all together was when I flew over for Brian's housewarming party in late June 1967. They were all very jolly with him and he with them."

He was a complex man. He seemed to know everyone although, remembers Taylor, "when I was ghosting his autobiography—such as it was—it became clear that he was lonely. He sought an exclusivity in his relationships. He didn't like sharing. In fact, he didn't want to share the Beatles with me, although I was his personal assistant and their press officer. He was funny, worldly, quite ready to tell stories against himself, terribly bad-tempered, romantic, sensitive to beauty—like gardens and rooms and royalty and all those nice things. But he was also a card-carrying supporter of Harold Wilson and got very excited about left-wing politics and made sure he voted Labour.

"He had other areas of his life, into which I didn't venture, and these caused him pain. We never knew where he went at night, and he frequently seemed unhappy. It was nothing that any of us could do much about. His father had died that summer, which hurt. And, like a lot of people with a full address book, there were times he couldn't reach anyone. If you are accustomed to being surrounded by a lot of people and nobody answers the phone, you get depressed. He got paranoid when that happened to him. He would think it was all over. And on one of those nights he died."

When told of Epstein's death, Lennon said: "I was scared. I thought: 'We've fuckin' had it.'"

Left: John Lennon, out of uniform, jamming with Chuck Berry. Born in Wentzville, Missouri, in 1926, Berry was persuaded by Muddy Waters to be a guitarist instead of a hairdresser in 1955. Subsequently, he became a hero for most of the British rockers. *Above:* George Martin and Paul McCartney.

All Along the Watchtower

On Thursday, May 29, 1969, at 7:45 p.m., six or seven policemen burst into the London home of Mick Jagger. Jagger said: "I didn't get a chance to say anything because one of them stuck his foot in the door. They kept me in the dining room while they searched the place." At Marlborough Street Magistrates Court the following morning, a large crowd gathered outside shouting: "We love you, Mick," while Michael Philip Jagger and Marianne Evelyn Dunbar (who sang professionally as Marianne Faithful) were being formally charged for the possession of cannabis. Television cameras peered at the front door of the court awaiting their exit. Jagger said: "It was all very boring." The charges were later dismissed.

A British opinion poll had shown that over fifty percent thought Jagger's

Mick Jagger, 1975, Fort Collins, Colorado.

previous conviction for possessing four pep pills—legally acquired outside Britain—had been too lenient. "I believe there can be no evolution without revolution," Jagger said himself. "Why *should* we try to fit in? I know I earn too much, but I'm still young and there's something spiteful in me which makes me hold on to what I've got." The Rolling Stones had been outlaws from the start: destructive in tone, arrogant in style, apocalyptic in performance, they more than any others had upended the notion of order being essential to art. It was proclaimed, very loudly, that art was chaos and chaos art. As Jim Morrison, lead singer of the Doors, said: "Erotic politicians, that's what we are. We're interested in everything about revolt, disorder, and *all* activity that appears to have no meaning."

For an early Rolling Stones record album, their manager, Andrew Loog Oldham, had written: "If you don't have enough bread to buy this disc, get that blind man, knock him on the head, steal his wallet and lo, behold, you have the loot. If you put the boot in, good: another sold." Admirably, the record company refused to endorse Oldham's sleeve notes. But when the Rolling Stones first visited California, some of their followers issued this proclamation: "Greetings and welcome, Rolling Stones, our comrades in the desperate battle against the maniacs who hold power. . . . They call *us* dropouts and delinquents and draft dodgers and punks. . . . But we will play your music in rock and roll marching bands as we tear down the jails and free the prisoners, as we tear down the schools, as we tear down the military bases and arm the poor, creating a new society from the ashes of our fires."

In fact, the message was essentially no different from that proclaimed at Monterey. Only the means had changed. Those who had watered the garden of flower power had discovered they were no more immune to entrepreneurial rip-offs than any other popular musician, black or white. The media and big business began to undermine the naïve optimism that had given strength to the music of

San Francisco and Liverpool. The Beatles, as befitted their role as leaders, attempted to stem the tide. "When we were touring and Beatlemania was at its peak of hysteria," McCartney remembers, "it would have been very easy to have used that power for evil purposes. But that was Hitler, that was what he wanted to do. There was, however, a desire to get power and use it for the good. We started off as a rock group, just playing what we wanted to play. But when Brian Epstein died, we found ourselves committed to record deals, music publishing contracts, films, and so on. So we tried to look and see whether we could do any better and get better deals. The idea of running our own affairs just snowballed from that simple beginning. All we wanted to do was to provide the kind of business situation that we always hoped there would be when *we* were trying to get a record contract or get into films or whatever. So now, instead of just taking all the profits out and being fat and rich, what we hoped to do was reinvest in things we believed in. For the first time, the bosses weren't going to want all the money back."

It was a noble ambition. "This *is* a business,"

Left: Janis Joplin. *Near right:* Timothy Leary provided the ideology for drugs; *far right:* Ken Russell provided an art derived from the ideology.

McCartney said at the time, "but we intend to have fun doing it." To that end, the Beatles held their first American board meeting on a hired Chinese junk that sailed, appropriately, it was thought, around the Statue of Liberty in New York Harbor. Liberty, after all, was what they intended to have; liberty to pursue their own schemes—such as putting a statue of British vaudeville comedian Bud Flanagan on every fire hydrant in London; liberty to run their own financial affairs and offer to others the kind of opportunity they claimed had been denied them. Their collective fortune was put into a multi-million-dollar entertainment, electronics, and merchandising enterprise called Apple

Corps Ltd. "It's a pun," Paul said, helpfully.

Then they appeared on the *Johnny Carson Show*, told the world what they were doing, and invited the world to participate. They set up offices in eight countries, with their headquarters in London's Savile Row. Occasionally, a Beatle drifted through in yellow satin frills and white bell-bottomed trousers. A thin girl behind the reception desk said: "I'm sorry, we're not equipped to handle poetry at present." Beads and bells and caftans wafted the worries away. London was thought to be swinging. Businessmen, cab drivers, secretaries, and society hostesses pushed and hustled for the weird and wonderful Apple artifacts. The Beatles opened two boutiques, patented an assortment of electronic inventions, began to build their own

recording studio—described by Paul as "the most technically sophisticated in the world"—planned four feature films, bought property including supermarkets, and carried along the hopes of a generation.

Eighteen months later, Lennon announced he was down to his last fifty thousand pounds, and that unless something was done, the Beatles would be broke within a year. An American businessman, Allen Klein, previously associated with the Rolling Stones, was brought in by John to administer a little organization. Jagger, in fact, had suggested the liaison. Lennon was nervous, but so was Klein. They met at London's Dorchester Hotel. "He told me

what was happening with the Beatles," Lennon once said, "and my relationship with Paul and George and Ringo. He knew every damn thing about us. He's a fuckin' sharp man." For his services, Klein took twenty percent of all the Beatles' earnings.

McCartney had meanwhile married Linda Eastman, whose brother John and father Lee were music business lawyers. The Beatles had almost signed themselves over to the Eastmans at one point. But Lennon didn't like them, and Klein, in spite of hostile rumors, seemed equally trustworthy. It was an expensive mistake. Derek Taylor, who had made some attempt to keep the ship afloat, says: "I had taken on too much, believing myself to be God. Apple was a dream and, of course, it ended and the Beatles woke up

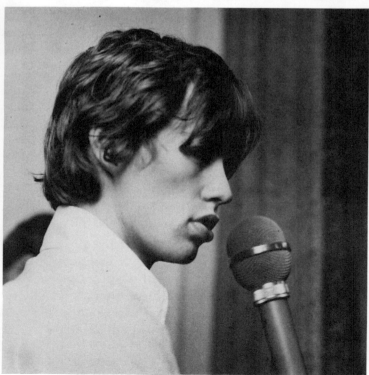

to discover they were still tired, even after a good night's meditation. Then it became a nightmare, and this time they didn't wake up. They broke up." The Apple shop closed, the movie section became a vehicle for individual Beatles' whims. The electronics division fused. The love so strong among the four was handed over for lawyers to work out. John and Paul quarreled. John told Paul he was leaving. In October 1968, John and Yoko Ono were busted for possession of marijuana. There were rows with the Eastmans, rows with Klein. The copyrights of their songs, now owned by a public company, were bought up by the very businessmen against whom Apple had been created. Within months, Paul took legal action to declare the Beatles dissolved. It was only three years after Monterey.

"The change had all begun very casually," Bill Graham recalls. "If a band was late, the public would say: 'Hey, man, cool it, we've got all night.' And there was one big group I couldn't believe. They walked up onstage—late—plugged in, turned their backs on the audience, and played the entire set watching the light show on the the backdrop. And the kids were happy. Nobody cared."

The new ideology of youth was blazingly direct: "Hope I die, before I get old," they sang. "They did themselves a great disservice," Graham continues. "It was so easy to say: 'Up against the wall, motherfucker—down with Nixon—we shall overcome.' They did nothing but speak negatively. Yet, if you'd taken a poll, ninety percent of them would have had nothing to complain about. Kids would come up to me and ask for spare change and I'd ask them what for? And they'd say: 'To see the show.' So I'd tell them the show was a luxury they'd have to pay for, they had to earn it. 'Should be free, man.' So I'd ask: 'What does your father do?' 'Bakery.' 'Then give me the address,' I said. 'I want free bread.' And they would look at me and say: 'Where you coming from, man?' They just didn't—couldn't—relate to any sense of reality."

"The idea in all our heads then was to ball every chick in sight," Eric Burdon, leader of the Animals, says. "That was the prime continual object: to have a permanent party. We didn't really care about the finances. We didn't know much about the ins and outs of business. We were involved in an attempt to make the whole world your front street." The mood was impatience, an unwillingness to postpone any satisfaction. I want to sleep—gonna sleep *now*. I want to make love—gonna do it *now*. Eat *now*; drink *now*; everything *now*. You want a flower? Take this flower or I'll break your arm. The affluence had enabled supposedly mature adults to behave like children. Yet the musicians themselves constantly denied any responsibility. As Bill Wyman, bass guitarist of the Rolling Stones, says today: "People were always telling us: 'You're in a position to influence the young, so you should set a good example.' But it had nothing to do with us. If a kid wants to let his hair grow long or wear strange clothes or play a guitar or do *anything*, that's got nothing to do with us. If he likes to listen to our music, that's great. Apart from that, we didn't have *any* responsibility."

"An artist would get onstage and say: 'Let's

Facing page: Alexis Korner (*bottom left*), the important, though relatively unknown, influence on British rock and blues, is credited with discovering the Rolling Stones, including Bill Wyman (*top left*), still the group's bass guitarist, and Brian Jones (*top right*). *Bottom right:* Michael Jagger; the artist as a young man. *Above:* Mick and Bianca Jagger immediately after their wedding. Mrs. Jagger desired stardom in her own right.

get together,' " Bill Graham remembers, "and fight and share and communicate. Then he'd get into his jet and fly off to his island and play with his sixteen-track machine. It was hypocrisy. The misuse of power was devastating. Do you realize what Jimi Hendrix could have done? Or Jim Morrison? Or Janis Joplin? Of course, they had a responsibility, which was to entertain. One of their main selling points, after all, was convincing the audience that they were all in it together. They were all against Washington, and all for the legalization of drugs. They were all against the war in Vietnam, and all in favor of everybody and everything being beautiful. But how many musicians went out onstage and said: 'Don't take acid, it ruins your head'? Not one. Not one. When I went out and told them bad drugs were being passed, the kids just laughed." Membership in the drug fraternity promoted a sense of togetherness and well-being; it also sold records.

Musicians were caught in a vortex of their own inspiration. Even if you were not involved with drugs, it was usually assumed you were. "I never took drugs in those days," Bill Wyman told me. "In the sixties, however, I was regarded as one of the worst heads. So was Charlie Watts, just because we looked like it. I just stood there on stage, yet people have said to me since: 'You were the heaviest junkie—you used to stand there with this mean look.' And if any of our group *was* busted for drugs, the papers always said: 'Rolling Stones Arrested.' It was outrageous." "*Help* was made on pot," Lennon has since admitted. "*A Hard Day's Night,* I was on pills." A softness for LSD he blamed on some "middle-class London swingers" who had "laid it on George, me, and our wives without telling us at a dinner party." As for heroin—it was "not too much fun. We sniffed a little when we were in real pain. I mean we just couldn't . . . people were giving us such a hard time." The middle-class swingers, presumably. And who had made them swingers? Mickey Mouse?

> *I'll shout and scream, I killed the King.*
> *I was around when Jesus Christ had his moment of doubt and pain.*

Killed the Tsar and his ministers . . .
   Pleased to meet you, hope you
      guessed my name.

Inside one album, the Rolling Stones are depicted at the aftermath of some squalid feast set in a decaying baronial hall. Jagger, in battered trilby, sneers at the camera, his mouth stuffed with an apple. Drummer Watts is slumped, feet on the head of the table. The others are splayed morosely among the remnants of an orgy that might have been, grins of seedy self-congratulation across their lips. The album, like the "revolution" they had so fervently espoused, was called *Beggars Banquet*. But the pickings were considerable. In 1968, over one hundred million rock records were manufactured and sold. One hit song would earn more in a year than ninety percent of the population would earn in a lifetime. The revenue of a single music publishing company during the preceding five years had exceeded the total famine relief received by India during the preceding ten.

The question was, whose profit? The success of the Beatles had encouraged the belief that rock and roll had at last freed popular music from the shackles of Tin Pan Alley; that youth had something valuable to contribute other than its youthfulness. Jagger and his imitators were poisoning this hope. Partly this had come about by familiar means. "He [Jagger] took my music," Muddy Waters says. "But he gave me my name." Partly this brash posturing, which had become essential for the well-bred rock star, hid a less comfortable reality. "It was a struggle for groups in those days, in spite of their apparent success," Keith Moon, drummer with the Who, says. "There were so many of them that agents just signed up anyone who came along. We were sent out to the most obscure places, one side of the country one night and the other side the next, and all for thirty dollars a night. But it would cost that to get

Top left: Jerry Garcia, born in San Francisco, 1942, later discharged as unfit for Army service, but good enough for the Grateful Dead. *Bottom left:* Eric Burdon, originally of the Animals, in Palm Desert, California. *Top right:* Jim Morrison of the Doors, under arrest; *bottom right:* Joe Cocker, British longshoreman turned pop singer, at Woodstock.

there and back. Most of our pocket money, therefore, had to be borrowed from the agents — and paid back with interest. In fact, you never really earned any money at all. The equipment was paid for by the agency, so was the van that took you to concerts and brought you home. And when the agents got paid for the work we had done, they kept most of it as repayment for loans and paid us ten or twenty dollars a week. The agents and the managers and the record companies had everything sewn up, and we were just getting further and further into debt."

The mid-sixties was littered with rock groups exploited in much the same way as many of the swing bands had been in the thirties. On tour, promoters would demand five or six performances a week; if the crowds were good, maybe a

seventh. Image was everything. Manfred Mann denied for years that he was married with a child, even though his family was everything to him. "People treated us like cattle," he says. "There was no respect for musicians at all. You couldn't go out for a walk, you couldn't go to the shops or lead a normal life. And though you could not afford anything else, you couldn't afford to be seen getting on a bus because pop stars weren't supposed to do that. Everyone was bothering you all the time, but you weren't getting paid for being bothered.

Left: Blood Sweat and Tears, first of the "super groups"? *Right:* Crosby, Stills, Nash and Young, the most successful of the "super groups." The former played rock in a jazz idiom; the latter made their first public appearance at Woodstock.

Meanwhile, the record companies were doing very well out of it. Managers and record companies had a totally different life-style. They despised us, on whom they depended, and hardly paid us any money. Those who were successful, like the Beatles, were really the exception. And even they had to pay in the end."

Against such a background, it might be argued, no one should be surprised that the talk of "revolution" was eagerly listened to. The ambitions which led to the foundation of Apple were perhaps understandable and worthy—the desire to put right seventy years of wrongs. But the attempt failed because of the manner in which this "revolution" was attempted, and because of the public behavior of some of its leaders, who were mostly seen to be lacking in honesty, integrity, and talent. The Beatles were brought down not by their inadequacies as businessmen, which were real enough, but by the hedonistic indulgence of those they inspired. John Lennon could claim, and has, that he never noticed the initials of "Lucy in the Sky with Diamonds" spelled LSD until a determined clergyman insisted it was so. No matter. Lennon was not believed. Roger McGuinn of the Byrds told me how a particularly unpleasant transatlantic flight had been the inspiration for their song "Eight Miles High." "But that song blew us out of the game," he says. "Everyone thought it was an LSD promotion. You only had to say the word 'high' to be associated with drugs. In fact, the Byrds did only one drug song, which was called 'Artificial Energy'—and that was against amphetamines." "It got to the point where people would look down their noses at you if you refused a joint," another musician, now retired, told me. Drugs had been used before the Rolling Stones; the Beatles had had their fill in Hamburg. Haight-Ashbury was in bloom before the Rolling Stones trampled across America. But Jagger, by his example (thought so chic by socialites the world over), epitomized the darker

Left: Jimi Hendrix, who spoke with his guitar; *top right:* Tina Turner, who returned to Africa, but didn't like the food; *bottom right:* Sly Stone, married in Madison Square Garden and divorced soon thereafter, in private.

side of this revolution once so full of promise. He was not the cause of its undoing, but he was certainly its most visible manifestation.

And then Brian Jones was drowned in a silent sadness, floating on the lake by Christopher Robin's house at Pooh Corner, which he had purchased. Jones had left the Rolling Stones two months before. He had been unhappy for a year, becoming increasingly tired and despondent. The French newspapers said he died of a heroin overdose. But he had never taken heroin and, shortly before his death, had been gathering a new band around him for new recordings. The funeral was in Cheltenham, full

of tweeds and prosperous upper-class ladies. "Everybody was around the grave," Bill Wyman remembers. "All his family and relatives were tranquilized. As the coffin was being lowered into the ground, the press was terrible— cameras poking into the grave, everyone asking questions. There was no respect. But when we drove away through Cheltenham, there were thousands of mourners, men with their hats off and women crying. I'd never seen anything like it."

The Beatles, with Yoko Ono in attendance, recording "Let It Be," an unwitting epitaph for their era.

And then there was Hendrix, James Mitchell Hendrix, described by *The New York Times* as "the black Elvis," possibly the finest instrumentalist of his generation, playing his guitar with his teeth, behind his back, or under his leg like T-Bone Walker, masturbating with it, caressing it, dragging from it sounds that no one knew existed. He, too, had advocated pot, which, he predicted in 1967, would be legalized within five years. "I am what I feel," he once told me. "I play as I feel and I act as I feel. I can't express myself in any conversation. I can't explain myself like this or that. It doesn't come out like that. But when I'm up on stage, it's all the world. It's my whole life." Until, one morning in London, drugged, alone, he slipped quietly into oblivion.

"Jimi realized what he was up against," Eric Burdon says, "how he was being manipulated. He knew what he wanted to do with his life and he knew that it just wasn't possible. He went out just like a plant that flowers overnight. It was total show business to go out the way he did. A lot of people did through lack of knowledge. But nobody can tell me that Hendrix didn't know what he was doing, because he played his life the way he played his acts."

Hendrix went crazy, smashing everything in sight. The audience got to its feet and cheered.

Hendrix had come from Seattle, Washington. He was part Mexican, part Negro, the grandson of a Cherokee. He had wanted to be an actor; he had wanted to be a painter; he really didn't know what he wanted to do. He left home at fifteen and never went back. He joined the Army Airborne and made Spec. 4. He went to New York. He was so broke that a girl friend bought him his first guitar. He began to play on every rock and roll tour he could find—Little Richard, B. B. King, Ike and Tina Turner, King Curtis, he played with all of them. One night, at the Café Wha? in Greenwich Village, he was heard by Chas. Chandler, one of the Animals. With his manager, Mike Jeffries, Chandler brought Hendrix to London, found him a couple of musicians, and put him to work in a variety of London clubs. "I remember thinking," Chandler said, "this cat's wild enough to upset more people than Jagger."

Hendrix was first and last an instrumentalist whose music was an extraordinary blend of black culture as interpreted by the Beatles and others and the original black music itself. Some British musicians, who emulated American blues artists, felt they had discovered in Hendrix the real thing. "He was the personification

of black music," Alexis Korner says. (Korner was largely responsible in Britain for the revival of American blues. He discovered and encouraged, among others, the Rolling Stones.) "Hendrix had this horrible feeling that he wasn't playing the blues," Korner remembers. "Such an idea coming from someone that was able to play the blues as well as he could I found very strange. The trouble was that he didn't play it in the watered-down form which had come to be accepted as the blues. Amazingly, he felt guilty because he was playing it perfectly."

The guilt had bizarre manifestations. Success had not been immediate. But at a concert in Munich, Hendrix was pulled from the stage by some overenthusiastic kids. As he jumped back, he noticed his guitar had been cracked in the fray and that several strings had been broken. The years of frustration exploded; he went crazy, smashing everything in sight. The audience got to its feet and cheered. Later Hendrix would strut around his stage like a six-foot parakeet, adorned with witchcraft charms, his hair on end as if in fright of his face. At Monterey, he burned his guitar, clowning like a musical gypsy rampaging around the sensibilities of the young. And all this from a man consumed by self-doubt, who liked dried flowers, lace, brocade, and Japanese canvases. "You can say my music is erotic, I don't care," he said. "When I die I want people just to play my music, go wild, freak out, do anything they want to do. Enjoy themselves. The mechanical life—where cities and hotel rooms all merge into one—has killed that enjoyment for me. So I've just got to get out. Maybe to Venus or somewhere. Some place *you* won't be able to find me."

Again, unlike Jagger, Hendrix's distress had understandable cause. "If you want to see what an American black is going through today, where his mind is at, go and see Jimi Hendrix," Eric Burdon told me at the time, "and you'll realize why there are race riots in America and why the country is close to civil war. He's a wizard on the guitar, but his music is so disturbed and explosive. He is exorcising generations of anger."

At the Woodstock Festival, Hendrix played

Bill Graham decided to close the Fillmores because audiences and performers alike had "become scary, ugly." The deaths of Brian Jones, Jim Morrison, and Jimi Hendrix (funeral, *near left*) were a warning.

"The Star-Spangled Banner" with a wrenching, tearing sound that left the two hundred thousand in the audience stunned. (The film version shows his performance being followed by hysterical applause. Clever film editing can prove anything.) Hendrix had already become passionately involved in the gangs of Harlem, in the growth of the Black Muslim Church. He planned to start a touring Band of Gypsies, a show where music and food and drink would be free, where those who came to listen would come to share. But in the pilfering gloom that pervaded popular music in the late sixties, such an ideal was absurd. It would have meant the end of the entire system on which the propagation of that music depended.

And then there were Jim Morrison of the Doors; Cass Elliott of the Mamas and Papas; Pig Pen, founding member of the Grateful Dead, gross, stupefied, majestic, surly, the embodiment (it was thought) of social challenge; all dead on beds, alone. Youth gathered at festivals not of life, but of death. Jagger watched while a fan was stabbed to death at Altamont. The show must go on; it did. "The musicians did it to themselves," Bill Graham believes. "They got involved in coke or mescaline or heroin on a regular basis, and it showed in their material, it showed in the lapsed time between their records. It got to the point where the public would go to shows just to see if musicians would turn up, and when they did turn up, it was an event. It was a macabre reason for going to a music show, but it was the truth. So many great musicians have gaps of whole years in their careers while they were hooked. And very few reached the potential they might have had they not consumed what they did. And have you thought of what happened to all those kids, those thousands of nameless kids, who followed blindly into the abyss simply because some rock star said it was okay? *What* was okay?"

Janis Joplin was born in Port Arthur, Texas, an industrial town described by her biographer, Myra Friedman, as a "plateau of mediocrity with an undercurrent of violence." She was an

Janis Joplin: "I'm the biggest singer in America, I'm the biggest singer in the world!"

intelligent and gifted painter with a reputation for being "unusual." Her friends loved taking her to parties because she would come on tough, swearing like a truck driver, affronting those who did not regard such behavior as proper to a young lady. She learned to sing, drink, and take drugs. She traveled to San Francisco.

There, she joined a group called Big Brother and the Holding Company, and with them performed at Monterey. Clive Davis was startled, and signed her up for Columbia. She seemed outrageous, and wanted to be thought so, particularly by men, most of whom she intimidated. There was nothing unusual, she thought, in the suggestion that she sealed her recording contract with Davis by fucking him. She swaggered around like the nigger-loving whore that Port Arthur thought she was, her parchment arms flailing like a berserk windmill. "Tell me I'm good, tell me I'm good," she cried out to her audience. With her bottle of booze placed proudly

Left: Mick Jagger and Keith Richard on tour. *Above:* Janis Joplin at home.

atop her amplifier, she paraded the stage like a debauched Carnival Queen, or King Kong in drag. She painted a blood-stained American flag on the side of her Porsche. Grisly, the ultimate in vocal overkill, she wanted to rename her group what she eventually called their first album, Cheap Thrills.

Myra Friedman came to know her after Monterey: "You wouldn't want to be on the bad side of her tongue when she got strong," Friedman told me, "and it took a while to break through. Janis wanted to seem a hard, tough girl. She was, of course, anything but that. She was not classically pretty in any sense of the word; in fact, she looked as though she had just crawled out of some Louisiana swamp. But she had tremendous energy and was determined to seem in command of everything. But she really wasn't. She, too, was just scared."

Frightened by her success, she could not believe she deserved it. She gloried in it, wanted it, yet could not cope with it. Once she screamed at a telephone operator: "Get Johnny Cash on the phone. I'm the biggest singer in America, I'm the biggest singer in the world!" Unsure of her sexuality, she put enormous effort into proving her desirability. She could and did behave like a nymphomaniac. But she could and did behave like an ice maiden. She showed Myra Friedman a picture of herself consumed,

she imagined, by lechery. "But it was just a little kid licking an ice cream," Friedman says. "It wasn't remotely sexy, although Janis thought it was."

In spite of her growing addiction to heroin, Joplin never missed a performance and never turned up late for a rehearsal or recording date. Friedman believes Janis only used heroin because it had become a part of her life, part of the expected behavior of a rock star. She was financially secure, and was managed with affection. But psychologically, she was adrift. Those who surrounded her assumed she was as tough as she wished to appear and did nothing to protect her from what she was doing to herself. She seemed, in fact, at her happiest the weeks before she died. "People are not always depressed when they kill themselves," Myra Friedman affirms. Janis had just made her most successful recording; she had found a relationship that pleased her. She had been off heroin for almost six months, although she still drank a lot. She was in high spirits, and then she picked up the needle and injected a massive, killing overdose into her body.

The Hells Angels insisted on supervising the "security" at the Rolling Stones concert at Altamont near San Francisco in 1969. *Above:* before the Angels arrived. *Right:* after the Angels took over; a youth was stabbed to death during the concert. It was only 18 months since Monterey.

Whatever Gets You Through the Night

By 1970, popular music had arrived at its worst crisis. The hopes of a generation had come to nothing. First Elvis, with his unique synthesis of black and white, then the Beatles, with their rejection of previously approved social and business attitudes: each had contributed beyond measure, Elvis as a performer, Lennon and McCartney as composers. Each had inspired a host of followers and radically changed the direction of an entire culture. Both had been frustrated by the limitations of the medium they had invaded and by the selfish naïveté of their cohorts. For the latter, there was no cure; the Stones and others had set loose a chain of self-destruction that had brought and would continue to bring its inevitable consequences. But as for pop music's limitations, Lennon and McCartney were too good as song writers, separately and together, to be

A group called Kiss, 1975.   David Cassidy.

diverted in the long run by entrepreneurial greed or imitative inanity.

In the years following the Beatles' retirement from live performance, the wealth they had earned gave them freedom to experiment in their electronic playroom, the recording studio. Their first LP, *Please Please Me,* had taken sixteen hours to record; *Sergeant Pepper* took nine months. But out of such experiments came a new awareness of their musical potential. They acquired a musicianship that years of one-night stands and shrieking fans and inadequate amplification equipment had denied them. Instrumentally, neither Lennon nor McCartney was particularly adept. But their example, their demonstration of the possible, gave heart to a growing number of musicians on both sides of the Atlantic for whom technical skill was becoming almost an end in itself.

The dilemma was very simple. The forms in which popular music outside the theater had flourished, or attempted to flourish, during the previous seventy years—whether the twelve-bar three-line blues, or the sixteen-bar four-line Tin Pan Alley song—were no longer sufficient to embrace the burgeoning instrumental skills of many rock performers. The search was on, therefore, to find such a form. McCartney once told me: "I was always frightened of classical music. And I never wanted to listen to it because it was Beethoven or Tchaikovsky and big words like that, and Schönberg! A cab driver the other day had some sheet music of a Mozart thing on his front seat. And I said: 'What's that?' And he said: 'Oh, that's high-class stuff, you won't like that. Highbrow!' And that's the way I always used to think of it. I used to think: Well, that's very clever all that stuff. But it isn't, you know, it's just exactly what's going on in pop at the moment. Pop music *is* the classical music of now."

But classical music has always had a multiplicity of forms within which to express itself. By comparison, popular music is primitive. What could be done with the virtuosity, for instance, of a guitarist like Jimmy Page of Led Zeppelin? For most rock musicians, jazz—the traditional refuge of instrumental virtuosi—seemed defunct, devoid of passion, stale, an obscurantist, barren language, "a painful halt," Leonard Bernstein says. Increasingly, these musicians turned to one another for satisfaction. John Lennon played with Keith Richard of the Rolling Stones; both played with Eric Clapton of the Yardbirds. Like their jazz forebears, rock musicians enjoyed matching their skills against each other. The business mind boggled. If only this casual jamming could be packaged, imagine the profits! Imagine a record that showcased Clapton, Dylan, and perhaps a Beatle. Police would need to be brought in to protect the record stores. And then it happened, on August 1, 1971. George Harrison brought in his friend the sitar player Ravi Shankar, Eric Clapton was there, and so was Bob Dylan, all performing in aid of the fledgling state of Bangladesh.

The concert was not a musical triumph, in spite of individual moments. But it spurred the industry to new efforts at shotgun marriages, most ending in early and acrimonious divorce. Eric Clapton remembers another such grouping: "It was fine until we got onto the stage and suddenly realized that we'd only rehearsed about four or five numbers. We frightened the lives out of ourselves." The irony for Clapton must have been particularly acute since it was he, along with bass player Jack Bruce and drummer Ginger Baker, who had pioneered one way out of popular music's dilemma. They had first played together as early as 1966 at the suggestion of Baker, one of the strongest drummers of his generation. Their method was to improvise around a given theme until mental and physical

exhaustion brought the song to an end. Ignoring the lessons of bebop, the trio decided there were to be no restrictions, rhythmically, harmonically, or melodically—the only limitations were to be their individual skills. With characteristic immodesty, Baker called the group Cream.

Cream was hailed as the musical savior of rock music. Every guitarist tried to soar like Clapton; every bass player wished to thank Bruce for bringing to the instrument a voice it had not seemed to possess before; and every drummer doubled the size of his drum kit. "Improvisation and performances which constantly renew themselves," affirmed Jack Bruce, "that's our goal." To Bruce's counterpoint, Baker gave rhythm; to Clapton's free-flowing skills, he gave shape. On their first tour together, Baker practiced so intensively that he left behind him a trail of hotel bills for broken furniture.

The instrumental prowess of these three musicians was matched only by the size of their egos. "We all thought we were virtuosi and had this dream about being the perfect band," Clapton says, "which wasn't the way to approach it

at all. All we were doing was producing aggressive music." Often, they would quite deliberately attempt to play one another right off the stage, as if to prove who was fastest or most tenacious. Clapton now claims that eventually the group was not even being honest to its audience, that they were just performing the same routine. It had probably occurred to all of them what had been obvious to jazz musicians for decades: improvisation, especially when it self-consciously lacks any relationship to form, is not enough.

Nor was the idea of a supergroup. Occasionally, the associations worked well and seemed worthwhile. The gathering of David Crosby, Stephen Stills, Graham Nash, and Neil Young embarked upon a 1974 tour of thirty concert dates, playing to combined audiences of over one million people. "Managements could be terribly restrictive," Stills says. "I used to play very well with Jimi Hendrix and we would have recorded together. And later, when Young left,

The theater of rock was more than a match for Artaud: Ian Anderson of Jethro Tull *(left)*; Slade *(right)*.

everybody kept nudging us to get back together for 'the business.' Luckily, Neil is much too stubborn for that. But one day Neil and I *will* make an album together, just the two of us, that will absolutely terrorize them."

The uneasy combination of rock groups with symphony orchestras did not work either. John Lloyd of Deep Purple attempted a concerto that succeeded in being neither good rock nor good orchestral music. One critic thought its structure was clumsy, its instrumentation banal, its invention feeble, and its claim to serious composition derisory.

Others were attracted by the notion of attempting a rock opera, by which they usually meant rock music with a story. The most notorious, and successful, was the Who's *Tommy*. Its composer, Pete Townshend, later denied he had described the work as an "opera." It had begun life as a record album; certainly, the music was richer and more complex than anything Townshend had composed before. It was a "concept" album like *Sergeant Pepper* — except that all the songs related to a story. What that story was, however, remained a mystery. For the most part, it seemed an inconsequential yarn about a deaf, dumb, and blind boy whose predicament was allegorical. Of what, remained obscure.

Tommy was performed in 1970 at New York's Metropolitan Opera House, although no attempt was made to stage its action. That was left to Ken Russell. His film, by its extraordinary inventiveness, transformed a collection of exquisite songs, previously crippled by philosophical claptrap, into a magnificent artifact. Yet it also demonstrated that the music appeared to have no operatic life beyond the film; the film was its only possible realization, other than the record. It weakened the notion that "rock opera" as a theatrical form merited prolonged consideration.

Nonetheless, with its emphasis on the vaudeville in rock music, *Tommy* unwittingly opened up another possibility. Since the glory days of San Francisco, rock had become increasingly absorbed in the idea of a "total experience," the creation of an environment in which the music could be heard to its best advantage. Bill Graham had made the first move in this direction by the use of light shows. Soon, no self-respecting rock concert was without psychedelia, which often dwarfed the musicians. Add to this the dense smell of marijuana, the required uniform of multicolored, loose-fitting garments, and the hip, thought-to-be-sophisticated talk lifted wholesale from black youth, and the belief grew that Utopia was right around the corner — well, at least, rock as theater, vaudeville rock, a grotesque reminder that the Beatles had joined together the substantial heritage of British music hall with the excitement and guts of black American music. That meeting produced the son of an Arizona Baptist minister, who described his band as "the ultimate, the end product of an affluent society."

Alice Cooper, born Vince Furnier, liked to dress on stage in gold lamé pants and a black leather jacket hooked together with thongs. His eyes blackened with mascara and eyeshadow, he would thrash his band with a whip, goading them on to ever louder and more raucous noise. A boa constrictor named Yvonne flailed obediently and obscenely between his legs. A trash can was dragged onstage and its contents hurled into the audience, while filthy smoke wafted through the auditorium. Deafening sounds of

battle brought the act to its conclusion, with live chickens being axed on stage, their still-warm, twitching, dismembered bodies hurled bleeding into the laps of the audience while Cooper himself was "beheaded" by a spastic executioner. "Violence and sex sell," Cooper said. His first four LPs averaged a million sales; with one, each buyer acquired a pair of female panties.

Cooper was not alone in such "entertainments." Dr. John the Night Tripper, otherwise Mac Rebennack, sought to re-create the mystique of New Orleans music by dressing himself in African dress woven out of vines, ivy, and snakeskins. His act included an assortment of mock sacrifices and voodoo incantations, performed on a darkened stage lit only by torches. Then there was David Bowie, heavily promoted as one of the world's greatest superstars. In appearance he was unusual: orange hair, laced high-heeled boots, false eyelashes, flowing silk scarves, cheek glitter, and lipstick. In interviews, he proclaimed his bisexuality. In performance, in particular of his declared masterwork *The Rise and Fall of Ziggy Stardust and the Spiders from Mars,* he sang about a cataclysm of universal dimensions that might have been World War III, pollution overkill, or a vision from the nether regions.

Bowie became the object of a cult—or so his management said. Sophisticated fans lauded their approval of Ziggy Stardust and the BBC investigated the phenomenon in a documentary. Whereas bubble gum performers such as David Cassidy or the Osmonds appealed to distinct age groups, it was pointed out, Bowie sold records to both the very young and their older brothers and sisters. Others thought Bowie the musician was lost in an image devoid of humanity. His androgynous body was illuminated by tatty imitations of those same San Francisco light shows. "I know that one day a big artist is going to get killed onstage," Bowie said, "and I keep thinking it's going to be me."

Rock as theater—it has rarely been anything else—received a further nail in its coffin with the advent of another British group called, portentously, Genesis. "At the moment, we are still at the first stage of the audio-visual," the group's ex-singer Peter Gabriel told me, "in much the same state as those first stereo engi-

Facing page: an early 1960s English rocker named Paul Raven found the answer: he changed his hair, his costume, and his name—and became a star as Gary Glitter. *Above:* Patti LaBelle and the Bluebells, from Philadelphia, Pennsylvania, recorded, "I Sold My Heart to the Junk Man" in 1962, and "Danny Boy" in 1964. Eleven years later, they appeared at the Metropolitan Opera House as, simply, LaBelle.

neers who experimented with trains passing from one speaker to another. We did not intend to create a Hollywood song and dance spectacular, however, but a concept whose visual and musical aspects can be expressed at the same time." To this end, he shaved the front of his scalp which gave the appearance of the last of the Mohicans. It was, he said, a "gimmick to make more money." In a black jumpsuit and harsh white make-up, he sang of (among other things) a woman who unzipped herself on a train and fell apart in halves. Another song, entitled "Supper's Ready," told of "the ultimate cosmic battle for Armageddon between good and evil in which man is destroyed, but the deaths of countless thousands atone for mankind, reborn no longer as Homo Sapiens." Ah.

At one concert, Genesis' drummer invited the audience to boo. "It gave them something to do which was not just a considered, automatic, and politely conceived response," he says. "We liked to conjure up an image of playfulness," Peter Gabriel added. "Our role as musicians is somewhere between the orchestra in the pit and the old-fashioned, but out-front, rock and roll group. Instead of the band being the focus of attention, therefore, it will be the mime or dance or whatever we are orchestrating. I appreciate that this may well be providing more bourgeois escapism."

In 1969, one Dave Robinson and his partner formed a promotion company whose principal, if not only, clients were a group of British pop musicians known as Brinsley Schwarz. Robinson decided to unveil the group for an expectant world by means of what he described as "the biggest hype of all time." He rented a transatlantic jet in London, and a fleet of black Cadillacs in New York. Then he invited a hundred or so British journalists to witness the group's triumphant debut at Bill Graham's Fillmore East. (After his success in San Francisco, Graham had opened up a second auditorium in New York.)

When the journalists arrived at the Fillmore,

> **White music, which has emasculated black music for decades, has now achieved the same result with itself.**

they discovered that Brinsley Schwarz was only the support band. The group played competently but briefly, the audience clapped politely, and the journalists were left composing articles to defend themselves against the accusation of having been influenced by promotional generosity. If popular music is measured by the number of gossip column inches, the expedition must be reckoned a success. But if popular music is about anything else, the hype was a disaster. Not a single record contract resulted, not even a favorable review. Instead, the group was left with a hideous debt. Robinson threw himself into what seemed an impossible job of recoupment. After three years of incessant touring of bars and clubs, school dances, college parties, and civic ballrooms, he did it. Musically, however, the group was finished. They made a few records, some of which were well received. But they never again achieved the first-night "glamor" of their debut at the Fillmore.

This attempt to impress the audience by the glossiness of the packaging was hardly new. But it was a measure of the creative bankruptcy of popular music in the early seventies that the rock public came to believe in glitter as an achievement. Paul Raven, who started his career as an entertainer when only fifteen, spent ten consistently unsuccessful years performing a passable imitation of what Elvis Presley was presumed to have been like in his early days. An experienced recording executive named Mike Leander, while casting about for a new act, saw Raven, dressed him in silver lamé— leaving bare an expanse of hairy chest—and changed his name to Gary Glitter. "Do You Wanna Be in My Gang?" gurgled Glitter. Who could resist?

Meanwhile, in Salt Lake City, Utah—a place known for its locusts, seagulls, saints, and predilection for soft drinks—a prolific family by the name of Osmond observed that black music could be turned into nice, clean, and prof-

---

David Bowie and the triumph of androgyny.

itable family entertainment. By chance, the five boys and a girl had voices as pretty as their faces; dutifully, they all went to work. Their music became known by the name of what could be seen exuding from the faces of their audience—bubblegum. Every time one of their voices broke, it became a national event, and ten percent of their enormous profits went clattering into the Mormon Church. The Ohio Express, early apostles of this bubblegum music, also oozed cleanliness, while singing to its adolescent audience, most of whom were female: "Yummy, yummy, yummy, I got love in my tummy,"

The most resplendent of this theatrical ragbag, however, was a British group called Roxy Music. Immaculate, whether in high cowboy drag or full Nazi regalia, whether languid in white tuxedos or rampant like horror movie drop-outs, they played the changes so fast that their faithful audience always seemed to be one costume behind. "For a long time, I couldn't really decide which I was more interested in, music or the visual arts," their leader, Bryan Ferry, says. "I'd always wanted to be a painter and, as a music fan, I'd always preferred to see the more exotic black American bands. They always presented themselves so . . . immaculately. The slick, visual appeal was an added bonus. That's why Roxy Music pays so much attention to presentation on stage and packaging for records."

"Roxy Music's audience in America," Lester Bangs, editor of the rock and roll magazine *Creem*, says, "is a bunch of young people who have picked up on their superficial stylistic mannerisms, reminiscent of the old Andy Warhol, and made it into the latest teen-age fad. They think it's hip to be gay, or act as though you were. The girls all dress up in 1940s outfits and walk around acting bored, while the boys mince around acting queer. They see it as a way

British and American pop stars proved that image could be more significant than performance. *Top left:* Roxy Music (Bryan Ferry second from right), who tried elegance; *bottom left:* the New York Dolls, who tried transvestism; *bottom right:* Dr. John, who tried Cajun fur and snakeskin; and *top right:* Elton John, who tried anything and everything.

of rebelling by nonassertion. The band is musically very sensitive to a lot of different things. But their vitality is severely limited due to the fact that the leader of the group is this fellow named Bryan Ferry, possibly the most vacuous excuse for a superstar yet to appear. It was my unfortunate experience to meet Mr. Ferry once at a party. I rushed up to him and said: 'Bryan Ferry, you're my hero. I love you, great record.' But this man was so bland. He stood there in his white tuxedo with his cigarette in his hand and said absolutely nothing. Somebody should have shoved him in a corner, put a martini in his hand, and forgotten about him. Like all glam bands, Roxy Music are more interested in getting their names in the social register and trying on different kinds of clothes than doing anything about real rock and roll. In Roxy Music, you see the triumph of artifice. Because what they are about is that they are not about anything.''

Ferry's silence, of course, could be reckoned preferable to mouthing revolution; musically, it might seem a little unfair to dump him with the Osmonds or Gary Glitter. His songs are superior in every way: better constructed, more challenging lyrically, more rewarding harmonically. But as Ian Anderson of Jethro Tull reminded me: "I think we helped spawn something in rock music which has become a very unhealthy trend: the ludicrously expensive theatrical element became so important, that the music couldn't keep pace at all. Who is going to pay more to see me than they would for a good hamburger?'' Lester Bangs recalls a Jethro Tull concert in which "they were laying down all their *sturm and drang* heavy metal music, when suddenly one of the group got dressed in a bunny suit and went hopping across the stage. Perhaps there was a message, but it escaped me. It was just the same old gunk music dressed up in new clothes.''

The rock and roll "revolution" appears to have come full circle. White music, which has emasculated black music for decades, rendering it harmless and making it culturally painless, has now achieved the same result with itself. In such a milieu, Elton John bounces to the top of the charts with unnerving regularity. He has brought to popular music a refreshing, extroverted vigor. But his music, although skillfully fashioned, is empty; for some, much of it might easily—although unfairly—be mistaken for Muzak. "We are usually compared with music,'' Lee Valvoda, an executive of Muzak's Memphis operation, says, "but that is not our purpose at all. It's easier to describe what Muzak is not than what it is. It is not background music and it is not piped music and it is not entertainment music. Because it is used specifically and entirely for commercial purposes, we call it functional music.''

Muzak had begun in the mind of Brigadier General George Squire, an officer with the Signal Corps during World War I. Squire thought that music might alleviate the boredom of soldiers bogged down in the trenches and under

Left: Alice Cooper in maternity drag; *right:* Alice with Yvonne, America's most successful boa constrictor.

fire for days on end. He conceived the idea of piping tunes down the field telephone cables, in between orders telling the men to advance and get killed. After the war, the idea lay dormant until an advertising executive, William Benton (who was also responsible for the jingle "You'll wonder where the yellow went, when you brush your teeth with Pepsodent"), using the local telephone company's lines, piped music into a number of restaurants.

Another war gave Muzak the boost it needed. In munitions factories all over England, the strains of total war were purged by the sound of music. The scheme was so successful that a number of academic studies were instituted to discover exactly what could be done to harness music power to dollar power. The research demonstrated that it was possible to stimulate the work rate with varied music patterns. Not any old pop tunes, that is, but carefully manufactured music whose purpose was "ear conditioning." "Each tune," Valvoda says, "has a degree of stimulation programmed against the worker's fatigue curve. If you were listening to music at seventy beats per minute, it would do nothing for you because that's your pulse rate. It would neither soothe you nor stimulate you. In fact, we never go below seventy beats because we are not interested in soothing people or putting them to sleep."

"Even if you brought me the Mona Lisa to sell," advertising executive Jack Brokensha says, "I'd find the right music. First, I'd lay down some really strange electronic sounds — we could have a lot of fun with moog synthesizers, principally because it would be so appealing to sell an old art situation with some ridiculous modern electronics. I once sold a telephone book with a bunch of clever lyrics, and sold a truck by getting some good funky down-home music and shouting slogans over the top of it. You can sell anything with well-selected music. I'm a bit of a jazz performer myself — I play a little jazz for my musical head."

Muzak and the jingle factory have ambitions similar to those of many contemporary popular music manufacturers. Sometimes, the brand name changes, but the goods remain the same. Black music, whether from Detroit or Philadelphia, has become slick and sterile, its blackness carefully dressed for the white supermarket. The product (they claim) is a manifestation of black power. An entire industry called disco music has been created to satisfy the theory that music is now "used specifically and entirely for commercial purposes."

Record executives now burrow deeper and deeper into the past for as yet unexploited material to coin their next millions. The rich seam of blues, jazz, and ragtime has been exhausted; folk music, Irish, medieval, Jamaican, anything, as long as it is old, continues to supply the occasional bonus; country music is obscured beneath a thick coating of lacquer. Instrumental skill, once thought to be a prerequisite for musicianship, has been lost in the rattle of rock theater. A misguided search for "true" music — exploitable, of course — consumes producers and performers alike. What was thought to be indigenous Jamaican music was given the name "reggae" or "blue-beat," usually recorded quickly, cheaply, and without concern for the

Left: Donny Osmond began his career as one of a clean-cut group of Mormon brothers who sang on the *Andy Williams Show;* as with David Cassidy, the audience was too busy watching to care about the sound. *Above:* the Bay City Rollers.

artists' well-being or payment. Much of it was uninspired, poorly produced, and out of tune; it seemed crude in an age of sophisticated studio recordings. Nonetheless, for a while it swamped the market and filled the coffers.

Black performers who have gone to Africa have not always found what they had expected. "I really get down as the food isn't good and I don't get any fantastic vibes from the people," Tina Turner told me, "so I'm really bored. I remember it was very damp, very humid. I didn't sleep comfortably and I got the feeling that Africans are very lazy people. They just want to live off the land. When Ike and I were there, I felt that they enjoyed our performance. But I still need to be inspired by something which is definitely not there." The myth that it all started in Africa begins to look like a belated and strident attempt to gain proper credit for the black contribution to popular music. It is more reassuring to place the origins of a music in the supposed freedom of another continent than in the degradation of a vicious slavery. But it didn't work.

Some groups took to the hills—literally. "We saw the Beatles' film *Help,* where they all lived in the same house, and we thought: That's for us," Jim Dandy of Black Oak Arkansas says. Subsequently, the six-man group, plus numerous retainers, purchased several hundred acres of forest in northern Arkansas, renovated an old tourist camp, constructed their own schoolhouse, bought the local post office, built a swimming pool, raised the flag, put up a stockade the U.S. Cavalry would have been proud of, and locked themselves inside. "Togetherness is security to us. We want to be independent and we don't want to have to rely on anybody. Thomas Jefferson said the best government has to govern the least. So we just try to look after each other and not strain the system too much. We believe in nature."

"We live humbly but tastefully." Dandy continues, "But what we are doing ties into rock and roll because we have independence. It's a statement of freedom, and that's what rock and roll today is all about. Yes, we're really living a pretty wholesome life up here."

Imagine...

"The essential misapprehension about popular music," Lester Bangs told me, "is that it is anything other than a totally capitalistic enterprise. In fact, it has absolutely nothing to do with anything except making money and getting rich. Some popular musicians start out with revolutionary rhetoric, but all they want is cars and girls and champagne. It's nonsense to think that popular music is about anything but conspicuous consumption and the good life."

Popular music now outgrosses the combined revenue of movies, theater, opera, ballet, and sport. While America celebrated the bicentennial of its independence, for example, the recording industry produced approximately a thousand new songs per week. Each one aspired to be a hit; that was the reason for its existence. Few people played or sang to express their own or other people's emotions. And when they did, the results were usually thought "freaky" or "uncommercial." The entire operation, performers and entrepreneurs alike, constantly strives in quest of the holy grail, the next and biggest hit of all. Talent must be bludgeoned into producing its maximum yield. Musicianship, a

Donovan, a bright talent laid waste by the excesses of stardom.

Helen Reddy (with Joey Heatherton and Rod McKuen) gives out the Grammys.

necessary although subservient quality, must be rendered useful rather than creative.

It's not just a cliché: great music, especially great popular music, has developed in conditions of squalor, even pain. Not the pain of boredom on the road in a highly lucrative tour, but the pain of having to fight every step of the way, to make it against the odds. Some of its brightest stars have fallen in the attempt: Billie Holiday, Bix Beiderbecke, Jimmie Rodgers, Jimi Hendrix. But the most copied, imitated, and stolen music of the twentieth century has been the music of blacks, consistently the most despised and exploited group in American society. Many have found that money cushions the hurt and chosen the easy life of social acceptability, and only those with determination as well as talent are now able to resist the blandishments of an industry where the legend of a new Rolls-Royce at the door the morning after an overnight success can be made a reality.

When an album called *Tubular Bells* by Mike Oldfield was issued in 1973, it was received with respect, albeit suspiciously. Much of the music was immediately attractive, although some of it seemed the familiar self-indulgent mumblings beloved of rock stars. Worse, no one was clear how it should be described. Lasting almost forty-nine minutes, it was obviously not a pop song or even rock music in any usual sense. Its construction, although loose, depended on a small number of interrelated themes developed along vaguely classical lines. Its texture owed much to Sibelius, Vaughan Williams, and Michel Legrand. Scored for a large ensemble of rock instruments including a battery of electric guitars, the work was unmistakably orchestral in range and imagination. Not surprisingly, its commercial progress—in terms of the charts, that is—was slow. Today,

however, it has sold over five million copies around the world.

In the United States, *Tubular Bells* outsold every other comparable contemporary British record. But then, there *were* no other comparable records. Oldfield had not only written the piece himself, suggested the design for the album cover, and engineered the sound, but had played almost the entire orchestra—grand piano, glockenspiel, bass guitar, various organs, flageolet, mandolins, timpani, numerous electric and acoustic guitars, assorted percussion instruments, and, of course, the tubular bells. More extraordinary, he refused to travel to America to promote his record —in fact, he refused to travel anywhere, de-

Walking away from Woodstock *(left).* Permanence in double chins, toupees, and Goo Goo bars. *Top:* Frank Sinatra, Gene Kelly, and Fred Astaire in Hollywood; *bottom:* Opryland.

clined with only a few exceptions to be interviewed, gave only one concert (at the Queen Elizabeth Hall in London), and then refused to be interviewed much about that, disliked being photographed and normally did not allow it, never spoke on television and only twice on radio, and remained apparently untouched by the riches that five million records must have brought him. He is shy to the point of embarrassment, diffident about his work, has never bought anything he felt he didn't need, and went to live in an isolated house in Herefordshire on the Welsh border, the exact location of which was more or less secret. "You went towards Wales," he says, "and it's the first hill on the right. I think."

Oldfield began his musical career singing and recording with his elder sister Sally as "Sallyangie," an acoustic folk duo. They made one record when he was fourteen, which was not a success either musically or commercially. Disagreements with his sister over the sound Oldfield was already striving for compelled him to go it alone. He formed a group called variously Barefoot and Barefeet. None of its other members understood a word Oldfield was saying.

Another dissatisfied musician, Kevin Ayers, previously with the avant-garde free-form pop group called Soft Machine, asked Oldfield to join his new ensemble the Whole World, as bass player. Oldfield was flattered and accepted. It was a lucky move. Not only did he come into contact with some of the more dedicated and musically accomplished of his contemporaries, Kevin Ayers and drummer Robert Wyatt among them, but he was introduced to David Bedford. Then thirty-one, Bedford was well established as a classical composer and pianist of consider-

Some consider Woody Herman's newest Herd *(top)* his best; yet many of its members were born after Herman began recording. Earl Hines *(center)* plays with three or four musicians instead of a large band; his recent arrangements are fresh, often daring. Ian Carr *(bottom)*, with Mike Gibbs, has revitalized jazz in England through invention, not imitation. *Right:* Dave Brubeck recently reunited with Paul Desmond; he also plays in an electrified group with his sons.

able promise, with commissions from Benjamin Britten's Aldeburgh Festival and the BBC Promenade Concerts. A former scholar at the London Royal Academy of Music, Bedford had studied with Italian composer Luigi Nono and now supplemented his earnings by playing rock. Not the teeny-bopper variety of David Cassidy, but music seriously attempting to find a way out of the cul-de-sac into which popular music had been led. Thus, when Oldfield began to explain the music he had imagined, Bedford understood and encouraged him. Most importantly, he gave Oldfield a copy of Frederick Delius' tone poem *Brigg Fair*, as for Bedford this seemed the nearest sound to that which Oldfield had described. Kevin Ayers, with characteristic pragmatism, gave Oldfield a two-track tape recorder and told him to go away and record what he was talking about.

The Whole World did not survive, but Oldfield took advantage of its demise to begin recording on tape what he had heard in his head. Without financial resources or backing, he began the arduous process of composition. He taught himself to read and write music and slowly put together what became *Tubular Bells*. At this stage, it was little more than a compilation of harmonies and chord sequences that had taken his fancy during his brief career as a performer.

Through Ayers, Oldfield also met Richard Branson, an English ex-private school boy (Stowe). Branson had started a mail-order discount record store called Virgin that offered at cheap rates the best LPs from both sides of the Atlantic. Later, he invested all his profits in buying and renovating a ramshackle sixteenth-century manor house near Oxford and equipped it with the best recording equipment he could afford. It would be an ideal setting for making music, he argued: the peace of the countryside, luxury accommodations, and total freedom from schedules, businessmen, and interfering journalists. The idea was so good, in fact, that almost no one came. Except, that is, Mike Oldfield, for whom the isolation was perfect. For months, he worked on his demo tape, occasionally helping out with a few other groups

that visited the unfinished manor, but mostly recording and re-recording himself and his music. Eventually, the tape was completed and Oldfield emerged convinced he had a masterpiece. He was just eighteen.

Alas, no one else shared his enthusiasm. Branson wanted to, but couldn't. He was almost broke. He wanted *Tubular Bells* for his new (as yet unformed) Virgin label but had to tell Oldfield he should go elsewhere. For a year, Oldfield trudged around to every record company in the Western world—literally. He was on the point of giving up. In fact, he had given up when, unexpectedly, Branson contacted him again. As one last and desperate attempt, Branson and his partner Simon Draper took the tape to MIDEM, the annual music publishers' conference held in Cannes. Only one record executive showed the slightest interest, and then on condition that Oldfield dub in some unspecified vocals to give the thing some "meaning." Oldfield had to turn to Branson. And Branson,

Left: Bob Dylan returned to the road in 1975, here as inverted Nigger Minstrel. *Right:* Joni Mitchell has applied her own language to the barrenness of rock lyrics.

cluding Mick Taylor, then of the Rolling Stones, David Bedford, and Kevin Ayers. The audience, among them Mick Jagger, was enthusiastic, though the hall was less than full. Some critics attempted to evaluate the piece in terms of fugue and counterpoint, references that have puzzled Oldfield ever since. Most were confused but agreed it was an impressive debut. The concert also persuaded Oldfield that performances were not for him; nor were the public, the press, and the machinery of rock promotion. He had dreaded the whole outing and went home to his father's house, where he occupied himself excavating a duck pond. Branson was faced with the nightmare of promoting a record the composer and central performer of which refused to have any part in selling.

What happened next was as absurd as it was lucky. The record had clocked up some success in America when film director William Friedkin decided he would use a section as theme music for his movie *The Exorcist*. Both Branson and Oldfield now wince at the mention of the film and Branson, at least, would like to persuade all comers that the immense box-office success of *The Exorcist* was irrelevant to the ultimate triumph of *Tubular Bells*. Certainly, the record was already selling quite well. But the crucial shift from commercial respectability to superstardom came after the release in America of a single called "Theme from the Exorcist." However, *The Exorcist* and its millions of dollars were irrelevant to Oldfield. He was building his duck pond and that was that.

still a believer, was left with no choice. He would have to launch his new shoestring label with a work nobody wanted. With flashy optimism, Branson gave *Tubular Bells* the number he felt it deserved, V 2001.

Oldfield returned once more to the studio for some additional recording—in fact, some twenty-three hundred recordings—and a few months later the acetates were ready. On May 25, 1973, the record was released. Branson now likes to think that it was an overnight success, although at the time its advent seemed less than spectacular. A month later came the Queen Elizabeth Hall concert. Oldfield assembled an impressive collection of instrumentalists, in-

Above: Ron Wood, Billy Preston, Mick Jagger, and Keith Richard, keeping the Rolling Stones together. *Near right:* Britain's Average White Band, whose synthesis of Motown and rhythm and blues brought them acclaim. *Far right:* Crosby, Stills, Nash and Young, whose solo efforts have been less challenging than their group work.

Success, of course, has occasionally bought its own protection. Led Zeppelin is among the most commercially successful groups in the entire history of popular music. In the first six years of its existence, the group made six LP records, each one selling at least two million copies. One, a double album called *Physical Graffiti*, entered all the American charts as number three, at the time the highest level of entry achieved by any record. Its advance sale alone was fifteen million dollars, a figure without precedent. One and one half million units were sold within the first two weeks. One key shop in New York reported selling upward of three hundred copies per hour. Zeppelin's records outsold those of the Rolling Stones three to one; the Beatles had experienced nothing comparable. In 1972, a year in which the group released no new LPs, Zeppelin represented almost eighteen percent of the total business of Atlantic Records. There is little doubt that had Zeppelin chosen, they could have re-released their earlier albums and had all six riding high in the charts, perhaps occupying the top six places. "We have so many statistics," says Danny Goldberg, then vice-president of their record company, "why have more?" "They are," says Ahmet Ertegun, Atlantic's boss, imprecisely, "the biggest unknown group in the world."

This is a group that, for its first three and a half years, doggedly refused to issue press

Led Zeppelin doggedly refused to issue press handouts; released no group photos (because they didn't have any); employed no PR department; cut no singles.

handouts; released no group photos (because they didn't have any); employed no PR department; cut no singles (the surest way to chart success); never appeared on television except in an abandoned pilot show; appeared live on radio just once, and that a long time ago. Their lead guitarist was almost the sole practicing survivor of the late-sixties school of technical wizards, a thin, almost inaudible ghost of a man, like a choirboy, dog-tired but smiling. "I've compared notes with other writers and artists," Jimmy Page says defensively, "to see what time of day is most productive. Writers seem to thrive on schedules. Poets, or composers like me, just go at it. I've lost all concept of time long ago."

Page began playing when he was fifteen. An only child, the son of a personnel manager, he grew up in Felton next to London's Heathrow Airport. He remembers distinctly the event that changed his life: he heard Chuck Berry singing "No Money Down" and knew (correctly) that in its primitive manner it touched a profound social nerve. No money down, live now and pay later—the whole gaudy never-had-it-so-good I'm-all-right-Jack trashy postwar materialism caught in that one song. And when his guitar was confiscated at school, Page knew how his life was to be. The energy of Little Richard startled him into action. He played anywhere and everywhere, and by the time he was twenty had become the youngest—and also the best—session guitarist in London. He worked with P. J. Proby, Dave Berry, the Kinks, the Who, and the Rolling Stones; he did a stint of one-night gigs around the country until he collapsed with fatigue. He cut a solo single called "She Just Satisfies" on which he sang and played all the instruments except the drums. It was rubbish; his work as a session player had become the same. At the end, he had no idea what he was doing or why. Eventually, he joined the Yardbirds as a replacement bass player.

He is unmarried—"I once told a friend: 'I'm

just looking for an angel with a broken wing, one who couldn't fly away.' " Obscene letters sent him by fans and others distress him inordinately. Death threats are frequent. He worries about the pace of being on the road, of constantly having to live up to his image, whatever that is. When he returns home, he can't eat or sleep or in any way relax for days, sometimes weeks. He longs to tour in an open wagon, stopping when and where the mood takes him. He lives only for his music. The rest is meaningless.

And what of the music? Stylistically, it is a tour de force, borrowing from Bo Diddley, the Stones, Cream, and Burt Bacharach, fusing jazz, rock, blues, flamenco. It is persuasive and snarling, whether acoustic or electric. It is deceptively facile, yet almost never overblown. It relies heavily on the blues for its emotional strength, yet has expanded the vocabulary of that ill-used idiom while remaining firmly locked within it. Some maintain that, like the best or the worst of rock, Page and his troupe have been schooled in the art of excess. They play too loud and too long. Yet the musical evidence dumbfounds such a view. A song like "Stairway to Heaven" is characteristic; it begins quietly with acoustic guitar playing an aching quasi-blues melody. The singer stutters out the simplest of themes. Gradually, but inevitably, the sound develops over ten minutes into a massive climax, the bass and drums providing an elemental roar from which the guitar (now electric) and singer tear a raging, hurting melody. Not all Zeppelin's songs are based on this pattern, but a sufficient number to recognize this as the group's signature. Again, it is the multiplicity of cross-references that makes the music arresting, as if the band were summing up rock and roll today and yet refashioning many of its conflicting elements into a new sound that has the possibility, thereby, of extended development. One hears snatches of the Beatles' chord progression, the miasmic, tortured blues line of Leadbelly, the rhythmic brutality of Pete Townshend. Yet the whole is different from the parts.

Of all those working in the rock milieu today, Page is the master craftsman. In groups like Cream, rock musicians took advantage of their considerable instrumental capabilities—but the question remained, what do you do with those capabilities? Concertos for Rock Group and Orchestra emerged, song cycles, cantatas, three-hour improvisations, the lot. But Page recognized that rock contained within *itself* the possibility of development. Recently, he wandered

Business goes on, too. *Left:* Peter Rudge, born in Wolverhampton, England, 1946, and Cambridge University educated, on the 1975 Rolling Stones tour of America he organized. *Below:* Clive Davis left Columbia Records under a cloud, and landed at Arista Records with Patti Smith. *Right:* Aretha Franklin.

around India listening to every sitarist he could find — just men in the street playing their instruments. "I felt very humbled by the quality of their musicianship. In fact, I felt embarrassed to be playing at all," he says. "You only get as much out of rock and roll as you put into it. There's nobody who can teach you. You're on your own." Today, in concert, as the group enters, the entire audience, twenty to thirty thousand, light matches or candles or lighters and stand in silent recognition of a sound, an achievement, that speaks eloquently for them and their longings. The sight of those flickering beacons, says Page, stops him dead in his tracks. It is, he says, a moment of true magic.

Time, Page says, ceases when he performs on stage. He has tried frequently to cut down Zeppelin's performance to two hours or so, but it always creeps back to well over three. As we talked, Page drew me further and further into his world. Time slipped away. We were perched high up in a Hollywood hotel, the drapes closed, a film projector standing idle, records stacked untidily on the floor, Page with a guitar in his hands, waiting — as he says — for "something to come through." Occasionally, the silence was interrupted by the need to move onto the next city for the next concert. Food was brought in, the armed guard ever watchful, the telephone more or less permanently off the hook, the television blank. That he is worth a fortune is clearly irrelevant to him, except insofar as it pays for his privacy. He has the isolation and knowledge of a monk. By remaining calm at the center of a disintegrating culture, he is providing an example for its future development.

Neither Page nor Oldfield has eschewed the financial rewards that popular music can bring. Both enjoy its more harmless pleasures though both have found ways of avoiding its more insidious effects. Each composes or performs for his own satisfaction, although each has chosen

Stevie Wonder, blind from birth. Born in Saginaw, Michigan, May 1951.

There is nothing original about Elvis Presley's music except Elvis Presley, and that is enough.

to work in a medium whose language is reckoned the common property of all. Between them, Page and Oldfield stand against the triviality of glitter rock, the destructiveness of such as Jagger, the banality of the Osmonds. Both have prospered within the system, demonstrating that the transition from obscure talent to million-dollar acclaim is not in itself damaging.

Yet both have embraced old music to create fresh musical experiences. Oldfield admits to using African melodies; Page uses Moroccan chants to spice his compositions. Both rely heavily on the tradition of Afro-American blues and jazz to provide instrumental and rhythmic flavor. But all composers, from Bach to Ives, have thrived on the absorption of popular dances and songs. It is not the use of such material that matters, but the manner of its recomposition. The unacknowledged theft of another man's music, which characterized the earlier progress of blues into rock, is despicable. David Bowie and a group called Sweet each released a single in 1973 that simultaneously and coincidentally used the same rhythmic riff. That riff had been heard on a Yardbird record seven years earlier. Twenty years before that, the same riff had been written by Bo Diddley. Had Bowie produced a record that revealed this common material in a new light, adding to one's understanding of the original without detracting from the uniqueness of Bowie's interpretation, his usage might have been worthwhile. To plunder the past in order to provide insight for the future has always been an essential requirement of the artist.

But such has not been the case in the development of popular music. Those who have suffered, from Pinetop Smith to Muddy Waters, are as much in need of praise as the grotesque superstars who now claim the stage. There is nothing original about Elvis Presley's music, except Elvis Presley, and that is enough. But those who control the popular music industry today have ensured that, despite a continuing and prolific outpouring of melody, there is little original about much of what is now sold as popular music; most of it is the mindless pap of a

culture cluttered by sound, unable to discriminate between noise and music.

In spite of the example Oldfield and Page have set, popular music carries on down its baubled sewer. It should not be thought that the commercialization of a naïve tradition necessarily cheapens the original. There is no logical reason why the progress of country music from the Ozarks to Nashville should have resulted in the stultification of the folk tradition. But the methods by which the music industry has chosen to sustain that progress have brought unexpected difficulties. According to Lester Bangs, "The problem of creating mythology with living people is that you have to watch them fall old and decay, or fall down and make fools of themselves. They can't live up to their own mythology. Mick Jagger is a perfect example. His face is turning all flabby and his big lips are hanging down. After all, he's getting old. Here's a guy

From left to right: Leo Sayer, who kept British rock going; Ginger Baker, who discovered rock in West Africa; Herbie Hancock who brought jazz into rock on the West Coast; Chick Corea, who brought rock into jazz on the East Coast; and Chuck Berry, who kept on rocking and maintained a high outrage quotient.

who's thirty-three—he's jumping around on stage, he's doing handstands, and he's getting more and more of a hangdog face all the time. This is, to say the least, unfortunate. Especially when you start singing songs about 'time isn't going to wait for me.' The Rolling Stones seem content to sing 'It's Only Rock and Roll,' and that's a perfect indication of the irrelevance of rock in the current context."

It is sometimes argued that the Rolling Stones, among others, are trapped on a financial merry-go-round from which there appears to be no escape. But Peter Rudge, who manages the Stones' tours, says: "Jagger is very concerned that something a little extra is given. Before the first date we had laid out a million and a half dollars. The actual cost of our 1975 North American tour was three and a half million dollars. Then there was American tax and promoters and commissions. The Rolling Stones themselves were left with only twenty or thirty percent of the money to be divided among the four of them. The gross for the tour, by the way, was in the region of eleven million dollars. So it's a living."

The popular music industry is now so colossal that it will not allow itself to atrophy.

The question remains, what can be salvaged; while Roy Acuff dreams of international audiences for the Grand Ole Opry, others are hammering at the gate. Doug Kershaw, who decided that Denver wasn't big enough for his second wedding, so moved it to the Houston Astrodome, has been pounding on Nashville's door for some while. Country rock may not be a revolutionary musical concept, but at least it has vitality. Others, like Bill Monroe, who have turned away from the Grand Ole Opry, seem to have preserved the spirit of their music without losing any of its commercial appeal. Some, like Pete Seeger, battle on in isolation.

Musicals, on the other hand, as conceived by Mamoulian and Rodgers and Hammerstein, mirror the paradox of all popular music—indeed, of all art that claims to be popular. As the musical has·developed, whether in sophistication of technique or subject matter, the audience has become more educated and expects more. But as more has been provided, the musical moved away from its origins, from vaudeville, revue, burlesque, operetta, from all the things that originally gave it life, and became something more akin to opera—which is precisely what its audience does not want. Tin Pan

Alley is no longer the arbiter of musical taste; its song writers are redundant. Those who have replaced them no longer need the musical theater as an outlet for their songs. So Broadway has become an anachronism, magnificent but moribund. Yet in such a milieu a work like *Pacific Overtures* has surfaced. Paradoxically, its strengths are also its weaknesses. It suffers because it is *not* opera. Although its theatrical and musical ambitions are considerable, it has been forced to measure those ambitions with the supposed demands of the commercial, musical theater. Its limited orchestration suggests that it is not opera; its subject matter and style of presentation make it neither musical comedy nor musical revue. Sondheim and others have raised the musical expectations of their audience to a level that, through no immediate fault of their own, they are unable to satisfy.

It could be that jazz will provide an escape route. "Jazz became corrupted by the western idea of what art is all about—that the audience is an accidental eavesdropper on a great performance," Ian Carr, a British jazz trumpeter, says. "But the fact is that when you become involved in what is jazz, then the audience plays a

crucial part. It's almost like preaching the gospel in the South—the congregation are part of the action. Too many jazz musicians believed they were just playing for themselves and regarded it as vulgar to want any involvement from the audience. Then the virtuoso took precedence over the ensemble. But I believe that both the music and the virtuoso should be subservient to the group. That produces a healthy sound. The good thing about the new 'jazz-rock' groups, or whatever label you want to stick on them, groups like those of Herbie Hancock and Chick Corea, is that they are producing a collective music in which the virtuoso performer is an integral part of the whole.''

Jazz took the strengths of two cultures—the European and the African—and welded them into a life force that was American. Its white practitioners were quickly gobbled up by entrepreneurs in search of a fast buck; their music diluted and adapted, the property of no one and the expression of nothing. Its black practitioners escaped for a time, upholding the possibility that jazz might become a flourishing art form. For a while they succeeded, and the early achievements of individuals such as Armstrong or Ellington gave the illusion that something substantial was being created.

Alas, it was not. The compromises involved in its acceptance were too great. Many black musicians—despite their protestations to the contrary—equated commercial success with cultural and social achievement, for both their art and their people. Commercial success could

Left: Jimmy Page, born in Middlesex, England, 1945. A distinguished Yardbird before becoming the pilot of Led Zeppelin. *Top left:* Bruce Springsteen, John Hammond's latest discovery. *Center left:* Eric Clapton, who lost himself. *Top right:* Rufus Thomas put on short pants, thus ensuring that the traditions of minstrelsy would never die. *Center right:* Stephen Sondheim, composer of opera, operetta, or musical? *Bottom:* although musically banal, reggae can make some claim to be a music by the people, for the people. Jamaican Premier Michael Manley successfully campaigned astride a reggae war song, ''Better Must Come''; the blandness of the sound should not lull one away from an uncomfortable awareness that Bob Marley and his Wailers represent black insurrection and power, a return to Africa, and a rage against Babylon—that is, whatever Marley reckons as the establishment. The sound is familiar, but so is the message and the manner of their exploitation.

only be attained, however, on the white man's terms. So these men either cooled their music to a temperature the whites would tolerate, or went in another direction, rendering it impenetrable and sterile. From the mid-thirties, only composers of Ellington's stature were able to survive the universal whitewash. Ellington's large-scale symphonic works, such as *Black, Brown and Beige*, were created in spite of rather than because of this trend. And it was surely no accident that Armstrong's greatest hit—it became almost his theme song—was a second-rate melody from a second-rate musical comedy, *Hello, Dolly!* By comparison, his stunning records of the late twenties and early thirties have been more or less forgotten except by aficionados.

Chick Corea joined Miles Davis's jazz band in 1969. His musical education encompassed Beethoven, Bach, Chopin, Stravinsky, and Art Tatum. Electric music, he felt, was indecent. He discovered, however, that electric keyboard instruments provided an unusual range of tonal qualities that were useful for composition. "The intention of most rock groups is quite different from the intention of a Stravinsky or a Bartók or a jazz musician," he explained to me. "Delicacy

of form is a prime consideration for classical and jazz composers, whereas for most rock groups, it is secondary. They are more con-

cerned with doing things to an audience in a particular way than with creating a form which might puzzle the audience at first but ultimately

Left: Opryland, for a change, put on a show. *Above:* at the Grammy Awards. From left to right, David Bowie, Art Garfunkel, Paul Simon, Yoko Ono, John Lennon, Roberta Flack.

yield a much greater satisfaction."

"Jazz is not dead," Corea says. "But it has become predictable. The music of Bach is an interesting and parallel example. Bach wrote an unbelievable amount of music, hundreds of composers copied him, his style was and is full of endless riches. Bach is Bach. The music is there, to be played and enjoyed. But it's not the *only* music, it's not the *only* form, although it's a treasure house from which endless jewels can be extracted. Jazz is the same. You can take from it elements to make new forms of music that are valid in their own terms, although recognizably jazz in origin. Rock music has rarely seemed to have that flexibility."

Corea's current band, Return to Forever, has also resolved the virtuoso problem. "Fortunately, everybody in the band is a master musician and they're all excellent composers. It is not our intention to create an art form, but it is our intention to make people feel really good with music. What you want to label this new music is not our responsibility. All the artist can do is take what he knows and create something from it, without thinking what it should be called."

"I hate my music being described as rock and roll," Jimmy Page told me. " 'Pop' as a name is ridiculous. They're both a long way from the truth. Anyway, I distrust all labels. And formal training—I survived just three hours—can shackle you for life. What we play is street music, folk music, and that's why we refuse to get involved with the media. If what we are saying has any truth, then people in the street will know. It won't need me or you to spell it out. What I do cannot be explained in an interview, or an article, or in any light-entertainment cliché. In the past, I got annoyed that contemporary music was abused by the press and television, by big business and by intellectual apologists. But I now see that as an advantage. Although I confess that in my present situation, I am a product of an immensely rich industry, to be spurned is the greatest boon I could have. It is my best chance of survival."

Mike Oldfield—with doves. Our best hope?

If popular music is to survive as anything more valuable than a source of revenue for innumerable merchants, it will require steady and purposeful criticism. Unlike literature or poetry or even classical music, popular music does not have an agreed upon language by which its product can be understood. Partly this arises because the music is not deemed worthy of proper analysis; partly because the music and the image it perpetuates are often thought interchangeable. Either way, the lack of reasoned evaluation, from whatever source, whether from religious leader or renowned critic, committed or otherwise, is the music's biggest handicap. Truth is abandoned.

Jack Wyrtzen is a mild, silken-haired missionary who runs a Word of Life community in upstate New York. Once a musician, he is now proselytizing for another faith. "I've seen naked savages, jungle dancers, and I can't see the difference between what our young people are doing around the world in rock and roll dancing. It all originated out of the jungles and I think rock and roll is taking us all right back to the jungles today. I believe we are living in sex without marriage, people are dancing and carousing and overindulging in eating and filth. Our big objection to rock music is not only the beat, which I think comes out of the jungles, but the words and what the words are spelling out. Look at the lives of these artists: the dress, the glasses they wear."

"The first time I saw Wet Willie," Lester Bangs once wrote, "I got excited as hell. You would do too, if you were in Macon, Georgia, whooping it up deep Friday night down at Grant's Lounge, the wildest bar this side of the frontier. Every slick black honker in town had just had his turn in the night's mighty tenor battle, and now the dazed stage is took by a bunch of high-steppin' Suthun lads who don't play no queerbait but they can jive as good as they want. Up front's a rangy-boned cussed-callow youth who looks just enough like Jagger without overdoin' it; he's a real rawhide power swaggerin' son of the soil and he commences to whoop out some of the hottest, nastiest, most needlin' to the point harp since early Paul Butterfield, with the rest of the band cookin' like ten Rastamaniacs straight behind him all the way."

"I believe it is demonic," Wyrtzen went on. "The dress, the glasses they wear. I believe it is tied into illicit sex. I guess the biggest pushers of rock music around the world would be the Beatles. Look at their lives. The immorality, the way they go to India with the yogis, get all wrapped up in the occult. And look at Elton John with his glasses and freaky clothes. And Elvis Presley who found he could tie in a lot of filthy language and go through sex motions with his hips."

"Wet Willie just limbers up the whole club with a good excursive and precisely economical few minutes of the Honerific [sic]," Lester Bangs continued, "and then he throws back his head and commences to shout:

> 'You're just hanging out
> At the local bar
> And you're wonderin'
> Who in the hell you are!
> Are you a bum, or
> Are you a star?
> Keep on smilin' through the rain.'

And you best believe, he gave me the chills."

"I believe Elvis Presley and the Beatles and the Rolling Stones are going to answer to God," Jack Wyrtzen concluded, "for all the pollution of youth around the world. All this rock culture is just stirring people up to do evil instead of to do good. Just as the people were doing in Noah's day. Just look at their dress and the glasses they wear. God is going to rain judgment upon earth—and this could happen at any moment with all the rock music and illicit sex and wine, women and the glasses they wear—and there will be a time of terrible tribulation when all hell will be let loose on earth. . . ."

Criticism does not replace enjoyment. It may limit that enjoyment. But it might, just occasionally, assist a better understanding of why the music is like it is. Then again, as Memphis Slim told me, "All blues singers are great liars."

(Entries in italics refer to captions.)

Abbott, George, *123*
Acid rock, 253–71
Acuff, Roy, 112, *179*, *184*, 189–90, 192, 301
Acuff-Rose, *188*, 190
Adams, Stanley, 109
Adderley, Cannonball, *53*
Addy, Mickey, 98–99, 103, 105–106
African music, 5–7, 299; influence of, on American music, 5–7, 9, 11; instruments, 6–7
Afro-American music, 5–15. *See also* Blues; Jazz; Ragtime; Rhythm and blues
Alhambra, the (Harlem), *60*, *70*, 104
Allen, Fred, 118
Allen, Gracie, *89*
Allen, Jules Verne, 187
Allen, Lou, *89*
Allen, Steve, 217
Almanac Singers, 196, 198
Altamont rock concert, 269, *270*
Ambrose, Bert, 146
American Bandstand, *223*, 225
American Federation of Musicians, 106, 137; strike (1942), 155, 189
American Negro Blues Festival, 73
American Negro music, 5–15
American Society of Composers, Authors, and Publishers. *See* ASCAP
Anderson, Bill, 193
Anderson, Ian, *275*, 282
Anderson, Ivie, *144*
Andrews, Julie, *135*
Andrews Sisters, *147*, 155
Animals, the, *243*, 249, 257, *259*, 266.

See also Burdon, Eric
Ann Arbor Blues Festival (1969), *171*
Antiwar songs. *See* War songs
Apollo Theatre (Harlem), 65, 70
Arcadia Ballroom (St. Louis), 44
Arista Records, *296*
Armstrong, Louis, xi, 33, *37*, 39, 43–44, 46, *59*, 70, 71, 140, *142*, 147, 155, 185, 303, 304
Arno, Peter, 137
Arnold, Eddy, 217
ASCAP (American Society of Composers, Authors and Publishers), *101*, 109, 111–12, 114, 155, 189
Astaire, Fred, *89*, 117, *124*, *126*, *128*, *131*, *132*, *288*
Atlanta, Ga., and country-western music, 179
Atlantic Records, 159, 165, 295
Austin, Gene, 106
"Austin High Gang," the, *41*
Autry, Gene, 187
Aux Frontières du Jazz (Goffin), 146
Avakian, George, *59*
Average White Band, *294*
Avery Fisher Hall (New York), *171*
A. W. Perry & Son, 21
AWARE, Inc., 207
Ayers, Kevin, 290, 293, 294

Bach, Johann Sebastian, 4, 299, 304, 306
Bacharach, Burt, 296
Bacon, Lloyd, *110*
Baez, Joan, *195*, *204*, 207, 209
Bailey, Mildred, *153*

Bailey, Pearl, *135*
Baker, Ginger, 274–75, *300*
Baker, Josephine, *75*, *86*
Baker, LaVern, 161
Balanchine, George, *124*, 135
Ballard, Florence, *167*
Balthrop, Carmen, *31*
"Band That Played the Blues, The," 145, *150*
Bangladesh concert, 274
Bangs, Lester, 282, 287, *300*, 310
Banya, 7
Baraka, Amiri, 15
Barber, Chris, 221
Barefeet, 290
Barnett, Charlie, 147
Barrett, Sweet Emma, 59
Barron's (Harlem), 45
Bartók, Béla, 304
Basie, Count, 45, 47, *50*, *66*, 69, 70, 71, 150, *154*, *168*
Bauer, Billy, 50
Bay City Rollers, *284*
Beach Boys, the, 245–47, 249
Beale Street (Memphis), 56–57, 58, 59, *65*
Beatles, the, 4, *15*, 218, 229, 231–43, 249, 254–57, 263, 265, 273–74, 276, 285, 295, 296, 310; American tours, *231*, 242, 246–47; and Apple Corps Ltd., 255, 257, 263; critics, 241; dissolution of, 257; early days, 237–39; and Brian Epstein, 239, 241, 249, 251; Hamburg engagements, 238–39; musical influences on, 237, 241; and *Sergeant Pepper* album, 235, 241. *See also* Harri-

Beatles (*Continued*)
  son, George; Lennon, John; Mc-
  Cartney, Paul; Starr, Ringo
Bebop, *47, 49–50, 148, 275*
Bechet, Sidney, *28*
Bedford, David, 290, 293, 294
Beethoven, Ludwig van, 5, 241, 274, 304
Beggars Banquet, 259
Beiderbecke, Leon Bix, *41, 43,* 44, 46, 155, 288
Benton, William, 284
Berkeley, Busby, *115,* 132
Berlin, Irving, 17–18, 30, 94, 97, 98, 101, *102,* 106, 107, *110,* 118, 123, *126, 128*
Bernard, Mike, 15, 28
Bernstein, Leonard, 118, *123,* 125, 135, 137, 241, 274
Berry, Chuck, 227, 232, 235, 237, 241, *247, 251,* 295, *300*
Berry, Dave, 295
Big Brother and the Holding Company, 247, 269. *See also* Joplin, Janis
Big D Jamboree, 182
Birdland (New York), 50
Birdsong, Cindy, *167*
Black, Bill, 212, 214
Black American music, 276, 284. *See also* Black musicians; Blues; Jazz; Ragtime; Rhythm and blues
Black Caribs, 5
Black caricature, *76*
Black Crook, The, 121
Black culture, 15; development of, 12–13
Black jazz, *140. See also* Jazz; White jazz
Blacklisting, *196,* 207
Black musicians, 13; in Africa, 285; exploitation of, 288, 299, 303–304; influence of, 140, 155; and segregation, 12–13, 55, 69–71; in white swing bands, 147. *See also* White music industry
Black Oak Arkansas, 285
Black Swan Record Company, *39,* 60
Blake, Eubie, 19, 21, *28,* 30
Blakey, Art, *148*
Bland, Bobby, 161, *171*
Blesh, Rudi, 19
Blind Tom, 26
Blood Sweat and Tears, *260*
Blue Caps, the, *216*
"Blue devils," 55
Blue Hawaii (film), 225
"Blue" notes, 9
Blue-beat, 284
Bluebells, the, *277*
Bluebird Records, 159

Bluegrass, *183, 188,* 190
Bluegrass Boys, *188*
Blues, the, 5–6, 15, 55–73, *169,* 267, 284, 296, 299; African heritage, 7, 9; and country-western music, 184; dissemination of, 59–61; as emotional response, 9, 55; and folk music, 209; and gospel, 163; harmonies, 9; and jazz, 9; and minstrels, 57–58, 59, 62; musical structure, 56; origins of, 11; origin of term, 55; and popular music, 9, 55–56; and ragtime, 9; and recording industry, 60–62, 64, 65; and rhythm and blues, 158, 159; subject matter, 56; types of, 59–60; and Tin Pan Alley, 114; and work song, 56; and white music industry, 59, 64–65, 67, 71, 73
Bob Cats, the, 147, *150*
Bolden, Buddy, 35
Bolton, Guy, *107*
Bonner, Captain M. J., 174
Boogie-woogie, 13
Boone, Blind, 25–26
Boone, Pat, *214,* 215–16
Boswell Sisters, *112*
Bowie, David, 277, *278,* 299, *305*
Bowman, Dave, *47*
Bowyers, Millyon, 225
Boy Friend, The, 135
Bradford, Perry, 60–61
Bradshaw, Tiny, 162
Brando, Marlon, 225
Branson, Richard, 293–94
Brenston, Jackie, 171
Brewer, Teresa, 171
Brice, Fanny, *91*
Brinkley, J. R., 188
Brinsley Schwarz, 278
British Broadcasting Corporation (BBC), 4–5, 208, 221–24, 277, 293; Light Entertainment Show, 218, 223
British folk revival, *209*
British jazz, *290*
British music hall, *75, 77,* 79–80, 83, 85, 86, 89, 91–93
British rock, 218, 221, *300. See also specific British groups*
Britten, Benjamin, 293
Broadcast Music Incorporated (BMI), 112, 114, 155
Broadside Ballads, *201*
Broadway, *97,* 122, 136–37, 301. *See also* Musicals
Broonzy, Big Bill, 59, 61, *69,* 73, 162, 237
Brothel songs, 59
Brown, Clarence, 161
Brown, James, *168*
Brown, Les, 155

Brown, Lew, 98
Brown, Roy, 163
Brown, Ruth, 161, 165
Brubeck, Dave, 50, *53,* 290
Bruce, Jack, 274–75
Bryan, Al, 107
Bryant's Nigger Minstrels, 202
Bubblegum music, 281
Buck, Gene, *102*
Buck and Bubbles, *89*
Bunny Hug, 39
Burdon, Eric, 232, *243,* 249, 257, *259,* 266, 267
Burlesque, 76–77, 79; and development of musical, 118, 121, 122
Burnett, Chester Arthur. *See* Howlin' Wolf
Burns, George, 89
Butterfield, Paul, *168,* 310
Byrds, the, 232, 243, 245, 247, 249, 263

Caesar, Irving, 97, 98, 103, 104, 107
Café Society (New York), 61, 69, 70–71, *153,* 196
Cakewalk dance, 15, 26–27
Calloway, Cab, *53,* 159
Cannon, Sarah. *See* Minnie Pearl
Canterbury Arms Music Hall (Lambeth), *77, 79*
Cantor, Eddie, 94, 106, *112*
Capone, Al, 44
Carmichael, Hoagy, *102*
Carnegie Hall (New York), 15, 45, *61,* 150–51, 218, *232*
Carr, Ian, *290,* 301, 303
Carr, Leroy, 162
Carson, Fiddlin' John, 179
Carter, Alvin Pleasant (A.P.), *174,* 182–83, *193*
Carter, Benny, *39,* 45, 140, 144
Carter, June, *174*
Carter, Maybelle Addington, *174,* 182–83, *196*
Carter, Sara, *174,* 182–83
Carter, W. H., 19
Cash, Johnny, *174, 193,* 270
Cassidy, David, 4, *273,* 277, 284, 293
Catlett, Sid, *39*
Chad Mitchell Trio, *204*
Chandler, Charles, 266
Channing, Carol, *135*
Charles, Ray, 161, *171,* 248
Chauvin, Louis, *21, 22*
Checkerboard Club (Chicago), 158
Cherokee tuning, 177
Chess, Leonard, 161
Chess Records, 159, 161
Chevalier, Albert, 89, *91*
Chevalier, Maurice, *118*
Chicago, 137

Chicago, 5, 62; and jazz, 10, *15, 41,* 43–44; and rhythm and blues, 158–59, 161, 163, *165*; and urban blues, 73, *171*
Chopin, Frederic, 304
Christensen, Axel W., 28, 30
Christian, Charlie, *47*
Church of God in Christ, 12
Civil rights movement, 207
Civil War, 11, 13, 56, 202
Clambake Seven, 147
Clapton, Eric, 4, *241,* 274–75, *303*
Clark, Dick, *223, 225*
Clark, Gene, 243
Clarke, Kenny, *47*
Clarke, Michael, 243
"Classic blues," 62, 65
Classic rags, 21
Classical music, 274
Clayton, Buck, 148
Clayton, Jan, *124*
Cleveland, Ohio, 11
Cliburn, Van, 4
Clooney, Rosemary, 171
Clovers, the, 164
Club Alabam (New York), 44
Coasters, the, 237, 241
Coasters, Mark II, the, *216*
Cocoanut Grove (Los Angeles), 155
Cochran, Eddie, 227
Cocker, Joe, *259*
Cohen, Leonard, *209*
Cohn, Harry, 105
Cohn, Irving, 98
Cole, Nat King, *148, 165, 171*
Coleman, Ornette, 52
Coleman, W. C., 26
Collins, Lottie, 93
Collins's Music Hall, 77
Colombo, Russ, 142
Coltrane, John, 52–53
Columbia Broadcasting System (CBS), 103, 152
Columbia Gramophone Company, *61*
Columbia Pictures, 105
Columbia Records, 50, 64, 65, 158, 232, 269, *296*
Comden, Betty, *123*
Comets, the, *229*
Como, Perry, 165, 166
Condon, Eddie, *47*
Connolly, Cyril, 241
Connor, Edward, 83
Cooke, Sam, *168*
Cooper, Alice, 276–77, *282*
Copland, Aaron, 4
Corea, Chick, *300, 303, 304*
Cornshuckers, the, 180
Cotton Club (Harlem), 45, *53,* 70, 161
Count Basie Orchestra, *154*

Country blues, 59, 62
Country Music Foundation, 180
Country Music U.S.A. (Malone), 177
Country rock, 301
Country-western music, 111–12, 114, 173–93, 218, 241, 284; commercialization of, 188 ff.; European heritage, 176–77; instruments, 177, 189; and radio, 173–74, 179, 180, 182, 188–89, 192, 193; and recording industry, 179, 183, 184; and singing cowboys, 187–88; survival of, 174, 176; use of term, 190; and western swing, 189
Coward, Noel, 123–24
Cowboy films, 187–88
Cowboy Ramblers, the, 187
Cowell, Sam, 86, 89
Cream, *241, 275, 296*
Creole Jazz Band, *37*
Creoles, influence of, on jazz, 35, 44
"Crib House," *34*
Crombie, Tony, 218
Crosby, Bing, 4, *41,* 106, 112, 132, *148,* 154–55, 166
Crosby, Bob, 145, 147, *150*
Crosby, David, 243, *247,* 275
Crosby, Stills, Nash and Young, *260, 294*
Cross-talk act, 83, *84*
Crudup, Arthur "Big Boy," *171,* 214
Crump, Ed, 58
Crystals, the, *227*
Curtis, King, 266

Dalhart, Vernon, 180
Damone, Vic, 166
Dance, use of, in musicals, 135–36
Dance bands: jazz, 38–39, 41, 44–45, 47; swing, 145 ff.
Dance routines, rhythm and blues, 165
Dandy, Jim, 285
Danks, Hart, 101
Dare, Phyllis, 204
Darin, Bobby, 225, 229
Dave Brubeck Quartet, *53*
Davies, Ray, 80
Davis, Clive, 232, 269, *296*
Davis, Miles, 50, *148,* 304
Day, Doris, 243
Day of Jubilee (Sept. 22, 1862), 11
Dean, James, 225
Debussy, Claude, 44
Decca Record Company, 142
Deep Purple, 276
De Forest, Dr. Lee, *110*
Delius, Frederick, 293
Delroys, the, *218*
Delta, the, 5, 56, 57, 73
De Mille, Agnes, *124,* 127–28
De Mille, Cecil B., 127

Dene, Terry, 223–24
Denton, Bobby, 229
Denver, John, *204*
De Paris, Wilbur, 35
Depression, the, 65, 111, 115, 122, 131, 140, 180, 189
Desmond, Paul, *53, 290*
Detroit, Mich., 11. *See also* Motown
Dibdin, Charles, 199
Dickson, Jim, 245
Diddley, Bo, *169, 296, 299*
Dietrich, Marlene, *202*
Disco music, 284
Dixie Hummingbirds, 163
Dixieland jazz, 44, 49. *See* Jazz
Dr. John the Night Tripper, 277, *281*
Dodds, Johnny, *37*
Domino, Fats, 161
Dominoes, the, 164, 241
Donegan, Lonnie, 221, 241
Donovan, *195, 249, 287*
Doors, the, 254, *259,* 269. *See also* Morrison, Jim
Dorsey, Jimmy, 45, 143, *148*
Dorsey, Tommy, 45, 143, 147, *148, 150,* 152, 153, 155
Douglas, Stephen A., 202
Draper, Simon, 293
Drifters, the, *162,* 164, 237, 241
Drifting Cowboys, the, 190
Driftwood, Jimmy, *184*
Drinking songs, 79–80
Drums: African, 9; suppression of, in slave states, 5–6
Dryden, Leo, 80, 83
Duncan, Tommy, 189
Dutrey, Honoré, *37*
Dylan, Bob, 4, *60,* 71, 73, *198, 204,* 208–209, 243, *247,* 274, *293*

Eastman, John, 255, 257
Eastman, Lee, 255, 257
Eastman, Linda, 255
Ebb, Fred, 137
Eckstine, Billy, *148,* 161, *171*
Eddy, Duane, 229
Eddy, Nelson, 132
Edison, Thomas, 60
Edmonds, Shephard N., 26
Edward VII, King of England, 91
Egyptian music, 7
Eight-tone scale, 7
Eldridge, Roy, *39, 142*
Ellington, Edward Kennedy "Duke," 4, *15,* 43, 45–47, 70, 71, 144, 150, 155, 303, 304
Eliot, T. S., 241
Elliott, Cass, 269
Ellis, Don, 50
Eltinge, Julian, 85
EMI Records, 241

Epstein, Brian, *232, 239, 249, 251, 254*

Epstein, Clive, 239, 249

Ertegun, Ahmet, 295

Ertegun brothers, 159

Essex Record Company, 168, 171

Estes, Sleepy John, *66*

Etting, Ruth, *70*

Everly Brothers, *188, 216*

Exorcist, The (film), 294

Fabian. *See* Forte, Fabian

Faithful, Marianne, 253

Fast piano style, 13

Feather, Leonard, 49, 52

Feist, Leo, 102, 106

Female impersonators, in music halls, 85

Ferber, Edna, 122

Ferry, Bryan, 281–82

Fields, Dorothy, *124, 128*

Fields, Gracie, *202*

Fields, Herbert, *124*

Fields, Joseph, *124*

Fields, Lew, *124*

Fields, W. C., *132*

Fiestas, the, *218*

Fifth Avenue Theatre, *84*

Fifty-Second Street (New York), 47, 49, *148*

Fillmore East, *267, 278*

Fillmore West, 247–49, *267*

Fischer, Fred, 97–98, 102

Fisher, Charlie, 105

Fisher, Eddie, 165, 166

Fisk Jubilee Singers, 161

Fitzgerald, Ella, *144*

Five Blind Boys, 163

Five Royales, the, *218*

Five Satins, the, *218*

Five-tone scale, 7

Flack, Roberta, *305*

Flamingoes, the, 164

Flanagan, Bud, *89, 255*

Flatt, Lester, *188*

Folies-Bergère, *86*

Folk music, 196, 206. *See also* Protest songs, War songs

Folk process, 196, 209

Folk songs, 18, *73*

Fonda, Henry, 245

Fonda, Jane, 245

Fonda, Peter, 245

Fontaine, Joan, *89*

Fontaines, the, 165

Fosse, Bob, 137

Forte, Fabian, *214, 229*

Foster, Stephen, *98*, 100–101, 107

Franklin, Aretha, *167, 248, 296*

Freddie and the Dreamers, *243*

Freed, Alan, 167–68

Freeman, Arnie, 41

Freeman, Bud, 34, *41, 43,* 152

Freeman, Harry Lawrence, 25

Friedkin, William, 294

Friedman, Myra, 269–70

Friml, Rudolf, 118, 122

Fruit Jar Drinkers' Band, *179*

Fuller, Jesse, *73*

Fulton, Johnny, 154

Gabriel, Peter, 277–78

Garcia, Jerry, *259*

Garfunkel, Art, 305. *See also* Simon and Garfunkel

Garland, Judy, 75–76, 85, *91,* 95, *112*

Gaylord, Charlie, 154

Gee, Jack, 66

Genesis, 277–78

George V, King of England, 91

George Smith College for Negroes, 21

Georgia Jazz Band, *59*

Gershwin, George, 41, 97, 98, 105, 106, 107, *109,* 118, *121,* 124–26, *128,* 131

Gershwin, Ira, 106, *107, 121,* 124–25, *126, 128,* 131

Gibbon, John Sloane, 204

Gibbons, the Reverend Ronald, 241

Gibbs, Mike, *290*

Gilbert, Wolfe, 102

Gilbert and Sullivan, 118

Gillespie, Dizzy, 47, 49, *50,* 52, 53, 71, *148, 171*

Ginsberg, Allen, 249

Glitter, Gary, *277, 278, 282*

Glitter rock, 273 ff., 299. *See also* Rock music

Goddard, J. R., 189

Goffin, Gerry, 227

Goffin, Robert, 146

Goldberg, Danny, 295

Golden Gate Park (San Francisco), 248

Golden Gate Quartet, *162,* 163

Golden Oldies, *221*

Goldkette, Jean, 44

Good, Jack, 218, 221, 222–25

Goodman, Benny, 15, *39,* 45, 47, *60–61,* 67, *140,* 142–47, 149–52, 153, 155

Goodman Quartet, 147

Goodman Trio, 147

Gordon, Roscoe, 171

Gordy, Berry, 157–58, *167*

Gore, David Ormsby, 243

Gore, Leslie, *214*

Gospel music, 9, 11, *73,* 182; and Beatles, 241; and blues, 163; origin of, 12–13; and rhythm and blues, *161, 162,* 163–64, *165, 167*

Gotham Theatre (New York), 95

Graham, Bill, *245, 247–48, 257–58, 267, 269, 276, 278*

Graham, Billy, 241

Graham, Charles, 101

Gramercy Five, *142, 147*

Grand Ole Opry, 112, 174, 177, *179,* 182–83, 189, 190, 192–93, 215, 217, 301

Grand Terrace (Chicago), 142

Grateful Dead, the, 247, *259,* 269

Gravitt, Ed, 19

Great Vance, the, 79

Greco, Juliette, 93

Green, Adolph, *123*

Green, Mrs. Juanita, 66

Green, Mitzi, *124*

Greenup, Bruner, 27

Grofé, Ferde, *41, 124*

Gugu-gugu drum, *7*

Gumm, Frances. *See* Garland, Judy

Gumm sisters, *76*

Guthrie, Arlo, *198*

Guthrie, Woody, 73, 183, 195–96, *198, 201,* 206, 207–208

Guy, Buddy, *171*

Hager, Fred, 59

Haggard, Merle, *188,* 193

Haight-Ashbury, 263

Hair, 136–37

Haley, Bill, 168, 171, 217, 218, 221, 222, 223–24, *229*

Hallelujah (film), *65*

Hamilton, Chico, 52

Hammerstein I, Oscar, 91, 111, 121

Hammerstein II, Oscar, 84, 118, 121, *124, 126,* 127–28, 130, *132*

Hammerstein, William, *15,* 84, 91, 128

Hammond, John, 47, *60–61,* 65, 66, 67, 69–71, 142, *167, 303*

Hampton, Lionel, 47, 147, *168*

Hancock, Herbie, *300, 303*

Handy, W. C., 35, 44, *56,* 57–59, 60, *65,* 73

Hanley and McDonald, 98

Harburg, E. Y., *107,* 115, 122, 132

Hard Day's Night (film), 258

Hardin, Lil, 37

Harding, Warren G., *179*

Harlem, 45, *47,* 53, *60,* 65, 67, 70, 104, 161

Harlem Opera House, *15*

"Harmonic clubs," 77

Harney, Benjamin Robertson, 27–28

Harrelson, Cecil, 229

Harrington, the Reverend Bob, 193

Harris, Chas. K., *98,* 99, 101, *102,* 121

Harris, Wee Willie, 223, *224*

Harris, Wynonie, 162

Harrison, George, 237, 242, 255, 274

Harrison, Rex, *135*
Hart, Lorenz, 122, *124*, 127, 130, *131*, *132*
Hawkins, Coleman, *39*, 44
Hawkins, Erskine, 162
Hay, George D., 174, 176, *179*, 182
Hayden, Scott, 22, *25*
Hayes, Isaac, 3
Haymarket, The (New York), 104–105
Hays, Lee, 198
Hayworth, Rita, *126*
"Head arrangements," 44
Heath, Percy, *53*
Heatherton, Joey, *287*
Hecht, Ben, *123*
Hegamin, Lucille, 61
Helburn, Theresa, 128
Hellerman, Freddy, *198*
Help (film), 258, 285
Henderson, Fletcher, *39*, 44–45, 47, 67, 140, 143
Henderson, Rosa, 61
Hendrix, Jimi, *221*, 235, 258, *263*, 266–67, 269, 275, 288
Hentoff, Nat, *47*, *144*
Hepburn, Katharine, *128*
Herbert, Victor, 98, *102*, 109
Herd, the, *290*
Herman, Woody, *91*, 140, 145, 147, *150*, 155, *290*
Hess, Bennie, 185
Heyward, DuBose, 125
Higginbotham, J. C., *47*
Hill, Joe, 198
Hill Billies, the, 180
Hillbilly music, 180, 182–85, 188, 189, 190. *See also* Country-western music
Hillman, Chris, 243, *247*
Hines, Earl "Fatha," 44, 47, 53, *142*, *148*, 185, *290*
Hoffman, Carl, 21
Hole in the Wall (Memphis), 57
Holiday, Billie, *49*, 67, 69, *70*, 71, 144, 288
Holiday, Clarence, 67
Holly, Buddy, 224, 237
Hollywood: musicals, 111, 130–32, 135; and Tin Pan Alley, 109, 111. *See also* Movie industry
Hollywood Club (New York), 45
Hootenanny, 207
Hope, Bob, *89*, 94, 132
Hopkins, Al, 179–80
Hopkins, Lightnin', *167*
Hoss-Hair Pullers, 180
Houston, Texas, 10
Houston Grand Opera Company, *31*
Howlin' Wolf, 161, 164, *169*, 171
How to Write a Popular Song (Harris), 99

Humes, Helen, *47*, *65*
Hunter, Alberta, 64
Hunter, Ivory Joe, 165
Hurok, Sol, 149–50
"Hurrah Sporting Club," *21*
Hylton, Jack, 146

Ian, Janis, *207*
Illinois Jacquet, 162, 165, *168*
Immigrants, *97*, 102
Ink Spots, the, 155, *157*, 164, 165, 212
Intuition, 50
Ives, Burl, *204*
Ives, Charles, 299
Ivey, William, 180, 182, 192

Jackson, Bullmoose, 161
Jackson, Mahalia, 161, 163
Jackson, Milt, *53*
Jackson, Aunt Molly, 198
Jackson, Tony, 10, *27*
Jackson, New Orleans Willie, *62*
Jacquet, Illinois. *See* Illinois Jacquet
Jagger, Bianca, *257*
Jagger, Mick, 253–54, 255, *257*, 259, 263–64, 267, 269, 294, 299, 300, 310
Jamaican music, 284–85. *See also* Reggae
James, Harry, 140, 144, 145, *148*, 152–53, 155
James Cleveland Singers, *162*
Jangdharrie, the Reverend Wycliffe, 66
Jardine, Al, *247*
Jazz, 5, 9, 33–53, 55, *56*, 58–59, 71, 139, 221, 284; and animal dance craze, 39, 41; and bebop, 49–50; Chicago influence, 43–44; "classical," 52–53; as collective improvisation, 43–44, 45, 52; Creole influence, 35, 44; dance bands, 38–39, 41, 44–45, 47; definitions of, 33–34; free-style, 50; and future of popular music, 301, 303, 304–306; instrumentation, 34–35, 37, 44; origins of, 9–11; as performing art, 34; and racial segregation, 47; and rhythm and blues, 159; small groups, 49; and solo playing, 44, 45, 303, 306; and swing bands, 140, 146–47, 155; and Tin Pan Alley, 107, 112, 140; white, 41, 44, 47, 50, 140; and white music industry, 38–39, 47, 50; and white musicians, 140, 146–47, 155, 299
Jazz blues, 59
Jazz criticism, 146
"Jazz-dancing," *12*
Jazz hot, le, 86
Jazz Hot, Le (Panassié), 146
Jazz-rock, 303

Jazz Singer, The (film), 41, 111
Jefferson, Blind Lemon, 13, 59, *62*, 196
Jeffries, Mike, 266
Jessel, George, 106
Jethro Tull, 282
Jewish immigrants, and Tin Pan Alley, 102–103
Jimmie Rodgers Life Story, The (Rodgers), 185
Jitterbug, *139*, 146
John, Elton, *281*, 282, 310
Johnny Cash Road Show, *174*
Johnson, Bunk, 49
Johnson, Florence, 21
Johnson, James P., *27*
Johnson, Willie, *196*
Jolson, Al, 41, 106, *109*, *110*, 111, 132, 153
Jones, Brian, 235, *257*, 264–65, *267*
Jones, Elmore, 161
Jones, Mrs. Eva Thompson, 174
Jones, Jonah, *39*, 69–70
Jones, Le Roi. *See* Baraka, Amiri
Joplin, Belle Hayden, 22, 25
Joplin, Janis, 4, 66, 235, 247, 254, 258, 269
Joplin, Scott, *17*, 19–25, 28, 30–31
Jordan, Joe, 22
Josephson, Barney, *61*, 70–71, *153*, *196*
Jug band, 18

Kalman, Emmerich, 118
Kalmar, Bert, *109*
Kaminsky, Max, *47*, *50*
Kander, John, 137
Kane, Helen, *110*
Kangaroo Hop, 39
Kansas City, 15, *21*
Kaufman, George S., *124*
Kaufman, Murray the K., 242–43. *245*
Kay, Connie, *53*
Kean, Edmund, 118
Keeler, Ruby, *109*, *115*
Keisker, Marion, 211
Kelly, Gene, *131*, 132, *288*
Kennedy, John, 221
Kentucky Club (New York), 45
Kern, Jerome, 102, 118, 121, 122, 124, 126–27, *128*, 131
Kershaw, Doug, 301
Kimball, Robert, 122
Kincaid, Bradley, 182
King, B. B., 161, 171, 266
King, Carole, *227*
King Creole (film), 225
King of Jazz, The (film), 41, 43
Kingston Trio, 207, *209*
Kinks, the, 80, 295
Kinney, Bill, 212

Kirby, John, *39, 49*
Kirshner, Don, 114–15
Kiss, *273*
Klein, Allen, 255, 257
KMA radio (Shenandoah, Iowa), *188*
Kohlman, Churchill, 167
Konitz, Lee, 50
Kora, *7*
Korner, Alexis, *257, 267*
Krell, William H., *25, 26, 27*
Krupa, Gene, 47, *140,* 142, 144, 145–146, 147, 152
Ku Klux Klan, 12

LaBelle, Patti, *277*
LaBelle, *277*
Ladnier, Tommy, *28*
Lafayette Theater (Harlem), 70
La Guardia, Fiorello, 95
Laine, Jack, 10
Lampell, Millard, 198
Lane, Burton, 132
Lanfield, Sidney, *126*
Langer, Lawrence, 128
La Rocca, Nick, 38–39, 41
La Rue, Danny, *93*
Las Vegas, Nevada, *94,* 95, *214, 229*
Lauder, Harry, 83, *84*
Laurents, Arthur, 135–36
Lawrence, Gertrude, *123*
Leadbelly, 183, *196,* 207, 296
Leander, Mike, 278
Leary, Timothy, *254*
Led Zeppelin, 274, 295–96, 299, *303*
Ledbetter, Huddie. *See* Leadbelly
Lee, Lieutenant George, 56–57, 58–59
Lee, Gypsy Rose, *91*
Lee, Peggy, *148*
Legrand, Michel, 288
Lehár, Franz, 118, 122
Leiber, Jerry, 73
Leiber and Stoller, *115, 171, 216*
Lennon, John, *235,* 237, 242, 249, 251, 255, 257, 258, 263, 273–74, *305*
Leon, Dan, 85, 91
Lerner, Alan Jay, *126*
Let's Dance, 143
Levant, Oscar, *43*
Levister, Dick, *218*
Lewis, Furry, *65*
Lewis, Jerry Lee, 229, 241
Lewis, John, 50, 52, *53*
Lewis, Ted, *91*
Leybourne, George, 79–80
Liberace, *94, 95, 214*
Lieberson, Goddard, 50
Light Crust Doughboys, 189
Light shows, 276
Lincoln, Abraham, 204
Lincoln, Paul, 223
Lincoln Gardens, 43
Little Richard, 221, 227, 266, 295

Little Walter, 161
Liverpool, 237, 254
Liverpool Cavern, *232,* 237, 239, *243*
Lloyd, Marie, *79,* 92
Loesser, Frank, 135
Log Cabin (Harlem), 67
Lomax, John, *196*
Lombardo, Guy, 143, 145
London Palladium, 43, *86,* 218
London Pavilion, 89, 204
London Theatrical Managers Association, 86
Lone Star Cowboys, the, 187
Lord, Jon, 276
Louis the Whistler, 105
Louisiana Hay Ride, 182, *187,* 215
Love, Mike, 246, 247
Lovin' Spoonful, 249
Lower East Side (New York), *91*
Lubitsch, Ernst, 121, 130
Ludlow's Summer Company, 83
Lynn, Bambi, *124*
Lynn, Loretta, *188,* 193
Lynn, Vera, *202,* 206

MacArthur, Charles, *123*
MacDermott, Galt, 136
MacDonald, Jeannette, 132
Macon, Uncle Dave, *179,* 182, 193
Macon, Dorris, *179,* 182
Mahara Minstrels, *56,* 57
Maharishi Mahesh Yogi, *231,* 239, 249
Mahogany Hall (Storyville), 37
Mailer, Norman, 249
Main Street (Memphis), *57, 58*
Makeba, Miriam, *207*
Male impersonators, in music halls, 85
Malone, Bill C., 177
Mamas and the Papas, the, 232, 249, 269
Mamoulian, Rouben, *118, 121,* 125–126, 127–28, 130–31, 301
Manhattan Opera House, 111
Manley, Michael, *303*
Mann, Manfred, *241,* 260
Maple Leaf Club (Sedalia, Mo.), 18–19, 21
Marable, Fate, *33*
Marks, Ed, 102, 104–105, 108
Marley, Bob, *303*
Marsden, Gerry, *243*
Marshall, Arthur, 21, 25
Martin, Dean, 80, 166
Martin, George, *232,* 241–42, *251*
Martin, Mary, 128, *132*
Marvelettes, the, 157
Marx Brothers, 132
Mathews, Charles, 83
Maynard, Ken, 187
McCarthy, Senator Joseph, 71

McCartney, Linda Eastman, 255
McCartney, Paul, xi, *89,* 208, 235, 237, 238, 242, *251,* 254–55, 257, 273–74
McDonald, Country Joe, 208, *209,* 232
McGuinn, Roger (Jim), 232, 243, 245, *247,* 263
McKuen, Rod, *287*
McPartland, Dick, 41
McPartland, Jimmy, *41*
McPhatter, Clyde, 161, 164
Medicine show, and country-western music, 177, 179, 184
Melcher, Terry, 243
Mellow Kings, *218*
Memphis, Tenn., 35, 212, 215; and the blues, 10, 56–57, 73; and rhythm and blues, 171
Memphis Blues Caravan, *65*
Memphis Slim, 56, 57, 61, *70,* 73, 310
Memphis Sound, the, 57
Meredith, James, 208
Metropolitan Opera House, 276, *277*
Meyer, George, 98
MGM, 75, 135
MIDEM (Cannes), 293
Midnight Jamboree Radio Program, 193
Midnighters, the, 164
Millender, Lucky, 162
Miller, Glenn, 152
Miller, Max, *91,* 94
Miller, Mitch, 158
Mills, Florence, 27
Mills Brothers, *162,* 165
Mingus, Charles, *53*
Minnie Pearl, "Cousin," 177, *179,* 182, 189, 192
Minstrel shows, 15, 18, 19, 26–27, 118, *303;* and the blues, 57–58, 59, 62; and music hall/vaudeville, 83–84
Minton's (Harlem), *47*
Miracles, the, 157, *165*
Mississippi, 56
Mitchell, Chad, *204*
Mitchell, Joni, *293*
Modern Jazz Quartet, 33, 50, 52, *53*
Monette's (Harlem), 67
Monroe, Bill, *183, 188,* 190, 214, 301
Monk, Thelonius, 47, 52, *53*
Monkees, the, *115*
Monroe, Charlie, *183*
Monterey Pop Festival, 231–32, 235, 249, 254, 257, 267, 269–70
Moon, Keith, 259–60
Moonglows, the, 164
Moore, Constance, *150*
Moore, Scotty, 212, 214
Moore, Whistling Alex, 59
Morello, Joe, *53*

Morgan, Richard, 65
Morrison, Jim, 254, 258, *259, 267,* 269
Morton, Benny, *47*
Morton, Charles, 77
Morton, Jelly Roll, 10, *25, 34, 35, 37, 56*
Mosby, Cash, 57
Mostel, Zero, *135*
Moten, Bennie, *66*
Motown, 157, *167, 294*
Mount Kisco Golf and Tennis Club, *61*
Movie industry: and cowboy films, 187–88; and musicals, 111, 130–32, 135; and Tin Pan Alley, 105, 109, 111
Movie Theaters, swing bands in, 144, 147–48, *150,* 151
Muir, Lewis, 98
Murphy, Louisa, 35
Musicals, 117–37; antecedents, 117–118; cost of producing, 137; and Hollywood, 130–32; music hall tradition, 95; and operetta, 118, 121; as paradox of popular music, 301; and unity of form, 121, 128, 131
Musical Spillers, the, *19*
Music Hall, Billy Rose's (New York), 142
Music halls, 75–95, 117, 132; and the Beatles, 241, 276; and British rock, 222; drinking songs, 79–80; English, *75,* 77, 79–80, 83, 85, 86, 89; home-sweet-home themes, 80, 83; origin of, 76; patriotic ballads, 80; and war songs, 204, 206
Music publishers, 26, 100; sheet music, 101. *See also* Tin Pan Alley
Mutual Broadcasting, 152
Muzak, 282, 284

Nash, Graham, 275
Nashville, Tenn., 243; and country-western music, 173, *179,* 182, 189–190, 192–93
National Barn Dance, 179, 182, *187*
National Broadcasting Corporation (NBC), 152
Negro spirituals, 9, 44, 71
New Orleans, 5, 9, *15;* and instrumental blues tradition, 59; and jazz, 33–34, 35, 37, 43, 221; and rhythm and blues, 161. *See also* Storyville
New Orleans Rhythm Kings, *41*
New York, *15;* and jazz, 38–39, 44–45, 47. *See also* Fifty-Second Street; Harlem
New York Dance Band, 98
New York Dolls, *281*

Newport-New York Jazz Festival, *49*
Niblo's Garden (New York), 121
Nichols, Red, 140, 142
Nigger Mike's Bowery Bar, *18*
Nigger Minstrel of Eastbourne, *80*
Niven, David, 98
Noebel, Reverend David, 241
Nono, Luigi, 293
Norvo, Red, 49, *153*

O'Day, Anita, *49*
Odetta, *207*
Of Thee I Sing, 124
Offenbach, Jacques, 118
O'Hara, John, 126
Ohio Express, the, 281
OKeh Records, 60–61, 179
Oklahoma!, 127–28, 130–31, *132,* 135, 136
Oldfield, Mike, 288, 290, 293–94, 299–300, *306*
Oldfield, Sally, 290
Oldham, Andrew Loog, 254
Oliver, Joe "King," 37, 43, 71
One String Sam, 65
Ono, Yoko, 257, *265, 305*
On Your Toes, 135
Operetta, and development of the musical, 118, 121, 124
Opryland U.S.A., *179, 193, 288, 305*
Original Carter Family, *174, 176,* 182–83
Original Dixieland Jazz Band, 34, 38–39, 43
Orioles, the, 165, *218*
Ory, Kid, 37
Osata, Sono, *123*
Osmond, Donny, *284*
Osmonds, the, *4, 277, 278, 281, 282,* 299

Pacemakers, the, *243*
Pacific Overtures, 301
Page, "Hot Lips," *50, 59*
Page, Jimmy, 274, 295–96, 299–300, *303, 306*
Page, Patti, 165
Palace Theatre (New York), 95
Palao, Jimmy, *37*
Palomar Ballroom (Los Angeles), 143–44
Pan, Hermes, *126*
Panama Trio, the, *27*
Panassié, Hugues, 146
Papp, Joseph, 136, 137
Paramount Theatre (New York), 62, 140, 144
Pariser, Alan, 232
Parker, Charlie "Bird," *28,* 47, 49–50, 71, *148*
Parker, Colonel Tom, 216–18, 221, 222, 225

Parnes, Larry, 221, 238
Parton, Dolly, 193
Pastels, the, *218*
Patterson, Sam, 22, 31
Patti, Adelina, 83
Paul Whiteman Orchestra, *43*
Peekskill Riot, *201*
Peer, Ralph, *176,* 179–80, 183, 185
Pelicans, the, *218*
Penguins, the, 164, *218*
Pepper's (Chicago), 158
Perkins, Carl, *193,* 216, 218, 229, 237
Peter, Paul and Mary, *204,* 207
Petit, Buddy, 35
Petrillo, James Caesar, 155
Phillips, Billy, 37
Phillips, John, 232
Phillips, Sam, *193,* 211–12, 214–17, 218, 227
Phoenix Theatre (New York), 69
Phonograph, invention of, 60. *See also* Recording industry
Piaf, Edith, 92–93, *94*
Picou, Alphonse, 35
Pied Pipers, *148*
Pierce, Webb, *187*
Pig Pen, 269
Pink Floyd, the, 5
Pittsburgh, Pa., 11
Platters, the, *165*
Pleasants, Henry, 146
Pluggers, 104–106
Plummer, Roy, 218
Pollack, Ben, 142, 152
Poole, Charlie, 179
Popular music: and American culture, xi; commercialization of, 287–88, 299–300; criticism of, 309–10; definitions, 4–5; exploitation of black music, 288, 299; future development of, 301, 303–306; industry, xi–xii, 287–88, 299–300; origins of, 5; survival of, 309–10
Porgy and Bess, 121, 125–26
Porter, Cole, 106, 118, 122–23, 124, *126, 128,* 131
Preservation Hall (New Orleans), *10*
Presley, Elvis, 4, 15, 73, *115,* 171, 173, *193,* 211–18, 223–24, 225, 227, 235, 237, 242, 247, 249, 273, 278, 299, 310
Presley, Jesse, 212
Preston, Billy, *294*
Preston, Jerry, 67
Previn, Dory, 66
Pride, Charlie, *193*
Primettes, the, *167*
Prince, Harold, 137
Prisonnaires, the, 212
Proby, P. J., 295
Procope, Russell, *39*

"Professors," 19, 21
Prohibition, 56–57, 65
Protest song, 73, 195–98, 206, 208–209
Purcell, Henry, 52

Queen Bee (Chicago), 158
Queen City Concert Band, 17, 19

Rabbit Foot Minstrels, 62
"Race artists," 159
"Race music," 161
Radio: and country-western music, 173–74, 179, 180, 182, 188–89, 192, 193; Mexican border stations, 188–89; and swing bands, 144, 152, 155; and Tin Pan Alley, 102, 103, 106, 108–109, 111–12
Radio Luxembourg, 222
Rado, James, 136
Rag, as distinct from ragtime, 21
Ragni, Jerome, 136
Ragtime, 9, 11, 17–31, 34, 355, 71, 284; acceptance of, 27; and cakewalk, 26–27; as distinct from rag, 21; early publications of, 26; instruction, 28; origin of, 18; and rhythm and blues, 158; and Tin Pan Alley, 106–107, 139; and vaudeville, 27–28, 30; and white music industry, 17–18, 30, 31
Ragtime opera, 25, 30–31
Rainbow Room (New York), 47, 70
Rainey, Ma, 43, 59, 62
Ramez, Marian, 12
Ramez, Martinez, 12
Randall, Bill, 215–16
Ravel, Maurice, 44
Ray, Johnnie, 166–67, 168, 171
RCA Victor Record Company, 103, 159, 217
Reconstruction, 11–13
Recording industry, 287; black companies, 39, 60, 159, 161; and the blues, 60–62, 64, 65; and country-western music, 179, 183, 184; Independent, 159, 161; invention of phonograph, 60; and rhythm and blues, 159, 161; and rock and roll, 259, 263; and Tin Pan Alley, 109, 140
Reddy, Helen, 287
Redgrave, Vanessa, 195
Redman, Don, 39, 43, 44, 45, 47
Reed, Jimmy, 161
Reggae, 284–85, 303
Reisenweber's Café (New York), 39
Reliance Band, 10
Return to Forever, 306
Revue, and development of musical, 117–18, 121, 122, 124, 132, 136

Revue Nègre, La, 86
Rhythm and blues, 5, 114, 157–61, 294; and Beatles, 241, 242; and black recording companies, 159, 161; and the blues, 158, 159; and gospel, 161, 162, 163–64, 165, 167; origin of term, 161; and white market, 164–65; and white music industry, 159, 161, 164, 165–67
Rice, Thomas, 83–84
Rich, Buddy, 50, 150, 152
Richard, Cliff, 225, 238
Richard Keith, 269, 274, 294
Riddle, Nelson, 155
Riders of the Purple Sage, the, 187
"Riffs," 44
Riggs, Lynn, 127
Ritchie, Jean, 198
Ritter, Tex, 193
Robbins, Jerome, 123, 135–36
Robertson, Eck, 176, 179
Robeson, Paul, 196, 201
Robey, George, 85
Robin, Christopher, 264
Robins, the, 216
Robinson, Dave, 278
Rock and roll, 5, 9, 11, 114, 167–68, 171, 211–29; and the Beatles, 229, 231 ff.; and British pop music, 221; and British television, 218, 221–25; and music hall tradition, 95; origin of term, 167; and Elvis Presley, 211–18; and recording industry, 222. See also Rock music
Rock music, 253–71, 273–83, 306; development of, 296, 299; and drugs, 253–54, 258, 263, 264, 266, 269, 270; exploitation of musicians, 260; and improvisation, 275; instrumental virtuosity, 274–75, 296; and musical forms, 274–77, 296; profits, 259; recording industry, 259, 263; supergroups, 275–276. See also Rock and roll
Rock opera, 276
Rodgers, Carrie, 185
Rodgers, Jimmie, 176, 183–85, 186, 190, 192, 288
Rodgers, Richard, 124, 127–28, 130, 131, 132
Rodgers and Hammerstein, 136, 301. See also Hammerstein II, Oscar
Rodgers and Hart, 106, 118, 122, 132, 135. See also Hart, Lorenz
Rolling Stones, 4, 65, 235, 247, 249, 254, 255, 257, 259, 263–64, 267, 273, 274, 294, 295, 296, 300, 310. See also Jagger, Mick; Jones, Brian; Richard, Keith; Watts, Charlie; Wyman, Bill
Romberg, Sigmund, 118, 122
Ronnie and the Hi-Lites, 211

Roosevelt, Franklin D., 196
Roosevelt Club (Chicago), 158
Rose, Billy, 123, 142
Rose, Fred, 189
Rose, Wesley, 188
Rose family, 179
Rosebud Café (St. Louis), 22, 26
Roseland Ballroom (New York), 39, 44
Rosenfeld, Monroe H., 22, 25, 102–103
Ross, Diana, 158, 167, 227
Ross, Kid, 37
Rosselson, Leon, 209
Roxy Music, 281–82
Royal Canadians, 143, 145
Royal Roost, the, 50
Rudge, Peter, 296, 300
Rural blues, 62. See also Blues, the
Rushing, Jimmy, 35, 65, 66
Russell, Ken, 135, 254, 276
Russell, Lillian, 80
Russell, Pee Wee, 47
Russell, William, 201
Rydell, Bobby, 225, 229
Ryman Auditorium (Nashville), 179
Ryskind, Morrie, 124

Sadler's Wells, 77
St. Louis, Mo., and ragtime, 21–22, 25
St. Louis World's Fair, 25, 30
Sainte-Marie, Buffy, 207
San Antonio, Tex., 10
San Francisco. See Fillmore West; Golden Gate Park; Monterey Pop Festival
Sandrich, Mark, 126
Satherley, Arthur, 187
Saunders, Coon, 145
Savoy Ballroom (Harlem), 144
Sayer, Leo, 300
Schönberg, Arnold, 50, 124, 274
Schoolboys, the, 218
Schwartz, Arthur, 107
Scott, James Sylvester, 27
Scruggs, Earl, 188
Sea of Tunes, 246
Sedalia, Mo., 17, 18–19, 21
Seeger, Pete, 196, 198, 206–207, 209, 247, 301
Segregation, 12–13, 55, 69–71. See also Black musicians, exploitation of; White music industry
Sergeant Pepper's Lonely Hearts Club Band, 235, 241, 274, 276
Seron, 7
Shankar, Ravi, 274
Shannon, Bookmiller, 184
Shapiro, Ben, 232
Shapiro, Nat, 47, 144

Shapiro and Bernstein, Publishers, 98
Shavers, Charlie, 49
Shaw, Artie, 45, 69, 139, 140, 142, 145, 146, 147, 149, 151–52, 155, 202
Shearing, George, 35
Sheet music, 108; packaging, 100; publishing, 101
Sheridan, Tony, 239
Shevelove, Burt, 115
Shilkret, Nathan, 126
Shirelles, the, 162
Show Boat, 121–22, 136
Shuffle Along, 28
Sibelius, Jean, 288
Silver, Frank, 98
Silvers, Louis, 110
Simon, Paul, 209, 305
Simon and Garfunkel, 4
Sinatra, Frank, 148, 150, 153, 155, 189, 242, 288
Sissle, Noble, 28
6.5 Special, 223
Skiffle, 221, 237
Skillet Lickers, the, 179
Slade, 275
Slaughter, Marion Try. See Dalhart, Vernon
Slavery, and development of American music, 5–7, 9, 11
Slye, Leonard, 187
Slye Brothers, the, 187
Smith, Ada "Bricktop," 45
Smith, Bessie, 43, 44, 55, 59, 60, 62, 64–67, 69, 70, 153
Smith, General George, 17
Smith, Mamie, 61–62, 179
Smith, Patti, 296
Smith, Pintop, 13, 299
Smith, Sarah, 17
Smith, Willie "The Lion," 35, 61, 140
Snow, Hank, 183, 184, 217
Snow, the Reverend Jimmy, 193
Society Orchestra, 28
Society Syncopaters, 33
Soft Machine, 290
Solitaires, the, 218
Sondheim, Stephen, 121, 124, 125, 130, 131, 135–36, 301, 303
Song slides, illustrated, 105
Sons of the Pioneers, the, 187
Soul music, 11, 158
Soul Stirrers, the, 163, 168
Sour rock, 253–71
Sousa, John Philip, 19, 102
South, Eddie, 47
Spaniels, the, 164
Specialty Records, 159
Spector, Phil, 115, 227
Spirituals, 9, 44, 71
Spivey, Victoria, 65
Sprague, Carl T., 187

Springsteen, Bruce, 303
Squire, George, 282
Stackhouse, Houston, 66
Stafford, Jo, 148
Staple, Roebuck "Pop," 162
Staple Singers, the, 162
Stark, John, 21–22, 25, 30, 31
Starr, Ringo, 237, 241, 242, 249, 255
Steele, Tommy, 218, 221, 222, 223, 241
Stern, Joe, 102
Stewart, Rex, 39
Stills, Stephen, 275–76
Stoll, Oswald, 79–80, 92
Stoller, Mike, 73
Stone, Lew, 146
Stone, Sly, 263
Stookey, Paul, 204
Story, Sidney, 9, 35
Storyville, 5, 9–10, 25; and jazz, 34, 35, 37
Strauss, Johann, 118
Stravinsky, Igor, 50, 304
Strayhorn, Billy, 47
"Stride piano," 27
String Band, 198
Striptease, 95
Sullivan, Ed, 217
Sullivan, Joe, 142
Sullivan, Maxine, 144
Sun Records, 193, 217
Supergroups, 275–76
Supremes, the, 157, 158, 167
Sutcliffe, Stuart, 237, 238
Sweet, 299
Swing, 9, 11, 13, 139–55, 158; European contribution to, 146; fans, 148–49; influence of black jazz, 140, 145, 146–47, 155; in movie theaters, 144, 147–48, 150, 151; origin of term, 145–46; and radio, 144, 152, 155; recording industry, 152; vocalists, 148, 150, 153–55
Sykes, Roosevelt, 61, 66

Taggart, Joel, 196
Talking drum, 9
Tar Heels, the, 180
Tarriers, the, 207
Tatum, Art, 43, 50, 304
Taylor, Derek, 232, 239, 242, 245, 246, 251, 255
Taylor, Mick, 294
Tchaikovsky, Piotr, 4, 5, 274
Teagarden, Jack, 43, 152, 155
Teetot, 190
Tenneva Ramblers, the, 183
Teschemacher, Frank, 41
Texas Playboys, the, 189
Tharpe, Sister Rosetta, 161, 163
Theatre Guild of New York, 127–28
Thomas, Rufus, 171, 303

Thompson, Uncle Jimmy, 174
Thompson, Lydia, 118
Thornton, James, 101
Thornton, Willie Mae, 73, 115, 171
"Thundering Herd," 150
"Ticklers," 19
Til, Sonny, 165
Tilley, Vesta, 83, 85
Tilton, Martha, 147
Tin Pan Alley, 95, 97–115, 118, 121, 122, 131, 132, 139–40, 189, 190, 217, 221, 259, 274, 301; and European immigrants, 102; and folk music, 196; location of, 103; and movie industry, 105, 109, 111, 147; origin of, 103; and phonograph, 109; pluggers, 104–105; and radio, 102, 103, 106, 108–109, 111–12, 114; record sales, 140; and rhythm and blues, 165; royalty payments, 106; singing cowboys, 187; stock arrangements, 104; and swing, 145, 152; and vaudeville, 118; versatility, 106–107; and World War I, 107–108
Tommy, 276
Tough, Dave, 41, 152
Town Hall (New York), 47
Town Hall Party, 182
Townshend, Peter, 276, 296
Tracy, H. E., 15
Travers, Mary, 204
Treemonisha, 30–31
Tristano, Lennie, 50
Trumbauer, Frankie, 44
Tubb, Ernest, 182, 184, 190, 192
Tubular Bells, 288, 293–94
Tucker, Sophie, 60, 91, 94, 153
Turkey Trot, 39, 41
Turner, Ike, 171, 266, 285
Turner, Big Joe, 65, 161, 171
Turner, Tina, 263, 266, 285
Turpin, Thomas Million, 21, 26, 27
Tuxedo Dance Hall, 37
Twitty, Conway, 214, 216, 227, 229
Two I's (London), 223

Urban blues, 59, 158, 165. See also Blues, the
Urban migration, 10–11, 13, 18, 43, 56, 101
Vallee, Rudy, 47, 94, 106, 109, 110, 114, 154
Valvoda, Lee, 282, 284
Vandellas, the, 157
Variety theaters, 76–77, 84–85; definition of, 79; sexual ambivalence in, 85
Vaudeville, 41, 75–95, 117, 118, 121, 128, 132; definition, 79; influence on Hollywood, 132; and minstrel shows, 83; and ragtime, 27–28;

Vaudeville (*Continued*)
and rhythm and blues dance routines, 165; and Tin Pan Alley, 97, 105–106, 118. *See also* Music halls
Vaudeville blues, 59, 61, 62
Vaughan, Sarah, *49*
Vee, Bobby, 229
Verdi, Giuseppe, *104*
Victor Talking Machine Company, 179, 183, 184
Victoria, Queen of England, 89, 91
Victoria Palace (London), 92
Vidor, King, *65*
Vietnam War, 199, 207
Vincent, Gene, *216*, 224, 237
Vinton, Bobby, 229
Virgin Records, 293–94
Vocal blues, 59
Von Tilzer, Harry, 97, 102, *102*–103

Wagner, Richard, *104*
Wailers, Bob Marley and the, *303*
Walker, Frank, 64
Walker, Nancy, *123*
Walker, T-Bone, 159, 165, 266
Wallace, Henry, 206–207
Wallace, Nellie, *80*
Waller, Fats, *43, 45, 49*
War songs, 198, 201–202, 204, 206
Ward, Billy, 164
Ward, Helen, 140, 153
Warfield, Charlie, 22
Warhol, Andy, 281
Waring, Fred, 145
Warner, Albert, *110*
Warner, Jack, 105, *110*
Warner Brothers, 111, 187
Warren, Harry, 111
Warwick, Percy, *25*
Washboard Sam, 158, 159
Washboard Wonders, *180*
Washington, Dinah, 144
Waters, Ethel, 118
Waters, Muddy, 161, *168–69, 171, 251*, 259, 299
Watts, Charlie, 258, 259
WBAP radio (Fort Worth), 174
Weavers, the, *196, 198, 207*

Webb, Chick, *144*
Webb, Clifton, 118
Webb, Harry, 225
Wells, Junior, *171*
West, Mae, 94, 132
West Side Story, 135–36
Western swing, 189
Wet Willie, 310
Wexler, Jerry, 159, 161, 162, 165, *167*
Wheatley, Mr., 121
Whitcomb, Ian, 98, 111
White, Bukka, 59, *66*
White, Josh, *196*
White blues, *70, 196*
"White covers," 165
White jazz, 41, 44, 47, 50, 140, 303
White music industry: and exploitation of black music, 15, 288, 299, 303–304; and the blues, 59, 64–65, 67, 71, 73; and jazz, 38–39, 47, 50; and protest song, 196, 206–207; and ragtime, 17–18, 30, 31; and rhythm and blues, 159, 161, 164, 165–67; and swing bands, 142
Whiteman Paul, 15, *39, 43,* 44, 124, 154, 155
Whitman, Slim, 215
Whitter, Henry, 180
Who, the, 232, *241,* 259, 276, 295. *See also* Townshend, Peter
Whole World, the, 290
Wilder, Thornton, *135*
Wilkins, the Reverend Robert, *73*
Williams, Allan, 237, 238
Williams, Audrey, 190, 192
Williams, Bransby, 91
Williams, Clarence, 64
Williams, Hiram "Hank," 190
Williams, Big Joe, *73*
Williams, Mary Lou, *70*
Williams, Tennessee, *204*
Williams, Vaughan, 288
Williams and Piron Music Publishers, 37
Williamson, Sonny Boy, 13, 159
Willis, Chuck, 227
Willows, the, *218*
Wills, Bob, 184, *187,* 189
Wilson, Brian, 246, *247*

Wilson, Carl, 246, *247*
Wilson, Dennis, 246, *247*
Wilson, Edith, 61
Wilson, Harold, 251
Wilson, Mary, *167*
Wilson, Murray, 246
Wilson, Teddy, 47, 69, 147
Winchell, Walter, 128
Windmill Theatre (London), 95
Winninger, Charles, *118*
WINS radio (New York), 168
Winters, Bernie, 222
Winters, Mike, 222
Witmark, Isadore, 102
WLS radio (Chicago), *179, 182,* 187
WMCA radio (New York), 70
Wolverines, the, 44
Wonder, Stevie, 157, *299*
Wood, Ron, *294*
Woods, Harry, 98
Woods, Johnny, *73*
Woodstock, *259, 260, 267, 269, 288*
Work song, 9, 13, 18, 44; and the blues, 56; and rhythm and blues, 164
World War I, 117; and Tin Pan Alley, 107–108
World War II, 189, 206
Wright, Eugene, *53*
WSM radio (Nashville), 174, *179, 184*
Wyatt, Robert, 290
Wyman, Bill, *249,* 257, 258, 265
Wynette, Tammy, 193
Wyrtzen, Jack, 309–310

XER radio (Mexico), 188
Xylophone, primitive, *7*

Yardbirds, the, *241, 274, 295, 299, 303*
Yarrow, Peter, *204*
Young, Lester, *50, 154*
Young, Neil, 275–76
Young, Skin, 154

Zahl, Hyman, 223
Zanuck, Darryl, *110*

Picture Credits

Joseph Abeles Studio
131, 132, 134, 135 top & bottom

H. Ainscough
232 l.

Arista Records
296 r.

A.S.C.A.P. (American Society of Composers, Authors & Publishers)
101 bottom l., 101 r., 109 top

Atlantic Records
281 bottom

B.B.C. Copyright Photographs
164 bottom, 255 r., 277 r.

Janice Belson
10 top, 67 l. & r., 73, 115 top & ctr., 188 top ctr., 199, 223 r., 245 bottom, 252, 258 top & bottom, 286, 290 top, 294 top l., 296 l., 301 r.

The Bettman Archive Inc.
75, 77, 85 top, 86 top & bottom, 92, 94 top l., 102 l., 178 bottom

Rudi Blesh Collection
16, 17, 19, 20 top l., top r., bottom, 23, 24 top l., top r., bottom l., bottom r., 25, 27 bottom l., 30, color page "The Entertainer"

Jack Bradley
33, 41 top, 51 top l. (Danny Barker), ctr. l. (Howard Morehead), 59 bottom, 66 r. (Duncan Scheidt), 117, 167 bottom, 168 top l. (U.P.I.), color pages "Mesmerizing Mendelssohn," "Swanee River Flows"

B.M.I. Archives (Broadcast Music Inc.)
53 top middle, 165, 167 top (Raymond Ross Photography), 169 top l., 176 bottom l., 184 l., 197 top r., 204 top r. (Bela Cseh), 208 l., 217, 226, 227 top, 250, 293 (Whitestone Photo)

Carnegie Hall Corp.
14, 15 bottom

David Cheshire (Chesarchive)
79, 81 top l., top ctr., top r., bottom l., bottom ctr., bottom r., 82, 83, 85 bottom, 224 ctr. l., ctr. r., bottom l., bottom r.

Consolidated Poster Service
130 bottom, 289 bottom

Thomas R. Copi
46 bottom r., 53 top r., 164 ctr., 170 top r.

Chick Corea
301 l.

Country Music Foundation
175, 176 r., 178 top l., middle ctr., 191

Culver Pictures, Inc.
18, 84, 88, 89 top r., bottom, 90 bottom l., bottom r., 91 r., 93, 94 bottom, 102 r., 103, 104, 107 l. & r., 110 top l., 112 ctr., 114, 116, 119 top, 120 bottom, 122 top & bottom, 123, 124 top & bottom, 125 top, ctr., bottom l., bottom r., 126 top, ctr., bottom, 129 top l., top r., bottom, 130 top, 133, 195, 202 ctr., bottom, 291, color pages "Bully Song," "Pershing's Crusaders," "I Didn't Raise My Boy . . . ," "America Here's My Boy," "We're Going Over"

Frank Driggs Collection a.k.a. Photo Files
3, 26, 27 r., 29, 32, 36 top, 40, 41 bottom, 42 top l. & top r., 44, 45, 46 top, ctr. l., ctr. r., bottom l., 48, 49 top & bottom, 51 top r., 52, 53 bottom ctr., 58, 60 top & bottom, 61, 62, 63, 65 l. & r., 66 l., 68, 70 l., ctr., r., 72 bottom l., 76, 80 top, 89 top l., 91 l., 110 bottom, top r.,

112 top & bottom, 113, 137 r., 139, 140, 141 top, 142, 143, 144, 145 top l., ctr., r., 146, 147, 148 top l., top r., bottom, 149 l. & r., 150 top, ctr., bottom, 151, 154, 156, 158, 159, 160 bottom l. & bottom r., 162 top, ctr., bottom, 163 l., ctr,, r., 168 top ctr., 169 top ctr., 169 bottom l., 176 top l., 180, 183 l. & r. (W. B. Coxe), 186 top, bottom l., bottom ctr., 188 top l. & top r., bottom r., 192 r., 197 top l. (Windmann Studio), bottom, 204 top l., 211, 215 top, bottom l. & bottom r., 216 bottom l., 219 top l., top ctr., top r., middle l., middle ctr., middle r., bottom l., bottom ctr., bottom r., 221, 243 ctr., 254, 294 bottom r., color page "Chili Sauce"

John Edwards Memorial Foundation
178 top r., ctr. l., 184 r., 212

Donald Everly
216 top r.

Raeburn Flerlage (Kinnara-Flerlage Photography)
64 r., 71, 72 bottom r., 188 bottom l., 197 top ctr., 207 l., 209 l., 290 ctr.

Henry Grossman
303 ctr. r.

Woody Guthrie Foundation
198 top l., r., bottom l., 200

Historic New Orleans Collection
2, 11, 34

Dezo Hoffman Ltd.
4, 233 bottom, 247 top, 248, 256 bottom r., 276 top r., 301 l. & r.

Houston Grand Opera
31

International Media Associates, Inc.
304–305

Island Records
303 bottom

Jazz Music Books
36 bottom

Barney Josephson
228

Keystone Press Agency Ltd.
87, 89 ctr., 115 bottom, 186 bottom r., 194, 202 top, 203, 224 top

Alexis Korner
256 bottom l. (Hamburger Abendblatt)

Liverpool Daily Post and Echo Limited
233 top ctr. upper, top ctr. lower

London Features International (L.F.I.)
168 top r. (David Ellis), 192 l., 238 r., 240 top, bottom l., 246 bottom, 256 top l. (Michael Putland), 261, 273 (Michael Putland), 277 l., 280 top, 281 top (Michael Putland), 282 (Michael Putland), 297, 298, 302 (Michael Putland), 303 top l. (Michael Putland), ctr. l. (Michael Putland)

Magnum Photos Inc.
173 (Danny Lyon), 174 bottom (Arthur Tress), 244 (Burk Uzzle)

Rouben Mamoulian
119 bottom l.

The Theatre Collection, Museum of the City of New York
15 top, 97, 99, 101 top l., 108 top & bottom, 110 top ctr.

Museum of Modern Art Film Stills Archive
96, 120 top, 259 bottom

New York Daily News
138, 141 bottom, 201, 267, 288

The New York Public Library
6 top, 38–39, 54

Tony De Nonno
170 top l., 263 bottom, 295

Freda Norris
232 r., 233 top l., top ctr. middle

North Carolina Division of Archives and History
172

Frederic Ohringer
136 r.

The Old Slave Mart Museum
6 bottom l. & bottom r., 8 bottom

Amy O'Neal
64 l., 67 ctr., 164 top, 169 top r.

Opryland
178 top ctr., 193, 304 l.

Players Theatre London
119 bottom r.

Webb Pierce
186 middle ctr.

Harold Prince Productions
136 l. & ctr.

Radio Times, Hulton Picture Library
12, 57, 74, 78, 80 bottom, 91 ctr., 98 l. & r., 109 bottom, 145 bottom l.

Redferns
53 top l., bottom l., bottom r., 168 bottom, 169 bottom r., 170 bottom, 208 r., 227 bottom, 228 top l., bottom (Stephen Morley), 235 bottom, 240 bottom ctr., bottom r., 247 bottom (Stephen Morley), 262, 263 top, 272 (Stephen Morley), 275 l. (David Ellis) & r. (David Ellis), 276 top l., 279, 280 bottom (David Ellis), 284, 285 (Collin Fuller), 290 bottom, 301 ctr.

Rex Features Ltd.
233 top r., 243 top & bottom, 251 (David Graves)

Rolling Stones Records
256 top r., 266 l.

Al Rose
Color pages "Pretty Baby," "Tin Roof Blues," "Don't Leave Me, Daddy"

Ethan Russell
264–265, 268

Bob Schanz Studio
287

Sears, Roebuck & Co.
7 top & bottom

Rufus Thomas
304 top r.

Tower News Service
206

United Press International
51 bottom, 90 top, 94 top r., 204 bottom, 207 ctr., 210, 213, 214 top l., 228 top r., 230, 231, 236 top, 238 l., 245 top, 246 top, 255 l., 283, 289 top

The University of Texas, Hoblitzelle Theatre Arts Collection
28, 56 (The Albert Davis Collection), 59 top (The Albert Davis Collection)

Virgin Records
306–307